D0907155

About Island Press

Island Press is the only nonprofit organization in the United States whose principal purpose is the publication of books on environmental issues and natural resource management. We provide solutions-oriented information to professionals, public officials, business and community leaders, and concerned citizens who are shaping responses to environmental problems.

In 2004, Island Press celebrates its twentieth anniversary as the leading provider of timely and practical books that take a multidisciplinary approach to critical environmental concerns. Our growing list of titles reflects our commitment to bringing the best of an expanding body of literature to the environmental community throughout North America and the world.

Support for Island Press is provided by the Agua Fund, Brainerd Foundation, Geraldine R. Dodge Foundation, Doris Duke Charitable Foundation, Educational Foundation of America, The Ford Foundation, The George Gund Foundation, The William and Flora Hewlett Foundation, Henry Luce Foundation, The John D. and Catherine T. MacArthur Foundation, The Andrew W. Mellon Foundation, The Curtis and Edith Munson Foundation, National Environmental Trust, The New-Land Foundation, Oak Foundation, The Overbrook Foundation, The David and Lucile Packard Foundation, The Pew Charitable Trusts, The Rockefeller Foundation, The Winslow Foundation, and other generous donors.

The opinions expressed in this book are those of the author(s) and do not necessarily reflect the views of these foundations.

ALIEN SPECIES AND EVOLUTION

ALIEN SPECIES
AND EVOLUTION

The Evolutionary Ecology of Exotic Plants,
Animals, Microbes, and Interacting Native Species

George W. Cox

Island Press
Washington • Covelo • London

Library of Congress Cataloging-in-Publication data.
Cox, George W., 1935–
    The evolutionary ecology of exotic plants, animals, microbes, and interacting native species / George W. Cox.
        p. cm.
    Includes bibliographical references and index.
        ISBN 1–55963–008–6 (cloth : alk. paper) — ISBN 1–55963–009–4 (pbk. : alk. paper)
        1. Introduced organisms--Environmental aspects. 2. Introduced animal—
Evolution.
    3. Exotic plants—Evolution.   I. Title.
    QH353.C69 2004
    578.6'2—dc22   2003027299

British Cataloguing-in-Publication data available.
Design by Brighid Willson

Printed on recycled, acid-free paper

Manufactured in the United States of America
10   9   8   7   6   5   4   3   2   1

Contents

Preface   ix

Part I.   Basic Concepts of Alien Invasion and Evolution   1

1.   Alien Species and Accelerated Evolution   3

2.   Adaptation of Alien Species for Dispersal and
      Establishment   17

3.   Founder Effects and Exotic Variability   32

4.   Introduction Sources, Cryptic Species, and Invasion
      Routes   47

Part II.   Processes of Evolutionary Change and Adaptation   61

5.   Hybridization and Evolution of Exotics   63

6.   Hybridization and Transgenic Organisms   76

7.   Invasion Resistance of Native Communities   89

8.   Adaptation of Alien Species to New Habitats   105

Part III. Evolutionary Interaction of Aliens and Natives   119

9.   Evolutionary Adaptation by Alien Herbivores   121

10.   Evolutionary Adaptation by Alien Predators and
       Parasites   134

11.   Adaptation of Alien Diseases to Hosts and Vectors   148

12.   Adaptation of Plants to Alien Herbivores and Diseases   161

13.   Adaptation of Native Herbivores to Alien Plants   174

14. Adaptation of Animals to Alien Predators, Parasites, and Disease Agents   188

15. Accumulation of Herbivores, Predators, and Parasites by Alien Species   202

Part IV. Global Evolutionary Consequences of Alien Invasions   217

16. Alien Species as Agents of Extirpation and Extinction   219

17. Evolutionary Ecology of Alien Biological Control Agents   232

18. Counteradaptation and Integration into the Biotic Community   245

19. Dispersing Aliens and Speciation   258

20. Permanently Altered Biotic Communities   272

Literature Cited   287

Glossary   345

Index   355

Preface

The phenomena of biological invasions and rapid evolution have come together in the last decade to reveal a host of cases of rapid evolutionary change by alien species and the native species with which they interact. All groups of organisms—plants, animals, and microorganisms of all types—are involved. These examples of rapid evolution are of great interest to theoretical biologists, but they include many aspects of applied importance, as well. The potential for the spread of transgenes from plants of economic importance to wild and weed relatives is substantial. The same is true of transgenes introduced into populations of animals, especially those of importance in aquaculture and biological control. The growing number of species introduced for biological control also means a growing potential for ecological and evolutionary shifts that enable these agents to attack nontarget hosts. More generally, the mixing of genomes of alien and native species through hybridization increases the potential for the evolution of new invasive forms.

Despite the numerous, well-publicized cases of evolutionary shifts in human disease agents and the diseases and pests of agricultural plants and animals, the public at large remains largely unaware of the accelerated pace of evolution resulting from the massive introduction of species to new geographical regions. In particular, systems of governmental regulation of alien species tend to regard them as stable genetic entities. In education, the concept of evolution is treated as a controversial theory of the history of life on earth, rather than an on-going process of great relevance to human welfare.

Recognition of the importance of rapid evolution involving alien species culminates more than a half century of interest in the biology of introduced organisms. In 1958, in perhaps one of the most forward-looking publications in ecology, Charles Elton characterized introductions of animals and plants to new regions as "one of the great convulsions of the world's flora and fauna." In the book *The Ecology of Invasions by Animals and Plants*, he pioneered the field now known as invasion biology.

Although recognized as a classic analysis, Elton's book did not immediately stimulate widespread research. In the 1970s, with growing concern about the endangerment and extinction of species, alien introductions were recognized as a major threat to native biodiversity. The risks to survival of island species and to the long-isolated biotas of regions such as New Zealand and Australia were recognized early. In the 1980s, research on the impacts of alien species expanded greatly, especially in North America, New Zealand, Australia, South Africa, and western Europe. Focused first on the impacts of aliens in terrestrial and freshwater environments, concern soon spread to the marine environment. With the availability of new techniques of genetic analysis in the 1990s, an explosion of research on population genetics and evolutionary change in alien species and interacting native species occurred. Research on alien species, and increasingly on their evolutionary biology, is now being pursued in almost all developed countries. Concern about alien species issues, however, still lags in many tropical countries.

The literature on alien species and their evolutionary biology is now growing at an enormous rate. The journal *Biological Invasions* (Kluwer Academic Publishers) began publication in 1999, and many other journals in both basic and applied areas of biology carry articles on aspects of alien species biology. The ecology and evolution of alien species are the subjects of frequent national and international meetings of scientists and environmental managers. Federal and state agencies are becoming increasingly active in efforts to control noxious alien species. Controversies relating to genetic engineering and biocontrol introductions have increased societal awareness of topics closely related to the evolutionary biology of alien species.

In this book, we will examine evolutionary issues of exotic species, drawing examples from all parts of the world and all major ecosystem types. The various technologies of analysis of the genetic composition of organisms and populations have enabled biologists to recognize evolutionary change in great detail. We have drawn from the numerous examples of recent rapid evolution that have been documented and that, more often than not, involve species that have invaded new regions within historical or postglacial time. We have also drawn from examples of natural invasions, many of which have occurred since retreat of the last continental glaciation. These give considerable insight into the patterns of evolution that are likely to result from the massive introduction of species to new geographical regions due to human activities.

To examine this rapidly developing field, in part I, we begin by examining several basic aspects of the evolutionary biology of alien species. These include the evolutionary dynamics of the dispersal and colonization processes that enable organisms to invade new areas and the patterns of genetic variability that are associated with these invasions. Within recent decades, powerful new techniques for characterizing genetic variability within populations have been developed. Among these are the well-known techniques of allozyme analysis and the more recent techniques of DNA fingerprinting and sequencing. These techniques are enabling breakthroughs in the detection of cryptic species, in describing the genetic structure of alien and source populations, in defining the number and location of establishment events, and in tracing the routes of alien species as they spread into new regions.

In part II, we examine basic relationships that determine the evolutionary potential of alien species in their new homes. These include the potential for hybridization with closely related native species or other aliens, the potential for gaining transgenes from genetically engineered species, the ability to overcome resistance of native communities to invasion, and the ability to adapt to basic abiotic and biotic conditions of the new environment. In the latter two challenges, the patterns of genetic variability that were considered in part I become key resources for adaptive evolution.

In part III, attention is turned to some of the most exciting examples of rapid evolution that have been documented in recent decades. These include the adaptation of alien species to the new native plant and animal species that they begin to exploit and the adaptation of native species to the new alien biotic agents that they encounter. Alien plants become suitable hosts for many native herbivores, whereas alien animals may exert selective influence either as enemies or as new prey or hosts. Alien plant and animal diseases or disease vectors also create strong new evolutionary pressures on many native species. For humans, understanding the evolutionary threats posed by alien species, as well as the capabilities of native species for their own evolutionary responses, is essential to sound environmental management.

Part IV provides an opportunity to look into the future, as alien invasions are a major component of global environmental change. Intentional and unintentional introductions of alien species are one of the principal causes of extirpation or extinction of native species. Additional introductions of alien species for biocontrol bring risks of similar impacts, especially because these species have the potential for evolutionary shifts in host use. In addition, alien species are becoming substantial components of biodiversity in almost all ecosystems, and it is thus essential to understand the potential of these ecosystems to assimilate them. Likewise, the potential for the aliens to stimulate speciation must be considered. Interacting with other aspects of global change, alien invasions are creating new community types and will play a major role in determining how ecosystems respond as global climates change. Humans have indeed altered the global evolutionary stage, and the evolutionary play has been speeded as a consequence.

I am indebted to many individuals for the help they have given in pulling together ideas and information from the extensive and scattered literature on evolutionary ecology of alien species. I especially thank the following individuals for reviewing one or more chapters and making valuable suggestions for improvement: Ellen Bauder, Amy C. Blair, Scott P. Carroll, Darla G. Cox, Melania E. Cristescu, Curtis C. Daehler, Margaret B. Davis, Jeffrey S. Dukes, Andrew P. Hendry, Bohun B. Kinloch, Jr., Christian Lexer, Svata M. Louda, Leroy McClenaghan, Megan McPhee, John Obrycki, Roger Peterson, Robert Ricklefs, Dolph Schluter, Kristina Schierenbeck, Craig A. Stockwell, Colin Townsend, David Truesdale, Thomas F. Turner, Kathy Williams, Lorne M. Wolfe, and Arthur Zangerl. I also thank the following individuals for helping me locate important literature: Janis Antonovics, Allison Colwell, Katie Beauchamp, Peter Bowler, Curtis C. Daehler, Jim Detling, Mark Dybdahl, Edwin D. Grosholz, Ronald Hedrick, Dan Herms, Stuart Hurlbert, Pat Johnson, James Juvik, Carolyn King, Lex Kraaijeveld, Svata Louda, Jim Mills, Gwen Mayo, Ray Newman, Jim Patton, Ian Payton, Sarah Reichard, Dave Rizzo, Dolph Schluter, Peter Sweetapple, and Lyndon Wester. Barbara Dean, executive editor for Island Press, gave many valuable suggestions for organization and presentation of the material.

GEORGE W. COX
Santa Fe, New Mexico

Part I.

Basic Concepts of Alien Invasion and Evolution

In this introductory series of chapters, we outline the basic issues of evolutionary biology of alien species and consider basic aspects of dispersal capabilities and genetic variability that are central to the study of evolutionary change by aliens.

In chapter 1, we begin our examination by reviewing the magnitude and economic impact of worldwide introduction of plants, animals, and microorganisms to new geographic regions. Patterns of rapid evolution associated with these introductions are then presented, and their general significance is described. The major evolutionary issues that will be examined in succeeding chapters are then outlined.

Chapter 2 begins our examination of specific evolutionary issues by considering the selective pressures that act on mechanisms of dispersal by species poised to invade new regions or exposed to the agents of long-distance transport that modern human technology has created. The adaptations and evolutionary responses that enable the individuals that reach new regions to become established and spread are also discussed.

In chapter 3, we consider the patterns of genetic variability that species bring with them to new regions. First, we review the most important techniques of assessing genetic variability in populations of species, both in their native source populations and in newly established alien populations. We then consider how the processes of introduction and establishment tend to influence the genetic structure of founder populations.

Finally, in chapter 4, we examine how analysis of the genetic composition of populations of alien species in their native regions and regions of introduction can reveal precise source regions and invasion routes. In addition, these analyses often are able to distinguish cryptic aliens— forms not previously recognized as alien or not clearly distinguished from each other in their morphology.

These introductory discussions prepare us to proceed to an examination of the processes by which evolutionary change and adaptation occur in alien species in their new homes.

1.

Alien Species and Accelerated Evolution

"A growing appreciation that organic evolution, like mountain building, is an ongoing rather than simply historical process has stimulated an infusion of evolutionary thinking into mainstream ecology. Foremost among the factors that have fostered this development are reports of remarkable adaptive evolution known to have taken place in recent decades. . . . "

—CARROLL ET AL. (2001)

Potato late blight (*Phytophthora infestans*) is a fungal disease of the Irish potato (*Solanum tuberosum*) and its relatives. The potato itself was domesticated in the Andean region of South America, whereas the blight fungus is believed to be native to the Toluca Valley of Mexico. The potato was introduced to Europe in the 1500s, and became a major food plant in Ireland and many other countries. A strain of the blight fungus somehow reached western Europe in the mid-1840s, where, coupled with weather conditions favorable to its development, it decimated potato crops. In Ireland, the almost total loss of the potato crop led to famine, in which 1.5 million people died and many more were forced to emigrate. Closely related strains of the fungus have since invaded all major potato-growing areas of the world. In the twentieth century, these strains have been more or less controlled by a combination of resistant potato varieties, fungicidal treatments, and sanitation.

Prior to the 1980s, strains of the blight fungus affecting potato and tomato (*Lycopersicon esculentum*) crops were of a single mating type, which reproduced asexually and showed little genetic variability. This genetic uniformity contributed significantly to the success of disease control. In the early 1980s, however, resurgence of late blight disease began to occur in the Old World, and by the late 1980s and early 1990s, severe outbreaks of the disease also affected potato crops in Canada and the United States (Fry and Goodwin 1997). These outbreaks were traced to new strains of late blight fungus that apparently originated in Mexico. The new strains were much more virulent and were resistant to one of the primary fungicides previously used to control late blight. These strains have already caused production losses measured in millions of dollars in parts of the Pacific Northwest.

Even more serious is the evolutionary potential created by these new forms of the late blight fungus. The new strains belong to the complementary mating type of the earlier fungus, so their arrival now makes possible sexual reproduction and resulting genetic recombination. Sexual reproduction has already been confirmed in several locations (Goodwin et al. 1998). New fungal strains that appear to be the result of recombination between different mating types have also been found on tomatoes in North Carolina (Wangsomboondee et al. 2002). Thus, the stage has been set for the rapid evolution of new genetic races of a fungus that is known to affect two of the world's most important crops, potatoes and tomatoes, both of which are members of a plant family containing a host of other cultivated plants.

The Economic and Ecological Impact of Alien Species

Invasive alien species are now recognized throughout the world as one of the most serious ecological and economic threats of the new millennium (Pimentel 2002). Alien plants are reducing the productivity of agricultural crops, pastures, and rangelands and are disrupting many natural terrestrial ecosystems. In addition, alien plants are choking waterways and altering the function of freshwater and marine ecosystems. Many of these plants are now legally designated as noxious weeds. Alien animals are also altering the biotic structure of land, freshwater, and marine ecosystems and are pushing many native species toward extinction. Introduced disease agents are infecting crops, livestock, fish and game animals, timber trees, and horticultural plants. Increasingly, introduced diseases and their vectors are posing new threats to human health as well. The worldwide total of species introduced to new geographical regions by human agency probably approaches half a million species (Pimentel et al. 2001).

The direct and indirect economic costs of these invaders are enormous. In the United States alone, alien plants, animals, and microbes are estimated to cause economic losses of $137.2 billion annually (Pimentel et al. 2000), with estimates for agricultural losses worldwide reaching $248 billion (Pimentel et al. 2001). An additional $4.2 billion loss occurs in the United States due to alien forest insects and pathogens. Additional direct losses result from damage by aliens to fisheries, navigation, and industry. Still other costs are incurred in fighting alien species that are endangering native plants and animals. Invasions of natural ecosystems by alien species are degrading their unique aesthetic and recreational values.

Invasions of alien species are certain to continue, in spite of increasing awareness and prevention efforts. Much of this invasion is likely to occur as a result of increasing international trade and travel (Ewel et al. 1999). For the period from 1920 to 1990, for example, Levine and D'Antonio (2003) examined the relationship between value of foreign imports to the United States and the numbers of alien mollusks, plant pathogens, and insects becoming established. The most conservative model predicted that between 2000 and 2020 some three species of mollusks, five species of plant pathogens, and 115 species of alien insects are likely to become established in the United States. Less conservative models gave numerical predictions more than tenfold greater. Increased internal trade and traffic, including exchanges of organisms mediated via the Internet (see, e.g., Kay and Hoyle 2001), also mean that the spread of alien species within the United States and other countries will be great.

Alien Species and Contemporary Evolution

These threats, however, are only the tip of an ecological and evolutionary iceberg (Palumbi 2001). The worldwide introduction of alien species is leading to rapid evolutionary change in both alien species and the native species with which they interact. Contemporary in the sense that they occur over tens to hundreds of generations rather than millions of generations, these patterns of evolution are the result of profound human influences on the natural world (Stockwell et al. 2003). The introduction of alien species is interacting with habitat destruction and degradation, overexploitation of plants and animals in natural ecosystems, and global climatic change to create an evolutionary revolution. Patterns of rapid evolution involve all groups of organisms and all patterns of organismal interaction: plant-herbivore, prey-predator, and host-pathogen systems (Thompson 1998; Gilbert 2002). Far from slowing evolutionary change, humans have accelerated evolutionary processes.

Despite the serious impacts of alien species, their dynamic evolutionary potential has received little recognition. In particular, systems of regulation and management of these species have failed to recognize this potential. Alien species are classified as beneficial, harmless, or harmful, based on an evaluation of a limited sample of individuals at a particular time, with the usual result that they are either permitted or prohibited in commerce. Little attention is given to the risk of evolutionary change by alien species once they become established in a new region.

As we shall see, all species, both native and alien, are at all times subject to evolutionary pressures that may maintain an evolutionary status quo or may lead to gradual or rapid change in genetic characteristics. Freed, in many cases, from the constraints of gene flow from their parent population and from biotic pressures of former enemies, alien species acquire exceptional evolutionary opportunities. Because populations of alien species have become established in new physical and biotic environments, however, they are subject to altered selection pressures that are likely to bring about rapid evolutionary change. In their new environment, alien species may encounter close relatives from which they had been isolated geographically. Hybridization with these relatives may enhance their evolutionary potential. Furthermore, those aliens that become abundant and highly invasive impose strong new evolutionary pressures on the natives with which they interact.

The example of late blight of potatoes is only one of many cases in which alien species pose threats to human interests through their evolutionary potential. Strong anthropogenic selection pressures imposed by pesticides, antibiotics, and environmental pollutants such as heavy metals have long been known to induce resistance in plants, animals, and microbes. Numerous plants have shown rapid evolution of resistance to heavy metals in spoil heaps associated with mining activity (Macnair 1987). Literally hundreds of plants, animals, and disease organisms, many of them alien to the regions involved, have evolved resistance to pesticides (see, e.g., National Academy of Science 1986). More than 100 plants now show resistance to herbicides, with more being recorded annually.

The potential for alien species in general to show rapid evolutionary responses to other pressures, however, has been appreciated only in the last quarter century. Numerous examples of such evolutionary responses are now available. A recent survey (Reznick and Ghalambor 2001), for example, documented 34 studies of rapid evolution in response to agents other than pesticides, antibiotics, or pollutant chemicals. Most of these studies involve evolutionary changes following the introduction of a species to an environment with novel characteristics or to a new location. Some 18 of these studies reflected rapid evolutionary changes by alien species—organisms that had invaded or been introduced to new geographical areas.

The risks of unexpected evolutionary responses of alien species have been increased by the rapidly expanding technology of genetic engineering. This is particularly true for genes that confer tolerance by crop species and other "beneficial" organisms to herbicides or other pesticides, or that confer systemic resistance to pests or diseases. The majority of these genetically transformed species possess close relatives that are cropland weeds or wild ancestral species with the potential to evolve weed races. The possibility of escape of such genes via rapid evolutionary change demands the utmost caution in their introduction to open agricultural systems.

Appreciation is also growing that evolutionary change occurs within a community context, with change in individual species both being influenced by many other species and having impacts on other aspects of the community and ecosystem. This appreciation has led some to propose community genetics as a new subfield of science (Neuhauser et al. 2003). Whether or not such a branch deserves formal recognition, the fact is that rapid evolutionary change involving alien species and the natives with which they interact is proceeding on a very complex and influential ecological stage.

Adaptation of Alien Species for Dispersal

Dispersal is a basic life history process for all organisms and one of central importance to alien species. All species possess a life history stage—spore, seed, egg, larva, or mature organism—that is adapted in some way for transport by wind or water currents, attachment to animal carriers, or active locomotion to sites that may offer suitable habitat. Plants and animals adapted to ephemeral or disturbed habitats have long been known for their ability to disperse widely and colonize new, often isolated sites. During human evolution, such species have proven to be well adapted to the habitats created by human activity. Many have followed humans as they migrated to new areas and often refined their life history traits to take advantage of humans, both as creators of habitat and as agents of dispersal. Such species are preadapted to spreading rapidly once they have been introduced to a new geographical region.

Many species have taken advantage of wheeled vehicles, seagoing ships, and airplanes as agents of transport, enabling them to cross major geographical barriers. Many of these species, especially plants, have been carried deliberately to new regions (see, e.g., Mack and Erneberg 2002), but others have hitchhiked. Modern systems of travel and commerce have become strong agents of selection for altered modes of reproduction and dispersal. The intimate association of weeds and other pests with crops and domestic animals, for example, is favored not only by the care that humans give to these domesticated species, but also by the enhanced probability that weed and pest progeny will be transported to new world regions (Gould 1991). Natural selection is constantly acting to fine-tune adaptations for dispersal by natural and human agency (Dieckmann et al. 1999).

Adaptation of Alien Species to New Environments

Alien species show diverse patterns of evolutionary adaptability when they arrive in new geographical regions. Each has a particular pattern of genetic variability that influences its potential for evolutionary change. In some cases, variability may be very limited due to the small number of individuals in the founding population. Genetic drift in small initial populations may further reduce variability by genetic bottlenecking. The genetic composition of a new population may be a biased sample of variability in the source population, the so-called founder effect. Thus, evolutionary responses may be constrained by lack of variability in many cases.

On the other hand, many colonizers, especially those of early successional or disturbed habitats, arrive with high phenotypic and genetic adaptability. Founder populations of crop weeds and arthropod pests may consist of many individuals, carrying much of the variability of their source populations. The potential for such species to evolve races adapted to local conditions has long been recognized (Baker 1974). Aquatic organisms, carried in large numbers in ballast water of cargo ships, may also possess high genetic variability. Many other aliens, especially plants, have been introduced deliberately and in abundance, and their high genetic variability is guaranteed by multiple introductions and sources.

Alien species may also acquire genetic variability after their arrival. Many weedy plants, for example, are able to hybridize with closely related crop plants. Such hybridization may provide a source of new genetic variability, including transgenes that have been introduced by genetic engineering. In addition, complex patterns of hybridization may occur among species that were once isolated geographically but have been brought together in new regions or introduced to regions where they have close relatives among native species. In addition, the genetic composition of alien plants and animals is increasingly being influenced by multiple introductions that bring together genetic races from different parts of their native range. The hybrids of such races may show greater genetic variability than individual races in the native region.

Evolutionary adaptability is favored by other genetic features (Lee 2002). In particular, the fraction of additive genetic variance within the genome strongly influences adaptive capability. Additive genetic variance represents allelic variability through which selection can progressively modify a quantitative characteristic by increasing the frequency of particular alleles. Genetic loci that show additive genetic variation are termed quantitative trait loci. Epistasis, an interaction in which one gene influences the expression of another, can also facilitate rapid evolutionary change. The potential for chromosomal restructuring by inversions, translocations, duplications, or other changes that can influence gene action is another influential factor. The extent to which selection results in trade-offs of adaptive gain in one feature and loss of adaptation in another can also influence the capacity for evolutionary change.

For those aliens with favorable genetic variability, the particular habitat conditions and biotic pressures of the new environment often result in rapid evolutionary adjustments (Thompson 1998). Physical and chemical conditions differing from those of the native region select for adaptation to the new habitat. Biotic pressures due to predators, parasites, disease agents, and competitors are also altered. In some cases, these conditions are relaxed, favoring rapid population growth and high reproductive success by aliens. In these cases, selection may favor reallocation of resources from defense to growth and reproduction. In other cases, new biotic associates may be exploited for food or for pollination and seed dispersal. In time, many of the new associates may begin to act as predators, parasites, diseases, or competitors.

In general, the population growth that often follows colonization of a new geographical area is highly favorable for rapid evolution (Reznik and Ghalambor 2001). The success of an invader in spreading through a new region is often the product of its ability to adapt to the new conditions it encounters (García-Ramos and Rodríguez 2002). High dispersal ability may introduce populations to new areas to which they are poorly adapted and in which they fail to become established. In time, however, evolutionary adaptation by more slowly spreading populations may result in successful establishment in the same new areas.

Alien Species and Evolutionary Change by Natives

Evolutionary change flows outward from established alien populations, affecting the entire biotic community to some degree. Alien plants can alter conditions of the physical environment, changing physical conditions such as light intensity, chemical conditions such as soil salinity, and resource conditions such as nutrient availability. Use of resources by alien plants or animals can bring them into competition with natives. Alien predators, parasites, and disease agents establish complex new relationships with both natives and other aliens. The aliens themselves also constitute resources for native species to exploit. The presence of alien species thus leads to reorganization of the community food web and associated pressures of natural selection.

The establishment of an alien species thus creates a nucleus of accelerated evolution within the invaded community (Carroll and Dingle 1996). The evolution of the alien itself is accelerated, as new selective pressures act on it. As the alien population grows, its influence accelerates evolutionary change by native species. Selection may favor traits that reduce negative impacts of the alien or that enable native species to take advantage of the resources the alien provides. These adjustments by native species, known collectively as counteradaptations, in time integrate the alien into an altered biotic community.

Local communities and entire regional biotas invaded by aliens are thus permanently changed. The ubiquity and abundance of many alien species virtually precludes their eradication. Some, in addition, establish mutually beneficial interactions with native species, in some cases making their eradication undesirable. Even when alien species can be removed, a community of species that has been changed by evolution remains. Return of native species to an original evolutionary state is impossible, and a "ghost of alien influence" will remain. Alien invasions, alone and in combination with the influence of global climatic change, have already created new community types in many locations (Walther 2000).

Evolution by Alien Species and Global Change

On regional and continental scales, the effects of alien invasions are now being compounded by global climatic and habitat change (Mooney and Hobbs 2000). Global change has many aspects: climatic warming, atmospheric carbon dioxide increase, increased nitrogen deposition, increased ultraviolet radiation intensity, deforestation, desertification, chemical pollution, habitat disturbance and fragmentation, and loss of biodiversity. These aspects of global change are now beginning to strain the adaptation of many native species to the conditions to which they have long been closely adjusted. Most of these changes also make it easier for alien species to become established and spread. As a result, the frequency and intensity of biotic invasions are likely to be increased by global change (Lodge 1993b;Vitousek et al. 1997).

Global change compounds the evolutionary pressures acting on invading aliens. Where communities are in disequilibrium, natural selection is likely to favor plants and animals with short life spans, high dispersal abilities, rapid population growth capacities, opportunistic patterns of resource use, and high evolutionary adaptability (Barrett 2000). Fragmentation of habitats is likely to favor species with high dispersal and colonization capabilities (Barrett 2000). Thus, increasing numbers of rapidly evolving alien species are likely to alter the composition and dynamics of all of the world's ecosystems.

Alien invasions possess the capacity to influence global climatic change (Mack et al. 2000). For example, the deliberate introduction of African tropical pasture grasses to the Amazon basin holds the potential to increase the importance of fire and inhibit the recovery of abandoned pasture areas to tropical forest. Flammable grasses would thus tend to convert forest areas into grasslands and savannas, with reduced biomass and transpiration. Such change would exacerbate the problem of atmospheric carbon dioxide accumulation as well as promote warmer and drier conditions throughout the region (fig. 1.1).

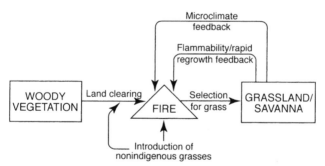

Figure 1.1. Relationships of forest, grassland, fire, and climate as affected by the widespread introduction of African pasture grasses to the Amazon basin. The positive feedbacks from the initial influences of land clearing and introduction of exotic grasses promote the increased influence of fire, which increases the tendency for transformation of the landscape from tropical forest to grassland and savanna. (Reprinted with permission from R. N. Mack, D. Simberloff, W. M. Lonsdale, H. Evans, M. Clout, and F. A. Bazzaz. 2000. Biotic invasions: causes, epidemiology, global consequences, and control. *Ecological Applications* 10:689–710. © 2000 Ecological Society of America.)

Time Lags in Impacts of Aliens

Many alien species show a substantial time lag—years or decades—between initial establishment and the appearance of strong ecological impacts (Crooks and Soulé 1999). Time lags can exist for both ecological and evolutionary reasons (Kowarik 1995). For example, a time lag can result simply from the fact that a new alien species requires time to disperse into favorable habitat patches throughout a region and to build up populations capable of producing abundant seeds or offspring. At some point, it then becomes capable of a major population explosion and serious ecological impact. Initial populations may also suffer from low reproductive success because low population density restricts beneficial social interactions among individuals, the Allee effect (Lewis and Kareiva 1993). An Allee effect appears, for example, to account for the slow increase in the eastern population and range of the house finch (*Carpodacus mexicanus*) between its introduction on Long Island, New York, in 1940 and the abrupt increase in its spread in about 1960 (Veit and Lewis 1996). Climatic shifts may also make environmental conditions favorable for invasive spread of a species long after its initial establishment.

On the other hand, an initial population may lack evolutionary adaptations that permit explosive population growth. After some time period, through genetic reorganization within the population, an evolutionary breakthrough may occur, enabling the alien to become an invasive species. A switch to earlier flowering, for example, has apparently enabled a ragwort (*Senecio inaequidens*) to become highly invasive in Europe (Kowarik 1995). Hybridization between species or between populations of a species from different source areas may be a major impetus for the evolutionary emergence of an invasive form after a time lag (Ewel et al. 1999; Ellstrand and Schierenbeck 2000).

Extirpation or Extinction of Native Species

Invasive alien species often cause the local extirpation and sometimes the complete extinction of native species. In particular, alien species introduced to insular environments such as islands, lakes, or rivers have caused numerous extirpations and extinctions in short periods of ecological time. Continental and oceanic areas are now beginning to experience these effects. Alien species may drive native species to extinction by competition, predation, or disease effects. Many native plants have suffered from hybridization and genetic swamping (Daehler and Carino 2001), as have some animals. The ability of native species to make the evolutionary adjustments necessary to prevent their extirpation or extinction varies greatly, and is a key concern of conservation biology.

The impact of alien species as agents of extirpation and extinction is of great concern because most habitats and regions of the world are being flooded by alien species in a very short period of ecological and evolutionary time. In most North American ecosystems, for example, more than 10% of species are now aliens, with more appearing every year. This rate of invasion exceeds by several orders of magnitude the invasion rate in pre-European time.

The extinction potential of this new era of alien invasions rivals the wave of extinction accompanying the colonization of the New World, Australia, New Zealand, and many oceanic islands by humans. More than half of the large mammals of North America disappeared at the end of the Pleistocene, coincident with the appearance and spread of human hunters through the New World. That human overkill is the probable mechanism of these extinctions is strongly supported by much evidence. Simulation of the population dynamics of the North American megafauna, species by species, confirms that human hunting is adequate to account for the extinction of almost all species (Alroy 2001).

In Australia, where 23 of 24 genera and 85% of species of large mammals disappeared about 46,000 yr ago, human colonization and its ecological impacts are among the most likely causes of extinction (Miller et al. 1999; Roberts et al. 2001). In New Zealand, recent data and analyses indicate that all 11 species of moas were hunted to extinction by humans in less than 100 yr, following arrival of Polynesians in the thirteenth century A.D. (Holdaway and Jacomb 2000). Throughout Melanesia, Micronesia, and Polynesia, colonization by humans between 1,000 and 30,000 yr ago resulted in extinction of more than 2,000 species of birds (Steadman 1995).

Evolutionary Responses of Native Species

One of the striking features of many invasions is a massive, early population outbreak that makes the alien form conspicuous and often highly destructive. In some species this outbreak may occur immediately after initial introduction; in others it occurs only after a delay of years, decades, or even a century. Following the outbreak, however, the population of the alien, as well as its ecological impact, may decline substantially. In many cases, native species also make ecological and evolutionary adjustments that shield them from the impacts of aliens. In addition, the population outbreak of the alien creates massive ecological and evolutionary opportunities for exploitation by members of the native community. Ecological responses may be rapid, as members of the native community learn to exploit the new community member as a food source and to avoid its direct detrimental influences. Later, evolutionary adjustments improve the ability of members of the native community to use the alien as a resource or to avoid the negative impacts of the alien.

Thus, over the long-term, evolutionary adjustments occur by members of the native community, and alien species may become integrated into the biotic assemblage. The sum of these responses or counteradaptations leads toward the reestablishment of a stable community. Stability, in this sense, implies that the alien has been accommodated at the level of dynamics of the landscape at large. That is, its regional population has stabilized, and its action in extirpation and extinction has ceased.

Not to be overlooked is the potential for pest species, native or alien, to evolve in response to selective pressures by deliberately introduced biological control agents. Although few such responses have been documented, most introduced biocontrol agents have been active only for a few years or decades. As we shall see, enough evidence has accumulated of this risk to require very detailed screening of prospective biocontrol agents and the inclusion of procedures to assess their evolutionary potential (Simberloff and Stiling 1996).

Alien Invasions and Speciation

In the short term, many biologists point out that the worldwide dispersal of alien species, combined with their role in extinction of species they encounter, is tending to homogenize the world's biota, creating, in a sense, a "New Pangaea" (Rosenzweig 2001). An often overlooked evolutionary result of the spread of alien species, however, is the establishment of new, independent evolutionary populations in different geographical areas. Over the long term, divergence and speciation of these populations will to a degree offset the extinctions that occur in the shorter term.

As we shall see, patterns of evolution of alien species and the native species with which they interact are rapid, diverse, and often startling. New species are arising before our eyes by hybridization and divergent evolution. The patterns of rapid evolution seen in species expanding their ranges into new regions in many cases involve multiple adaptive traits and multiple genes (Reznick and Ghalambor 2001). The capacity for evolutionary change in areas where competition is low and the potential for rapid population growth high is considerable. Under these conditions, strong directional selection by conditions of the physical or biotic environment can cause rapid genetic change. Invasions by alien species thus carry two potentials: a short-term threat of extinction and a longer term promise of speciation.

Alien Species, Evolution, and Conservation

A major issue now exists in defining what is and what is not an alien. Global climate change has now permitted many species to extend their ranges into regions that formerly were climatically unsuitable. Should species be regarded as aliens if they invade new areas in response to regional climatic change that makes such new areas suitable? Considering such species alien fails to recognize that range shifts in response to changing environmental conditions have always occurred, and thus are, in a sense, natural. Should the goal of conservation be to confine species to ranges defined at some arbitrary date, even in the face of changing climate? Such a strategy could lead to extinction of species if environmental change exceeds their ability for evolutionary adaptation. A modified view of what constitutes an alien will certainly be necessary.

Rapid evolution in alien environments also has major conservation implications. For example, populations of endangered species increasingly are being held in captivity or translocated to areas of habitat that are considered safe, the objective being to maintain populations that can be used to reintroduce individuals to their native areas at a future time. Rapid evolutionary change in such "safe" habitats, however, may reduce the suitability of the population for reintroduction to their original native habitats (Conant 1988). The ubiquity of rapid evolutionary change by populations introduced to new environments means that the genetic composition of endangered species must be managed as a reserve of evolutionary potential, not as gene pool locked in time (Stockwell et al. 2003).

The rapid rate of introduction of species to new geographical regions has opened a Pandora's box of evolutionary change. From the perspective of human interest, many of the evolutionary responses of aliens themselves are detrimental. Responses of native species, on the other hand, tend to mitigate some of these detrimental impacts. Thousands of uncontrolled experiments in evolution thus are being played out, giving theoretical biologists new insights about evolutionary processes and applied biologists new challenges to environmental management.

In the next chapter we shall begin to examine these issues in detail, beginning with a consideration of dispersal processes. Our objective will be to see how alien species are adapted for dispersal and the extent to which rapid evolutionary adaptation for human-assisted dispersal is occurring.

2.
Adaptation of Alien Species for Dispersal and Establishment

"Founding events provide one circumstance in which rapid changes in the external and internal (genetic) environment might occur. These events provide a possible escape from the homogenizing effects of large populations, or perhaps alter the balance of advantages in pleiotropic genes such that one of the characters they control is no longer disadvantageous. . ."

—GRAY (1986)

From 1981 to 1991, Martin Cody and Jacob Overton (1996) censused vascular plants on small islands in Barkley Sound on the west coast of Vancouver Island, British Columbia, Canada. These censuses revealed many cases of colonization and extinction. Colonization by most species resulted from seeds that were adapted for wind dispersal and were blown from mainland areas. This raised several interesting questions. First, were the seeds that reached the islands different from those that did not? Second, were the seeds of plants that maintained populations on the islands different from those of mainland plants? Third, did seed structure change through time for plants that maintained populations on the islands? For three species of wind-dispersed annual or biennial herbs of the aster family, Cody and Overton were able to compare seed morphology for populations on island and mainland areas, and, for two of the three, for islands varying in the length of time since colonization.

One species, woodland ragwort (*Senecio sylvaticus*), showed no differences between mainland and island areas, but the other two did. For one

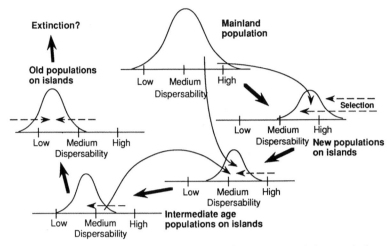

Figure 2.1. Dynamics of dispersal and natural selection on wind-dispersed plants invading islands such as those in Barkley Sound, British Columbia, Canada. New island populations tend to be founded by seeds likely to be carried farthest by wind. Once established on islands, selection favors lower tendency to be carried far by wind, since this increases the chance that seeds will be blown off the island. The curved arrows indicate the most likely patterns of dispersal. The dashed arrows indicate the influence of natural selection on dispersability and the thick arrows indicate stages in the evolutionary sequence. (Reprinted with permission from M. L. Cody and J. Overton. 1996. Short-term evolution of reduced dispersal in island plant populations. *Journal of Ecology* 84:53–61. © 1996 British Ecological Society.)

of the latter, hairy cat's ear (*Hypochoeris radicata*), seeds of island plants were about 25% larger and the volume of the feathery pappus about 34% less than for seeds of mainland plants. For the third species, wall-lettuce (*Lactuca muralis*), populations varying in age from 1 to more than 10 yr were available. Newly established populations showed smaller seeds than those of mainland plants, but seed size increased significantly with population age. Pappus volume also showed a tendency to decrease over time. Experiments also indicated that wind-carried seeds of both *Hypochoeris* and long-established *Lactuca* fell to the ground more quickly than seeds of mainland plants or newly established island plants. The significance of these changes was twofold. The seeds of *Lactuca* that were able to colonize remote islands were light and had a large pappus that favored their long-distance transport. Once established on an island, however, selection favored heavier seed with a smaller pappus, as these seeds would more likely remain on the island (fig. 2.1).

Evolutionary Adaptation for Dispersal and Establishment

Cody and Overton's study (1996) clearly shows that characteristics related to dispersal and establishment of species in new areas are subject to strong pressures of natural selection. All three of the plant species examined are aliens in North America, and part of their success is probably due to their evolutionary adaptability. For these and many other plants, animals, and microorganisms, systems of human transport and the altered environments that humans have created are influencing the evolution of basic life history features related to dispersal and establishment (Sakai et al. 2001).

Invasive species are almost by definition preadapted for dispersal into new regions and habitats that are unoccupied or that possess resources that are not fully utilized. Most such species originally evolved adaptations for dispersal by nonhuman agents, but increasingly, their long-distance dispersal is being carried out by humans. The most successful alien invaders are those that combine effective mechanisms of natural and human-assisted dispersal. Over the past millennia, especially since humans began practicing agriculture, many mechanisms have evolved to enhance the likelihood of dispersal by human agency. Successful invaders must also be adapted for quick establishment in new locations and must possess specific mechanisms for quickly capturing the resources required for growth and reproduction.

Adaptations for natural dispersal by different organisms include spores, seeds, larval stages, or other propagules that can be carried great distances by wind or water. The spores of plant pathogens such as rusts and other fungi can be carried across oceans, as well as over thousands of kilometers within continental areas (Brown and Hovmøller 2002). Plants as diverse as ferns, dandelions, milkweeds, cattails, and cottonwoods produce enormous quantities of spores or seeds that are carried long distances by wind. Pines and other forest trees produce winged seeds that are dispersed appreciable distances by strong winds. A number of invasive plants practice a "tumbleweed" mode of seed dispersal that has proven very effective. Many newly hatched spiders disperse by "ballooning," in which they produce a silk thread that enables them to be carried by wind. Most aquatic plants and animals produce seeds or larvae that are transported by water currents. Some aquatic plants simply break into fragments that can be carried to new locations, where they grow and reproduce. Floating plants, such as duckweeds (*Lemna* spp.), reproduce vegetatively and can be carried by currents to new locations.

Many plants also possess adaptations for dispersal by animals by a variety of techniques, such as burs that entangle in animal fur or spiny joints that embed in animal skin. In central Mexico, a surprising number of cropland weeds possess burrs, hooks, or awns that appear to adapt them for dispersal on the clothing of farmers (Vibrams 1999). Other plants produce fruit that contains seeds that pass intact through the digestive tract of animals. In most cases, animal-assisted dispersal functions only for short distances. Although waterfowl and other plant-feeding birds may fly long distances on migration, the probability of transport of viable seed in their digestive tracts to distant, yet suitable, habitats is small (Charalambidou and Santamaría 2002; Clausen et al. 2002). Most seeds eaten by waterfowl prior to migratory flights, for example, are probably discharged within 300 km of the feeding area.

Many animals possess active means of dispersal by locomotion on land or through air or water. Aquatic animals that live attached to the substrate as adults produce larvae that can swim or float to new locations. Insects with flightless aquatic or terrestrial larvae disperse as winged adults. For many terrestrial and aquatic animals with moderate locomotion capabilities, dispersal tends to follow closely the distribution of suitable, closely spaced habitat areas. Vertebrates and many invertebrates that are capable of long-distance movements often rely on complex behavioral and sensory abilities to recognize appropriate new habitats.

Dispersal and establishment by parasites and diseases require a suitable host plant or animal and, in some cases, a different alternate host or required vector species. Parasites or diseases with direct life cycles, in which the infective agent or its reproductive stage is transferred to a new host without using an alternate host or vector, are more likely to invade new regions (Dobson and May 1986). Parasites of freshwater fish, for example, show this pattern, with 39 of 48 parasites that are successful invaders being capable of direct transmission.

Natural dispersal mechanisms, however, seem to play a very small role in the dispersal of alien species across major geographical barriers such as major mountain ranges, deserts, and oceans. In particular, dispersal of plants across ocean barriers by wind or water currents is not known to have led to the recent introduction of invasive plants anywhere in the world (Mack and Lonsdale 2001). Within continental areas, however, natural dispersal mechanisms have enabled many arriving alien species to spread rapidly through areas of favorable habitat.

Dispersal of vertebrate animals introduced to new continents has often been extremely rapid. In North America, birds such as the house sparrow

(*Passer domesticus*), European starling (*Sturnus vulgaris*), and cattle egret (*Bubuculus ibis*) showed exponential population growth that enabled them to colonize suitable habitat from coast to coast in 50 yr or less (Cox 1999). The Eurasian collared dove (*Streptopelia decaocto*) is now spreading through the United States and Mexico in a similar manner. In Italy, gray squirrel (*Sciurus carolinensis*) populations introduced to a broad-leafed woodland area in 1970 are now spreading exponentially and are likely to spread throughout broad-leafed forests of Europe and Asia (Bertolino and Genovesi 2003).

Inadvertent Human-assisted Dispersal

Humans have assumed major roles as unknowing agents of dispersal of plants, animals, and microbial species. On a local scale, seeds, spores, and other propagules are often dispersed in mud on tires of motor vehicles and shoes of hikers (see, e.g., Jules et al. 2002). Plant seeds are carried by almost all types of transport vehicles, so the dispersal of many invasive plants tends to follow railroad lines and highways. On a broader scale, human-assisted dispersal is responsible for the vast majority of intercontinental and interoceanic introductions of alien species. Cargo ships and aircraft carry propagules of all types of organisms across previously insurmountable barriers. They provide rapid mechanisms of dispersal to which some species are preadapted and to which others may evolve adaptations.

Perhaps the most common inadvertent means of introduction of alien plants to new continents has been via crop seed contaminants. In the northeastern United States, 6–7% of the alien plants that became established before 1900, and are now thoroughly naturalized, were introduced via contaminated crop seed (Mack and Erneberg 2002). Many of these species introductions were truly inadvertent, their seeds being accidentally included because of inadequate techniques of seed cleaning. In some cases, however, they were deliberately added by seed merchants to increase the volume of their seed sales.

Cropland Weed Adaptation for Dispersal by Humans

Many cropland weeds have capitalized on dispersal as crop seed contaminants. These species have evolved races that show patterns of growth and reproduction that mimic those of crop plants (Barrett 1983). These forms, known as agroecotypes, are largely restricted to stands of cultivated crops. Agroecotypes are often weedy races of the crop plant itself, with the mimicry being enhanced by gene exchanges between crop and weed races. In some cases, the mimicry is largely confined to vegetative similarity, and the weedy plant simply produces and drops seed at or prior to crop harvest. In other cases, mimicry extends to seed characteristics, ensuring that weed seeds are harvested, and thus dispersed and planted, with those of crop plants. The germination, growth, and reproduction of the weed race typically match the phenology of the crop plant. These adaptations have led to the introduction of many agroecotypes to new continental areas as contaminants of grain used for seed.

Perhaps the most remarkable set of agroecotypes is that associated with rice (Barrett 1983). Some of these are wild relatives and weedy races of cultivated rice (*Oryza sativa*). Others are races of barnyard grass (*Echinochloa crus-galli*) that have evolved to mimic the phenology, vegetative appearance, and seed morphology of cultivated rice. Two chromosome races of *E. crus-galli*—the tetraploid race, *phylopogon*, and the hexaploid race, *oryzoides*—are worldwide in distribution in areas where irrigated rice is grown. These races are essentially restricted to rice fields, although other forms of *E. crus-galli* occur as weeds outside rice fields. Needless to say, dispersal from their Asian region of origin has been as a contaminant in rice seed.

Crop mimicry is perhaps most frequent among grain crops but is by no means limited to grains (Barrett 1983). An agroecotype of vetch (*Vicia sativa*), for example, possesses flattened seeds that mimic those of lentils (*Lens esculenta*). False flax (*Camelina sativa*), a member of the mustard family, is a mimic of cultivated flax (*Linum usitatissimum*).

Dispersal by Deliberate Introduction

Characteristics that make plants and animals valuable or attractive to humans are, in a sense, preadaptations for their dispersal to new geographical regions. Crop, forestry, and horticultural plants, domestic animals and exotic wildlife, aquacultural fish and shellfish, species prized by the pet and aquarium trade—all have gained access to new geographical areas because of their value or attractiveness to humans.

European colonization of many world regions led to the deliberate introduction of many plants and animals. Many plants were introduced to North America and other world regions from Europe in early Colonial times because of their agricultural, medicinal, or herbal properties. Numerous grasses and legumes were widely introduced, also beginning in Colonial times, because of their real or supposed value as forages. Introductions for forestry and horticulture become important somewhat later and have continued to the present. In the eastern United States, between 61 and 68% of plants, depending on location, that were introduced before 1900 and have become thoroughly naturalized were deliberately introduced (Mack and Erneberg 2002). These percentages are likely to be low because the manner of introduction of 31–37% of naturalized species could not be determined with certainty. For Hawaii, about 57% of naturalized species were deliberately introduced (Wester 1992). Since 1900, the percentage of naturalized plants that were deliberately introduced has tended to be even higher in many areas, including the United States, Australia, and New Zealand (Mack and Erneberg 2002).

Many species of trees have been introduced to new regions for timber production, fuelwood, creation of windbreaks, stabilization of stream banks, or wetland reclamation. Australian eucalypts have been introduced throughout the world for timber and fuelwood production and for use as windbreaks. Russian olive (*Eleagnus angustifolia*) and Siberian elm (*Ulmus pumila*), together with other species, were planted extensively in central North America as windbreaks and landscaping trees. Several varieties of tamarisk (*Tamarix* spp.) were used for stabilization of stream banks in the southwestern United States in the early twentieth century. In Florida, Australian melaleucas were planted in hopes that they would help reclaim marshland by increasing transpiration of water. Russian olives, tamarisks, and melaleucas have become very serious invaders in their areas of introduction in North America.

In terms of number of alien species, horticultural attractiveness accounts for more introductions of invasive woody plants in the United States than any other perceived value (Reichard and White 2001). In Australia, similarly, 65% of all plants that have become naturalized were introduced for horticulture. Deliberate introduction for horticultural and related use is responsible for establishment of many plants that reproduce vegetatively (Pyšek 1997).

Animals have also been deliberately transported to new areas. Domestic livestock, including cattle, horses, sheep, goats, and rabbits, have been introduced to many oceanic islands or have become feral after their introduction for husbandry. Various game and fur-bearing animals have been released on islands or new continental areas or have escaped from farms. Game birds and songbirds have been introduced to new geographical areas for sport and pleasure. Game fish have been freely translocated to new waters, both within and between continents. Fish and invertebrates introduced for aquaculture or aquarium display have escaped or been released into natural waters and established wild populations. The ecological impacts of many of these introductions are substantial (Cox 1999). We shall examine the role of some in extirpation and extinction of native species in chapter 16.

History of Human-assisted Dispersal

Long-distance human transport of plants falls historically into three phases: accidental, utilitarian, and aesthetic (Mack and Lonsdale 2001). The accidental phase, which began with the first colonial settlements in the Americas, Australia and New Zealand, and many other world regions, involved the unintentional introduction of ruderal plants—those that inhabit roadsides and wasteland areas—and crop weeds to these areas from Europe. Within 50 yr of the first settlements in New England, for example, at least 22 European plants had become common yard and garden weeds. Most of these probably arrived as contaminants in crop seed or animal fodder. Others reached new continents as seeds in soil used as ship ballast, which was usually dumped onshore following a transoceanic voyage. The utilitarian phase of introductions comprises the numerous deliberate introductions of plants for herbal and medicinal use, pasture improvement, and forestry. The aesthetic phase constitutes deliberate introduction of plants for horticultural purposes. Obviously, these phases overlap, and today introductions still occur for all of the reasons cited above.

With the development of transoceanic ship travel and commerce, many characteristics of aquatic plants and animals became preadaptations for accidental long-distance dispersal. These adaptations now function for dispersal of organisms across ocean areas, along marine coastlines, and to and from interior seas and large lakes. These characteristics include sessile growth in shallow marine habitats, which preadapted plants and animals for growth on the hulls of ships, and tolerance of conditions in ballast water that came into use by modern transoceanic shipping. Ballast-water transport has been responsible for introducing about 35 species of fish to new areas throughout the world (Wonham et al. 2000). Broad salinity tolerance has been a major factor in the recent ballast-water introductions of invertebrates and fish from the Black, Caspian, and Azov seas of Asia to the North American Great Lakes, for example (Ricciardi and Rasmussen 1998).

The ability to survive as seeds, eggs, larvae, or adults for periods of weeks or months has enabled many plants and animals to stow away in cargo carried by ships, railroads, and land transport. The rapid naturalization and spread of alien plants in North America during the late 1800s, for example, was probably promoted by the expansion of railroad systems and commerce (Mack 2003). The enormous growth of air cargo now enables many alien species to reach new areas in a matter of hours.

A little-appreciated mode of dispersal of alien species is via public or private mail and parcel post systems. Regardless of federal and state laws prohibiting the transport of designated species across national or state lines, it is easy to mail such species almost anywhere. The growth of e-commerce has increased this risk. Kay and Hoyle (2001), for example, found that almost every aquatic or wetland plant that carried a state or federal designation as a noxious weed could be ordered from an aquatic plant nursery somewhere. Plants federally designated as noxious weeds in the United States could be obtained from nurseries in both North America and Europe.

Dispersal Capabilities and Invasiveness

Reaching a new region and establishing a population there are only the first phases of the invasion process (Shigesada and Kawasaki 1997). Some alien species sooner or later undergo an expansion phase that introduces them into suitable habitat throughout the new region. Many other adaptations function to enable this expansion or invasion phase and determine its pattern and speed (National Research Council 2002). For seed plants, biologists have searched with only moderate success for characteristics that would serve as predictive tools for plant invasiveness. Invasive plants are quite varied in their characteristics, and the attributes that create invasiveness are still not clearly understood.

Many aggressive alien weeds are self-fertilizing, apomictic (meaning that they produce seed without fertilization), or have vigorous modes of vegetative reproduction (Brown and Marshall 1981). The climbing ferns (*Lygodium* spp.) that are rapidly spreading in Florida, for example, possess gametophyte stages in which self-fertilization is common (Lott et al. 2003). This enables single sporophyte plants, established by wind-carried spores, to reproduce once they become established in a new location.

Several seed plant features show a high statistical relation to invasiveness. For woody plants, these include small individual seed mass, short generation time, frequent large seed crops, and high mass-specific relative growth rate (Rejmánek 1996a; Grotkopp et al. 2002). Small seed size is in turn correlated with small nuclear DNA content and small cell volume, which seem to be correlated with rapid growth to maturity and seed production. Small seed mass also correlates with large seed number, wider seed dispersal, high germination, and a short chilling period needed to break seed dormancy. These characteristics, derived from an analysis of invasive and noninvasive species of pines, have proven useful in identifying invasive plants among a wide range of woody angiosperms (Rejmánek 1996a).

Experimental studies of growth ʹrates of invasive and noninvasive species of pines, carried out by Grotkopp et al. (2002), concluded that the best distinguishing factor was growth rate per unit mass of plant tissue. This, in turn, was closely related to specific leaf area—the area of leaf surface per unit of leaf mass. This study also supported the importance of small seed size and short generation time as predictors of invasiveness of pines.

Based on an analysis of a global data set of agricultural weeds, invasive species were found to show statistical tendencies to be pollinated and dispersed abiotically (Daehler 1998). For species known to be invaders of natural vegetation, however, species capable of nitrogen fixation and species with a vine growth form were more frequent than expected (Daehler 1998; Pyšek 1997).

Altogether, these adaptations suggest a pattern of growth that enables invasive species to preempt resources, either in time or space. Rapid germination and growth enable invasives to preempt resources early in a growing season. Clonal growth and abundant seed production permit plants to capture resources in horizontal space and, through their climbing ability or rapid vertical growth, to gain the light resource by overtopping competitors.

Another major set of factors related to the success of alien species are those to which members of invaded communities are not adapted. For example, chemical inhibition has been suggested as a mechanism underlying the success of some invasive plants (Callaway and Aschehoug 2000). Diffuse knapweed (*Centaurea diffusa*), native to Eurasia, has become a serious invasive weed in parts of western North America. This plant produces root exudates that inhibit the growth of perennial bunchgrasses in North America, although not of related Eurasian bunchgrasses. Similarly, herbivores and predators that invade island areas previously free of such animals encounter plants and prey lacking adaptations to avoid their easy exploitation.

A number of other correlations exist with respect to invasive plants, although these do not yet give a clear indication of an underlying adaptive mechanism. For example, some studies have suggested that the most pernicious invasive species are members of genera that do not occur in the invaded region. A few examples include trees such as ailanthus, casuarina, Brazilian pepper, tamarisk, and Russian olive in North America and various species of pines in South Africa (Rejmánek 1996a). Studies in Hawaii, on the other hand, suggest that in most plant families invasive species tend to belong to genera that are already present rather than new genera (Daehler 2001). Whether this represents a consistent difference between continental and insular regions is not yet clear.

Additional sets of statistically significant correlations involve the tendency for invasive plants to have an extensive range in their native region and to be invasive in more than one geographical region. In eastern Canada, for example, Goodwin et al. (1999) studied 165 pairs of European plant species, one member of which had invaded eastern Canada and one of which had not. They found that 70% of the Canadian invaders could be predicted from their distribution in Europe. In an analysis of 235 species of alien woody plants that have become naturalized in North America, Reichard and Hamilton (1997) found that invasiveness in other regions was the most reliable predictor of whether or not a species would be invasive in North America.

Biological features related to invasiveness for animals are similar to those of plants in many ways. Ehrlich (1986) noted, for example, that invasive animals tended to be have broad feeding habits, high adaptability to physical conditions, short generation times, high genetic variability, and a tendency for association with humans. Lodge (1993a) also noted that invasive animals showed high dispersal rates, phenotypic plasticity, and often asexual reproduction. For aquatic organisms, McMahon (2002) found that Eurasian zebra mussels (*Dreissena polymorpha*) and Asian clams (*Corbicula fluminea*) contrast sharply with native North American clams in having extremely high fecundity, rapid growth, early maturity, and short life span. Nonnative ants, particularly those with worker castes that fight in competition with other ants, tend to be smaller-bodied than congeneric native species (McGlynn 1999), although the benefit of small size is not certain.

For introduced land bird species, Cassey (2002) found that habitat generalism tended to favor establishment success, together with nonmigratory behavior and lack of sexual dimorphism in plumage. Dietary and nest site flexibility have also been related to establishment success of birds introduced to islands (McLain et al. 1999).

Rapid Evolution of Enhanced Dispersal

The introduction of species to new geographical areas, coupled with global climate change that is altering the locations of climatically suitable habitats, means that selection for enhanced dispersal capability is acting on many species. Modeling studies show that in many cases selection should favor higher dispersal tendencies in populations at expanding edges of their range (Travis and Dytham 2002). However, for species showing a strong Allee effect—reduced population growth effects at densities below some optimum—selection for increased dispersal capability may be low (Lewis and Kareiva 1993).

A few studies have examined rapid evolution of characteristics related to the actual dispersal process. As we saw at the chapter outset for annual plants that colonized islands in Barkley Sound, British Columbia, such characteristics can be subject to intense selective pressures (Cody and Overton 1996). Cwynar and MacDonald (1987) found that seed mass of lodgepole pine (*Pinus contorta*) was smallest in the northernmost and most recently established stands in the Canadian Rocky Mountains. Seed mass increased significantly with estimated time since founding of stands as lodgepole pine migrated north following glacial retreat. Similar selection pressures are especially likely to act on species colonizing any sort of fragmented habitat. Roff (1990) concluded, for example, that among insects, the loss of flight capability was lowest in species that use patchy habitats. Inasmuch as habitat fragmentation is a major feature of global environmental change, alien species in particular will experience strong selection for the ability to colonize such habitats (Barrett 2000).

Similar selection has acted on animal species, such as the speckled wood butterfly (*Pararge aegeria*), a widespread species in the western parts of Europe and North Africa. In the United Kingdom, the species greatly expanded its range during the latter part of the twentieth century. Sometime between 1976 and 1985, it also colonized the island of Madeira, about 540 km west of Morocco. Hill et al. (1999) compared the body size and morphology of recent colonist populations with those where the species had long been resident. Colonists tended to be larger in body size, and in the case of the subspecies in the United Kingdom, to have larger thoraxes, where wing muscles are located, and broader wings. These differences were suggestive that selection favored particular adaptations for flight in source populations of colonist butterflies.

In England, two species of bush crickets have been expanding their ranges northward from areas along the southern coast (Thomas et al.

2001). One, the long-winged cone-head (*Conocephalus discolor*), possesses two forms, short-winged and long-winged. Localities colonized within the past 20 yr show higher frequencies of the long-winged form than do localities occupied for more than 20 yr. The evidence is strong that this difference is at least partly genetic. The second species, Roesel's bush cricket (*Metrioptera roeselii*), also has two forms, a flightless short-winged form and a long-winged form capable of flight. The long-winged form shows higher frequencies in more recently colonized localities. Similar observations exist for ground beetles expanding their ranges northward in southern Canada (Niemalä and Spence 1991). In these cases, it appears likely that under climatic conditions favoring range expansion, the more dispersive forms of these insects are favored. Under stable climates, the more sedentary forms may be favored. We shall consider this relationship in more detail in chapter 20.

For organisms dispersed over long distances by vehicles of transport and commerce, strong selection exists for tolerance of the special conditions of these agents. For example, broad salinity tolerance should favor the survival of aquatic organisms during transoceanic voyages, during which ballast water exchanges may occur (Ricciardi and Rasmussen 1998). Broad salinity tolerance should also favor establishment in areas into which ballast water is ultimately discharged. Whether or not rapid evolutionary responses have occurred as a consequence of such selection is not yet known.

Rapid Evolution of Enhanced Establishment Capability

Strong selection also exists for reproductive success by individuals that have reached new, favorable environments. Genetic variants that have a reduced reliance on outcrossing or on biotic pollination mechanisms are likely to be favored in small, isolated populations. Gradual evolutionary shifts from outcrossing to self-fertilization may be one of the evolutionary processes underlying the time lag phenomenon associated with the rise of many introduced species to the status of seriously invasive species.

In several cases, introduced plant species have rapidly evolved higher rates of self-fertilization (Brown and Marshall 1981). Smooth cordgrass (*Spartina alterniflora*), introduced to San Francisco Bay in the mid-1970s, has spread over open mudflats to form discrete, circular, clonal patches with varying degrees of isolation from each other. This species is normally strongly outcrossing in its reproductive mode. The San Francisco Bay colonies are derived from a few individuals, however, and the flowering times of the different patches vary considerably. Although inbreeding depression is high in many self-fertilizing plants, many highly self-fertile clones exist and carry out most of the seed production in the overall population. The relatively unoccupied mudflat habitat also favors successful germination and growth of seeds produced by selfing plants that might have failed in their native range on the Atlantic coast. In this case, selection is apparently favoring self-fertilization, at least during the early stages of the invasion process (Daehler 1999).

Selfing mating systems, in general, have been postulated to evolve in species that follow a strategy of colonization of new or newly created habitats (see, e.g., Holsinger 1988). Genetic bottlenecking that results from small founder populations may eliminate the advantage of genetic recombination and thus favor increased certainty of reproduction through selfing.

On the other hand, shifts toward increased outcrossing have been documented in a number of introduced plants (Brown and Marshall 1981). In Australia, soft brome (*Bromus mollis*) and subterranean clover (*Trifolium subterraneum*), both primarily selfing plants, have shown increases in outcrossing rates. This shift presumably increases the level of genetic recombination, which may increase adaptability of these species to local environmental conditions.

Rapid adaptation of seed production and germination characteristics of several plants have been documented. Common groundsel (*Senecio vulgaris*) exhibits a variety *vulgaris* that occurs in both ruderal habitats and agricultural habitats, such as cropland, orchards, and plant nurseries. Populations in these two habitats are genetically differentiated ecotypes (Leiss and Müller-Schärer 2001). The ecotype from agricultural habitats produced more flowering heads and, when fertilized, showed a greater increase in seed production than the ruderal ecotype. Similar results were obtained for common chickweed (*Stellaria media*) by Sobey (1987).

The Chinese tallow tree (*Sapium sebiferum*) was introduced to Georgia in the late 1700s. Subsequently, in the early twentieth century, trees were introduced to Louisiana and Texas from an undocumented source. The latter introductions have proven invasive, in contrast to the Georgia plants (Siemann and Rogers 2001). In a common garden experiment in which trees were grown from seedlings for 14 yr, 60–70% of those from Louisiana and Texas began to set seed, whereas less than 20% of those from Georgia or from Taiwan, where the species is native, became reproductive. Thus, it appears likely that an invasive, early reproducing geno-type evolved in the southeastern United States.

Seed dormancy is another characteristic that has evolved rapidly in several alien plants. Cheatgrass (*Bromus tectorum*), an annual, has invaded open habitats throughout much of North America. For such a plant, germination must be timed to correspond with the season of assured moisture availability, not just irregular rainfall events. Allen and Meyer (2002) examined the germination behavior of cheatgrass from populations in different environments in the western United States. Plants from the Mojave Desert had strong dormancy and required prolonged after-ripening drying. In the Mojave, seeds ripen in June, but assured moisture is not available until the following winter rains. Thus, the dormancy mechanism prevents germination during occasional summer thunderstorms that do not provide enough moisture for plants to mature. Plants from mountain areas, on the other hand, show little dormancy. These plants mature in late July, when both temperature and moisture conditions are often favorable for immediate growth. These dormancy patterns are genetic and have evolved in about 100 yr.

Differences in seed dormancy and germination have been found in several other weedy plants. Variety *vulgaris* of common groundsel, in fact, is derived from *Senecio denticulatus* ssp. *vulgaris*, from which it differs in lacking seed dormancy (Moritz and Kadereit 2001). Canada thistle (*Cirsium arvense*) also exhibits ecotypes differing in seed dormancy and germination patterns (Moore 1975).

Dispersal Adaptation and Genetic Variability

Thus, we can see that a diverse set of characteristics can preadapt organisms to be successful invaders of new geographical regions, especially with the assistance of the rapidly expanding systems of international travel and commerce. These transport systems, coupled with the massive human modification of landscapes, place strong selection pressures on plants and animals. Patterns of rapid evolution in response to these pressures are only recently being recognized.

The evolutionary responses that dispersing and newly established aliens are able to make depend on the genetic variability that exists among this select group of individuals. The number of colonists, their geographical origins, the frequency of dispersal events, and the mode of reproduction all influence the evolutionary potential of an alien colonist. We shall examine these important variables in the next chapter.

3.
Founder Effects and Exotic Variability

"The initial genetic structure of a successful invasive population depends on several factors, including the effective size of the introduction event(s), the genetic diversity of the source population(s), and the number of founding sources."

—STEPIEN ET AL. (2002)

The Argentine ant (*Linepithema humile*) is native to South America and was introduced to the United States in about 1891 in ocean cargo shipped to New Orleans. It quickly made its way to California, where it has become a serious pest of agriculture, urban residential areas, and natural environments. Argentine ants reach very high densities and displace most native ant species, as well as many other ground-living arthropods. In doing so, they are threatening a specialist ant-feeder, the coast horned lizard (*Phrynosoma coronatum*). In Argentina, in contrast, Argentine ants are not nearly as abundant and do not displace other ant species.

Analysis of the genetics of the introduced populations, using the DNA microsatellite technique (see below), shows that the three microsatellite loci examined have only 47% of the variability that is seen in populations in Argentina (Suarez et al. 1999). The microsatellite alleles present in California are also a subset of those noted in Argentina. The frequency of heterozygous individuals was about 9% in California, compared to about 30% in Argentina. This clearly indicates that the population introduced in

New Orleans carried only a fraction of the genetic variability of the native South American population.

The greatly reduced genetic variability in the California population may be a major contributor to its pest status. In Argentina, this ant is much less abundant than it is in California, and ants from different nests show high levels of aggression toward each other. In California, ants from different nests show little or no aggression, so neighboring nests form "supercolonies" over large areas. Individual ants, both workers and queens, are able to move freely among these nests. This lack of aggression seems to result in part from the genetic homogeneity of the population. In effect, the ants do not show recognizable differences that would identify them as being from different nests. A similar pattern of low aggression is shown by Argentine ants in central Chile, where they have also been introduced.

In addition, following introduction of Argentine ants to North America, natural selection now is apparently acting against spread of genetic variability within the continental population (Tsutsui et al. 2003). Ants from colonies of low genetic diversity attack and kill those from more genetically diverse colonies. This behavior tends to reinforce the supercolony structure of the overall population.

Assessing Genetic Variability

The case history of the Argentine ant in North America demonstrates that the degree of genetic variability of an alien species may have major implications for its impact. In this chapter, we shall examine the patterns of genetic variability that exist in populations of alien plants and animals. Many techniques are now available for assessing genetic variability within populations and determining the degree of genetic similarity among populations (Parker et al. 1998). Thus, we are able to compare variability in populations of introduced species to variability in their populations in areas to which they are native. We can also evaluate how the level of genetic variability in introduced populations influences their evolution in the new environment.

Techniques for assessing genetic variability in samples of individuals from populations involve analysis of variability in enzyme structure (see, e.g., Buth and Murphy 1999) and in nuclear or organelle DNA and RNA structure (Hillis et al. 1996; Krawczak and Schmidke 1998). These techniques include allozyme analysis, various DNA fingerprinting techniques such as DNA fragment length polymorphism analyses, microsatellite analysis, mitochondrial DNA (mtDNA) analysis, chloroplast DNA (cpDNA) analysis, and sequencing of DNA and RNA genes or sectors. DNA analysis, in particular, is an active and rapidly developing field.

Allozyme Analysis

The oldest and least expensive form of genetic analysis is enzyme electrophoresis, a technique for detecting variation in the genes coding particular enzymes. Allozymes are different forms of an enzyme coded by different alleles at a single genetic locus. From 20 to 40%, or sometimes more, of the loci coding enzymes show variability in different groups of organisms (Parker et al. 1998). Allozyme analysis can detect patterns of heterozygosity as well as allele frequencies.

For an allozyme analysis, enzymes are first extracted from macerated tissue. The extract is then placed in a starch gel, cellulose acetate gel, or other gel medium and subjected to electrophoresis. An electrophoretic gradient is created by placing the gel in contact with two trays containing a buffer solution and connected to a power source. Several buffer solutions may be used, depending on the enzymes chosen for analysis. In the electrophoretic gradient, different molecular forms of enzymes migrate through the gel at different rates. After migration has occurred, an enzyme-specific stain is applied to the gel to define bands corresponding to the points to which different enzyme forms have migrated. Allozyme analyses are usually carried out on many enzymes. The number of different forms present in individuals or populations can thus be determined for each enzyme, and variability within and among populations can be evaluated from results for all enzyme analyses.

DNA Fragment Length Polymorphism Analyses

DNA fragment length polymorphism analyses are based on the action of restriction enzymes, which cut double-stranded DNA at points where a specific sequence of four to eight nucleotides occurs (Parker et al. 1998). DNA is first extracted from the plant or animal material. One or several restriction enzymes are then used to cut the DNA into fragments. Differences due to nucleotide substitutions, additions, subtractions, or rearrangements may exist within these fragments. Depending on the objective of the analysis and knowledge of specific gene structure, various approaches may be followed to detect these differences.

Restriction Fragment Length Polymorphism (RFLP)

The RFLP procedure is most suited to analysis of variation within a species or among closely related species. The objective usually is to determine if allelic variation exists for a particular gene. To detect allelic differences, the products of digestion by restriction enzymes are hybridized with a radioactively labeled DNA probe. This probe is a short sequence of DNA, chosen to match a portion of the gene under analysis, combined with a label such as a radioisotope. The DNA fragments created by use of restriction enzymes are separated by gel electrophoresis and hybridized with the probe. Then the positions of the hybridized fragments are identified on an x-ray film. If genetic variations exist that affect the length of DNA fragments containing the gene, bands will appear at slightly different positions on the electrophoretic gel.

Amplified Fragment Length Polymorphism (AFLP)

In the AFLP technique, double-stranded DNA is digested with two restriction enzymes, one that cuts at a specific six-nucleotide section and one at a specific four-nucleotide section. Specific double-stranded DNA adapters, usually about 25–30 base pairs in length, are then ligated to the ends of restriction fragments. DNA primers, complementary to the adapters except for a specific extension of three nucleotides, are then used to prepare a subset of the restriction fragments for amplification by the enzyme DNA polymerase, a procedure termed polymerase chain reaction (PCR). These primers attach to the fragments with the complementary adapter and extension sequence. The DNA region amplified thus depends on the primers. These may be specific to a particular region of the genome, such as a specific gene. Only the fragments that hybridize with the primers are amplified. Amplification involves the annealing of the double-stranded DNA, that is, its separation into individual strands, and its replication by DNA polymerase. This process is repeated 30–40 times, and the fragments with attached primers are increased enormously in abundance. The amplified DNA fragments are then separated by electrophoresis on a polyacrylamide gel. The locations of these fragments are then determined by staining or application of a radioactive probe.

Random Amplified Polymorphic DNA Analysis (RAPD)

The RAPD technique is similar to the AFLP technique but usually does not involve the use of restriction enzymes (Williams et al. 1990). The primers used in RAPD are only 10 bases in length and consequently find many more binding sites than 20-base primers. Several to many primers can be used. These primers work throughout the genome and attach at points where their structure matches that of a DNA segment. Primer pairs that attach with an orientation toward each other define the segments that are to be amplified. Amplification is carried out by PCR, using a procedure similar to that in AFLP. Binding sites flanking DNA segments up to about 2,000 or so base pairs in length can be amplified. The resulting amplified fragments are from unknown locations and are considered to be of random origin within the genome. Within these amplified segments, differences in DNA arrangements may exist. After amplification, the DNA segments are separated by electrophoresis and stained. When a series of many primers is used, up to 100–200 electrophoretic bands typically can be seen, some or many of which will show polymorphisms. For example, in a study of variability of water spinach in Florida, Van and Madeira (1998) used 18 primers and found 188 different bands, 31% of which were polymorphic. Analyses such as this allow both the degree of polymorphism and the similarity of samples from different populations to be assessed.

Microsatellite Analysis

Another indicator of genetic variability is variation in DNA microsatellites, which are present in the genomes of many organisms. Microsatellites are sections of DNA in which a sequence of one to about six nucleotides is repeated along DNA strands. For example, the bases ATT (adenine-thymine-thymine) might be repeated along a strand of DNA in a sequence of 12 successive units (ATTATTATT . . . ATT). These sequences do not code for protein. They tend to be localized in centromeric or noncoding regions of the chromosomes. Although their origin and function are still not fully understood, evidence is accumulating that microsatellites have organizational or regulatory functions within the genome (Li et al. 2002). The number of microsatellite units at a particular location varies, however, so they can be analyzed in a manner analogous to alleles of a DNA gene. Microsatellites mutate by changes in the number of repeated units. The mutation rate of these units is much higher than the rate of point mutation at nuclear gene loci, leading to extensive variation in the number of repeats. These mutations are believed to occur either by slippage of complementary DNA strands during replication or by unequal recombination between complementary DNA strands (Li et al. 2002).

For microsatellite analysis, genomic DNA is extracted and treated with restriction enzymes. The microsatellite sequences are usually flanked by special DNA sequences that allow specific primers to be used to amplify the microsatellite sections. Using DNA polymerase, microsatellite sections are then amplified and units of different length are separated by gel electrophoresis.

Microsatellites can thus be used to determine the degree of variability within a population or the similarity of individuals from different populations. The degree of heterozygosity of individuals can also be assessed, since individuals possess two microsatellite sequences, one from the male and one from the female parent. Population differences can sometimes be detected by analysis of microsatellites when little difference appears in analyses of allozymes or mtDNA.

Mitochondrial DNA Analysis

Animal mitochondria contain a circular DNA molecule about 15,000–20,000 base pairs long. The DNA codes for subunits of several mitochondrial enzymes and for several forms of RNA. It also possesses a noncoding control region that is highly variable. Mitochondria occur in the cell cytoplasm, and in animals more than 99.9% of mtDNA is inherited from the female parent. In almost all species, mtDNA is transmitted without recombination to offspring. Most cells contain between hundreds and thousands of copies of the mtDNA molecule, making it a relatively easy form of DNA to obtain. It is also the form of DNA most likely to survive for long periods after the death of an organism. Some museum specimens, for example, are good sources of mtDNA, although it is usually impossible to extract DNA from specimens preserved in formalin.

The noncoding, control region (d-loop) of the mitochondrial genome shows a higher rate of evolutionary change than nuclear DNA. Analysis of mtDNA involves extraction of the DNA, amplification of the control region portion of the molecule with primers and DNA polymerase, and sequencing of the resulting DNA. The sequences obtained can be examined to determine the degree of variability within populations or the degree of similarity among populations. Portions of the mtDNA molecule can also be examined by RFLP.

Mitochondrial analysis can also be conducted for plants. Plant mtDNA is more variable in size and structure than that of animals or fungi. The mtDNA of higher plants has noncoding segments interspersed through the DNA molecule, as well as coding segments introduced from nuclear DNA.

Chloroplast DNA Analysis

Chloroplast DNA is a maternally inherited genome in most higher plants and, like mtDNA, does not undergo recombination during plant reproduction. Chloroplast DNA is larger than mtDNA; it is estimated at 120,000–150,000 base pairs in many plants. Chloroplast DNA accumulates mutations more slowly than does nuclear DNA, however. Analysis is carried out by sequencing or use of the RFLP or RAPD techniques.

DNA and RNA Sequencing

Genes or segments of DNA or RNA can be captured by primers and amplified as in AFLP analyses. The specific nucleotide sequences of these units can then be determined by standard sequencing procedures (Krawczak and Schmidke 1998).

Founder Effects and Genetic Bottlenecking

Genetic variability among alien species varies greatly. When introductions involve only a few founder individuals from a limited part of their native range, only a fraction of the genetic variability of the source population is introduced. This "founder effect" may be compounded by genetic drift that leads to the loss of alleles from small founder populations. When a founder population remains small over several to many generations, the loss of genetic variability by genetic drift, termed genetic bottlenecking, may lead to loss of almost all variation in the population (Allendorf 1986). Thus, the size of the founding population and how quickly this population increases are important determinants of the genetic variability of alien populations.

The European starling (*Sturnus vulgaris*) in North America provides a good example of genetic bottlenecking and at the same time shows that low genetic variability does not always limit the success of an alien species. The North American population, now continent-wide in distribution and enormously abundant, is derived from about 100 individuals released in New York City in 1890 and 1891 (Cabe 1998). Allozyme analysis showed that the North American population lacks about 42% of the alleles that occur at loci showing variability in Europe. Furthermore, starlings from different parts of North America show no significant variation in genetic makeup. Even without a high degree of genetic variability, however, this behaviorally adaptable species has colonized a wide range of habitats in North America.

On the other hand, founder populations often consist of many individuals or result from repeated introductions of individuals from different parts of their native range. In such cases, alien populations may have high genetic diversity. Many of these species have not only proven to be seriously invasive but have also shown genetic adaptation to different environments within their new range.

Kudzu (*Pueraria lobata*), one of the most troublesome alien plants of the southeastern United States, exemplifies this latter category (Pappert et al. 2000). Allozyme analysis of 14 loci showed that individual populations varied in polymorphism, some having as few as four and some as many as 12 polymorphic loci. Overall, population analyses from 20 localities showed that 13 of the 14 loci examined were polymorphic. The high diversity of kudzu evidently reflects its deliberate introduction on many occasions over about 50 years. Kudzu was repeatedly introduced to the southeastern United States as an ornamental and forage plant, as well as for erosion control. Coupled with sexual reproduction, multiple introductions have made this species one of the most variable alien invaders of North America.

Evolutionary adaptability is one of the key characteristics of many, if not most, invasive alien species. In turn, adaptability reflects especially the degree of additive and epistatic genetic variability, together with the potential for acquiring additional variability through mutation, hybridization, and chromosomal rearrangement. Additive genetic variation represents the component of genetic variation that consists of alleles that have an overall quantitative effect proportional to their number (Lee 2002). In diploid species, for example, instead of being dominant or recessive, some alleles may have an additive effect, so when they are present on both chromosomes of the pair, their effect is greater than when only one member of the chromosome pair contains the allele. In many polyploid species, in which the number of complete sets of chromosomes is greater than two, the potential for accumulation of alleles with additive quantitative effects can be high because a particular gene locus exists on more than two sets of chromosomes. Epistasis refers to the influence of alleles at one locus on the expression of alleles at a different locus.

Additive genetic variation is usually regarded as the material for rapid evolutionary change, such as that seen in many alien species and native species with which they interact. Carroll et al. (2003b), however, found that epistasis is an important component of adaptation by the soapberry bug (*Jadera haematoloma*) to new alien host plants. We shall examine this case in detail in chapter 13.

Genetic Variability Among Alien Plants

Levels of genetic variability seen in populations of alien plant species vary greatly. Almost all alien plants that are dioecious or monoecious but which reproduce by obligatory outcrossing show levels of genetic variability equal to or only slightly below that of their source populations. Some of these species, such as tree of heaven (*Ailanthus altissima*), are highly invasive. A few, however, exhibit somewhat reduced variability, reflecting small founding populations or genetic bottlenecking following introduction.

Many introduced plants that are self-fertilizing, apomictic, or vegetatively reproducing show lower genetic variability than do populations in their native regions. White bryony (*Bryonia alba*), for example, is an apomictic herbaceous vine that was introduced from central and eastern Europe to parts of the northwestern United States in the mid- to late-twentieth century (Novak and Mack 1995). Populations have become established in three somewhat separate areas: southeastern Washington and adjacent Idaho, western Montana, and southeastern Idaho and northern Utah. If the species had been introduced as a small number of plants from a single Old World source, one would expect that the population in the United States should show little genetic variation. Allozyme analysis showed that populations in the two northern areas were polymorphic in about 19–20% of the loci examined, whereas the southern population is polymorphic in only slightly more than 7% of loci. Strong differences were evident among populations, however, and it is likely that at least two and possibly three independent introductions, of white bryony occurred in the United States.

Populations of alien plants that are self-fertilizing, and thus do not experience genetic recombination, tend to show low genetic variability if they originate from a small founder population. Witchweed (*Striga asiatica*), a self-fertilizing plant parasitic on grains such as sorghum and maize, is a relatively recent introduction to the eastern United States. In this case, allozyme analysis found that plants from two populations in North and South Carolina showed no allele differences at any of 32 enzyme loci, although this plant is quite variable in many characteristics in different parts of Asia and Africa (Werth et al. 1984).

Cheatgrass (*Bromus tectorum*) is another example of a successful alien plant with low genetic variability. It is one of the most widespread, abundant, and ecologically disruptive alien plants in North America (Mack 1981). A short, predominately self-fertilizing, annual grass, Linnaeus named it *tectorum* ("of roofs") because it grew commonly on sod roofs of European houses. Cheatgrass has been recorded from every U.S. state, including Alaska and Hawaii. It has proven to be a highly invasive plant in open habitats throughout western North America. In semiarid regions of the Columbia Plateau and Great Basin, cheatgrass invasion leads to increased wildfire frequency that can transform sagebrush steppe to pure stands of cheatgrass. One can hardly imagine a more successful invader.

Allozyme analyses of cheatgrass plants from 60 sites across North America reveal little overall genetic variability (Novak et al. 1991a). About 4.6% of the loci examined were polymorphic in individual populations. Furthermore, in a sample of more than 2,000 individuals, no individual was found to be heterozygous for any of 25 genetic loci. Most of the variability that does exist is among, rather than within, populations, suggesting that some adaptation to local environments may be occurring. Analyses of microsatellite markers, a somewhat more sensitive indicator of variability, from four locations in Utah and Nevada revealed 15 different genotypes (Ramakrishnan et al. 2001). At one site, however, all 52 individuals were identical in their microsatellite genotype. The various genotypes also showed some tendency to sort out by habitat differences in seasonal temperatures.

Nevertheless, genetic variability in cheatgrass is relatively low in North America. Not surprisingly, in its native range, which extends from western Europe to Afghanistan, greater overall genetic variation exists (Novak and Mack 1993). Almost twice the number of loci showed polymorphism in Eurasia as in North America. The differences among these populations are also greater than in North America. Surprisingly, however, the variability within individual Eurasian populations was actually less than in North America, averaging slightly more than 2%. This suggests that North American populations, although possessing less genetic variability overall, are probably derived from seed originating from several parts of the Eurasian range. This has apparently led to the greater variability within populations in North America than in Eurasia.

Many alien plants show high levels of genetic variability, usually indicating that they were introduced several or many times and, in some cases, from different parts of their native range abroad. High genetic variability can be shown both by species that are outcrossing and by those that are self-fertilizing, apomictic, or clonal.

Yellow starthistle (*Centaurea solsticialis*) is an example of a self-incompatible annual weed that shows high genetic variability as measured by allozyme analysis (Sun 1997). For 22 populations in Washington, Idaho, and California, allozyme analysis showed that 43% of loci were polymorphic and that 38% of individual plants were heterozygous for polymorphic loci. Little genetic divergence has yet occurred among populations, however, with the exception of a small, outlying population in San Diego County, California, which shows reduced variability.

Slender wild oat (*Avena barbata*), on the other hand, is a primarily self-fertilizing grass that maintains levels of allozyme variability in California comparable to those existing in Old World populations (Clegg and Allard 1972). The high variability of this grass is apparently due to its introduction on numerous occasions.

Leafy spurge (*Euphorbia esula*) is one of the most serious plant invaders of rangeland in western North America. As a sexually reproducing, outcrossing species, a fairly high genetic variability was not unexpected. Analyses of cpDNA by RFLP and RAPD techniques showed that variability of maternally inherited patterns was very high (Rowe et al. 1997). This indicates that a number of introductions from different sources in the Old World probably occurred.

In North America, bulbous bluegrass (*Poa bulbosa*) presents an interesting example of high variability in spite of the fact that it reproduces almost entirely by the asexual production of bulblets (Novak and Welfley 1997). Like cheatgrass, bulbous bluegrass is continent-wide in distribution, occurring in 40 U.S. states. One would expect this reproductive strategy to be associated with low genetic diversity, especially if a genetic bottleneck occurred at the time of introduction. Allozyme analysis showed that bulbous bluegrass has an unexpectedly high level of variability, with about 47% of loci being polymorphic. Heterozygosity was also high, and many individuals showed three alleles at each locus, a consequence of the North American populations apparently being autopolyploids. Multiple introductions have probably contributed to the high genetic variation.

Genetic Variability Among Alien Animals

Analyses of the genetic variability of alien animals also reveal very diverse patterns. Many alien aquatic invertebrates show high levels of genetic variability, suggesting that the founding populations consisted of numerous individuals or involved multiple introduction events. Many of this introductions have occurred by transport of attached organisms on ship hulls or release of ballast water from transoceanic cargo ships. Asian sea anemones (*Diadumene lineata*), which reproduce largely by clonal growth, have apparently been introduced on several occasions, so several or many genotypes are present in many alien populations (Ting and Geller 2000). Introductions to the North American Great Lakes, such as those of zebra and quagga mussels (*Dreissena polymorpha, D. bugensis*), typically involve massive founding populations that carry a large fraction of the genetic variability of source populations (Stepien et al. 2002). On the other hand, some introduced marine mollusks appear to show reduced genetic variability (Holland 2000).

A well-documented example of high genetic variability in an alien species is provided by the brown mussel (*Perna perna*), native to the South Atlantic and Indian Oceans, which appeared in the Gulf of Mexico in 1990. It has subsequently spread rapidly along the coast of Texas and Mexico. Analyses of microsatellites for populations in the Gulf of Mexico and various native localities in South America and South Africa showed very high levels of allelic diversity in both alien and native populations (Holland 2001). The high level of diversity in the Gulf of Mexico indicates that the initial population was established by a large founder population that carried most of the genetic variability of the source area.

A quite different pattern is shown by several alien ant species in North America and Hawaii. Two species of alien ants have been highly successful in continental North America. Both the Argentine ant, described at the chapter outset, and the red fire ant show genetic variability that is low compared to populations in their native regions. Alien populations of these species, together with those of several other invasive ants, tend to form enormous supercolonies, which can have a severe impact on native animals (Holway et al. 2002). In all likelihood, invading populations of these species have experienced genetic bottlenecks during their invasion of new geographical regions (Tsutsui et al. 2000).

In the case of the red fire ant (*Solenopsis wagnerî*), two forms exist: monogyne ("one queen") and polygyne ("many queens"). The monogyne red fire ant was introduced from South America to the Gulf Coast near Mobile, Alabama sometime between 1933 and 1945. It has spread widely through the southern United States and has established colonies in California. In this case, the high density achieved appears to be the result of release from predators and parasites that exist in South America.

The polygyne form of the red fire ant in the United States, first reported in the 1970s, appears to lack many of the alleles present in South American populations (Ross et al. 1993). In particular, loss of variability at the locus involved in sex determination results in a preponderance of diploid, homozygous, sterile males at the expense of haploid, fertile males (Ross et al. 1996). Multiple queens are produced in each nest, and many of these queens migrate to other nests. As a result, in North American polygyne populations, the number of egg-laying queens per nest is much higher than in South American populations. These queens tend to be unrelated to each other and to worker ants of the nest in which they are reproducing. Together with the lack of intercolony aggression, these ants are thus able to maintain a very high density of interconnected nests (Holway et al. 2002).

The Mediterranean fruit fly (*Ceratitis capitata*) is another insect for which worldwide spread can be correlated with patterns of loss of genetic variability (Gasparich et al. 1997). Mitochondrial DNA analysis showed that greatest variability occurred in sub-Saharan Africa, where eight haplotypes were found in the DNA section examined. In the Mediterranean region of Europe, where the fly appeared in the early 1800s, two of these haplotypes were found. Most New World populations showed one, or occasionally two, haplotypes. The predominant, and often only, haplotype differed in eastern South America, the Andean region of South America, and Central America, suggesting at least three independent colonizations from the Old World. In Australia and Hawaii, only one haplotype was found.

Recent appearances of the Mediterranean fruit fly in California and southern Florida have created controversy about whether reappearances were separate invasions or simply recovery of populations from levels that were continually present, but undetectable. In southern California, in six outbreak years between 1975 and 1994, most localities showed populations fixed for one haplotype. In 1992, however, an additional haplotype appeared in both central and southern California. Thus, it appears that at least two colonization events occurred in California but that the recurring outbreaks in southern California might be occurring from small resident populations. In Florida, on the other hand, the haplotypes that appeared in 1962–63 were different from those in 1984, 1990, and 1994. In addition, the haplotype that appeared in 1984 differed from that in 1990, but it reappeared in 1994. Thus, outbreaks in Florida may be due to independent colonizations.

Among terrestrial vertebrates, genetic variability in alien populations varies greatly. The marsh frog (*Rana ridibunda*), introduced to England from Hungary as a translocated group of only 12 adults, would have been expected to show greatly reduced genetic variability. Rapid growth of the new population apparently prevented a significant genetic bottleneck, so the resulting population in England showed a pattern of genetic diversity similar to the source population in Hungary (Zeisset and Beebee 2003).

On the other hand, some birds, such as the European starling in North America, discussed earlier in the chapter, show low variability and evidence of a genetic bottleneck associated with small numbers of colonist individuals and a period of low initial population size. In other cases, colonization of new areas may be effected by only a handful of individuals, carrying very limited genetic variability. The red fox (*Vulpes vulpes*) was introduced to Australia in the late 1800s for rabbit control and as a game animal. In the state of Victoria, the founding population consisted of only a few individuals, but population growth was rapid and little loss of alleles by genetic drift evidently occurred (Lade et al. 1996). Foxes reached Phillip Island, about 0.5 km from the mainland of Victoria, in 1907. The founding population there may have been only a mated pair or a pregnant female. Analysis of microsatellites of island and mainland animals showed that the current island population has much reduced genetic variability.

Many passerine birds introduced to various locations show little or no evidence of severely reduced genetic variability (Merilä et al. 1996). The European starling was introduced to New Zealand on 13 occasions, with founding populations totaling about 653 individuals. New Zealand starlings showed essentially equal variability with European populations, in sharp contrast to the situation in North America. The greenfinch (*Carduelis chloris*), with a founding population much smaller than the 653 founder starlings when it was introduced to New Zealand, nevertheless increased rapidly in numbers and did not experience a genetic bottleneck (Merilä et al. 1996). Common mynahs (*Acridotheres tristis*) introduced to many locations in the Pacific and South Africa showed an intermediate condition, with somewhat fewer polymorphic loci and fewer alleles per locus (Baker and Moeed 1987; Fleischer et al. 1991). The South African population showed the most severe reduction in genetic variability, reflecting a small group of founders (table 3.1).

Table 3.1. Genetic variability patterns for populations of
the common myna (*Acridotheres tristis*) in regions where
it is native and introduced. (Data from Baker and
Moeed 1987.)

	Alleles per Locus	*Polymorphic Loci (%)*	*Heterozygosity (Average)*
NATIVE			
India	1.43	31.5	0.05
INTRODUCED			
Australia	1.30	23.1	0.05
New Zealand	1.24	19.5	0.05
South Africa	1.15	12.9	0.03
Fiji	1.30	20.6	0.05
Hawaii	1.20	18.0	0.06

Genetic Variability among Alien Microorganisms

Microorganisms and fungi that cause disease in plants and animals also
show diverse patterns of genetic variability. However, RAPD analysis of
butternut canker (*Sirococcus clavigignenti-juglandacearum*), a fungal disease of
North American butternut (*Juglans cinerea*), shows complete lack of variation (Furnier et al. 1999). This indicates that it is a very recent introduction of a single fungal strain. Even so, it is proving highly virulent to butternut trees. As we shall see in chapter 11, other fungal diseases show
much higher levels of genetic variability.

Genetic Variability and Invasiveness

Analyses of genetic variability thus show that alien species differ greatly
in variability and that low, as well as high, variability can contribute to
their invasive capabilities. Analyses of genetic variability can also reveal
other information. Cryptic species—forms that are genetically distinct
but were previously unrecognized—are being identified through such
analyses. DNA fingerprints can also help identify the source locations of
alien populations, a useful step in the search for potential biological control agents. We shall turn to these topics in the next chapter.

4.

Introduction Sources, Cryptic Species, and Invasion Routes

"Identifying the geographical source of invasive species is a critical component of invasion biology. . . . Because historical human records are often incomplete, inaccurate or simply nonexistent, molecular genetics offers a powerful tool for identification of putative source populations."

—Tsutsui et al. (2001)

Clouded salamander (*Aneides ferreus*) is the name that was first given to a salamander that occurs in forests along the Pacific coasts of northern California and Oregon, on Vancouver Island, and at one spot on the adjacent mainland of British Columbia, Canada. Oddly, this salamander is absent from the coast of Washington. All other known forest plant and animal species that occur on Vancouver Island and also in coastal Oregon are also found in coastal Washington State. The discontinuity of the clouded salamander distribution raised the question, "What is the relationship of the British Columbia population to the populations in Oregon and California, and how did the British Columbia population originate?"

Todd Jackman (1998) undertook a genetic analysis of animals from populations at 25 localities throughout the range of this salamander. He used allozyme analysis, mitochondrial DNA (mtDNA) analysis, and examination of chromosome structure. His results revealed a surprising relationship. British Columbia salamanders were nearly identical to those of California and differed from those along the Oregon coast. This finding suggested that the British Columbia population might have been introduced from California. An examination of historical records then revealed that the bark of tanoak (*Lithocarpus densiflorus*) was shipped from California in large quantities to tanneries on Vancouver Island in the late 1800s. Since clouded salamanders are good climbers and often hide under the loose bark of trees, they were likely transported to Vancouver Island with the bark of tanoak.

Jackman's study not only revealed the source of the British Columbia populations but also showed that the Oregon populations were distinct from those of California and British Columbia in many genetic features. He also located a zone of overlap between the two salamanders near the Smith River in northern California. Hybridization occurred in this zone but was quite limited. Jackman concluded that the two forms deserved recognition as separate species. Thus, a new species name was proposed for the California and British Columbia form: *Aneides vagrans*, the wandering salamander, an appropriate name for a species that traveled north from California and invaded British Columbia!

Molecular genetic analysis now provides a very powerful set of tools for characterizing populations of alien species and relating them to populations in their native range. Genetic analyses also hold the potential for distinguishing cryptic species, aliens as well as natives. Of great practical importance is the ability to pinpoint the locality of origin and route of invasion of alien forms. As we shall see, pinpointing the locality of origin is often of great value because it can help narrow down the search area for potential biological control agents of harmful aliens. Knowledge of the precise region of origin of alien species can also help us understand the degree to which release from competitors, predators, parasites, and diseases has enabled alien species to do well in their new homes.

Genetic Analyses and Discovery of Cryptic Species

Cryptic aliens are species that were not recognized as alien in origin or, in some cases, not distinguished from other aliens. Many cryptic species are probably the products of recent evolutionary divergence, although some may be strongly conserved genotypes of ancient origin. Many examples of cryptic aliens involve marine invertebrates. Marine polychaete worms of the genus *Marenzelleria*, for example, are native to the Atlantic coast of North America. They appeared in coastal waters of Scotland in 1979 and in the Baltic Sea in 1985 (Bastrop et al. 1998). These polychaetes have since become a major component of coastal and estuarine habitats throughout much of western Europe. Mitochondrial DNA fingerprints of animals from various locations on both sides of the Atlantic revealed that three distinct, but morphologically indistinguishable, forms were present, two in Europe and three in North America. Each of the three forms differed from the others by up to five mutations. The three North American forms had evidently been considered to belong to one species, *M. virens*. Of these three forms, as yet unnamed, two had apparently been transported to European waters, probably in the ballast water of cargo ships, in separate introduction events. One form, from the northern coastline of the United States, was apparently introduced to an area in the North Sea and has appeared along the coasts of Scotland and the Netherlands. The second, from the southern Atlantic coast of the United States, was apparently introduced directly into the Baltic Sea. Thus, molecular genetic analysis revealed three cryptic species and pinpointed the region of origin of the two alien forms that had appeared in Europe (Bastrop et al. 1998).

In similar fashion, a jellyfish of the genus *Aurelia* appeared in a lagoon in southwestern San Francisco Bay in 1988 (Greenberg et al. 1996). It appeared to differ morphologically, however, from the common *A. aurita* of the outer coast of California. Allozyme analysis upheld this difference and showed it to be similar to a form of *Aurelia* in Japan. The Japanese *Aurelia* also had been regarded as *aurita*, so the molecular genetic analysis not only pinpointed the origin of the San Francisco Bay population, but showed that it and the Japanese form were probably a distinct species. The exact relationship of this yet-unnamed species to other members of the genus *Aurelia* is still to be unraveled.

Another marine invertebrate example is provided by European crabs of the genus *Carcinus* (Geller et al. 1997). These crabs have invaded the east and west coasts of North America, as well as the coasts of South Africa, Tasmanian Australia, and Japan. Presumably, these invasions were the result of ballast water transport in cargo ships. Two similar species occur in Europe, *C. maenas* along the Atlantic coast and *C. aestuarii* in the Mediterranean Sea. Using mtDNA fingerprints, these species can easily be distinguished. Analysis of specimens from the invaded regions revealed that all *Carcinus* crabs on both the east and west coasts of North America and in Tasmania were *maenas*. In both South Africa and Japan, where only one species or the other previously had been detected, however, both species were found to be present.

Uncertainties about the species status and region of origin also exist among alien vertebrate animals, as indicated by the example at the chapter outset. Another case involves swamp eels, large predatory fish of the genus *Monopterus* that are native to southern and eastern Asia, the East Indies, and West Africa. During the 1990s, isolated populations of introduced animals were discovered near Atlanta, Georgia, and Tampa, Miami, and Homestead, Florida. These fish pose a very serious threat to native wetland vertebrates of all types. The alien populations were provisionally identified as the Asian swamp eel (*Monopterus albus*), a widely distributed form of southern and eastern Asia for which considerable uncertainty exists about systematics and taxonomy. Analyses of mtDNA sequences of eels from North American and Asian localities indicated that at least three independent introductions to North America had occurred (Collins et al. 2002). Eels from near Miami and Tampa, Florida, showed high similarities to each other and to eels from China. Those from near Homestead, Florida, grouped with eels from Malaysia, Vietnam, and Indonesia. Eels from the population near Atlanta, Georgia, were distinct from other North American animals and did not show a close relationship to any of the Asian populations sampled. Although the potential for North American populations to interbreed is unknown, it appears likely that these eels represent two or three biological species.

Other analyses that have led to recognition of cryptic species among alien animals include studies of *Corbicula* clams in North America (Siripattrawan et al. 2000), cladocerans in the Great Lakes (DeMelo and Hebert 1994), and amphipods in central European waterways (Müller et al. 2002).

Cryptic species have also been identified among other kinds of organisms by DNA fingerprinting. Dogwood anthracnose, a fungal disease of shrubs of the genus *Cornus*, first appeared on flowering dogwood (*C. florida*) in eastern North America in 1976. It has since become a major cause of dogwood mortality and has spread to the Pacific dogwood (*C. nuttallii*) in the western United States and Canada. The fungal agent associated with the disease was found to be a member of the genus *Discula* and was named *D. destructiva*. Subsequently, however, studies of *Discula* forms from dogwoods have revealed a second, as yet unnamed, form of *Discula*.

Studies of these *Discula* fungi are complicated by the fact that their reproductive stages have not been observed. The difficulties of identifying and distinguishing fungi in their mycelial stages make molecular genetic analysis advantageous. Trigiano et al. (1995) examined DNA fingerprints of *Discula* cultures obtained from flowering dogwood and Pacific dogwood. These analyses showed that *destructiva* and the unnamed form were quite distinct. They also showed that *destructiva* was nearly uniform in genetic characteristics in the various populations sampled in eastern and western North America, whereas the unnamed form showed greater variability. These results suggested that *destructiva* is an alien species that entered North America and has spread rapidly. The unnamed form, in contrast, appears likely to be a native fungus that has coevolved closely with North American dogwood and is less virulent. The native region of *destructiva* is not yet known, but the fungus could have been imported on horticultural stock, such as Japanese dogwood (*Cornus kousa*), which is native to Japan and Korea.

Source Areas Revealed by Genetic Analyses

For many other alien species, including plants, animal, and microorganisms, genetic analyses have helped to pinpoint source areas. Source areas are often those suspected from other evidence, but many unexpected patterns of origin are also revealed.

Hydrilla (*Hydrilla verticillata*) is one of the most troublesome aquatic weeds in the southern United States. Two forms occur in the United States. One, a dioecious plant, was introduced near Tampa, Florida, in the early 1950s and has spread through many southern states and west to California. The other, a monoecious form introduced to the Potomac River near Washington, D.C., in the 1970s (Steward et al. 1984), is distributed from South Carolina northward in coastal states to Connecticut and in California and Washington (Madeira et al. 2000). Hydrilla is widespread in Australia, New Zealand, eastern Asia, and islands of the southwest Pacific and also occurs in localized areas of Europe and Africa. Considerable effort has been made to find biological control agents for this weed, so source areas of the North American invasive forms are of great interest.

Using DNA fingerprinting by the random amplified polymorphic DNA analysis (RAPD) technique, Madeira et al. (1997) examined the relationships of 44 hydrilla samples from most of the world regions where it occurs. The dioecious form in the United States was most similar to a sample from Bangalore, a city in southern India. This agrees with an earlier report that hydrilla was introduced to Florida by a plant dealer who obtained the material from Sri Lanka, an island country close to the southern tip of India. The monoecious form closely matches a sample from Seoul, Korea, which perhaps accounts for its adaptation to more northern areas in the United States. The hydrilla sample from New Zealand, where it first appeared in 1963, appears most similar to forms from Australia, where hydrilla is widespread and has long been present.

Garlic mustard (*Alliaria petiolata*) is an invasive alien plant in forests of eastern North America. This species has a wide distribution in the Old World. Its original distribution extends from England and western continental Europe eastward to Russia and Asia Minor and southward to North Africa. This invasive herb was introduced to eastern North America in the 1860s and now occurs in at least 30 U.S. states and six Canadian provinces. DNA fingerprinting that compared North American populations to those in Scotland and those in western continental Europe indicated that the greatest similarity of most alien populations was to the Scottish populations (Meekins et al. 2001). Some populations in eastern Canada and Maryland did not show close relationships with the Scottish material, however, and may have been introduced separately from other European sources.

The native regions of several plant pathogens have been identified from similar evidence. Sorghum ergot (*Claviceps africana*) is a fungal disease of plants of the genus *Sorghum*. This fungus was unknown in the Western Hemisphere until 1995, when it appeared in Brazil, either by introduction in contaminated seed or by long-distance dispersal of spores. Within 2 years, however, it had spread north to the United States. This ergot fungus is widespread in Africa, Asia, and Australia. Amplified fragment length polymorphism analysis revealed that the Western Hemisphere strain is most closely related to strains in Africa and also showed that despite lacking a sexual stage, the American strain has high genetic diversity (Tooley et al. 2002).

In other cases, the likelihood that a new plant disease is alien has been revealed, although the source area remains in doubt. An example is butternut canker (Furnier et al. 1999), which has caused widespread mortality of butternut (*Juglans cinerea*) in eastern North America. Genetic fingerprinting by the RAPD technique was used to examine 86 samples of this fungus from throughout the range of butternut. No variability was found in these samples. This, together with the very recent appearance of the disease, indicates that it is a recent introduction, probably from a location in Asia. A fir canker also showed much lower genetic variation in North America than in a location in Sweden, suggesting that it, too, was a recent introduction to North America (Wang et al. 1997).

Among marine invertebrates, the colonial ascidian ("sea squirt") *Botryllus schlosseri* is now a nearly cosmopolitan marine invertebrate that has been introduced to new coastal regions by oceanic ships. *Botryllus* is a fouling organism that grows commonly on the hulls of ships and is believed to be native to the Mediterranean Sea. This ascidian first appeared on the North American east coast in the early 1800s, apparently introduced by ships from Europe. Much later, in the 1940s, it colonized the west coast of North America from California to Alaska. Analysis of microsatellite alleles showed that *Botryllus* populations on the New England and California coasts were quite distinct, making it unlikely that west coast populations were introduced from the North American east coast (Stoner et al. 2002). Thus, it appears that the populations on the North American west coast are derived by an independent introduction from Europe or from Asian localities to which the species has been introduced from Europe. Although genetic analyses have not yet been conducted to test these alternatives, ascidian colonies from Japan and California are so similar genetically that they will grow together into a single colony. Numerous other alien marine invertebrates have been introduced to California from Japan.

In some cases, the locale of origin has turned out to be quite unsuspected. Two of these cases involve crustaceans. The Chinese mitten crab (*Eriocheir sinensis*), native to eastern Asia, has recently become established on the Pacific coast of the United States. The volume of trans-Pacific shipping would suggest that the most likely source was directly from Asia in ballast water. Analysis of mtDNA samples, however, showed that this population was derived from a source in Europe, where the species was introduced more than 100 years ago (Hänfling et al. 2002).

Another cladoceran that has recently appeared in North America, *Daphnia lumholtzi*, is widespread in Australia and India, with populations in several locations in Africa. Although Australia might seem the most likely source for this species, allozyme and mtDNA analyses indicated that alien populations were most similar to those of India and Africa (Havel et al. 2000). This, combined with other evidence, suggests that *Daphnia lumholtzi* was accidentally introduced from East Africa with fish that were brought to North America for aquaculture.

Among terrestrial animals, useful information on the sites of origin of alien pests has also been revealed. Studies of the genetics of native and introduced populations of the Argentine ant (*Linepithema humile*) using mtDNA fingerprinting and microsatellite analysis have pinpointed the source area of this alien in both North America and Europe (Tsutsui et al. 2001). When North American populations were compared to populations from 12 sites in Brazil and Argentina, they were found to be most similar to those from Rosario, Argentina, a major port city located on the Parana River northwest of Buenos Aires. Argentine ants from colonies established in South Africa and near Rome, Italy, however, may have come from one or more locations between Buenos Aires and Rosario. As we noted in chapter 3, the genetic impoverishment of these introduced ants has played a major role in their impact.

Similarly, the regional origin and native plant hosts of grape phylloxera (*Daktulosphaira vitafoliae*), an aphid pest of cultivated grapes worldwide, have been pinpointed by mtDNA analysis (Downie 2002). In Europe, grape phylloxera is derived entirely from aphids native to the frost grape (*Vitis riparia*) of the northeastern United States. This genetic race of aphids has also been introduced to several other world regions where grapes are grown. A second source of phylloxera aphids is the winter grape (*Vitis vulpina*) of the southeastern United States. This form was apparently introduced to California and from there to Australia, New Zealand, and Peru.

Vectors of human disease also can be traced to their regions of origin. The Asian tiger mosquito (*Aedes albopictus*) is a recent colonist of the New World. This mosquito is a vector for various viral diseases, including dengue fever. Analyses of mtDNA from the United States indicated that tiger mosquitoes were very similar to those of eastern Asia, including Japan (Birungi and Munstermann 2002). Other evidence suggested that tiger mosquitoes arrived in the United States as larvae in pockets of water in automobile tires shipped from Japan. Asian tiger mosquitoes appeared soon afterward in Brazil. The mtDNA haplotypes predominant in Brazil, however, are quite different from those in both the United States and Japan, so the precise origin of the Brazilian populations is still uncertain.

The origins of some disjunct mammalian populations have been traced by means of mtDNA analysis. The common vole (*Microtus arvalis*), for example, occurs on the Orkney Islands, which lie north of the northern tip of mainland Scotland, but not in the rest of the British Isles. The species is widespread in mainland Europe, and the closest population is in Denmark. To investigate the precise source area of voles, tissue samples were obtained from animals from the Orkney Islands and from 26 localities throughout the range of the species in mainland Eurasia (Haynes et al. 2003). Mitochondrial DNA was extracted from these samples, and the cytochrome *b* gene was amplified and sequenced. Numerous haplotypes were found, but the greatest similarity was between haplotypes of voles from the Orkney Islands and those from France and Spain. Since the Orkney Islands were covered by ice during the last glaciation, voles must have been introduced following glacial retreat. Apparently, the common vole was brought to the islands by Neolithic human settlers from southwestern Europe, a conclusion that perhaps sheds light on the origin of the early human settlers of these islands.

Perhaps not surprisingly, genetic analyses sometimes raise as yet unanswered questions about the origin of alien species. The round goby (*Neogobius melanostomus*), an invasive fish native to the Black and Caspian seas and major inflowing rivers, appeared in the North American Great Lakes in 1990 and has now established populations in all five lakes. The goby also appeared in the Gulf of Gdansk, Poland, in the same year. Analyses of mtDNA from these alien populations did not closely match those of gobies from the northern Black Sea, nor did the Polish and North American gobies show strong similarity. Thus, the exact source of the founding fish for these alien populations is still unknown (Dillon and Stepien 2001).

Source Areas of Species with Multiple Introductions

Genetic analyses can also reveal information about the number of introductions of individual alien species. For many aliens, multiple introductions are the rule. The numerous opportunities for transport of both aquatic and terrestrial plants and animals make multiple introductions increasingly frequent. In Australia, for example, the discovery of three new populations of the invasive marine alga *Caulerpa taxifolia* in New South Wales, Australia, led to a series of analyses of ribosomal DNA to try to determine their sources (Schaffelke et al. 2002). One was confirmed as originating from populations along the coast of Queensland. The remaining two populations, which are different from each other, apparently came from other sources, as yet unknown.

One of the best examples of multiple introductions of an alien plant comes from ongoing studies of cheatgrass (*Bromus tectorum*). As noted in chapter 3, cheatgrass has a wide native distribution in the Old World. Novak and Mack (2001) examined samples from 164 localities throughout the species' native and introduced ranges, using allozyme electrophoresis. These studies led to the identification of a number of genetic markers that are specific for locations in the species' native range. Using these markers, they are able to infer the source areas of populations in regions to which the species has been introduced.

In North America, at least seven or eight independent introductions of cheatgrass have occurred (Novak and Mack 2001; Bartlett et al. 2002). Most of these seem likely to have been direct introductions to western North America, since the genetic markers do not occur in the East. Two may have been to eastern North America, with subsequent spread westward to the Pacific Northwest. In other areas of the world, at least two introductions, from the Iberian peninsula and Morocco, appear to have occurred to the Canary Islands. At least two introductions have also occurred to Argentina, both from localities in eastern Europe.

One result of the multiple introductions of cheatgrass is a mosaic pattern of population genetics (Novak et al. 1993). For example, cheatgrass populations in southern British Columbia possess high frequencies of a genetic marker derived from a source area in eastern Europe. In eastern Washington, populations possess high frequencies of a genetic marker of unknown origin. In spite of the reduction in genetic variability that usually characterizes individual founder populations, genetic variants from different parts of the native range also may come together as populations grow and spread. Thus, in north-central Washington, cheatgrass populations possess both of the above markers.

Multiple introductions are also implicated for a cladoceran known as the long-spined water flea (*Bythotrephes longimanus*). Changes in the frequency of various gene loci between 1989 and 1996 demonstrated that there has been a continuing introduction to North America of water fleas from Lake Ladoga in western Russia. The present genetic structure of North American *B. longimanus* is more similar to that of the organisms in Lake Ladoga than it was originally (Berg et al. 2002). The genetic structure of long-spined water flea populations in 1989 showed strong founder effects, including an excess of heterozygote genotypes at one gene locus. By 1996, the genetic structure of the North American populations closely matched that of populations in Lake Ladoga, and the frequency of homozygote and heterozygote genotypes matched the Hardy-Weinberg expectation for stable populations.

One of the most interesting and complex patterns of introduction of an alien species to much of the world involves the Mediterranean fruit fly (*Ceratitis capitata*). Gasparich et al. (1997) examined nucleotide variation in portions of the mitochondrial gene for NADH dehydrogenase for flies from more than 100 populations in Europe, Africa, North and South America, and Australia. The greatest diversity of haplotypes was found in sub-Saharan Africa, where the number of haplotypes, or individual chromosomal arrangements, was greater than in all other areas of the world combined. Mediterranean fruit flies became established around the Mediterranean Sea in the early 1800s, and their populations now show only two common haplotypes of those represented in sub-Saharan Africa. By the early 1900s, Mediterranean fruit flies had invaded the New World. The pattern of haplotypes in Central and South America is complex. Most populations in Central America and northern South America possess only a single haplotype, but the specific haplotype is different in Central America, Venezuela-Brazil, and the region from Colombia to Peru. In Argentina, a still different haplotype, unique to this world region, is common. These patterns indicate that multiple introductions have occurred to the New World from the Mediterranean region or Africa. Single haplotypes occur in fruit fly populations in Hawaii and Australia. Australian populations might have been founded by flies from the Mediterranean region or the Andean region of South America. Hawaiian populations probably came from the Venezuela-Brazil area of eastern South America.

Mediterranean fruit flies have appeared occasionally in Florida, Texas, and California (Gasparich et al. 1997). These small outbreaks have been attacked vigorously with baited traps, release of sterile males, and insecticidal sprays, the result usually being that eradication was claimed. Each outbreak has usually been considered as a new invasion, rather than an upsurge of a population reduced to an undetectable level. In California, for example, six outbreaks were recorded between 1975 and 1994 (Carey 1996). The locations of several of the outbreaks are similar and suggest that an established population exists. Haplotypes of most of the fruit flies in the six outbreaks match that common in Central America (Gasparich et al. 1997), so one or more introductions from this region may account for most outbreaks. In 1992, however, a different haplotype appeared in both northern and southern California, indicating that an independent introduction from a region other than Central America had occurred. Thus, at least two introductions, and possible more, have led to the California outbreaks.

In Florida, five outbreaks of Mediterranean fruit fly occurred between 1962 and 1994 (Gasparich et al. 1997). None of the haplotypes appearing in Florida can be traced to Central America. Furthermore, the haplotypes appearing in 1962–63, 1984 and 1994, and 1990 were different, indicating that four independent introductions probably occurred. Thus, multiple introductions have played a major role in the invasion of various world regions by this insect pest, with resurgence of populations from very low levels very likely playing a role in sudden outbreaks of the species in California. In any case, a very complex evolutionary potential is now present because of the existence of Mediterranean fruit fly populations of differing genetic makeup in different world regions.

Invasion Routes of Alien Species

Genetic analyses can help to identify major invasion routes, particularly those followed by aquatic invaders. The spiny cladoceran (*Cercopagis pengoi*), a native of the Black and Caspian Seas of western Asia, colonized the

Baltic Sea region of Europe and subsequently, in 1982, the North American Great Lakes. It was presumed that this colonization occurred through ballast water transport, but the proximate source of the North American invasion was not known. Cristescu et al. (2001) sequenced two mitochondrial genes to characterize spiny cladoceran populations in Europe, Asia, and North America and infer routes of invasion (fig. 4.1). The forms of the spiny cladoceran in the Black and Caspian seas differed in the haplotypes represented, so much so that the divergence of these two forms is estimated to have occurred 800,000 years ago. The Baltic Sea population showed one DNA haplotype that is among the several that occur in the Black Sea population. In turn, the Great Lakes population contained only the haplotype present in the Baltic Sea.

As we noted earlier, another spiny cladoceran, *Bythotrephes longimanus*, that has invaded North American lakes was determined to have come

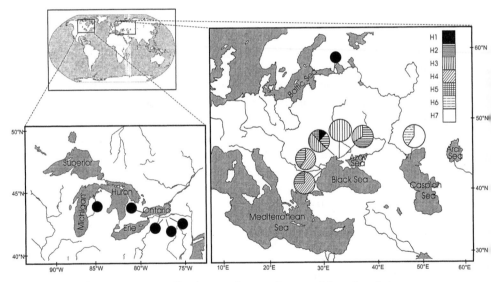

Figure 4.1. Frequencies of haplotypes for populations of the spiny cladoceran (*Cercopagis pengoi*) in its alien range in North America and in its native range in Eurasia. These haplotype patterns indicate that the North American Great Lakes populations came from the Baltic Sea region and that the Baltic Sea population probably derived from the Black Sea. (Reprinted with permission from M. E. A. Cristescu, P. D. N. Hebert, J. D. S. Witt, H. J. MacIsaac, and I. A. Grigorovich. 2001. An invasion history for *Cercopagis pengoi* based on mitochondrial gene sequences. *Limnology and Oceanography* 46:224–229. © 2001 American Society of Limnology and Oceanography.)

from Lake Ladoga, Russia (Therriault et al. 2002). The Neva River connects this lake to the Gulf of Finland in the eastern Baltic Sea at the port of St. Petersburg, Russia. Thus, the North American populations were apparently introduced in ballast water of cargo ships coming from St. Petersburg.

Studies of these cladocerans have helped identify a major invasion corridor for exotic invaders of the North American Great Lakes. In particular, they have revealed the importance of the connection between the Caspian Sea and the Baltic Sea (Berg et al. 2002; Ricciardi and MacIsaac 2000). The Volga River, which flows into the Caspian Sea, is connected by a series of rivers, canals, and lakes to the Gulf of Finland in the eastern Baltic Sea. Several alien species from the Caspian region, including *Cercopagis pengoi*, have followed this corridor and made the final stage of the trip in ballast water of commercial ships traveling from the eastern Baltic Sea to North America. These and other planktonic cladocerans have shown a rate of invasion roughly 50,000 times that of natural invasions of North America from Eurasia (Herbert and Cristescu 2002). At least 12 other species that have dispersed along the Eurasian portion of this corridor are poised to make the final jump to North America (Berg et al. 2002).

Disproving Cases of Supposed Human Introduction

Molecular genetic analyses have also been used to determine that some populations are not recent human-assisted introductions, as once thought. The European periwinkle (*Littorina littorea*), widespread on the Atlantic coast of North America, has been considered by many to be a recent historical introduction because of its sudden appearance in many locations in the late 1800s. Analyses of mitochondrial and nuclear DNA, however, showed many differences between North American and European populations (Wares et al. 2002). The most recent date for the likely spread of the European periwinkle to North America is about 16,500 years before present. It now appears likely that this species was present but very restricted in distribution along the North American coast and rapidly expanded its range in response to ecological changes that occurred in recent time.

Source Areas and Biological Control Potential

The ability to determine the precise source areas of introduced aliens has major implications for classic biological control. Source areas represent the most likely places to find effective biocontrol species. In the case of

Argentine ants, described above, the region near Rosario, Argentina, appears to be the logical location to search for possible biological control agents. It has been suggested that the success of Argentine ants in areas to which they have been introduced is due to escape from particular parasitoids, a fly of the family Phoridae. Phorid flies are known to attack other ants of the genus *Linepithema* in Brazil, but not the Argentine ant itself. In any case, these parasitoids are not known from the Rosario area. Thus, it appears that other possible biocontrol agents should be sought in the areas now known to be the source of Argentine ant introductions.

Genetic studies of variability and source areas have additional implications for biological control. For example, given that butternut canker is an introduced fungus with low genetic variability (Furnier et al. 1999), a search for resistant butternut genotypes may well be worthwhile. The low genetic variability of the canker fungus may limit its ability to overcome such resistance.

Introduction Sources and Evolution

This chapter emphasizes the fact that modern systems of transport bring together populations of alien species from many world regions. Often, the populations of a single species are the product of multiple introductions, in some cases from very different parts of their native range. Furthermore, some alien forms, on detailed genetic analysis, turn out to be related but distinct taxa. These forms are being introduced to geographical regions that often contain related species from which they have been isolated in space. Thus, intercontinental dispersal of species is creating the potential for interbreeding of related but previously isolated taxa. In the next chapter, we will examine the processes of hybridization that result and explore their evolutionary significance.

Part II.

Processes of Evolutionary Change and Adaptation

In this series of chapters, we examine some of the major mechanisms of evolutionary change and how they relate to adaptation of alien species to the new physical and biotic conditions they encounter.

Chapter 5 considers the increased frequency of hybridization that results when closely related forms, whether they be different alien forms or alien forms and related natives, are suddenly brought together. Some of the most remarkable examples of the origin of invasive taxa can be traced to hybridization and subsequent reorganization of the hybrid genomes. Hybridization also holds the potential for the escape of transgenes from genetically engineered plants, animals, and microorganisms to wild forms, many of which are already problem aliens in various world regions. The evolutionary consequences of acquisition of transgenes by wild plants, animals, and microorganisms are of great current concern and will be examined chapter 6.

The potential for invasion and adaptation to new ecological systems depends on the evolutionary adaptability of aliens to the biotic and abiotic conditions encountered. Success depends on the ability to flourish in the new biotic environment. In chapter 7, we shall examine factors that determine the degree of resistance of biotic communities to invasion by aliens and the factors that enable aliens to overcome such resistance. In chapter 8, we consider patterns of evolutionary adaptation to these new physical and biotic conditions. As we shall see, adaptive breakthroughs often appear to be responsible for the sudden explosive change of alien species from forms with only minor impacts to highly invasive forms with serious impacts.

Having examined these basic aspects of adaptation of aliens to their new environments, we will proceed to examination of the more specific evolutionary interactions of aliens and the native species with which they interact.

5.

Hybridization and Evolution of Exotics

"It is interesting to note that two Old World [*Rhamnus*] species
that have been brought together to a habitat on a different continent,
away from their place of origin, have hybridized naturally and probably
produced several generations of fertile hybrids. . . . The aggressive nature
of these new hybrids should be of concern to local stewards and naturalists."

—GIL-AD AND REZNICEK (1997)

In 1879, a new salt marsh cordgrass appeared along the coast of Hampshire, England. To some, it seemed to be a luxuriant form of the native salt marsh cordgrass, *Spartina maritima*. Others deemed it a new species and named it *S. townsendii*. The new form spread slowly along the coast, but in the late 1880s, a change occurred that initiated a rapid acceleration of its spread. As it turned out, that change was a chromosome doubling that created a plant that was eventually named *S. anglica* (Gray et al. 1991). Further study revealed that *S. townsendii* is actually the sterile hybrid of *S. maritima* and *S. alterniflora*, a North American salt marsh cordgrass that had been introduced to the coast of England. These two cordgrasses are close relatives with similar chromosome numbers (Baumel et al. 2002a). Chromosome doubling restored the fertility of *S. anglica* and simultaneously isolated it reproductively from its parental forms.

Thus, a new species arose through hybridization and chromosome doubling. Furthermore, *S. anglica* proved to be highly competitive and invasive, eventually colonizing estuary areas all around the British Isles, the coast of France, and elsewhere. The parental genomes of *S. anglica* have remained remarkably stable since formation of the hybrid and doubling of its chromosome number (Baumel et al. 2002b). It has displaced the native cordgrass in many areas and now occupies areas of formerly open mudflat that were important as wintering habitat for shorebirds such as the dunlin (*Calidris alpina*). It has also stimulated increased sediment deposition, with accumulation reaching 4 cm/yr. The genetic uniformity of *S. anglica* apparently also makes it highly susceptible to infection by an ergot fungus (*Claviceps purpurea*). Extensive diebacks of this cordgrass occur, at which times massive amounts of silt are flushed into salt marsh channels (Gray et al. 1991). The spread of this new species has been accompanied by profound ecological changes in coastal salt marshes.

Hybridization and Origin of Invasive Aliens

Spartina anglica was one of the first examples of the evolutionary potential that is created by the introduction of alien species to new regions, where they meet native species or other aliens that are close relatives. Hybridization can occur between alien species, between aliens and natives, or between hybrid forms and other aliens or natives. Hybrid forms involved in these further hybridizations can be of spontaneous origin or can be artificial hybrids created and released by humans. Hybridization, in the broadest sense, can also occur between members of populations of a single species that come from different source areas. The potential for origin of novel genetic forms is therefore quite complex (fig. 5.1).

Hybridization is likely to be one of the important stimuli for the development of an invasive exotic after a significant time lag (Ewel et al. 1999; Ellstrand and Schierenbeck 2000). Hybridization may result in genetic recombination that produces a genotype better adapted to the new environment than its parents (Abbott 1992). It may also lead to greater genetic variability among hybrid offspring than that shown by parental populations, so offspring may occupy a wider range of microhabitats than can parents. Genetic mechanisms such as allopolyploidy, the doubling of chromosome number following hybridization, can stabilize the genetic structure of hybrids. Such individuals may possess substantial hybrid vigor, giving them an adaptive advantage over their parents. Finally, hybridization may eliminate effects of fixed detrimental alleles that have accumulated in parental populations.

The reproductive capability and vigor of hybrid species vary greatly. If the hybridizing forms are similar enough for chromosomes to pair and

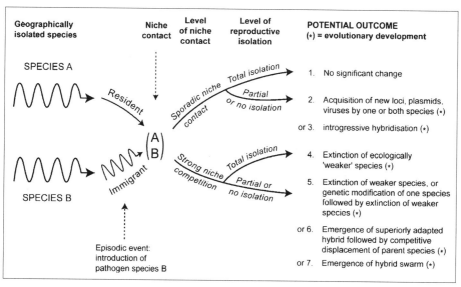

Figure 5.1. Possible evolutionary consequences of contact between a native species and an introduced species of pathogen. Similar evolutionary interactions also can occur between higher plants and animals. (Reprinted with permission from C. M. Brasier. 2001. Rapid evolution of introduced plant pathogens via interspecific hybridization. *BioScience* 51:123–133. © 2001 American Institute of Biological Sciences.)

behave normally in meiosis, hybrid forms may be fertile. If hybridization is frequent and widespread, the parental forms may essentially merge to form one reproductive complex. This process, known as introgressive hybridization, may enhance genetic variability, and the progeny may show hybrid vigor. If substantial chromosomal or genetic differences exist, the hybrid offspring may show reduced fertility or complete sterility. In plants, however, doubling of the chromosomes of sterile hybrids can occur, restoring fertility, since chromosomes are able to pair and behave normally in meiosis. This, in fact, occurred with the cordgrasses discussed at the chapter outset.

The potential for hybridizations involving alien species is great. For example, the plant genus *Centaurea*, to which the knapweeds and starthistles belong, contains about 1,350 species, among which at least 232 hybrids have been recorded (Roché and Roché 1991). In the British Isles alone, 95 putative hybrid plants involving one or more aliens have been recorded (Stace 1991). In Ontario, Canada, 34 hybrids involving one or more alien plants have been reported (Vilà et al. 2000). The potential for hybridizations to produce invasive new plants is also great. In a survey of invasive plant taxa apparently derived from interspecific hybridization, Ellstrand and Schierenbeck (2000) identified 27 cases in which hybridizations involving one or both alien members have given rise to invasive forms.

Hybridization Between Alien Plants

One of the most striking examples of hybridization and its consequences involves plants of the composite family, genus *Tragopogon*, known commonly as salsify or goat's beard. In eastern Washington, hybridizations occur among all three combinations of members of the genus: *Tragopogon pratensis, T. dubius,* and *T. porrifolius* (Owenby 1950). Hybrids of *T. pratensis* and *T. dubius* have given rise by polyploidy to a fertile form considered to be a new species: *T. miscellus.* Hybrids of *T. pratensis* and *T. porrifolius* have similarly given rise to a second new species: *T. mirus.* Although these new species have not proven to be noxious or highly invasive, they have spread well beyond their points of origin (Novak et al. 1991b).

The plant genus to which willows belong (*Salix*) is notorious for hybridization among species that have been planted in new locations. Many hybrids involving both native and introduced species occur in North America. Numerous species and varieties of willows also have been introduced to Australia, where the genus is entirely alien (Cremer et al. 1995). These forms have produced at least nine hybrids, some between two and some among three species. Several of these hybrids have proven to be invasive.

The complexity of potential hybridizations among alien plants is illustrated by knotweeds of the genus *Fallopia* in Britain and continental Europe (Bailey 1999). Two forms of *Fallopia japonica,* varieties *japonica* and *compacta,* have been introduced to Britain. Variety *japonica,* an octoploid with a chromosome number of 88, is male sterile but spreads vegetatively by rhizomes and is a very aggressive invader of disturbed habitats. Variety *compacta,* a tetraploid (n = 44), is a much less invasive form but has male-fertile as well as male-sterile plants. Another widely introduced knotweed, *Fallopia sachalinensis,* a tetraploid (n = 44), also has both male-fertile and male-sterile forms. A third introduced species, *Fallopia baldschuanica,* has a chromosome number of 20 and produces fertile pollen. Male sterile varieties of *Fallopia japonica* are frequently pollinated by *sachalinensis* or *baldschuanica* and in many cases produce viable seed. Hybrids of *japonica* with both other species, varying in chromosome number from 44 to 88, have been found in nature. These hybrids are very widely distributed in Britain. Viable seeds with a chromosome number of 32 have also been produced from other crosses or backcrosses. Similar patterns of hybridization also occur in continental Europe. The frequency and diversity of these patterns of hybridization gives a considerable evolutionary potential to this plant complex. New, fully fertile knotweeds that are better adapted to European climates and soils might well appear. *Fallopia japonica* has also been introduced to other world regions and is a widespread invasive plant in Canada and the United States (Sieger 1997).

Weedy forms have also arisen by hybridization between aliens in many other plant genera, including *Carduus* (Warwick et al. 1989), *Centaurea* (Talbott-Roché and Roché 1991), *Lonicera* (Harrington et al. 1989), *Rhamnus* (Gil-ad and Reznicek 1997), *Rhododendron* (Milne and Abbott 2000), *Tamarix* (Gaskin and Schall 2002), and *Onopordum* (O'Hanlon et al. 2000). Johnsongrass (*Sorghum halepense*), one of the world's most noxious agricultural weeds, is also suspected to have arisen by hybridization, in this case between two species of wild sorghums in Africa (Paterson et al. 1995). Soft brome (*Bromus hordaceus*), another invasive grass of regions of Mediterranean climate, is a tetraploid derivative of hybridization between two other Old World grasses (Ainouche et al. 1999).

Many hybridizations involve introduced crop plants and alien relatives. In northern California, for example, a weedy form of the genus *Secale* has evolved by hybridization of cultivated rye (*Secale cereale*) with *S. montanum*, a grass that was introduced to an experimental station in Washington. The hybrid has become established in the wild in the Pacific Northwest (Sun and Corke 1992). Many other such cases are known. Enhanced weediness has resulted from gene flow from crops to weedy relatives for seven of the world's most important crop species (Ellstrand et al. 1999).

Hybridization Between Alien Animals

Alien animal hybridizations also produce new forms that can become aggressive invaders. Many of these involve aquatic organisms, especially fish. Fish hybrids, many of artificial origin, are common among tilapias, salmonids, centrarchids, esocids, and various ornamental fish.

The major commercial species of tilapia include the Mozambique tilapia (*Oreochromis mossambicus*), blue tilapia (*O. aureus*), Nile tilapia (*O. niloticus*), Warm River tilapia (*O. urolepis hornorum*), and the redbelly tilapia (*Tilapia zillii*) (Chapman 1992). Tilapia are now farmed worldwide. In the United States, commercial tilapia culture is concentrated in Arizona, California, and Florida. Several tilapia forms, which may be in part the result of hybridization, make up most of the commercial stock. These hybrids are believed to have originated mostly from crosses of blue tilapia with Nile, Mozambique, and Zanzibar tilapia. Some genes from other species also seem to be present. Two of the most popular hybrids are the Florida red, a cross between blue and Mozambique tilapias, and a hybrid between blue and Nile tilapias. The blue tilapia is favored as one parent because of its tolerance to cold water. Active breeding programs for tilapias are being conducted at several locations.

Several tilapia, including some that are likely to be hybrids, occur in the wild in the southwestern United States (Courtenay et al. 1984; Costa-Pierce and Doyle 1997). Nile tilapia, possibly including fish with hybrid contributions from blue tilapia, are established in the lower Colorado and Gila Rivers and irrigation canals in southeastern California and south-western Arizona (Courtenay et al. 1984). Fish similar to Mozambique tilapia, but possibly with hybrid contributions from Warm River tilapia, occur in Los Angeles County, the Salton Sea, and some irrigation ditches in southern California (Courtenay et al. 1984). Other hybrids have been reported from central Arizona and southeastern California, but their status is uncertain (Courtenay et al. 1984). Redbelly tilapia also occur in the Salton Sea (Costa-Pierce and Doyle 1997).

Hybrid sport fish of several types have been produced and stocked in fresh waters. For instance, several hybrids between species in the salmonid genera *Salmo* and *Salvelinus* have been produced in captivity and the fish stocked in Canadian lakes (Crossman 1984). In the family Centrarchidae, hybrids have occurred naturally and been produced in captivity with several sets of close relatives (see, e.g., Epifanio et al. 1999). Hybrid sunfish, for example, are usually a cross between the bluegill (*Lepomis macrochirus*) and the green sunfish (*L. cyanellus*). These and other centrarchid hybrids are commonly stocked in ponds used for sportfishing. Another sport fish, tiger muskellunge, is a sterile hybrid between northern pike (*Esox lucius*) and muskellunge (*E. masquinogy*). Although these hybrids occasionally occur naturally, most tiger muskellunge are artificially propagated and stocked. This hardy hybrid has been stocked in numerous lakes and rivers in eastern North America.

Hybridization Between Alien Microbial Species

The potential for origin of new invasive forms by hybridization extends to fungi and other microbial forms. Molecular genetic techniques have been instrumental in the identification of forms of fungi and in recognition of patterns of hybridization among them. Many of these fungi also hold the potential to cause widespread mortality of host plants when a virulent form arises or is introduced to a new location.

A detailed example of the role that hybridization can play in fungal virulence is provided by the Dutch elm disease fungi, which are ascomycetes of the genus *Ophiostoma* (Brasier 2001). Three forms of *Ophiostoma* that act as biological species and attack elms are known: *O. ulmi*, *O. novo-ulmi*, and *O. himal-ulmi*. *O. novo-ulmi* also shows two subspecific forms, known by the acronyms EAN and NAN. *O. ulmi* and *O. novo-ulmi* have been involved in the pandemics of Dutch elm disease in western Eurasia and North America. *O. himal-ulmi* is, as yet, restricted to the western Himalaya Mountains, where it appears to be a relatively nonvirulent associate of native elm species.

The Dutch elm disease fungi have been transported intra- and intercontinentally by transport of elm logs and timber. The vector in the fungi's spread through elm populations is bark beetles of the genus *Scolytus*, which occur throughout the world distribution of elms.

The first major outbreak of Dutch elm disease began in Europe in about 1910, in North America about 1927, and in central Asia in the late 1930s. This outbreak was caused by the arrival in these areas of *O. ulmi* from some as yet unknown source. In the 1940s, *O. novo-ulmi* initiated a second outbreak in two areas, eastern Europe, where the EAN form was involved, and the Great Lakes region of North America, where the NAN form was involved. In Europe, the EAN form spread both westward to the Netherlands and eastward into central Asia. The North American outbreak spread continent-wide, and the NAN form was introduced to the British Isles and western Europe in the 1970s and 1980s. NAN and EAN forms of *O. novo-ulmi* now overlap in Italy and parts of central Europe to the north. In the course of the spread of *O. novo-ulmi*, *O. ulmi* has likely been competitively eliminated in much of the northern hemisphere (Brasier and Buck 2001).

Although *O. ulmi* and *O. novo-ulmi* tend to behave as reproductively isolated species, some interchange of genes, and also of viruses, has occurred. The genetic interchanges seem to have involved the transfer of vegetative incompatibility genes from *O. ulmi* to *O. novo-ulmi*. These genes prevent the fusion of cells of different compatibility types and, most importantly, the transfer of viruses between these types. The viruses in question are capable of destroying the fungi. Thus, interspecific hybridization has strengthened the overall virulence of *O. novo-ulmi*.

Additional hybridization is now occurring between the NAN and EAN forms of *O. novo-ulmi* in central Europe. These hybrids and their backcrosses represent a series of active centers of evolution of *O. novo-ulmi*, the outcome of which cannot be predicted. In addition, the potential exists for hybridization with other forms of *Ophiostoma*, including not only *O. himal-ulmi* but also members of the genus associated with other trees.

Another example of introduced fungal parasites of higher plants that can interbreed to produce hybrids with new host infection capabilities is provided by fungi of the genus *Phytophthora*. These fungi produce blight on a wide variety of higher plants. In the British Isles, a *Phytophthora* blight appeared on alders in the 1990s, killing many trees (Brasier et al. 1999). DNA fingerprinting revealed that this agent is a highly diverse polyploid resulting from hybridization of *Phytophthora* species alien to the British Isles but not known to attack alders. Although the typical form is polyploid, much of its diversity is related to variation in chromosome number. The parental forms appear to be two *Phytophthora* species that are not European natives but that can occur together on plants of the genus *Rubus*—raspberries and blackberries.

Additional examples of hybridization between alien fungi are provided by rusts in New Zealand and North America (Frey et al. 1999; Spiers and Hopcroft 1994). These hybrids have occurred among rusts of the genus *Melampsora* that occur on trees of the genus *Populus*.

Hybridization Between Alien and Native Plants

Many other hybridizations involve alien and native species, with consequences similar to those described for alien-alien hybridizations. Among plants, another cordgrass example is provided by the alien, smooth cordgrass (*Spartina alterniflora*), and the native species, California cordgrass (*S. foliosa*), in San Francisco Bay, California (Daehler and Strong 1997a; Antilla et al. 1998, 2000). Smooth cordgrass, native to the east coast of North America, was introduced deliberately to San Francisco Bay in the 1970s. DNA fingerprints using the RAPD technique were made of both species, together with plants in the field that were thought to be hybrids. In 1995, the presence of hybrids was confirmed. Hybridization occurs with either species as the pollen parent, but smooth cordgrass produces much more viable pollen than does California cordgrass, so where the two species occur in proximity, smooth cordgrass promotes heavy hybrid seed set.

Recent work (Antilla et al. 2000) has shown that hybrid-dominated populations of cordgrass are rapidly pushing California cordgrass toward extirpation in south San Francisco Bay. Whereas smooth cordgrass flowers later than California cordgrass, hybrids have an intermediate flowering period that overlaps for a longer period with California cordgrass. The various cordgrass forms have the same chromosome numbers and are interfertile. Hybrid cordgrass, which possesses the higher pollen production of its smooth cordgrass parent, thus backcrosses extensively with California cordgrass.

Like *Spartina anglica* in the British Isles, smooth cordgrass and its hybrids with California cordgrass are able to invade open mudflats at tidal levels lower than those occupied by California cordgrass. Thus, the ecological impact of smooth cordgrass and the hybrid forms may be great. It also appears likely that smooth cordgrass or hybrid cordgrass forms will eventually become established outside San Francisco Bay.

In California, extensive hybridization occurs between two species of sea figs, *Carpobrotus chilensis*, a rose-flowered native, and *C. edulis*, a yellow-flowered alien (Albert et al. 1997; Gallagher et al. 1997). Most fitness characteristics of hybrids were similar to or intermediate between those of the two parents (Vilà and D'Antonio 1998). Overall estimates of seed and seedling survival showed that survival probabilities were highest for *C. edulis*, second highest for hybrids, and lowest for *C. chilensis*. The fact that 74% of plants examined in a series of coastal transects were hybrids, however, suggests that additional factors may give hybrids some advantage over both parents.

Many other cases of hybridization between alien and native plants exist. In Florida and the Bahama Islands, the alien *Lantana camara* hybridizes with the native *L. depressa* (Sanders 1987). On Madagascar, the invasive bramble *Rubus alceifolius* has hybridized with the native *R. roridus*, yielding an apomictic form. In turn, this form has invaded La Réunion and other Indian Ocean islands (Amsellem et al. 2001). In Germany, the alien cress *Rorippa austriaca* has hybridized with the native *R. sylvestris* to give rise to a complex of invasive hybrid forms (Bleeker 2003). *R. austriaca* has a diploid chromosome number of 16, whereas *R. sylvestris* is a hexaploid with a chromosome number of 48. Only some of the hybrids, with ploidy levels ranging from 3X to 5X, reproduce sexually, but their populations are spreading into areas where neither parent occurs.

Artificial hybrids created by crop and horticultural plant breeding must also be considered as forms that can encourage the flow of foreign genes into native plant species. More than 100 such crop hybrids and thousands of horticultural hybrids have been created (Daehler and Carino

2001). With horticultural hybrids in particular, the parentage of derived forms may involve species from widely different geographic regions and is often held secret by the breeder. These hybrids in at least some cases hold the potential for further hybridization with native species. In regions such as the Hawaiian Islands and Florida, where thousands of horticultural forms have been introduced, the risk of such hybridizations is high.

Hybridization Between Alien and Native Animals

Hybridization between introduced and native invertebrates is probably more common than yet documented (Perry et al. 2002). Some of these hybridizations are cryptic and have only been detected by molecular genetic techniques. For example, an allozyme analysis of 64 populations of the cladoceran *Daphnia galeata* from North America and ten populations from Europe revealed that several populations in Ontario, Canada and New York were hybrids of North American and European forms (Taylor and Hebert 1993).

Crayfish are a group of freshwater invertebrates that have been introduced to new waters both accidentally and deliberately and both intra- and inter-continentally. These introductions have had many effects, including displacement of natives (see chapter 16). In northern Michigan and Wisconsin, *Orconectes rusticus* has been introduced to many lakes containing the native crayfish *O. propinquus* and *O. virilis*. In Trout Lake, Wisconsin, where *O. rusticus* was introduced in 1979, allozyme analysis and mitochondrial DNA fingerprinting have revealed that hybridization has occurred with *O. propinquus* (Perry et al. 2001a). Hybridization has not occurred with *O. virilis*, which is also present.

The hybrid crayfish in Trout Lake arise primarily from matings of *rusticus* females and *propinquus* males. These hybrids have high fecundity and survivorship but in addition show greater competitive ability than either parent. The least competitive form, *propinquus*, however, is being displaced rapidly, and since the female parent of most hybrids is *rusticus*, the mitochondrial genome of *propinquus* is disappearing rapidly. Thus, as pure *propinquus* crayfish disappear, the first-generation hybrids between the two species, which show enhanced competitive ability, will become less frequent. The genome that will eventually characterize the surviving population may contain some component of *propinquus* genes, however. Thus, in a sense, *O. propinquus* will have effectively been extirpated in Trout Lake, but *O. rusticus* will have undergone some evolutionary change as a result of genetic introgression.

Among insects, the spread of African honey bees (*Apis mellifera scutellata*) in the New World following their introduction to Brazil in the late 1950s has involved hybridization between this form and domesticated European subspecies. The African subspecies has spread through tropical and subtropical regions as feral populations that interbreed with the European forms in managed apiaries (Hall and McMichael 2001). The representation of European genetic markers declines gradually in apiary populations, and in time, European genotypes are expected to disappear completely (Clarke et al. 2001).

A recent concern among insects is the possibility of invasion of North America by the Asian form of the gypsy moth (*Lymantria dispar*). In the Asian form, the female is able to fly, rather than being flightless, as in the case of the established European strain (Liebhold et al. 1996). The Asian and European strains hybridize freely, and the consequences of such an interaction are difficult to predict but could likely lead to a greatly increased rate of spread of this destructive insect. Several incipient populations of the Asian form have been detected in North America, all of which have either failed or been eradicated.

Examples of hybridization between aliens and natives are numerous among fish (Leary et al. 1995). Most of this result from the deliberate stocking of alien species for the supposed improvement of sportfishing. In these cases, much of the conservation concern also relates to genetic extinction of the native (see chapter 16). In addition, substantial evidence now exists that the stocking of hatchery-reared fish into wild populations of the same species can reduce fitness of wild populations. The hatchery environment selects for several morphological and behavioral characteristics in Atlantic salmon (*Salmo salar*) and Pacific salmon (*Oncorhynchus* spp.) that confer reduced fitness in the wild (Fleming and Einum 1997; Reisenbichler and Rubin 1999).

Through hybridization between fish of hatchery and wild origin, the fitness of some populations spawning in the wild is also reduced. In Denmark, using DNA microsatellite analysis, Hansen (2002) found that wild brown trout (*Salmo trutta*) populations were in some cases highly introgressed and others only weakly introgressed by heavy stocking of hatchery fish. Hatchery trout appeared to be poorly adapted as anadromous fish, as opposed to permanent residents in freshwater, so interbreeding with wild fish may have reduced fitness of the anadromous wild population. In British Columbia, Canada, chinook salmon (*Oncorhynchus tshawytscha*) captured in the wild are spawned in aquacultural facilities, and the resulting fry are released back into streams to supplement natural reproduction. This procedure tends to select for high fecundity and small egg size (Heath et al. 2003). Offspring from small eggs have been shown to have lower survival than those from large eggs. In rivers that have received heavy supplementation with fry from hatchery spawning, significant reductions in egg size have been noted in the wild population.

Few cases of hybridization between aliens and natives are known among terrestrial vertebrates. Among mammals, hybridization occasionally occurs between domestic dogs (*C. familiaris*) and other canids, such as the gray wolf (*Canis lupus*) and the Ethiopian wolf (*Canis simiensis*) (see, e.g., Andersone et al. 2002; Gottelli et al. 1994). Feral domestic cats (*Felis catus*), derived from the North African race of the wildcat (*Felis sylvestris*), have also hybridized with the Scottish race of the wildcat, which is the last remaining wild race of the species (Beaumont et al. 2001).

More interesting is the interaction between the coyote (*C. latrans*) and the gray wolf. In eastern North America, coyotes expanded their range eastward and northward during the 1900s (Thurber and Peterson 1991). Animals in the eastern areas of range expansion also tend to be larger and heavier, especially in parts of New England. This difference is probably at least in part genetic. We shall consider this example in more detail in chapter 10.

Hybridization Between Alien and Native Microbial Species

Introduced fungal parasites can also hybridize with native forms. In the Netherlands, *Phytophthora nicotianae*, an introduced form, has hybridized with *P. cactorum*, a native, to produce a new blight fungus that attacks plants of the genera *Primula* and *Spathiphyllum* (Man in't Veldt et al. 1998).

In the Pacific Northwest, hybridization has occurred between the rust, *Melampsora occidentalis*, native to the black cottonwood (*Populus trichocarpa*), and the introduced *M. medusae*, native to the eastern cottonwood (*P. deltoides*) (Newcombe et al. 2000). The original geographical ranges of these trees and their rusts are nonoverlapping. A hybrid of the two species of *Populus* has been produced and grown as clones in commercial plantations in the Pacific Northwest. These hybrids were resistant to *M. occidentalis*. In 1991, *M. medusae* appeared on the hybrid cottonwoods, and since 1995, hybrid rusts (*M.* × *columbiana*) have been detected. By 1997, the rust hybrid had apparently displaced its parental forms in the Pacific Northwest. This hybrid form is capable of infecting not only the black and eastern cottonwoods but also the three other close relatives of these species that occur in North America. The hybrid also shows substantial genetic variation (Newcombe et al. 2001). Whether or not it will prove to be a more virulent pathogen than its parents remains to be seen.

Overall Significance of Hybridization

Thus, hybridization between and among alien species and between alien and native species has proven ability to give rise to new invasive forms, especially in the case of plants and plant disease agents. As the last example of cottonwoods and their rusts shows, deliberate hybridizations by plant and animal breeders are likely to increase the complexity of unintended hybridizations by their parasites and diseases.

The invasive forms resulting from some hybridizations have the capacity to transform habitats and biotic communities. Hybrid cordgrasses and willows can modify the physical habitats that they tend to dominate. Hybrid parasitic fungi have greatly altered the biotic structure of the communities they have invaded. The risk of origin of new, highly invasive organisms by hybridization is enormous, especially among fungi and other microorganisms about which our knowledge of introductions to new areas is fragmentary.

Issues involving hybridization are not limited, however, to those of the origin of invasive forms as considered in this chapter. In the next chapter we shall examine a special issue related to hybridization: the risks of transfer of engineered genes from crop plants and domestic animals to their wild relatives.

6.
Hybridization and Transgenic Organisms

"Organisms with novel combinations of traits are more likely to play novel ecological roles, on average, than are organisms produced by recombining genetic information existing within a single evolutionary lineage."

—TIEDJE ET AL. 1989

"Genes do not belong to an organism, they are at best part of a family of genes that may be very widespread."

—BERINGER 2000

Crop sorghum (*Sorghum bicolor*) is one of the world's most important grain crops, both in developed areas such as North America and in underdeveloped Africa, its native region. Many varieties, all annual and diploid in chromosome number, are under cultivation. Johnsongrass (*Sorghum halepense*) is a perennial, usually tetraploid, grass native to the Mediterranean region. Reproducing both by seed and vegetative means, it is one of the world's most troublesome weeds, especially of grain crops. Johnsongrass is now sympatric with crop sorghum in most areas of cultivation. Although both grasses tend to be self-pollinating, significant outcrossing occurs, and many Johnsongrass populations in the United States have experienced genetic introgression from cultivated sorghums.

Arriola and Ellstrand (1996) conducted experiments at two field stations in California in which Johnsongrass was planted at distances of

0.5–100 m from the edge of sorghum plots 0.2 ha in area. Enzyme electrophoresis was used to detect hybrids among the progeny of the Johnsongrass plants. In spite of the difference in chromosome number, substantial hybridization was detected, the rate being up to 2% for plants 100
m from the sorghum stand and up to more than 10% near the edge of the
stand. This frequency of hybridization is significant since sorghum varieties have been engineered with genes for herbicide resistance. Herbicide
resistance genes can obviously be transferred from crop sorghum to Johnsongrass. Widespread use of herbicide-resistant sorghums, coupled with
heavy use of herbicides, could easily select for herbicide-resistant Johnsongrass, which could be exceedingly troublesome because of its ability
to spread both vegetatively and by seed.

Crops and their weed races and close relatives form complexes of
plants of largely alien composition in most areas. The remarkable examples of rapid evolution that are occurring in these species complexes will
almost certainly be influenced by genetic engineering of the crop species
involved, followed by hybridization with related forms. In addition to
plants, animals and microorganisms are likely to be influenced by the
technology of genetic engineering.

Natural Hybridization and Gene Exchange

As we have seen in the previous chapter, hybridization between species is
a natural process that has played an important role in evolution, especially
in plants. The majority of plant species may, in fact, have originated
through a process involving hybridization (Grant 1981). The general role
that such hybridization has played in weed evolution has also long been
known. Hybridization between crop plants and weed races or related
species, most of which are aliens in many world regions, has been known
for a long time. Of the world's 13 most important food, oil, and fiber
crops, for example, genetic data indicate that 12 hybridize with wild relatives somewhere (Ellstrand et al. 1999). Hybridization with wild relatives
also occurs with many other cultivated plants, including crop, forage, timber, and horticultural species. In the United Kingdom and Netherlands, a
quarter to a third of cultivated plants hybridize with wild plants (Ellstrand
et al. 1999).

The hybridization process of primary concern for escape of introduced
genes, termed transgenes, is pollination of wild or weedy relatives with
crop pollen (Kirkpatrick and Wilson 1988; Klinger et al. 1991, 1992; Arias
and Rieseberg 1994). The potential for such hybridization is influenced

by the degree of self-incompatibility of the plants involved, the mode of pollen transport, and many conditions of the physical habitat. In the case of the common sunflower (*Helianthus annuus*), for example, crop varieties are highly self-compatible, whereas wild plants are self-incompatible. Both are insect-pollinated, primarily by bees. This relationship creates a strong potential for crop pollen to be transferred to wild plants, with the insect pollinators being capable of long-distance transport (Arias and Riesberg 1994). Crop and wild sunflowers occur in close proximity throughout most of the area of sunflower cultivation in the Unites States, and hybridization of crop and wild varieties is very frequent (Burke et al. 2002). For other species, including sorghum, radish, and squashes, hybridization resulting from insect pollination has been detected up to 1 km from crop plantings. Most grain crops, on the other hand, are wind pollinated and strongly self-compatible. Crop sorghum (*Sorghum bicolor*), for example, has an outcrossing rate of only about 10–15% and John-songrass, with which it is capable of hybridizing, is also primarily, but not completely, self-pollinating (Arriola and Ellstrand 1996), as we noted at the chapter outset. Field experiments have nevertheless detected hybridization between sorghum and Johnsongrass at distances of 100 m from sorghum plantings.

Experimental studies have revealed that genetic engineering itself can influence the frequency of outcrossing. The annual crucifer *Arabidopsis thaliana*, used widely in laboratory studies of plant genetics, is normally self-pollinating. Various transgenic lines carrying a gene for herbicide resistance differed substantially in outcrossing frequency, with several showing increased outcrossing tendency. One line was 17 times more likely to outcross than untransformed plants (Bergelson and Purrington 2002).

Genetic Engineering and Transgenes

Genetic engineers now have perfected techniques for transferring genes between microorganisms, from microorganisms to higher plants and animals, or from one higher plant to another. The genes themselves may vary in structure depending on their source and may be modified in structure before being inserted into a host organism. The performance of such transgenes depends to some extent on the location at which they are inserted in the host genome. Thus, many different transgenic lines of host organisms may be created, even with a single gene. Several types of genes are now being inserted into crop plants. These include genes for resistance to different classes of herbicides; for resistance to viruses, fungi, and insects; for male sterility; and for various growth, composition, and fruiting characteristics. With herbicide resistance, genes for resistance to more than one herbicide can be combined in the crop genotypes. For potato (*Solanum tuberosum*), for example, varieties with resistance to certain viruses, beetles, and lepidopterans, combined with resistance to several herbicides, can be created (Barber 1999). For maize (*Zea mays*), male sterility, resistance to lepidopteran pests, and multiple herbicide resistance can be combined. Genetic engineering is being extended to other organisms, as well.

The area of transgenetic crops as of 2001 exceeded 52 million ha worldwide (Dale et al. 2002). About three-quarters of this was in the United States (Letourneau et al. 2002). Crops with engineered herbicide resistance are grown on more than 20 million ha worldwide (Barber 1999). Transgenic maize, cotton (*Gossypium hirsutum*), and potato varieties that contain genes derived from the bacterium *Bacillus thuringiensis* for an insecticidal toxin occupy more than 8 million ha worldwide (Barber 1999). Despite some public resistance to genetically engineered foods, the area of transgenic crops is growing rapidly.

This transgene technology, applied to crop plants, has raised a number of concerns (table 6.1). One is the possibility that genes for resistance to diseases, pests, or herbicides might be transferred to already invasive weeds by hybridization, increasing their aggressiveness. A second is the possibility that nonweedy plants might be transformed into invasive weeds by the acquisition of transgenes. A third is that the spread of transgenes from crops to weeds might increase the selection pressure for pest insects and disease organisms to overcome the effects of genes intended to protect crop species. Although only quantitatively different from what plant breeders have been doing for decades, transgene technology has a much greater potential to influence the evolution of crop relatives and the organisms with which they interact.

Gene transfers can occur in both directions between crops and wild plants. Our main concern, however, is the flow of genes, especially certain kinds of engineered genes, from domesticated plants to wild species. In many cases, the wild species are troublesome aliens. More than 60 crop and tree species have been genetically engineered to contain genes for resistance to herbicides, diseases, or pests, or for other characteristics (Barber 1999). As of 2001, transgenic cultivars of eight major crop species have

Table 6.1. Potentially detrimental impacts of genetically modified crop plants. (Modified from Dale et al. 2002.)

DIRECT IMPACTS
- Impacts on nontarget organisms
    - –Effects of Bt and other endotoxins on nonpest animals
    - –Effects of pesticidal toxins on soil organisms and processes
- Altered crop plant behavior
    - –Increased postharvest persistence in cropland
    - –Invasiveness in natural habitats

INDIRECT IMPACTS
- Gene flow to noncrop plants and selection for transgenic characteristics
    - –Transgenic resistance to one or more herbicides
    - –Transgenic biotic or abiotic stress resistance
- Evolutionary influences of increased herbicide and other pesticide use
    - –Selection for herbicide resistance by noncrop plants
    - –Selection for animal pest resistance to Bt and other endotoxins
- Ecological effects of altered pesticide use patterns
    - –Effects of altered herbicide use on noncrop plant species and communities
    - –Effects of altered pesticide use on nonpest animal species and communities

been approved for distribution in North America and some other areas: oilseed rape, cotton, maize, potato, soybean, sugar beet, tobacco, and tomato (Hilbeck 2001). Transgenic maize (*Zea mays*), oilseed rape (*Brassica napus*), and cotton (*Gossypium hirsutum*) are all widely cultivated, especially in the Americas, and are all capable of interbreeding with wild relatives. Many more transgenic crop plants are being tested experimentally and are likely to be approved for release in the near future.

To date, transgenes from crop plants do not appear to have become established in noncrop races or species. Hybridization of different crop races of oilseed rape and possibly maize, however, has been shown to lead to the transfer of transgenes (Ellstrand 2001). In the case of oilseed rape, plants that combined transgenic resistance to three herbicides were found in a field situation in Alberta, Canada. Two sequential hybridization events were required to produce these plants from the individual oilseed rape varieties containing individual herbicide resistance genes. Thus, it appears to be only a matter of time until transgenes become established in some noncrop plants.

Potential for Exchange of Transgenes between Crops and Crop Weed Races

In many cases, hybridization can occur between transgenic crops and weed races of the same species. Such hybridizations are usually very frequent and involve little or no reduction in offspring vigor. Cultivated sunflower (*Helianthus annuus*) is one such example. Wild sunflowers occur throughout the United States and Mexico and in some states are designated as a noxious weed because of their influence on cultivated sunflower. Hybridization between crop and wild sunflowers can occur over distances as great as 1 km, and little or no reduction in fecundity is seen in hybrids (Arias and Rieseberg 1994). Crop-specific genetic markers spread to wild sunflower populations have been shown to persist for at least five generations (Whitton et al. 1997). Gene flow from crop sunflowers to adjacent wild populations is so extensive that the wild populations actually consist of plants derived from several generations of hybridization and backcrossing (Linder et al. 1998).

In addition, one of the most widely used transgenes, the *Bacillus thuringiensis* (Bt) endotoxin gene, not only has no fitness cost to wild sunflower plants, but increases their seed production, as well (Snow et al. 2003). In field situations, transgenic wild sunflowers produced 55% more seeds in Nebraska and 14% more seeds in Colorado than wild sunflowers lacking the Bt gene. Thus, genes introduced into crop sunflower for traits such as insect resistance could easily become established in wild sunflower populations and are almost certain to confer increased fitness on wild plants.

A second example of hybridization between crops and weed races of the same species involves radish (*Raphanus sativus*). Radishes are primarily outcrossing plants pollinated by insects. Klinger et al. (1991) examined gene flow from crop radish to weed radish planted at distances of 1–1,000 m from crop radish stands in California. A genetic marker in the crop plants that could be recognized by allozyme analysis permitted the recognition of hybrid offspring. For weed radish planted within 1 m of crop radishes, hybrids ranged from 14 to 100% of all offspring. Hybrid offspring were also noted in the weed plantings 1,000 m from crop radish stands. In addition, the hybrids themselves showed increased fitness, producing more seed than wild plants (Klinger and Ellstrand 1994). The variability in incidence of hybridization with distance from crop plantings was very great, so the average distance at which hybridization was noted was a very poor estimator of the risk of transgene escape (Klinger 2002).

Still another example shows the complexity of relationships that can occur among crop and noncrop plants. For beets (*Beta vulgaris*), several cultivated forms, the wild progenitor subspecies, and several weedy varieties exist. The cultivated forms include table beet, Swiss chard, fodder beet, and sugar beet. All beet forms are fully interfertile and exist in close contact in parts of Europe. Cultivated beets are exclusively biennial, whereas wild forms range from annual to perennial. Weed forms are primarily annuals, carrying a dominant gene for the annual habit. Weed beets have become a major problem for sugar beet cultivation in Europe and to a lesser extent in California. Transgenic varieties of sugar beets with resistance to herbicides and certain virus diseases have been developed, so the possibility of escape of transgenes to weed beets and other close relatives is real (Desplanque et al. 2002).

In Italy, alleles that are usually rare in the wild form (sea beet, *B. vulgaris* ssp. *maritima*) are common in this form where it occurs near plantings of table beets and Swiss chard (Bartsch et al. 1999). In California, sugar beets hybridize freely with wild sea beets that were apparently introduced as a contaminant of crop beet seed. They also hybridize with a second wild European beet, *B. macrocarpa* (Bartsch and Ellstrand 1999). Transgenic herbicide-resistant varieties of sugar beets are now available, and it is clear that their use will probably lead to gene escape into populations of wild and weedy forms (Boudry et al. 1993; Bartsch et al. 2001).

Other examples of hybridization between crop and weed races of the same species involve squash (*Cucurbita pepo*), carrot (*Daucus carota*), celery (*Apium graveolens*), and asparagus (*Asparagus officinalis*) (Spencer and Snow 2001; Ellstrand and Hoffman 1990; Wilson and Payne 1994).

A particular risk exists for genetic engineering of plants that are both beneficial and weedy. Bermuda grass (*Cynodon dactylon*), for example, is both a pasture grass and one of the most troublesome weeds of natural ecosystems (Ellstrand and Hoffman 1990). Transgenes introduced into this grass would almost certainly spread to grass populations outside the pasture environment, making this plant even more difficult to manage in areas devoted to natural vegetation.

Potential for Exchange of Transgenes between Crops and Other Plant Species

Many other hybridization routes exist for the transfer of transgenes between crop plants and other related species. Well-studied examples include the crop sorghum and Johnsongrass case described at the beginning of the chapter, as well as several other cases involving important crop plants.

One of the most extensively studied cases involves the possibility of transfer of genes for herbicide resistance from oilseed rape (*Brassica napus*) to field mustard (*B. rapa*). Oilseed rape has been bred to possess genes for resistance to three basic herbicide groups, and field evidence exists that these genes can move among plants of oilseed rape itself. Although oilseed rape is an allotetraploid and field mustard a diploid, hybridization is frequent and backcrosses of hybrids can occur to field mustard. Snow et al. (1999) examined the possibility that genes for glufosinate herbicide resistance could be transferred to field mustard through hybridization and backcrossing. They found that third-generation backcrosses with herbicide resistance could be obtained easily and that these plants showed survival and fecundity levels equal to normal field mustard plants. Furthermore, hybridization between these two plants has been documented in field conditions (Hansen et al. 2001). Thus, flow of herbicide resistance genes from oilseed rape to field mustard is likely and could lead to serious weed infestations by herbicide-resistant field mustard. In Denmark, transgenic herbicide-tolerant oilseed rape shows a high frequency of hybridization with *Brassica campestris*, with the hybrids carrying the transgene and backcrossing easily to this weed species (Jørgensen et al. 1998). Transgenes for other characteristics, such as content of specific oils, can also be passed from oilseed rape to *Brassica rapa* (Linder and Schmitt 1995). Oilseed rape hybridizes with at least four other species of the mustard family, some belonging to other genera, so the potential for transfer of transgenes to weedy plants is extensive (Jørgensen 1999).

Another example of potential interspecific transfer of a resistance gene involves wheat (*Triticum aestivum*) and jointed goatgrass (*Aegilops cylindrica*), a frequent grain field weed that often hybridizes with wheat. In an herbicide effectiveness study in Washington State, spontaneous hybrids occurred between wheat and jointed goatgrass. These hybrids carried herbicide resistance derived from the wheat parent (Seefeldt et al. 1999). Although most such hybrids are sterile, a small percentage are fertile and can backcross to jointed goatgrass (Guadagnuolo et al. 2001). Thus, backcrossing of hybrids to jointed goatgrass might easily introduce herbicide resistance to a very troublesome weed.

Many other examples of crop-weed systems with the potential for flow of transgenes to related species exist. Cultivated radish can exchange genes not only with weedy forms of the crop itself, as described earlier, but also with wild radish (*Raphanus raphanistrum*), a widespread distinct species (Snow et al. 2001). Other species known to exhibit this potential include quinoa (*Chenopodium quinoa*) (Wilson and Manhart 1993), squashes (*Cucurbita* spp.), maize (*Zea mays*), wheats (*Triticum* spp.), rice (*Oryza* spp.), soybean (*Glycine max*), barley (*Hordeum vulgare*), cotton (*Gossypium* spp.), millets (*Eleusine* and *Setaria* spp.), beans (*Phaseolus* spp.), and sugar cane (*Saccharum officinarum*) (Ellstrand et al. 1999; Wilson 1990).

Transgenes and Microorganisms

The potential also exists for transfer of transgenes from crops to microorganisms and among microorganisms themselves. Oilseed rape (*Brassica napus*) carrying an antibiotic resistance gene was found to transfer the gene to *Aspergillus niger*, a soil fungus (Hoffman et al. 1994). Recent studies of bacterial genomes have shown that many bacterial genes are subject to horizontal gene transfer, that is, exchange between different bacterial species (Smalla and Sobecky 2002). Genetically engineered bacteria introduced into soil microcosms have been shown to transfer engineered genes to other soil bacteria (Doyle et al. 1995). RNA transgenes for plant resistance to specific viruses can also be incorporated into the genome of certain viruses by recombination (Greene and Allison 1994; Tepfer 2002).

The behavior of transgenic microorganisms in the environment is still poorly understood. How transgenic viruses designed to attack insect pests behave depends on such factors as virulence, effectiveness of transmission between host organisms, survival over periods of host inactivity, and other factors (Dushoff and Dwyer 2001). Transgenic bacteria have been found to influence soil ecology in ways that are unsuspected (Doyle et al. 1995; Holmes and Ingham 1995). Transgenic forms can compete with indigenous microorganisms, modify metabolic processes in the soil, alter the community composition of the soil biota, influence symbiotic relationships between microorganisms and higher plants, and introduce novel metabolic products into the soil system. A potential also exists for rapid evolution of many microorganisms carrying transgenes, especially under conditions of environmental stress; consequences are difficult to predict (Velkov 2001).

Ecological Implications of Transgene Escape from Crop Plants

The release of domesticated plants with transgenes has major ecological implications. A potentially serious consequence is invasion of natural communities by transgenic crop plants or the creation of highly invasive weeds that carry transgenes for various characteristics. So far, major crops that carry genes for Bt endotoxins or resistance to herbicides do not appear to be more invasive into natural communities than their conventional varieties (Crawley et al. 2001). Most geneticists believe that species that acquire extra genes will experience a fitness cost except in situations in which the added gene exerts a strong beneficial effect (Tiedje et al. 1989). This suggests that escaping transgenes are not likely to benefit most weed species in nonagricultural settings. Many studies, however, have not shown such reductions in fitness (see, e.g., Snow et al. 1999). The persistence of crop sunflower alleles in wild sunflower populations over many generations suggests that genes that have little fitness cost can persist in wild populations indefinitely (Whitton et al. 1997). Studies with *Arabidopsis thaliana*, discussed earlier, show that fitness of transgenic lines carrying herbicide resistance is reduced considerably in herbicide-free settings (Bergelson and Purrington 2002). Much more research is needed on this question, and it appears likely that the answer will vary, depending on many aspects of the ecological situation.

Transgenetic crop plants carrying herbicide resistance genes are designed to tolerate the use of heavier applications of the herbicides in question. Thus, although this use will immediately control certain weeds, weedy plants not inhibited by the particular herbicide will gain greater ecological and evolutionary potential to exploit what amounts to an empty niche. Shifting patterns of weed infestation are likely to result.

More intense use of chemical herbicides will also select for increased herbicide resistance in weedy plants. A worldwide survey of herbicide-resistant weeds in 1995–96 revealed 183 resistant varieties of 124 weed species (Heap 1997). Resistance has evolved to all major chemical groups of herbicides, with many weeds showing multiple resistance patterns. Although the number of new varieties showing herbicide resistance has been roughly constant at about nine per year in recent years, major intensification of herbicide use would likely speed the evolution of resistance.

Transgenes that escape from crop plants to weed races or wild relatives of the crop may affect many nontarget organisms. The Bt endotoxin, which has been introduced to a number of major crop plants, might affect many nontarget species of lepidoptera that feed on crop relatives (Letourneau et al. 2002). Information on the feeding habits of such potential nontarget species is very incomplete, so the potential of such impacts is very uncertain. Benefits of transgenic insecticidal crop varieties may also be offset by declines in populations of natural enemies of crop pests induced by the transgenic crop itself (Obrycki et al. 2001).

For some plants, such as corn (*Zea mays*), pollen containing Bt endo-toxin may be carried by wind to areas outside cropland, where impacts on nontarget species might occur. At least 206 nontarget species of lepidoptera in the United States belonging to 20 families have been recorded from plants growing near enough to corn fields to be affected by corn pollen (Losey et al. 2002). The species of greatest concern is the monarch butterfly (*Danaus plexippus*), a migratory species that winters in very local-ized areas, some of which are becoming subject to severe human impacts. Monarch larvae feed on various species of milkweeds (*Asclepias* spp.), many of which tend to occur in weedy fields and fencerows, often near cornfields. Pollen of Bt corn deposited on milkweed leaves has been shown experimentally to increase the mortality of monarch larvae (see, e.g., Jesse and Obrycki 2000). Whether the risk from this factor exceeds that from the use of insecticides that are an alternative for control of corn pests, however, is uncertain.

Transgene effects may also influence ecological processes at higher trophic levels. Shifts may occur in insect pest or disease problems in crops carrying genes for specific resistance to pest organisms of these types. Genes that encode Bt endotoxins, for example, could affect predatory insects. The endotoxins produced in crop plant tissues may be transferred through food chains to foliage-eating insects and to soil organisms (Hilbeck 2001; Groot and Dicke 2002). Bt endotoxin taken in by a moth feeding on transgenic maize, for example, increased mortality and delayed development in green lacewings (*Chrysoperla carnea*) that fed experimen-tally on the moth larvae (Dutton et al. 2002). The potential for secondary effects such as this is not well understood.

Heavier use of herbicides and other pesticides has serious implications for native biodiversity. Nontarget plants and animals are more likely to be affected as use of pesticides intensifies. Heavier use of pesticides, com-bined with increased pest resistance, will make control of alien plants and animals in natural areas much more difficult.

Transgenes and Counterevolution

Many transgenes considered for introduction to crop plants act against arthropod pests or plant disease agents. As in the case of chemical pesti-cides, the potential exists for pests and disease agents to evolve resistance to these transgenic agents. This possibility has been considered for crops with the Bt endotoxin transgene. Several crop insect pests have evolved resistance to Bt endotoxin, in most cases at a fitness cost in an endotoxin-free environment. In the case of the diamondback moth (*Plutella xylostella*), however, resistance in some populations does not appear to reduce fitness, and the protein endotoxin itself may be metabolized with benefit to the moth larva (Sayyed et al. 2003).

For Bt maize, a strategy to delay the evolution of resistance by insect pests has been to couple plantings of Bt maize with refuge plantings of susceptible maize. Although selection for resistance might be high in fields of Bt maize, the high production of insects without resistance in refuges would delay the spread of resistance genes in the insect population at large (Alstad and Andow 1995). Unfortunately, the level of compliance to this strategy by farmers is far from complete (Dale et al. 2002).

Regulatory Issues

The technology of genetic engineering is tending to evolve more rapidly than regulatory capability. At present, evaluation of potential risks is based on short-term evidence that cannot evaluate the long-term potential for reorganization of genomes of wild organisms into which transgenes have escaped. The situation in this regard is similar to that of introduced alien species, in which only a fraction of those that become established become serious problem species. As Williamson (1993) noted, the fraction of genetically modified organisms that lead to problems is likely to be small, but the impacts of those that do could potentially be very serious.

Regulatory procedures have not adequately come to grips with the complexity of the genetic manipulations that are being performed. Introducing a specific gene into a specific organism, for example, may result in multiple transgenic lines that have different biological properties (Bergelson and Purrington 2002). Regulatory requirements for risk assessment are also far from adequate. Requirements for replication and duration of tests for nontarget impacts of plants carrying the Bt endotoxin transgene are inadequate to detect real effects in most cases (Marvier 2002). Furthermore, the required laboratory testing does not come to grips with the complexity and variability of conditions that exist in the open ecological systems into which these plants would be introduced.

Future Trends in Genetic Engineering

The potential of genetic engineering to modify the genetic structure of plants, animals, and microorganisms has only begun to be realized, as have the risks of spread of transgenes to nontarget organisms. The diversity of characteristics that can be engineered is increasing. Combining multiple genetically engineered traits in individual crop varieties is also becoming increasingly common. Efforts are being made to modify insecticidal transgenes, such as the gene for the Bt endotoxin, so they are effective against a wider range of insect types.

Genetic engineering is being extended to many new groups of organisms, and it is already being employed in biological control programs for pests such as the pink bollworm (*Pectinophora gossypiella*), in which a gene for a fluorescent protein is being introduced to the bollworm as a genetic marker (Thibault et al. 1999). Genetic engineering is spreading to domesticated and semidomesticated animals, forestry and horticultural plants, and aquacultural animals. Genetically engineered fish of several species that grow faster and reach larger sizes in aquaculture have been developed (Muir and Howard 2002). Genes for tolerance by plants and other organisms to insecticides, fungicides, and other pesticides are being sought to permit the increased use of increased dosages of these agents in a manner comparable to the present use of herbicides with herbicide-tolerant crops. Developments such as these would considerably broaden the impacts of pesticide chemicals on all living organisms.

Thus, genetic engineering is setting the stage for future evolutionary change by many organisms. Intensified selection for counter-responses by weeds and animal pests within the crop environment will certainly occur. Because of the potential for transgenes to escape to wild and weedy plants in grasslands, forests, and other environments, however, these evolutionary effects will extend much farther.

How natural ecosystems will be affected by the spread of alien species carrying transgenes is difficult to predict. Questions of what factors make natural ecosystems vulnerable to invasion by alien organisms and what factors enable alien species to invade such ecosystems are themselves of great evolutionary interest. We shall consider these in the next chapter.

7.

Invasion Resistance of
Native Communities

"Current hypotheses or generalizations about traits that distinguish both successful invaders and vulnerable communities all concern some extraordinary attributes or circumstances of the species or communities. And all are based on retrospective explanations for past invasions."

—MACK ET AL. (2000)

Diffuse knapweed (*Centaurea diffusa*) is an annual or short-lived perennial Eurasian forb that has become one of the most serious rangeland weeds in western North America. In native areas of the Republic of Georgia, it grows in steppe communities with bunch grasses closely related to those of the shrub steppe communities it invades in Washington, Oregon, Idaho, and other western states and Canadian provinces. Diffuse knapweed is a highly competitive invader, reducing the abundance of many native range plants. In the Republic of Georgia, however, its abundance is small and its impact minor. In eastern Washington, its annual economic damage is estimated at several million dollars.

Laboratory competition experiments between diffuse knapweed and three pairs of closely related species of bunch grasses, each pair consisting of one North American species and one Eurasian species, revealed some surprising results (Callaway and Aschehoug 2000). Diffuse knapweed exerted a much greater inhibition of growth on North American grasses than on those with which it coexists in Eurasia. When the experiments were repeated with activated carbon, which absorbs many organic substances, mixed into the soil of the pots in which the plants were grown, North American bunch grasses showed increased growth and knapweed reduced growth. Eurasian grasses, on the other hand, showed reduced growth in competition with knapweed in the activated carbon-enriched soils. These results suggested that diffuse knapweed releases some sort of chemical growth inhibitor into the soil to which North American grasses were sensitive but to which Eurasian grasses had adapted. It also indicated that Eurasian grasses were dependent on some chemical agent of their own, perhaps to counteract the substance released by knapweed.

In this case, the experiments showed that evolved adjustments existed between Eurasian grass species and diffuse knapweed and that the success of diffuse knapweed in North America was probably due in part to escape from these coevolved relationships. Coevolutionary adjustments of species to each other can thus be a major factor in determining the invasiveness of alien species, as well as the resistance to invasion by the communities they encounter.

Coevolved Relationships in Biotic Communities

The degree to which the plants, animals, and microorganisms in biotic communities are coadapted to each other by evolutionary processes has been a topic of intense debate among ecologists over the past century. This question has now come to be at the center of research about the conditions that permit the invasion of communities by alien species. Early in the past century, many ecologists viewed communities as integrated supraorganisms, in which member species were linked together almost as tightly as cells and tissues of an organism. Later, especially during the 1970s, an individualistic view largely replaced this organismal concept (McIntosh 1998). Species that occurred together were viewed simply as having similar, but independent, patterns of adjustment to conditions of the physical and biotic habitat. Although habitat conditions could be structured or influenced by other organisms, closely evolved adjustments between particular species were the exception. Among these exceptions were various mutualisms and symbioses. More recently, however, with the advent of detailed studies of ecophysiology and molecular genetics, renewed interest has appeared in coevolution and the adjustment of coexisting species to each other (Thompson 1994, 1999a).

To some degree, opportunities for coevolutionary adjustment among species depend on the nature of the physical environment. Natural environments differ greatly in basic features that are related to the ease of establishment of new individuals, whether they be native or alien. Some habitats present physical conditions that are extreme, others conditions that are benign. Some provide resources in abundance, others in very limited quantities. Coevolutionary adjustments of different organisms to each other seem to be favored by abundant resources and benign habitat conditions.

In addition, stability and predictability of the environment are factors of great importance to coevolution. Some communities occupy habitats that are relatively stable, exhibiting nearly constant conditions or showing seasonal patterns of change that are highly predictable. Spring-fed streams, tropical lakes, and tropical rain forests experience nearly constant conditions. Temperate rain forests and arctic/alpine tundra show strong, but highly predictable patterns of seasonal change. Other communities are subject to irregular events that influence physical conditions and resource abundance. Examples include most streams and lakes fed by surface runoff of water from heavy rains, riparian communities bordering streams subject to flooding, arid-land communities subject to violent weather events, and terrestrial communities subject to fire. In addition, many communities and intensively used lands are subject to disturbance by activities such as farming, grazing, timber harvest, vehicular use, and waste discharge. Stability and predictability of the environment also favor coevolution.

Stability, Predictability, and Alien Invasions

Disturbance often sets the stage for alien invasions. Environments with low stability and predictability often present areas of unoccupied habitat where competition for resources is low. These conditions favor the establishment of new individuals, aliens as well as natives (Davis et al. 2000). Many such environments, such as riparian areas subject to flooding, are also very rich in resources such as water and nutrients. Even though such habitats may possess a high diversity of native species, many alien species can also be successful because of the availability of establishment sites and resources. Some types of disturbance may also create conditions to which alien species from regions where human disturbance has long been a powerful evolutionary force are well adapted and native species are not (Byers 2002).

Since aquatic environments often show instability and unpredictability, it is also perhaps not surprising that some aquatic ecologists hold the view that invasion success is influenced principally by abiotic conditions of the habitat. Moyle and Light (1996), for example, argued that the success or failure of introduced fishes to become established in California depends on whether or not abiotic conditions are appropriate, rather than biotic characteristics of the recipient community.

On the other hand, in more stable and predictable environments, communities do exhibit some degree of coevolved organization. This is reflected in the presence of symbiotic relationships that are to some degree species-specific (Richardson et al. 2000). These vary from species-specific mutualisms, parasite-host interactions, and predator-prey relationships to less specific food chain, pollination, seed dispersal, or other relationships in which interactions are limited to a certain subset of the total community members. For plants, mycorrhizal fungi and nitrogen–fixing microorganisms are symbionts of varying specificity that can influence the success of alien plants. Absence of these symbionts may prevent the establishment of an alien in a new region. Host-specialized herbivores, predators, and parasites constrain the growth and productivity of many species in their native regions. These relationships suggest that success of some aliens is due to release from biotic constraints that exist in communities of their native region—the so-called enemy release hypothesis. This is also evident in the success of biological control strategies that involve identification and importation of natural enemies of alien species from their native regions. We examine the enemy release hypothesis in more detail below.

Species Diversity and Invasion Resistance

In 1958, Charles Elton hypothesized that communities rich in species were more resistant to invasion than less diverse communities. His hypothesis has proved to be stimulating but very difficult to test. The determinants of species diversity in biotic communities are complex and include processes operating on temporal scales ranging from long evolutionary time to short ecological time. A long history of evolution under conditions favorable to growth of organisms favors high species diversity. Tropical rain forests and coral reefs, for example, are ancient ecosystem types that have accumulated species over long evolutionary time. Other determinants of diversity are biogeographic factors, such as geographic isolation. Islands, where only small populations can develop, are subject to colonization and extinction dynamics that set a low evolutionary limit to species richness. Still other determinants involve events on an ecological time scale, especially disturbances such as fire, flood, or drought. An intermediate frequency or intensity of disturbance, for example, tends to promote species diversity by preventing a few dominant species from crowding out all others (see, e.g., Connell 1978). Riparian ecosystems, subject to flooding and often fire, exemplify this last relationship.

The greatest opportunities for coevolution of species exist in communities of high species diversity and stable or predictable habitat conditions. Natural communities differ greatly in species diversity, the number of species, and their equitability of abundance. The theoretical models of Robert MacArthur and others in the 1950s–1970s also suggested that species-rich communities were less subject to invasion and population fluctuations. In general, recent mathematical models of community composition also support the idea that invasibility decreases with an increase in species richness (Levine and D'Antonio 1999).

On the other hand, several analyses show that richness of alien species tends to increase with richness of native species. Lonsdale (1999) examined richness of native and alien plants in 184 sites ranging over many orders of magnitude in area. This analysis showed that the number of alien plants, but not their percentage as a component of the flora, increased with native plant species richness. He suggested that this indicated that there is no causal relation between the two diversities at the scale of analysis considered. The sites Lonsdale considered, however, were not communities of species that could potentially interact, but rather landscapes occupied by several to many community types.

Stohlgren et al. (2003) examined data sets for U.S. Forest Service vegetation monitoring plots and for plant diversity records by county recorded by the Biota of North America Program. These analyses also showed that alien plant richness increased with native plant richness, especially for large monitoring plots and county and state units. For plots of 1 m^2, the increase of alien diversity with native plant diversity was weak. In earlier studies (Stohlgren et al. 1999) in the grasslands of the north-central United States, plots of this size showed a decrease in alien diversity with increase in native diversity. Plots of the same size in the Colorado Rocky Mountains, on the other hand, showed the opposite pattern. Although these correlations are interesting, it is clear that understanding the influence of species diversity on invasion dynamics requires examination of how successful alien species are in invading a community of interacting, potentially coevolved species.

Some field studies have also shown that invasibility sometimes increases with increase in species diversity. In general, these results have been obtained in field situations subject to strong seasonal change, which affects resource availability. Examples include Mediterranean annual grassland (Robinson et al. 1995), successional Great Plains grassland (Foster et al. 2002), communities of streamside herbaceous plants (Levine 2000), and high mountain forest (Wiser et al. 1998; Fornwalt et al. 2003). Invasibility in these cases seems to reflect conditions that create abundant, underutilized resources. To test this idea about the influence of resource availability, Davis and Pelsor (2001) imposed a regime of watering, drying, and physical disturbance on grassland plots at the Cedar Creek research area in Minnesota. Their results showed that regimes that created short-term increases in resource availability favored the establishment of invader species. These observations suggest that the availability of unutilized resources, rather than native species diversity per se, determines invasibility in many situations.

Considerable experimental evidence is now accumulating that, other factors being equal, species-rich communities are less easily invaded. Field experiments on the role of species diversity in preventing invasion of alien plants have been carried out in grassland communities at Cedar Creek, Minnesota, over a number of years. On plots planted with different numbers of grassland plants, Knops et al. (1999) and Kennedy et al. (2002) tested the role of diversity in affecting the number of spontaneous invaders. In one experiment, plots 3 by 3 m in size were seeded with equal total amounts of seed of 1 to 24 herbaceous plant species. Plots were weeded during the first two years to maintain the desired diversity levels. In the third and fourth years, the richness and biomass of invaders were determined, along with measures of soil nitrate level and light penetration into the vegetation. The results were that both the number and biomass of invaders declined with increases in plot diversity. More diverse plots also had lower levels of nitrate and light, suggesting that resource availability was the mechanism inhibiting potential invaders. Other studies at the same location suggest that the presence of diverse functional groups of plants, such as legumes, nonlegumes, C_3 grasses, and C_4 grasses, contributes to the resistance of grassland communities to invasion (Symstad 2000).

Studies focused on individual invader species, in which disturbance and other external factors could be controlled, also suggest that community diversity impedes alien invasion. Naeem et al. (2000) analyzed the growth of narrowleaf hawksbeard (*Crepis tectorum*), an alien Eurasian annual, in field plots and greenhouse containers in relation to diversity of neighboring grassland plants. Neighborhood plants included species belonging to four major functional groups of native grassland herbs: C_3 and C_4 grasses, legumes, and nonlegumes. In both field and greenhouse experiments, hawksbeard growth declined strongly as the diversity of species forming its neighborhood increased. Diversity of different functional groups of plants likewise appeared to limit the success of yellow starthistle (*Centaurea solsticialis*) in microcosms of Mediterranean grassland species in California (Dukes 2001, 2002).

Somewhat similar results have been obtained for communities of aquatic organisms. Working with communities of sessile marine invertebrates in New England, Stachowicz et al. (1999) created artificial communities of one to four native invertebrates by placing together tiles, each 2 by 2 cm in size, on which individual species were growing. In an array of five by five tiles, five additional tiles with a 1-week-old recruit of an alien ascidian (*Botryllus schlosseri*) were interspersed. Survival of the alien ascidian decreased in linear fashion from more than 60% to less than 20% with an increase in diversity of the overall community.

Shea and Chesson (2002) developed a model that integrates many of these relationships. They proposed that factors such as disturbance interact with community organization to influence invasibility. For any given level of supply of basic resources, the richness of a local community in native species and the integrated pattern of resource use they exhibit limits the ability of alien species to invade. When some factor has prevented such a local community from reaching its greatest diversity, or when disturbance interferes with resource use, opportunities for alien invasion exist. In larger geographical regions, where major differences exist in basic resource supply for communities, native communities contain more species, but factors that create disturbance or interfere with community organization also result in invasion by more aliens (fig. 7.1). These factors may also interact with escape of alien species from natural enemies, as discussed later.

Another model, based on competition for resources by species in an assemblage, also showed that scale can modify the invasibility of a community (Byers and Noonberg 2003). For a given number of resource types, this model shows that increasing the number of species reduces invasibility. Increasing the number of resource types, on the other hand, increases invasibility. Thus, in both models (Shea and Chesson 2002; Byers and Noonberg 2003), resource availability patterns strongly influence the likelihood of invasion success.

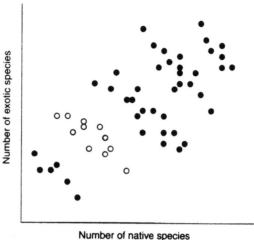

Figure 7.1. Hypothesized interaction of diversity of native and alien species across local environments that vary in resource richness and native biotic diversity of mature communities. For each group of species (such as the group with open circles), environmental conditions and availability of resources are assumed to be the same, and as native species diversity increases, exotic species diversity declines. With more favorable conditions and more abundant resources, the diversity of both groups generally increases, as suggested by the groups of species farther along the number axes (Reprinted with permission from K. Shea and P. Chesson. 2002. Community ecology theory as a framework for biological invasions. *Trends in Ecology and Evolution* 17:170–176. © 2002 Elsevier Publishing Company.)

Vulnerability of Insular Communities

That insular communities with low species diversity are so vulnerable to biological invasions also suggests that the degree of community organization and complexity influences the probability of invader success—the so-called biotic resistance hypothesis. Ecological release, the expansion of habitat and resource use seen in many recent island invaders, is an indication that the organization of most insular communities is weaker than that of comparable continental regions. The absence of particular animal groups, such as large terrestrial herbivores and predators, from many oceanic islands also means that constraints to the establishment of many kinds of plants and animals are almost completely lacking.

Alien plant species exceed 20% of the flora of many oceanic islands, and in several cases, exceed 80% (Rejmánek 1996). The highest percentages of alien plants on oceanic islands tend to be in the tropics, a pattern opposite to that seen in the representation of alien plants in continental floras. Patterns of human occupation, landscape disturbance, and plant introduction vary greatly in tropical island and continental areas, but the great difference in representation of alien species suggests that islands do indeed offer less resistance to invasion. A similar pattern exists for alien animals. The Hawaiian Islands provide one of the best-documented cases. Alien vertebrates in Hawaii include 8 amphibians, 15 reptiles, 21 mammals, and 28 birds; alien invertebrates number more than 2,500 species (Cox 1999).

Invasive Species and Escape from Coevolved Relationships

Only recently has attention been given to the possible role of coevolutionary adjustments among community members in creating resistance to invasion by alien species. In experiments examining species richness and invasibility, the assumption is usually that if many species use resources completely, it is because they have been sorted by ecological processes rather than adjusted to each other by evolutionary selection. Indeed, in many experiments, the species mix employed includes alien species that obviously have not had time to coevolve with natives.

Many examples are now available of alien species that have escaped coevolved relationships. Classical biological control, the identification and release of natural enemies of a pest, rests on this fact. Many pest species, both plants and animals, have been partially or largely controlled by the importation and release of such enemies. In this effort, of course, extensive research must be done to show that the probability that the introduced biological control agent will itself cause damage is very small (see chapter 17).

Several studies now suggest that many alien species have experienced release from restrictions that exist in their native region, an idea known as the enemy release hypothesis (Keane and Crawley 2002). This hypothesis suggests that plants that invade distant geographical areas have usually left most of their specialist herbivores behind and should not be quickly colonized by specialist herbivores in the new region. Although they may be attacked by generalist herbivores in the new region, generalist impacts should be heavier on native plants than the invading aliens. A survey of 13 studies that quantified herbivore impacts and differentiated between specialist and generalist herbivores supported these predictions (Keane and

Crawley 2002). A surprising number of specialist herbivores were found to use alien plants, but their impact was small. In all but two studies, generalist impacts were lighter on alien than on native plants.

A recent study provides a good example of release from herbivores and disease agents. White campion (*Silene latifolia*) is a European weed introduced to North America in the mid-1800s. It is now widespread, occurring in 43 states and several Canadian provinces, and in some areas is considered a noxious weed. Wolfe (2002) examined 50 populations in Europe and 36 in North America, recording the presence or absence of phloem-feeding aphids, anther smut fungi, herbivore damage to the flowers, and fruit or seed predation. The results (fig. 7.2) showed that all forms of herbivore and fungal damage were much more frequent in Europe than in North America. Overall, the frequency of damage was 17 times as great

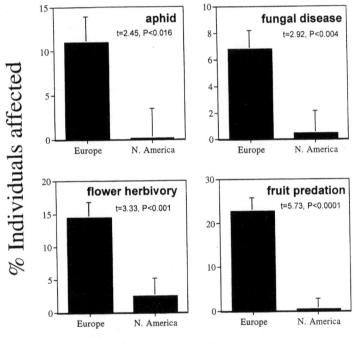

Figure 7.2. Frequency of occurrence of phloem-feeding aphids, anther smut fungi, flower herbivory, and fruit or seed predation in populations of *Silene latifolia* in Europe and North America. (Reprinted with permission from L. M. Wolfe. 2002. Why alien invaders succeed: support for the escape-from-enemy hypothesis. *American Naturalist* 160:705–711. © 2002 University of Chicago Press.)

in Europe as in North America. Two of the most frequent species to damage white campion in Europe were specialist organisms that are absent or rare in North America. Further studies of plants from numerous localities in Europe and North America have shown that the North American populations have evolved a more vigorous growth and reproduction pattern (Blair and Wolfe, forthcoming). North American plants germinated more quickly, grew larger, and branched and flowered more than did European plants. The rate of seed germination was greater in North American plants, as was the probability of overwinter survival. For female plants, on the other hand, the density of spiny epidermal hairs on the calyx, which encloses the maturing fruits, was less for North American than European plants. These observations strongly suggest that North American plants are investing more in growth and reproduction and less in herbivore defense than are European plants.

Scotch broom (*Cytisus scoparius*), native to the British Isles, has become a highly invasive shrub in the North American Pacific Northwest. Broom is attacked by many specialist herbivores in the British Isles, but few of these are present in western North America (Waloff 1966). Some 23 species of pod- and seed-feeding insects attack Scotch broom in Britain, none of which are present in the Pacific Northwest. Of the five species of true bugs of the family Miridae that occur on broom in Britain, only three occur in western North America. Release from herbivores is evident in late summer in the Pacific Northwest, where the foliage of broom lacks the insect damage that it shows in Britain. Specialist herbivores are also deficient on broom in Australia and New Zealand (Memmott et al. 2000).

The success of Australian eucalypts when introduced to other world regions is certainly due in part to escape from specialist insects that exert heavy herbivory in Australia. Although many native insects have begun to feed on eucalypts in areas to which these trees have been introduced, economically significant damage is rare (Ohmart and Edwards 1991). In California, for example, eucalyptus trees of many species have been introduced, beginning in the mid-1800s. Until recently, these species have been free of herbivorous insects that feed on them in Australia. Since 1984, however, about 15 species of herbivorous insects have been introduced, with many trees showing heavy damage from their feeding (Paine et al. 2000).

Release from herbivory is also responsible for the improved performance of a number of South African shrubs introduced to Australia and of Australian plants introduced to South Africa (Weiss and Milton 1984). For example, *Chrysanthemoides monilifera* (a South African native) and *Acacia longifolia* (an Australian native) both exhibit enhanced flower and seed production in the region to which they are not native.

Many invasive plants have also benefited from escape from fungal and viral enemies. Mitchell and Power (2003) surveyed fungi and viruses infecting 473 species of alien plants in the United States and in their native ranges. In the United States, these plants, on average, were attacked by 84% fewer fungi and 24% fewer viruses than in native regions. In these cases the fungi and viruses included both those that had been introduced to the United States with the host plant and species that had become associated with the plants after their introduction. For the 401 plant species that were not deliberately planted or heavily used by humans, the incidence of fungal enemies was much lower than for the 71 species heavily used by humans. This was believed to reflect the fact that heavily used plants had been introduced more frequently and in greater numbers than species not heavily used. In addition, species that were designated as noxious by many states or listed as invasive in natural communities by many states and nongovernmental organizations tended to show the greatest release from fungi and viruses.

Release from constraints other than predators and parasites can also occur. At the beginning of this chapter, we considered the case of diffuse knapweed and its allelopathic relationships with grasses in its native region and in North America (Callaway and Aschehoug 2000). Release from coevolved relationships with Eurasian grasses may thus contribute to the invasiveness of diffuse knapweed in North America. Russian knapweed (*Centaurea repens*) and spotted knapweed (*C. maculosa*) also owe a lot of their invasive capability to similar allelopathic behavior (Goslee et al. 2001; LeJeune and Seastedt 2001; Ridenour and Callaway 2001). For spotted knapweed, the allelopathic agent has recently been identified as one of the isomers of the organic molecule catechin (Bais et al. 2002). Many plants contain the (+)-catechin isomer, which is an antioxidant that protects tissues against oxidative damage and microbial attack. The (-)-catechin isomer, on the other hand, is a highly phytotoxic molecule. Spotted knapweed produces both isomers, with the (-)-catechin isomer being released into the soil. This molecule causes rapid death of the roots of many grasses and broad-leafed herbs, including perennial grasses native to North America (Bais et al. 2003). As for diffuse knapweed, Eurasian grasses appear to show greater resistance to spotted knapweed allelopathy.

Similar relationships hold for many alien animals. Torchin et al. (2003) examined the parasites of 26 species of invasive animals, including marine and freshwater molluscs, marine crustaceans, fish, amphibians, reptiles, birds, and mammals, in both native and invaded regions. On average, 16 species of parasites were recorded from these species in their native regions, whereas only about seven species were noted in invaded areas. Of these seven, only about three were parasites from the native region. The remaining four were new acquisitions in the areas invaded. The small fraction of parasites from native regions was presumably due to a low probability of parasites being included with the founding host group, their accidental loss from the host population after founding, or lack of suitable alternate hosts in the new region. In addition, the average prevalence of parasites among individuals of the host was only about 26% as great in the invaded regions as in the area where the hosts were native. Thus, this set of invasive host species experienced substantially reduced parasite pressure.

The European green crab (*Carcinus maenas*), introduced to the east and west coasts of North America, as well as to South Africa and Australia, is a good example of the extent of release of alien marine species from parasitism (Torchin et al. 2001). In their native range in Europe, these crabs are frequently parasitized by internally parasitic barnacles and isopods that stunt growth and block reproduction. These so-called "parasitic castrators" are absent in areas to which green crabs have been introduced. The frequency of other internal parasites of several groups is also less than 10% in areas of introduction, compared to more than 90% in Europe. Predation intensity, as measured by the incidence of limb loss, however, is similar in areas of introduction to that in Europe. The net effect of reduced parasitism is that green crabs reach larger sizes in areas to which they have been introduced, either because of faster growth or longer life span. A sibling species of the European green crab, *Carcinus aestuarii*, which has been introduced to waters around Japan, is also virtually free of parasites in areas of introduction.

Similar patterns exist for many invasive insects. In their native region in southern Brazil, Argentine ants, for example, are parasitized by phorid flies (*Pseudacteon* spp.), which lay eggs in the bodies of the ants. The presence of these flies makes the ants cease foraging and return to their underground nests (Orr and Seike 1998). In areas in North America and Europe to which Argentine ants have been introduced, they are freed from this parasitoid.

Among vertebrates, the European house sparrow (*Passer domesticus*) and the European starling (*Sturnus vulgaris*) have both flourished following their introduction to North America. Both species have experienced a substantially reduced parasite load. In North America, house sparrows have only 37 species of parasitic arthropods, compared to 60 species in Europe (Brown and Wilson 1975). Similarly, in North America, European starlings have only 22 species of parasitic worms, compared to the 70 species recorded in Europe (Hair and Forrester 1970). Mammals introduced to oceanic islands also tend to show reduced parasite loads (Dobson 1988).

Enhanced Growth and Performance of Alien Species

Several investigators have suggested that plants typically show more luxuriant growth in regions to which they are alien than in their native region. Crawley (1987), for example, compared published information on plant height for species of European plants in Europe and in their introduced range in California. For 228 species, he found that in California 99 species were taller, 66 shorter, and 63 about the same in height. He concluded that escape from natural enemies might have contributed to the significantly greater number of species that were taller. Blossey and Nötzold (1995) likewise suggested that many alien invasive plants show greater competitive ability, expressed as increased vegetative growth, in areas to which they have been introduced, compared to their native region. Increased growth capability was hypothesized to result from reduced allocation to herbivore defense. Testing this hypothesis with purple loosestrife (*Lythrum salicaria*), a native of Europe, Blossey and Nötzold found that plants from North America grew taller and produced more biomass than did plants from Europe. Tests with native European root-feeding weevils, natural herbivores of the plant in Europe, also showed that larvae of these insects showed higher survival and reached greater weights on North American plants than on European plants. Willis et al. (1999) also conducted experiments on purple loosestrife growth and performance of foliage-feeding insects. Shoot mass of North American loosestrife did tend to be higher than that of European plants. The concentration of phenolic compounds, which often function as herbivore repellents, in North American plants also tended to be lower than that in European plants. Larval development and adult size of foliage-feeding insects, however, did not differ for North American and European plants.

Other studies have failed to show consistent differences in plant growth between European plants in native and alien regions (Willis et al. 2000). Thébaud and Simberloff (2001), for example, conducted a more comprehensive analysis, comparing published information on native

European plants in Europe, California, and North and South Carolina, and native North American plants in California, the Carolinas, and Europe. They found no tendency for species to grow taller in areas where they were alien, whether in North America or Europe. In fact, North American natives tended to grow taller in California and the Carolinas. Thus, growth, at least as measured by general information on height published in regional floras, does not seem to be consistently greater for plants in alien environments.

On the other hand, in many specific cases, reproductive performance of alien plants has been shown to exceed that of native species that are closely related or are their principal competitors. In Hawaii, fountain grass (*Pennisetum setaceum*) has become an aggressive invader of dry habitats. Fountain grass experiences much less seed and ovule damage by insects and fungi than does its main native competitor, pili grass (*Heteropogon contortus*) (Goergen and Daehler 2001a, 2001b). In Tennessee, the alien shrub *Ligustrum sinense* experiences much less foliage damage by insect herbivores and realizes much greater fruit production than *Forestiera ligustrina*, a similar native shrub of the same family (Morris et al. 2002).

Invasive Species and Mutualistic Relationships

The ability of many alien species to become established in new geographical regions depends on the establishment of beneficial relationships with other organisms. For plants, these include organisms such as mycorrhizal fungi, nitrogen-fixing microorganisms, pollinators, and seed dispersal agents (Richardson et al. 2000). In Hawaii, for example, Carino and Daehler (2002) found that a small, alien, nitrogen-fixing legume appeared to facilitate the establishment of fountain grass (*Pennisetum setaceum*), a highly invasive plant with serious impacts. For animals, mutualistic interactions may develop with organisms that both provide food and are benefited by animal activities. Mutualists may be former associates from the native area or sometimes new associates from the region invaded. In Oregon, for example, alien sunfish apparently facilitate the establishment of the alien bullfrog (*Rana catesbeiana*) by reducing the density of dragonfly larvae that attack small bullfrog tadpoles (Adams et al. 2003). Parasitic species may likewise require the presence of specific hosts to become established.

With the increase in kinds of organisms and numbers of species being introduced to new regions, mutualistic and other interspecific interactions appear to be playing a greater role in promoting the establishment and success of new invaders (Richardson et al. 2000). The introduction of pollinator insects, for example, has favored the success of many plants that are native to areas where these pollinators are native. Seed dispersal interactions between alien plants and alien or native animals also favor the success of both alien plants and alien animals in many cases. The presence of a wide variety of alien microorganisms, plants, and animals now appears to be facilitating the establishment of still other alien species.

New Habitats Mean New Evolutionary Pressures

Alien species are successful because they encounter not only favorable conditions of the physical habitat, available resources, and mutualists, but also because they have often escaped biotic limitations that existed in their native region. Nevertheless, all aspects of their new environments are different from their native region to some degree. Thus, conditions favorable to population growth combine with altered pressures of natural selection, both biotic and abiotic. For many species, the result is rapid evolutionary adaptation to the new conditions. We shall examine the evidence for such adaptation to new habitat conditions in the next chapter.

8.

Adaptation of Alien Species
to New Habitats

"Founder effects, genetic drift, and natural selection can all lead to genetic differentiation in populations of an invading species, relative to the invader's source population."

—DAEHLER AND STRONG (1997b)

In about 1894, smooth cordgrass (*Spartina alterniflora*) was accidentally introduced to Willapa Bay, Washington, apparently becoming established as a single clone. In a little over a century, the species has spread over more than 1,000 ha, partly through vegetative spread and partly by reproduction by seed. Smooth cordgrass is native to the Atlantic coast of North America, where it has a specialist herbivore, the planthopper *Prokelisia marginata* (Order Homoptera). *Prokelesia* is absent from Willapa Bay, but occurs in populations of smooth cordgrass that were introduced into San Francisco Bay in the 1970s.

Daehler and Strong (1997b) examined the susceptibility of smooth cordgrass from Willapa Bay, San Francisco Bay, and Chesapeake Bay, Maryland, to herbivory by *Prokelesia* over two growing seasons in a greenhouse. They also examined the preference of *Prokelesia* for plants from these three populations. Cordgrasses from San Francisco Bay and Chesapeake Bay showed little or no reduction in biomass production compared to plants protected from herbivory. The Willapa Bay plants, under experimental herbivory by *Prokelesia*, showed an 88% average reduction in biomass production by the second greenhouse growing season, and some clones experienced 100% mortality. The Willapa Bay plants also exhibited levels of leaf nitrogen about 70% higher than those of the other two populations and were highly preferred by leafhoppers.

It is likely that the higher leaf nitrogen levels of Willapa Bay plants are at least partly due to a founder effect—the initial plant that became established in 1894 was by chance a high-nitrogen genotype. But the lower resistance of many Willapa Bay plants to leafhopper herbivory is more likely the result of genetic drift or natural selection (Daehler and Strong 1997b). Willapa Bay plants also showed slower growth and shorter, thinner stems and leaves than plants from the other populations, suggesting that selection has favored these characteristics at the expense of resistance to *Prokelesia* herbivory. Thus, in a little more than a century, smooth cordgrass had adapted to new habitat conditions characterized by reduced herbivore pressure.

Rapid Evolution to New Habitat Conditions

Invasion of a new environment by a species is an experiment in evolution. A subset of genotypes of a species is introduced into an environment that is similar in some physical and biotic features, but different in many others. Just as natural selection tends to promote genetic adaptation of populations to local conditions within the native range, the same process tends to occur in the new alien environment. In most cases, the new alien population has a high degree of spatial isolation from populations in the native region, precluding strong gene flow that might offset the action of natural selection under the new conditions.

Given adequate genetic variability, invading species thus are often able to make rapid evolutionary adjustments. In a laboratory selection experiment with plants, for example, velvet-leaf (*Abutilon theophrasti*) and green amaranth (*Amaranthus retroflexus*) showed significant genetic shifts in just four generations of selection under treatments involving different soil moisture levels, competitor diversity regimes, and intraspecific densities (Zangerl and Bazzaz 1984). Shifts involved many biological features: vegetative structure, photosynthetic rate, flowering phenology, and reproductive allocation. In field experiments, tall fescue (*Festuca arundinacea*) cultivars exhibited significant shifts in patterns of genetic variation in only 3 yr of selection under grazing and nongrazing regimes (Vaylay and van Santen 2002).

Adaptation of Plants to New Habitats

Among plants, basic life history features may be altered by natural selection. Many Eurasian plants introduced to North America have shown ecotypic adaptation to latitudinal differences in climate. Wild carrot (*Daucus carota*), for example, showed genetically based variation in age of reproduction along a latitudinal gradient from North Carolina to Ontario (Lacey 1988). This pattern is estimated to have evolved over about 150 generations. In Chile, burr medic (*Medicago polymorpha*) is naturalized over a 1,000-km range extending from the arid north to the humid south of the country (Del Pozo et al. 2002). In common garden tests, plants from different localities varied over a range of 46 days in time of flowering, as well as in winter growth vigor and other characteristics. Curly dock (*Rumex crispus*) (Hume and Cavers 1982), barnyard grass (*Echinochloa crusgalli*) (Roy et al. 2000), and common cocklebur (*Xanthium strumarium*) (Tranel and Wassom 2001) likewise showed ecotypic adaptation over their alien ranges. Recently, populations of salt cedar (*Tamarix ramosissima*) in Arizona and Montana were found to differ genetically in seedling investment in root biomass, with greater investment in northern populations (Sexton et al. 2002).

Detailed studies of common St. John's wort (*Hypericum perforatum*) over its latitudinal range in North America suggested that this species has shown rapid adaptation to habitat conditions (Maron et al. 2004). Genetic analyses indicated that this species was introduced to North America on multiple occasions and shows high genetic variability. North American populations showed distinct patterns of latitudinal adaptation, just as they do in Europe. Populations in particular North American locations, however, were not always derived from European populations occupying similar climatic regimes. Thus, it appears that natural selection has played a major role in adapting this species to latitudinal habitat differences in about 150 yr or less, corresponding to about 12–15 plant generations.

Shifts in mating systems are often seen in alien species. Genetic shifts toward self-fertilization, apomixis, or vegetative reproduction are often seen in alien plants (Brown and Marshall 1981). Presumably, the selective value of such shifts is increased reproduction in favorable environments in which, at least initially, the opportunity for outcrossing is very limited. On the other hand, shifts toward increased outcrossing are seen in some species (Brown and Marshall 1981). Where an introduction unit is genetically diverse, this may reflect strong, new selection pressures favoring recombination genotypes produced by outcrossing.

A clear example of a shift from sexual to asexual reproduction is provided by bulbous bluegrass (*Poa bulbosa*). This grass is widespread in western Europe, where it reproduces primarily by sexually produced seed (Novak and Welfley 1997). Bulbous bluegrass has become established widely in North America, but here its primary reproductive mode is by asexually produced bulblets. Many of the individual grass florets develop directly into these bulblets, and others develop into flowers that normally do not set seed. Some sexual reproduction may occur, however, since this species maintains a high level of genetic variation in North America.

In some cases, a shift from sexual to asexual reproduction may only occur in small, isolated populations of alien plants. Yellow starthistle (*Centaurea solsticialis*), as noted earlier, is an aggressive forb invader of rangelands in much of western North America. Most populations have remained strongly outcrossing. A small population in San Diego County, California, however, shows a high level of inbreeding (Sun and Ritland 1998). A strong genetic bottleneck during the establishment of this population may have eliminated alleles, leading to inbreeding depression and a reduction in the frequency of genotypes among which outcrossing could occur.

Examples of a shift toward outcrossing are less frequent. An increased frequency of outcrossing has been seen in weedy grasses in areas to which they have been introduced (Brown and Marshall 1981). Slender wild oat (*Avena barbata*) and soft brome (*Bromis mollis*) exhibit less than 1% outcrossing in European populations. Slender wild oat outcrosses at 2–7% in California and soft brome at 10% in Australia.

Other basic life history patterns, such as a shift from annual to perennial habit, may also occur as a result of strong selection in the alien environment. In annual bluegrass (*Poa annua*), for example, perennial ecotypes tend to develop in areas of intensively mowed turf (McElroy et al. 2002). This species, native to Europe, is a problem grass in lawns and golf courses.

Alien plants, both perennial and annual, have shown a variety of patterns of adaptation to physical habitat conditions of their new environment. Rose clover (*Trifolium hirtum*), for example, was introduced to California from the Mediterranean region of Eurasia in the late 1940s as a forage plant (Jain and Martins 1979). From pasture plantings, it has spread, in some places, to roadsides and other disturbed habitats in central and northern California. Comparison of the morphology and population dynamics of pasture and roadside populations showed that several differences existed between these populations. In roadside populations, the flower calyces of plants tended to be hairier than those of plants in pasture populations and to remain attached to the fruits after they fell from the plant. This was correlated with higher seed germination, but lower seedling survival, in the following season. In greenhouse experiments under identical conditions, roadside plants also tended to flower earlier and to produce about 22% more flowering heads. Thus, over a period of only about 20 yr, evolutionary differentiation of pasture and roadside populations of rose clover had occurred. Subterranean clover (*Trifolium subterraneum*) in Australia, introduced both deliberately and inadvertently, similarly shows a number of strains distinct from planted varieties (Cocks and Phillips 1979). Some of these may have originated by interbreeding and natural selection in Australia.

In California, slender wild oat (*Avena barbata*), an alien introduced from Europe, has evolved distinct races. One race is adapted to the semi-arid grasslands and oak woodlands of the Central Valley and lower foothills and the other to the valleys of the coastal mountains and the higher foothills of the Sierra Nevada Mountains (Clegg and Allard 1972). Populations in the grassland and oak woodland habitat are characterized by black, hairy lemmas and a series of five enzyme loci that are monomorphic. Coastal mountain and higher Sierran foothill populations show paler, less hairy lemmas and high levels of polymorphism for enzyme loci.

Many other annual forbs and grasses show genetically based patterns of adaptation to local habitat conditions, especially in characteristics related to reproduction. In Europe, common groundsel (*Senecio vulgaris*) shows differentiation of ruderal and cropland populations, with cropland plants having larger leaves and more flowering heads (Leiss and Müeller-Schärer 2001). Charlock mustard (*Sinapis arvensis*) and corn poppy (*Papaver rhoeas*) exhibit population differences in seed dormancy (Garbutt and Whitcombe 1986; Lane and Lawrence 1995). Canada thistle (*Cirsium arvense*), a noxious weed in many temperate regions, also shows ecotypes differing in phenology and disease resistance (Donald 1994). Among annual grasses in North America, red brome (*Bromus rubens*) populations differ in flowering phenology and seed mass in different habitats (Wu and Jain 1978) and cheatgrass (*Bromus tectorum*) varies in flowering phenology, seed mass, and the response of seed germination to temperature (Rice and Mack 1991; Meyer and Allen 1999).

Forage plants, both forbs and grasses, have been transported worldwide. These plants exhibit a complex pattern of genetic variation due to both artificial and natural selection. Many artificially selected cultivars and locally evolved ecotypes of white clover (*Trifolium repens*), for example, occur throughout the world (e.g., Gustine et al. 2002).

Rapid evolution of ecotypes adapted to new conditions also occurs in aquatic plants. In 1984, a strain of a tropical marine green alga, *Caulerpa taxifolia*, is believed to have been released accidentally into the Mediterranean Sea from the Oceanographic Museum of Monaco (Meinesz 1999). This strain apparently arose through selection in European aquaria and is characterized by vigorous clonal growth, resistance to cold water, and lack of sexual reproduction. This strain has not only spread over thousands of hectares of shallow coastal waters along the northern coast of the Mediterranean Sea, but has appeared in coastal waters of southern California and coastal waters far south of its native range in eastern Australia. *Caulerpa* contains a series of toxins that provide defense against grazing animals and organisms that might attach to its surfaces (Ribera Siguan 1996). Thus, evolutionary change under human selection may create alien forms that are highly invasive in new environments.

Adaptation of Animals to New Habitats

Evolutionary changes in life history features also occur in animals introduced to new regions. Adler and Levins (1994) have described an "island syndrome" of adjustments in morphology, behavior, and demography made by rodents on islands in the ocean or large freshwater lakes. These include increased body mass, delayed sexual maturity, altered territorial behavior, increased population density, increased survival, and greater population stability. In most cases, the species examined are not recent invaders, so these changes may be the result of long-term ecological and evolutionary adjustment. Populations of the house mouse (*Mus musculus*) on Corsica, for example, show several of these demographic responses, together with more sedentary behavior (Navajas y Navarro et al. 1989). Birds also exhibit a distinct "island syndrome" (Blondel 2000) involving many features of ecology, reproductive biology, and behavior. Again, many of these changes are long-term evolutionary responses, which we will examine in more detail in chapter 18.

Rapid evolutionary change in life history characteristics can be seen in many recently introduced alien animals, however. Among invertebrates, very rapid changes are apparently occurring in several alien species in North America. Zebra mussels (*Dreissena polymorpha*), for example, were introduced to North America in 1986 (Elderkin et al. 2001). First appearing in Lake St. Clair, between Lakes Erie and Huron, this species has now invaded the entire length of the Mississippi River. Allozyme analysis of mussels from seven locations from Minnesota south to Louisiana revealed large differences in allele frequencies for two of the six loci examined. Because gene flow from upstream to downstream localities in the Mississippi River must be substantial, these differences indicate that selection for different alleles at different latitudes must be strong.

Other recent North American invaders have shown rapid evolution. The fruit fly *Drosophila subobscura* has evolved a geographical cline in wing length comparable to that in its Old World range, since its introduction in about 1978 (Huey et al. 2000; Gilchrist et al. 2001). This cline apparently evolved in a period of between 10 and 20 yr. The Asian tiger mosquito (*Aedes albopictus*) shows allozyme variation within its rapidly expanding new range (Black et al. 1988a, 1988b). Much of this variation, however, appears likely to be due to genetic drift in the small local populations that are typical of this species both in North America and in its native Asian range. In Florida, however, rapid selection for loss of photoperiodically induced egg diapause has apparently occurred (Lounibos et al. 2003). Within about 10 yr, the percentage of eggs hatching under short photoperiods (10 h) increased from less than 2% in Georgia to more than 30%, in the Miami, Florida, area.

Among vertebrates, anadromous fish introduced to new regions show some of the most extensive evolutionary responses. Chinook salmon (*Oncorhynchus tshawytscha*), native to the Pacific coast of North America, were introduced to New Zealand in 1901–1907. From the initial introductions, salmon have colonized several river systems along the eastern coast of South Island. These populations now differ genetically among themselves and from their source population in California in several morphological and reproductive features, changes that have occurred in about 30 generations (Kinnison et al. 1998a, 1998b; Quinn et al. 2001). The timing of spawning migrations into freshwater differ as much as 7 wk among the several major river systems occupied. Fish also differ genetically from each other in ways related to the length of the migrations from the ocean to spawning areas in different river systems in New Zealand (Kinnison et al. 2001). In general, fish with longer upriver spawning runs tend to be larger bodied and to have a smaller ovary mass and smaller eggs. Experimental releases of salmon fry in 1994–1995 and recovery of adults in 1997–1998 showed that fish migrating to spawning areas 86 km farther inland and 413 m higher in elevation experienced greater losses of body and ovary mass than fish migrating to spawning areas near the coast. Thus, the difference in energy demand for migration is quite likely the major factor in selection for differences among populations.

Life history features have also been modified in shad (*Alosa sapidissima*), another anadromous fish. Shad were introduced to rivers in the Pacific Northwest from the mid-Atlantic coast in the late 1800s (Carroll and Dingle 1996). In these Pacific rivers, shad now show an increased frequency of repeat spawning and greater numbers of eggs than do fish from their mid-Atlantic origin. In these characteristics, they are more like shad from more northern areas of the Atlantic coast.

Similar evolutionary responses have been noted in freshwater fish. In Norway, Koskinen et al. (2002) documented rapid evolutionary change in grayling (*Thymallus thymallus*) introduced to lakes 80–100 yr ago. These fish, introduced first to Lake Lesjaskogsvatn in 1880, were then translocated from there to two smaller lakes in 1910. From these lakes, they colonized a fourth lake in 1920 by natural dispersal. Thus, only an estimated 11.8–22.0 generations separate these four populations from a common ancestor. Several life history traits now differ significantly among the four populations. In addition, the magnitude of the differences is incompatible with their origin by genetic drift, so selection for adaptation to local lake conditions seems to be responsible. The lakes differ substantially in prevailing water temperature, and experimental studies (Koskinen et al. 2002) found that fish from cold, intermediate, and warm lakes showed the highest survival rates in water of corresponding temperature.

The western mosquitofish (*Gambusia affinis*), native to North America, has shown rapid evolutionary change in several locations to which it has been introduced (Stearns 1983a; Stockwell and Weeks 1999). Stearns noted adaptive genetic changes in life history characteristics of mosquitofish introduced to Hawaii over a period of about 70 generations. Stockwell and Weeks (1999) found genetic change in body fat content and size at maturity in populations of mosquitofish introduced to thermal springs in Nevada. In this case, the changes probably occurred over about 110–165 generations (Table 8.1). Meffe et al. (1996) observed selection for increased temperature tolerance in populations of a related species (*Gambusia holbrooki*) over 60–90 generations in a power plant cooling pond in South Carolina.

Some alien birds also have shown rapid evolutionary adjustments to the habitat conditions and resource availability patterns of their new environments. The house sparrow (*Passer domesticus*), for example, has been introduced to North America and many other temperate regions from its home in Europe. It now occupies a broad range of climates from deserts

Table 8.1. Characteristics of populations of western mosquitofish in four springs in Nevada after translocation from a population at Fallon, Nevada. (Data from Stockwell and Weeks 1999.)

Spring	Temperature range (°C)	Length at maturity (mm)	Fat content (%)
#1	34–36	22–26	11–16
#2	34	20–21	14–22
#3	28	19–22	8–10
#4	12–40	16–18	6–7

to the subarctic in North America. Populations show a gradient of body size from large in northern localities to small in southern areas. This pattern, which follows Bergman's Rule of increasing body size of warm-blooded animals in colder regions, is usually interpreted to be adaptive in body temperature regulation (Johnston and Selander 1964; Johnson and Klitz 1977). This body size gradient appears to have a strong genetic component. Adjustment of basal metabolic rate to prevailing local temperature is also evident (Blem 1974; Kendeigh and Blem 1974).

The action of natural selection on house sparrows can be seen in comparisons of individuals surviving severe Kansas winter conditions with birds present in the preceding fall (Johnston and Fleischer 1981; Fleischer and Johnston 1982). The winter of 1978–79 in Kansas was one of the coldest and most snowy on record. Males surviving winter conditions were significantly larger and females significantly smaller than birds in the previous fall (Johnston and Fleischer 1981). For males, this is in agreement with Bergman's Rule, but for females other factors must be important. Both males and females also showed a decreased surface to mass ratio, however, which presumably promoted lower metabolic heat loss (Fleischer and Johnston 1982).

The house finch (*Carpodacus mexicanus*), native to western North America, has provided a particularly interesting case of rapid evolutionary change following its recent introduction to and colonization of new areas (Able and Belthoff 1998; Badyaev and Hill 2000). This species was introduced to Hawaii sometime between 1850 and 1870. In 1940, house finches were released on Long Island, New York, by a bird dealer. Between 1960 and 1990, this population spread over much of eastern North America, reaching Michigan and Alabama by 1981. In western North America, house finches native to the eastern Rocky Mountains also expanded their range northward into Montana in the period between 1940 and 1955.

The source of the house finches released on Long Island was southern California, where the population is strongly sedentary, with only 2–3% of birds showing seasonal movements of more than 80 km (Able and Belthoff 1998). By 1960, substantial migratory movements were documented in New York State and Pennsylvania, and by the 1980s, long-distance movements of birds from northern states to wintering areas in Florida and the Gulf Coast had developed. In contrast to southern California birds, the movements of eastern birds were oriented in a northeast-southwest direction. As the population of house finches spread outward from the area of introduction, the distances of seasonal movement increased markedly, suggesting that colonists of new areas were individuals tending to be more migratory in nature. Overall, however, the eastern North American population is only partially migrant. The fraction of birds moving more than 80 km between summer and winter is about 36%—much higher than in their southern California source area. Altogether, the pattern of development of migratory behavior in house finches of eastern North America is most consistent with the hypothesis that selection has favored genetic traits related to migration. These traits appear to have existed at low frequency in southern California populations, enabling rapid evolution of migratory patterns in the new eastern populations.

Badyaev and Hill (2000) analyzed the general morphology of populations of house finches in several of these recently occupied regions and compared them to long-established populations in California and Mexico. They found complex, multidirectional patterns of evolutionary change in bill, wing, tail, and tarsus length and body mass in newly established populations. For example, Hawaiian birds changed little in many factors but showed substantial reduction in bill length. Several populations showed increased sexual dimorphism in one or more characteristics. Alabama birds, for example, showed significant sexual dimorphism in all five major characteristics, whereas California birds were dimorphic only in wing and tail length.

In Montana, where house finch breeding activity was observed over 4 yr, Badyaev and Martin (2000) found that selection, judged by reproductive success, was acting strongly on sexually dimorphic characteristics. This result indicated that this newly established population was still evolving toward a morphology adjusted to the local environment. Additional studies examined selection based on pairing success, fecundity, and overwinter survival of birds in Alabama, Michigan, and Montana (Badyaev et al. 2000). These studies found different responses in the three areas but showed that the most successful birds of each sex were those with morphological characteristics matching those resulting from selection acting since the populations were founded.

A number of vertebrates in the Australasian region have shown rapid evolution following their introduction or invasion of new areas. The gray-breasted silvereye (*Zosterops lateralis*) expanded its range in the Australasian region in the 1800s and early 1900s. From Tasmania, the species invaded South Island, New Zealand in 1830. From there, it spread to Chatham Island and New Zealand's North Island in 1856 and throughout New Zealand by 1865. In 1904, it reached Norfolk Island, northwest of New Zealand. Along this progressive colonization sequence, populations showed gradual reduction in genetic diversity and increased genetic differentiation (Clegg et al. 2002). The changes at each colonization step, however, were small. Nevertheless, after three or four colonization events, founder effects and genetic drift led to a degree of differentiation comparable to that of silvereye populations isolated for periods of a few thousand years.

Among mammals, the European rabbit (*Oryctolagus cuniculus*), introduced to Australia in 1859, has evolved differences in body size and ear shape in different climatic zones (Williams and Moore 1989). These differences appear to be related to body temperature regulation. Rapid evolutionary changes also have been noted in several rodents introduced to oceanic islands (Pergams and Ashley 2001). The house mice (*Mus musculus*), introduced to the small British islands of Skokholm in about 1907 and Festur in 1939, has shown morphological changes in several characteristics. Black rats (*Rattus rattus*) introduced to the islands of Baltra and Santa Cruz in the Galapagos, Ecuador, have also shown morphological divergence in many skeletal characteristics (Patton et al. 1975).

New Zealand is a hot spot of evolutionary adjustments by introduced land vertebrates, as well as by the chinook salmon discussed earlier. The common myna (*Acridotheres tristis*), introduced in the late 1800s, shows latitudinal variation in morphology (Baker and Moeed 1979). Several other alien birds exhibit reduced clutch sizes compared to their native regions (Yom-Tov et al. 1986). Other European birds introduced in the 1800s show reduced genetic variability, compared to European populations, that appears to be the result of founder effects and genetic drift (Ross 1983; Parkin and Cole 1985; Baker et al. 1990).

The brush-tailed opossum (*Trichosurus vulpecula*) was introduced to

New Zealand from Tasmania and mainland Australia on various occasions beginning in 1837 (Yom-Tov et al. 1986). This foliage-feeding herbivore has spread throughout the country and is a serious pest in native forests. Examination of specimens from throughout New Zealand revealed that populations show a latitudinal trend of increasing size southward. Because introductions were not made to latitudes corresponding to the Australian source areas, this trend has evolved since introduction. In all probability, it developed within the first 30–35 generations following introduction.

Experimental Study of Evolution by Invading Species

How rapid the adaptation of introduced animals to new habitat conditions can be is illustrated by the results of experimental introductions of *Anolis* lizards to small, lizard-free islands in the Bahamas (Losos et al. 1997, 2001). Small groups of the lizard *Anolis sagrei* were introduced to 14 small islands in 1977 and 1981. The vegetation on the source island, Staniel Cay, was varied, but included scrubby coppice and moderately tall forest. The experimental islands had few trees and, in general, consisted of plants with very thin branches.

In 1991, 10–14 yr later, anoles were collected on the experimental islands and their morphology compared to that on Staniel Cay. Lizards on the experimental islands showed generally shorter limbs, wider toe pads, and somewhat greater body mass than animals on the source island. Overall morphology was related, however, to the maximum height of vegetation on the various small islands. Limb morphology was correlated specifically with the diameter of the perches used on different islands. Thus, adaptation had occurred to habitat conditions in only a few generations. The degree to which these changes reflect natural selection versus phenotypic plasticity, however, is still uncertain.

Adaptation to New Biotic Conditions

Evolutionary adjustments by both alien plants and animals are made to the changed biotic environment, as noted for smooth cordgrass at the beginning of the chapter. Blossey and Nötzold (1995) proposed that plants in general follow an optimal defense strategy, in which evolutionary trade-offs occur in allocation of resources to maintenance, growth, storage, reproduction, and defense. Thus, when invasion of a new region leads to reduced pressure from herbivores, selection should favor a shift from defense to other processes. To test this hypothesized strategy, Blossey and Nötzold compared plants of purple loosestrife (*Lythrum salicaria*) from their native range in Europe with plants taken from invading populations in North America. These plants were grown in a common garden in New York State. The North American plants grew substantially taller and produced much greater biomass than the European plants. Furthermore, tests with a root-feeding beetle (*Hylobius transversovittatus*) showed that its survival was more than three times as great on the North American plants as on the European plants, suggesting that some defense against this insect had become weakened.

Invasive forms of the Chinese tallow tree (*Sapium sebiferum*) in Louisiana and Texas appear to be a recently evolved ecotype with foliage that has reduced chemical defenses against herbivores (Siemann and Rogers 2001). Chinese tallow trees in North America do not yet appear to have accumulated a significant fauna of herbivores. Thus, even with reduced defenses, they are able to grow larger and produce more seeds than the original Asian ecotype introduced to the southeastern United States (Rogers and Siemann 2002).

The occurrence of trade-offs between growth or reproduction and herbivore defenses in plants such as purple loosestrife and Chinese tallow tree is thought to be frequent among invasive alien species. As Siemens et al. (2002) pointed out for field mustard (*Brassica rapa*), however, chemicals that defend against herbivores may have other functions that remain active in the alien environment. In addition, Koricheva (2002), through a meta-analysis of studies that have measured fitness costs of anti-herbivore defenses, showed that such defenses are part of a complex adaptive syndrome and are not easily evaluated by short-term measurements. Although many of the studies Koricheva examined did not involve alien plants, her analysis showed that adaptive trade-offs may not always be obvious for plants introduced to new biotic contexts.

Introduction of animals to new regions can also lead to rapid evolutionary adjustment to new biotic conditions, particularly the predation regime. Tammar wallabies (*Macropus eugenii*) were originally widespread in mainland Australia, where they were adapted to a variety of large predators. They were introduced to predator-free Kawau Island, in the Haruaki Gulf, North Island, New Zealand, in the 1870s. From there, they were introduced to the mainland of the North Island, near Rotorua, in 1917. Thus, these animals have lived free of large predators for more than 130 yr. Blumstein (2002) tested the behavioral responses of Rotorua wallabies to visual and acoustic stimuli of large predators. He found that they showed reduced recognition of all but the large marsupial wolf (*Thylaci-*

nus cyanocephalus) and that they did not respond to the foot-thumping alarm sounds of other animals. He concluded that relaxation of predator recognition was due to reduced selection over the years in New Zealand. Berger (1998) also noted reduced predator recognition in ungulates that had lived in predator-free areas for 50–100 yr.

Beyond Adaptation to Habitat

A wide range of plant and animal studies show that evolutionary responses to habitat conditions, some very rapid, often follow the introduction of species to new geographical regions. These adjustments include adaptation to new conditions of both the abiotic and biotic environments. Changes in conditions of the physical habitat, release from constraints of gene flow in native regions, and escape from biotic enemies in the native region all favor rapid evolutionary adjustments.

Adjustments of alien species to their new biotic environment, however, go far beyond the general response to the predation regime suggested by the studies of Blossey and Nötzold (1995). In the next three chapters, we shall examine adaptation by alien species to the new biotic resources they encounter. Introduced herbivores, for example, usually encounter a greatly altered range of potential food plants. In the next chapter, we shall examine some of the evolutionary responses shown by alien herbivores to this new array of potential foods.

Part III.

Evolutionary Interaction of Aliens and Natives

Some of the most dramatic examples of rapid evolution as a consequence of alien introductions involve species linked by food chain relationships. These examples include evolutionary change by the alien species themselves, the native species with which they interact, or, in many cases, both alien and native forms. In addition, various alien species brought together in new geographic regions often exhibit evolutionary interactions.

In chapters 9, 10, and 11, we examine patterns of rapid evolution of alien herbivores, predators, parasites, and disease agents to the new prey and hosts they encounter. Often freed from their own enemies and encountering prey or hosts lacking specific defenses, aliens may show rapid evolutionary change. Successful alien species in turn may stimulate evolutionary responses by natives. In chapters 12, 13, and 14, we turn our attention to evolutionary changes by native species. These include the ability of natives to exploit these species and to evolve ways to mitigate the detrimental impacts of alien predators, parasites, and disease agents.

Finally, in chapter 15, we describe how alien plants and animals accumulate herbivores, predators, and parasites from the new native biota that they have entered. These patterns of accumulation represent the first step toward ecological integration of the aliens.

These evolutionary interactions are the focus of some of the most active current research. How these interactions play out on a global scale will be the focus of part IV.

9.

Evolutionary Adaptation
by Alien Herbivores

"These data [on variability and selection] indicate that change and the potential for change are so great that the current patterns of host use should probably be seen as ecologically dynamic and not an end result of coevolutionary processes over millennia."

—BERNAYS AND GRAHAM (1988)

The codling moth (*Laspeyresia pomonella*), native to the Middle East, is a pest of apples, pears, plums, and apricots throughout temperate regions of the world. This moth reached North America in about 1750 and spread rapidly through fruit-growing areas, reaching the Pacific Coast in less than 25 yr. In California, where it had appeared by 1873, it first was a pest of apples (*Malus pumila*) and pears (*Pyrus communis*). In the early 1900s, however, it began to attack English walnuts (*Juglans regia*), and by 1930, it had become a major walnut pest (Phillips and Barnes 1975) and had begun to attack plums in the Los Angeles area. Still later, in the 1960s, it became a serious pest of plums (*Prunus domestica*) in the San Joaquin Valley.

Host shifts by the codling moth have involved the evolution of distinct races specializing on apple, walnut, and plum. Oviposition preference tests, for example, showed that the apple race only rarely would oviposit on walnut or plum, whereas the walnut and plum races strongly preferred walnut (Phillips and Barnes 1975). Attempts to condition the walnut and plum races by forcing them to oviposit on apple for up to13 generations showed that the preference for oviposition on walnut and plum was still strong and evidently genetic. Studies of the seasonal emergence of the three races also showed that the plum race appeared nearly 2 wk earlier in the season than the apple and walnut races because plum orchards are about 2–3 wk ahead of apple and walnut orchards in their seasonal development. To achieve the earlier emergence requires genetic adaptations in the mechanism of breaking diapause and in developmental heat requirements. Thus, adjustments in several genetic systems were probably involved in the evolution of these races. Circumstantial evidence suggests that the walnut race differentiated from the apple race, and the plum race from the walnut race.

The codling moth is just one of many alien herbivores that have been introduced to new regions, both inadvertently and deliberately. Arthropod pests of crops, forages, horticultural plants, commercial forest trees, and even weeds tend to track the introductions of these plants to new world regions. Often, they arrive without their own competitors, predators, parasites, and diseases. Vertebrate herbivores have likewise been introduced accidentally and deliberately, the latter for real or imagined benefits. Increasingly, in addition, deliberate introductions are being made for anticipated biological control benefits. All of these species are subject to selective pressures that may lead to evolutionary shifts in their patterns of plant feeding.

Coevolution of Plants and Herbivores

Although in this chapter we focus on evolutionary changes by alien herbivores, we should note that these patterns represent only one side of a coevolutionary process (Thompson 1994, 1999a). Techniques of molecular biology and chemical ecology are revealing that plant-herbivore interactions lead to evolutionary shifts by both members. Plants evolve protective chemicals in response to herbivore damage, and herbivores in turn evolve ways to overcome these defenses (Cornell and Hawkins 2003). In the case of many interactions involving plants and alien herbivores, these interactions tend to occur in patchy environments, in which details of the evolutionary setting vary. In some locations, which represent coevolutionary "hot spots," particular plants and herbivores may show very tight patterns of mutual evolutionary adjustment (Thompson 1999b). In other situations, corresponding to evolutionary "cold spots," the degree of mutual adjustment may be weak due to disruptive influences of other evolutionary pressures. Thus, a geographic mosaic of strongly and weakly coevolved populations of plants and herbivores is likely to exist.

Unfortunately, most studies of evolutionary adaptation have only begun to examine the full complexity of herbivore-plant interactions. Few studies have attempted to analyze reciprocal relations of herbivores and plants in the field situation. Thus, we are able to present only the first sketch of evolutionary processes involving alien herbivores and the plants with which they interact. In chapter 12, we shall examine patterns of adaptation by plants to alien herbivores and disease agents.

Herbivore Specialization for Plant Hosts

Herbivores show varying degrees of specialization for plant taxa. In general, vertebrate herbivores are adapted to plants of certain life forms, such as grasses or woody plant foliage, or to feeding on particular plant products, such as fruits or seeds, rather than to specific plant species. Herbivorous invertebrates tend to be specialized for feeding on particular plant parts, such as roots or leaves, or plant components, such as vascular fluids or leaf tissues. They vary enormously, however, in the variety of plant taxa used. Some are polyphagous, feeding on a wide variety of plant species or higher taxa. When introduced to new geographical areas, polyphagous species often begin to utilize a wide range of new plant species. For example, the wheat stem sawfly (*Cephus cinctus*), now known to have been introduced to North America from Asia (Ivie 2001), feeds on a wide range of cultivated, introduced, and native grasses. The principal criterion for suitable grasses appears to be relatively large stems that are able to accommodate the developing sawfly larvae.

Many other herbivores, however, are specialized for feeding on plant taxa that are characterized by the presence or absence of particular secondary chemicals. Many herbivorous insects tend to specialize on closely related species of plants belonging to a single family (Strong et al. 1984). This specialization is apt to limit their tendency to shift immediately to new plant hosts when they are introduced to new geographic regions. Monarch butterflies (*Danaus plexippus*), introduced from North America to locations such as Hawaii and Australia, for example, still depend on introduced milkweeds (*Asclepias* spp.) as their host plants.

Many herbivorous arthropods exhibit host races or biotypes adapted to different plant species (Futuyma and Peterson 1985). Some biotypes are nongenetic, but many have a genetic basis (Diehl and Bush 1984). In some cases, these forms are the result of polymorphic variation among individuals in a population. In other cases, they constitute geographic races or races adapted to different hosts and consist of individuals that are capable of interbreeding. In still other cases, they may constitute distinct, but perhaps unrecognized, biological species that essentially do not interbreed. For forms capable of interbreeding, some differences may exist because of genetic drift, but consistent differences must be maintained by natural selection in the face of the tendency of gene flow to maintain genetic homogeneity.

Ecological, and ultimately, evolutionary shifts of host plants by herbivorous invertebrates do occur, however. Even species with relatively restricted host preferences tend to show some genetic variability in host preference, and selection can often alter such preferences rapidly. Under experimental conditions, for example, oviposition preferences of some herbivorous arthropods could be changed in as few as 10–16 generations (Bernays and Graham 1988). Under artificial selection, the rice planthopper (*Nilaparvata lugens*) was converted to a biotype capable of attacking a formerly resistant rice variety in only 10 generations (Claridge and den Hollander 1980). The ability of such species for adaptation to new hosts or hosts with altered characteristics is essentially universal. In most cases, however, the new plant hosts are likely to be close relatives of former hosts (Futuyma 2000).

In some cases, the shifts are encouraged when alternate plant hosts provide "enemy-free space" that compensates for any reduction in growth and survival that the herbivore may experience on the new host plant (see, e.g., Gratton and Welter 1999). That is, a new host plant may provide a reduction in predator or parasitoid pressure on the herbivore, reducing its mortality due to these agents. If this benefit exceeds the growth and survival detriments due to feeding on a new plant host, natural selection will favor the host plant shift. In time, selection may also improve the growth and survival performance of the herbivore on the new host.

In other cases, the availability of alternate food plants with low herbivore utilization may permit host plant shifts or expansion. Funk and Bernays (2001), for example, suggested that the ragweed aphid, *Uroleucon ambrosiae*, which primarily uses a giant ragweed (*Ambrosia trifida*) in eastern North America, has recently expanded its range into the southwestern United States and Mexico, where it utilizes a wide range of host plants of the same family. Although aphids from southwestern populations still show the highest preference for giant ragweed, they accept other host plants more readily than do eastern aphids. Bernays and Funk (2000) found that olfactory organs of the antennae of ragweed aphids from the southwestern United States were fewer in number and possessed a smaller sensory surface than those of eastern aphids. This modification may be related to the expanded host plant use by southwestern aphids.

All apparent host plant shifts may not be adaptive, however. Zangerl et al. (2002) examined the shift of the parsnip webworm (*Depressaria pastinacella*) from its principal European host, wild parsnip (*Pastinaca sativa*), to cow parsnip (*Heracleum lanatum*) in North America. In this case, not only is survival of webworm larvae poorer on cow parsnip, a North American native species, than on wild parsnip, but predation by birds appears to be much higher. Cow parsnip thus may represent a population sink that is maintained only by high reproductive success on wild parsnip. Why the webworm continues to use cow parsnip as a host is unclear but may result from loss of genetic factors for host discrimination as a founder effect when the webworm was introduced to North America.

The wild parsnip and parsnip webworm relationship appears to fit Thompson's (1993) geographic mosaic pattern. Each species can act as a selective agent for the other (Berenbaum et al. 1986; Zangerl and Berenbaum 1993). Wild parsnip contains a set of five defensive chemicals known as furanocoumarins for which the webworm has specific detoxifying metabolic systems. In different populations of wild parsnip in Illinois and Minnesota, Berenbaum and Zangerl (1998) found that the patterns of abundance of different furanocoumarins were matched by the activity of detoxifying enzyme systems in the webworm, suggesting that these populations were coevolutionary hot spots. In later studies in Illinois (Zangerl and Berenbaum 2003), this matching pattern was also observed in many populations. In other populations, particularly those near populations of cow parsnip, the degree of matching was weak. The relative abundance pattern of furanocoumarins in cow parsnip differs from that in wild parsnip, so the presence of both plants alters the coevolutionary pattern for both wild parsnip and the parsnip webworm. Thus, the presence of cow parsnip tended to create a coevolutionary cold spot.

Ecological Host Shifts by Introduced Herbivores

Introduced vertebrate and invertebrate herbivores use many species of plants native to their new homes. In general, vertebrate herbivores use the same range of plant life forms as they used in their native region. Most invertebrate herbivores, especially terrestrial forms, tend to be more selective. For example, about 2,000 species of alien insects have become established in North America, about 400 of which are herbivores that feed on woody plants (Niemalä and Mattson 1996). About three-quarters of these herbivores are from Europe. Most of them have colonized the same genera of woody plants that they feed on in Europe. Only 12 species of European herbivores have expanded their feeding to genera of North American woody plants that do not occur in Europe; six of these are species with a diet including many genera in their native area.

Interestingly, the invasion of Europe by herbivorous insects from North America has been much weaker (Niemalä and Mattson 1996). Only 34 North American forest insects have become established in Europe, and most of these are apparently successful because of the introduction of their North American host plants. Several historical reasons may account for this remarkable imbalance. North America has a richer vascular plant flora than Europe, especially among gymnosperms. Many genera of woody plants that became extinct in Europe during the Pleistocene, in particular, have survived in North America. Thus, there may be more potential hosts for European invaders. European trees also appear to have a greater diversity of herbivorous insects than do North American trees, a relationship that may have favored selection for strong competitive ability. Physiologically, European insects from higher latitudes may also have less difficulty in dealing with photoperiod patterns at lower latitudes in North America than would species moving in the opposite direction. The combined impacts of repeated glacial cycles on forest distribution and the long history of human disturbance may also have selected for efficient dispersal and colonizing ability. Parthenogenetic reproduction, for example, is unusually common in European forest insects, many of which are successful colonists of North America. These patterns, in general, suggest that Europe may have been an evolutionary crucible for species unusually well adapted for invading North American areas with extensive forests, a diverse flora of woody plants, and low native herbivore diversity (Niemalä and Mattson 1996).

A recent example of a European invader is the European pine shoot beetle (*Tomicus piniperda*), which first appeared in North America in 1992. The first occurrences were at Christmas tree farms and pine tree nurseries. The beetle prefers Scotch pine (*Pinus sylvestris*) and Austrian pine (*P. nigra*), which are Eurasian natives. In North America, however, it can carry out its life cycle on most pines, including widespread native pine species such as red (*P. resinosa*), ponderosa (*P. ponderosa*), and jack (*P. banksiana*).

Although Europe has been the most important source of North

American forest pests, the potential for invasions from eastern Asia is great (Baranchikov 1997). Many of the genera of woody plants of western North America are represented in Siberia, and about 90 species of forest insects of significant economic potential occur there. A recent North American invader from this region is the Asian long-horned beetle (*Anoplophora glabripennis*), which appeared on Long Island, New York, in 1996. This wood-boring beetle has established infestations in New York and Illinois and has attacked at least 18 species of deciduous trees belonging to 12 genera (Smith et al. 2002).

Numerous herbivorous pests of agriculture, forestry, and horticulture have shifted or expanded their feeding activity to include native plants in areas to which they have been introduced. The Hessian fly (*Mayetiola destructor*), for example, is able to use many species of North American grasses, such as western wheatgrass (*Elymus smithii*), which belongs to the tribe to which its principal hosts, various wheats, belong (Jones 1938, 1939). Similarly, the cabbage butterfly (*Pieris rapae*), introduced worldwide from its native region in Europe, is able to complete its life cycle on many plants of the mustard family native to the United States. The gypsy moth (*Lymantria dispar*) feeds on a wide variety of woody plants in North America. Several major dipteran pests of fruits, including the Mediterranean fruit fly (*Ceratitis capitata*), Mexican fruit fly (*Anastrepha ludens*), and oriental fruit fly (*Bactrocera dorsalis*), are capable of attacking many species of plants. The corn earworm (*Helicoverpa zea*), a lepidopteran, feeds on a wide variety of crop and wild plants.

Numerous host shifts by deliberately introduced insect herbivores also have been recorded. Pemberton (2000) summarized information on host shifts by invertebrates introduced for biological control of weeds in the United States, the Caribbean, and Hawaii. Of 114 species, 15 have been recorded to use nontarget species. In all but one case, these were members of the same genus or genera closely allied to that of the target plant. So far, instances appear mainly to involve ecological adaptation, and genetic specialization by the introduced invertebrate for the new hosts is rare (see chapter 17).

A recent example of ecological host shifts by an introduced biological control agent involves a weevil (*Rhinocyllus conicus*; Coleoptera: Curculionidae) intended for control of musk thistle (*Carduus nutans*) and other species of this genus in North America (Louda et al. 1997). By 2000, this weevil had been recorded from 23 species of thistles of the genus *Cirsium*, most of which are native North American species, and several of which are of conservation concern (Pemberton 2000). We shall examine this phenomenon in detail in chapter 17.

Evolutionary Adaptation by Introduced Insect Arthropods

Most studies of alien herbivorous arthropods have concentrated on applied topics such as developing methods of control and counteracting evolution of resistance to chemical control. Arthropods have shown an extraordinary ability to evolve new genetic races in the agricultural environment. More than 500 species have evolved resistance to insecticides, in many cases exhibiting resistance to several major chemical groups of insecticides (McKenzie 1996). For example, the diamondback moth (*Plutella xylostella*), an insect pest of various crop plants of the mustard family in tropical and subtropical areas, has evolved resistance to every chemical pesticide used against it and also to the bacterial pesticide, *Bacillus thuringiensis* (Talekar and Shelton 1993). Evolutionary adaptability in response to strong selective pressures, such as those imposed by several pesticides, has also been shown by many vertebrates, including fish, amphibians, birds, and mammals. Recently, for example, European rabbits (*Oryctolagus cuniculus*) resistant to sodium monofluoroacetate (compound 1080) were found in southwestern Australia (Twigg et al. 2002).

Experimental evidence has shown that many herbivorous arthropods have the potential for rapid evolution of new host plant relationships (Jaenike 1990;Via 1990). Gould (1979), for example, examined the potential for host plant adaptation by the two-spotted spider mite (*Tetranychus urticae*), an herbivorous species known to feed on more than 180 species of host plants. Mites collected from the wild were reared for 8 months on bean plants that were a favorable host for the species. At this point, the mite population was divided into two groups, one that continued to feed on bean plants, and one that was given a combination of bean and mite-resistant cucumber plants. In this experiment, the availability of bean plants in the bean and cucumber mix was manipulated so that mites were forced to feed exclusively on cucumber for periods of up to 3 wk. During this time, their populations declined and selection for individuals most able to feed on cucumber occurred. The experiment was continued for 21 months. Results showed that mites in the bean and cucumber population improved substantially in survivorship and fecundity. When survivorship was tested at the end of the experiment on the most toxic cucumber leaves, for example, mites from the bean and cucumber population exhibited survivorship more than 40% greater than mites from the bean population. Mites from the bean and cucumber population, however, lost a small but significant degree of fitness on their original bean host. In similar experiments, Agrawal (2000) obtained similar results.

Fry (1989) extended the studies of Gould (1979) by examining the ability of the two-spotted spider mite to adapt to two other hosts that were initially only marginally acceptable: tomato (*Lycopersicon esculentum*) and broccoli (*Brassica oleracea*). In laboratory populations, mites showed reduced mortality and increased acceptance of these plant hosts in less than ten generations. Thus, rapid evolutionary adaptation by this mite is possible to plant hosts differing considerably in defensive chemistry.

Many of the major insect pests of agricultural crops have made ecological and evolutionary shifts from wild plants to crop species since their domestication. In some cases, these insects show high phenotypic and genotypic variability and are able to adapt to many host plants. The green peach aphid (*Myzus persicae*), for example, is known to feed on more than 400 species of plants belonging to more than 50 plant families (Weber 1985). Although they reproduce parthenogenetically, populations of this aphid exhibit numerous genotypes. Within crop fields, selection for certain genotypes may occur during an individual growing season, as Weber (1986) found in crop fields in Germany. This pattern of rapid, fine-scale adaptation has been observed in a number of native and alien insects (Mopper 1996).

A more restricted pattern of feeding on multiple hosts is shown by the southern cowpea weevil (*Callosobruchus maculatus*), native to sub-Saharan West Africa. This weevil is also able to use many host species, but within only one plant family, the Fabaceae. In addition, the southern cowpea weevil shows somewhat closer evolutionary adaptation to particular host species. This weevil has become a cosmopolitan pest of legume seeds in field and warehouse situations. Although its original host was probably the wild relative of the cowpea or black-eyed pea (*Vigna unguiculata*) in Africa, it now shows biotypes adapted to a wide variety of crop legumes (Wasserman 1986). The weevil now attacks crop legumes belonging to at least nine genera and more than a dozen species of legumes. Specific host races of the cowpea weevil show genetically based oviposition preferences presumably related to differences in host plant chemistry. The pea aphid (*Acyrthosiphon pisum*) shows a similar pattern of biotype formation on plants in the legume family (Auclair 1978).

A still more restricted pattern of host use is shown by the boll weevil (*Anthonomus grandis*), one of five closely related weevils whose ancestral host plants are members of the genus *Hampea*, a tropical American genus of the family Malvaceae, to which cultivated and wild species of cotton (*Gossypium* spp.) also belong (Jones 2001). The boll weevil itself uses two species of *Hampea* that occur on the Gulf Coast of southern Mexico. Analysis of the phylogenies of *Hampea* and the *Anthonomus* weevils that use them indicated that the use of *Gossypium* is a relatively recent ecological and evolutionary shift. The range of the two species of *Hampea* used by the boll weevil coincides with the region of the Mexican Gulf Coast considered to be the probable site of domestication of upland cotton (*Gossypium hirsutum*). The boll weevil has followed cotton to many parts of the world where this crop is grown and exhibits at least two ill-defined crop races in North America: "southeastern" and "Mexican." Since the boll weevil first appeared in the United States in Texas in 1892, the differentiation of the southeastern form is probably quite recent. The boll weevil also shows a race that appears to be confined to the wild species, *Gossypium thurberi*, in southern Arizona and northern Mexico. Based on analyses of mitochondrial DNA, the Thurber and southeastern races of the boll weevil differ markedly in haplotypes, although their morphology is very similar (Roehrdanz 2001). Since the crop race of the boll weevil was eradicated in Arizona in 1992, no evidence has been found that the race on wild cotton has moved into cultivated cotton.

Rapid evolutionary shifts or adaptation by a number of alien herbivores have been documented, as illustrated by the codling moth example introducing this chapter. The western corn rootworm (*Diabrotica virgifera*), native to Central America, provides a similar example. This crop pest has invaded regions of maize (*Zea mays*) cultivation in much of North America and became established in maize-growing areas of eastern Europe in the mid-1990s. In North America, damage by the larvae of this beetle approaches $1 billion annually. One of the tactics for dealing with this pest has been crop rotation in which maize is alternated with soybeans (*Glycine max*). Recently, however, a genetic form of corn rootworm with preference for oviposition and feeding on soybean has appeared in areas where this rotation has been practiced (Sammons et al. 1997). Genotypes of the western corn rootworm that have extended diapause have also appeared, enabling larvae to survive the rotation period with soybean and infect the next maize crop (Levine et al. 2002). The northern corn rootworm (*Diabrotica barberi*) has also evolved a biotype with extended diapause, enabling it to survive for a year during which another crop is alternated with corn (Krysan et al. 1986; Levine et al. 1992). These developments, together with genetic resistance to various insecticides, illustrate the complexity of evolutionary responses that alien invaders such as these corn rootworms can show in agricultural ecosystems.

The European corn borer (*Ostrinia nubilalis*), a moth, is another example of an insect pest that has shifted from one crop plant to another. It was apparently introduced to North America near Boston, Massachusetts, in about 1914 in broom corn or sorghum (*Sorghum vulgare*) material imported for the manufacture of brooms. This insect quickly became a major pest of maize (*Zea mays*), as well as many other crop plants. It also infests a wide range of wild native and alien plants. Since its establishment, biotypes differing in host specificity and number of annual generations have appeared (Hudon and LeRoux 1986). Three forms have been distinguished, characterized by one (univoltine), two (bivoltine), or several (multivoltine) generations during the year.

Pornkulwat et al. (1998) used random amplified polymorphic DNA analysis to distinguish these biotypes. The multivoltine biotype, characteristic of the southern United States, farthest from the presumed point of introduction in Massachusetts, was most distinct. It is likely that the form introduced was univoltine or bivoltine and that the multivoltine biotype has evolved in North America. It is also possible that separate introductions of corn borers differing in life history patterns occurred. Additional studies of these biotypes of the corn borer in New York State and Italy showed that they differ in the isomer composition of attractant pheromones produced by females (Cardé 1983). These differences may reflect a founder effect associated with the introduction of the corn borer to North America. In New York, however, three races of univoltine and bivoltine forms differing in pheromones have been noted in corn borer populations (Glover et al. 1991). One pheromone type shows a bivoltine annual cycle, the other both univoltine and bivoltine patterns. Some hybridization occurs, but the two pheromone races show partial reproductive isolation. Thus, some of these forms may represent incipient species (Cardé et al. 1978).

The Hessian fly (*Mayetiola destructor*) provides a good example of another evolutionary pattern: the ongoing evolutionary interaction between an insect herbivore and a set of host species. This species is perhaps the most serious insect pest of wheat throughout the world. Hessian fly also attacks barley, rye, and occasionally oats. Both wheat and the Hessian fly are alien species in North America and many other world regions. In North America, the Hessian fly appeared on Long Island, New York, in 1779, perhaps having been introduced in wheat straw used as bedding for horses of European soldiers during the Revolutionary War. The Hessian fly now occurs throughout wheat-growing areas of North America. Wheat breeders are engaged in an ongoing battle to create varieties that are resistant, with 60 such varieties released between 1950 and 1983. The mechanism of resistance is the production by the wheat plant of substances that kill the larvae hatching from eggs laid in plant tissues. Even on resistant varieties, however, some flies survive and reproduce. A gradual selection of a new virulent fly biotype thus occurs over a period of years. At least 16 Hessian fly biotypes are now known, and two or more are likely to occur in any area where wheat is grown (Ratcliffe et al. 2000).

Host plant shifts from native plants to introduced crop plants and then to other native or alien plants in other regions have also been documented. The Colorado potato beetle (*Leptinotarsa decimlineata*), for example, expanded its host range from native plants to cultivated potato (*Solanum tuberosum*) when potatoes were introduced to the western United States (see chapter 13). This beetle then spread through eastern North America where potatoes are grown. In the eastern United States, the potato beetle has adopted horse nettle (*Solanum carolinense*), a widespread native plant, and bittersweet (*S. dulcamara*), a European introduction, as hosts (Hare 1983; Hare and Kennedy 1986). In North Carolina, where the beetle has been present only since the late 1800s, it has evidently made an evolutionary adjustment to horse nettle, so its survival on this species is equal to or greater than on potato (Table 9.1). In Connecticut, on the other hand, survival is considerably lower on horse nettle than on potato. This difference may be related to the seasonal difference in potato growing in North Carolina and Connecticut relative to the phenology of horse nettle. Potatoes are grown earlier in the season in North Carolina than in Connecticut, so after harvest, a long period exists when horse nettle is an available host plant. During this period, two generations of potato beetles can develop on horse nettle, so selection for adaptation to this host may be strong.

Ongoing Evolution

These examples of rapid evolution by introduced herbivores appear to be the tip of an adaptive iceberg. Laboratory studies show that the potential for rapid evolution is widespread, and the examination of populations in agricultural ecosystems has now revealed clear examples of rapid evolution. Very likely, similar patterns will be detected in alien forest herbivores. As we shall see in the next chapter, alien predators and parasites are also

Table 9.1. Survival, fresh weight, and development time of Colorado potato beetles (*Leptinotarsa decemlineata*) on cultivated potato (*Solanum tuberosum*) and horse nettle (*Solanum carolinense*) in Connecticut, New Jersey, and North Carolina (Data from Hare and Kennedy 1986).

| | Survival (%) | Weight (mg) | Development Time (days) | |
			Male	Female
CONNECTICUT				
Potato	44.2	111.8	21.2	20.9
Horse Nettle*	3.3–6.7	83.9–98.2	28.0–36.0	26.5–28.8
NEW JERSEY				
Potato	47.5	103.5	21.2	21.3
Horse Nettle*	17.5–19.2	96.6–104.5	24.3–24.4	22.5–24.0
NORTH CAROLINA				
Potato	55.8	96.8	21.5	21.3
Horse Nettle*	60.8–62.5	94.0–102.2	21.9–23.8	21.5–22.8

* Figures in italics are for horse nettle plants from North Carolina and figures in Roman type are for plants from Connecticut.

adapting to the new prey and host environments they encounter. With these species, many more cases of rapid evolution have been documented, and both vertebrates and invertebrates have shown rapid evolutionary responses.

10.

Evolutionary Adaptation by
Alien Predators and Parasites

"In our opinion, there is no doubt that competition acts as a diversifying evolutionary force in freshwater fish communities, intraspecifically when other species are absent and interspecifically when they are present. The common claim that little evidence exists for character displacement and release is simply untenable. . . . "

—ROBINSON AND WILSON (1994)

The small Indian mongoose (*Herpestes javanicus*) is native to southern Asia, ranging from Iran and Iraq in the west to China and Java in the east. In the late 1800s and early 1900s, it was introduced to Mauritius in the Indian Ocean; Okinawa, Fiji, and the Hawaiian Islands in the Pacific; islands in the Adriatic Sea; many islands in the West Indies; and several other island areas (Simberloff et al. 2000). The motivation for these introductions was a supposed role in biological control of snakes and rodents.

In its native Asian range, the small Indian mongoose shows variation in body size and sexual dimorphism, depending on whether or not two other species of congeneric, but slightly larger, mongooses occur in the same area. In the easternmost part of its Asian range, these congeners are absent and the small Indian mongoose is larger and shows greater sexual size dimorphism, males being larger than females.

The source of populations introduced to oceanic islands was eastern India and Bangladesh, where the small Indian mongoose is sympatric with its congeners. An analysis of specimens from throughout the Asian

Table 10.1. Upper canine tooth diameters and skull lengths for the small Indian mongoose in eastern India and Bangladesh versus on various islands to which the species has been introduced in the absence of its congeners (Data from Simberloff et al. 2000).

Locality	CANINE TOOTH DIAMETER (MM)			SKULL LENGTH (MM)		
	Male	Female	% difference★	Male	Female	% difference★
E. India and Bangladesh	2.65	2.39	9.8	61.9	58.0	4.7
St. Croix, U.S. Virgin Islands	3.26	2.89	11.3	65.7	61.1	7.0
Hawaii, HI, USA	3.11	2.70	13.2	65.7	60.5	7.9
Oahu, HI USA	3.09	2.73	11.6	66.5	62.0	6.8
Mauritius	3.15	2.77	12.1	65.5	60.5	7.6
Viti Levu, Fiji	3.14	2.86	8.9	65.5	61.4	6.2
Okinawa, Japan	3.14	2.81	10.2	65.5	60.0	8.4

★ Difference from value for males.

and introduced insular range of the small Indian mongoose, however, showed that males from the island areas have increased in size and that sexual dimorphism has increased relative to Asian populations with sympatric congeners (Simberloff et al. 2000). Skull length of island population males averages 5.7–7.4% longer and canine tooth diameter 17–23% greater than for males from eastern India and Bangladesh (Table 10.1). These differences are intermediate between those of animals in eastern India and Bangladesh and those in easternmost Asia. Sexual dimorphism of animals in island populations is similar to that in the easternmost Asian populations.

That these patterns are consistent for mongoose populations on islands in widely separated ocean areas suggests that the changes are evolutionary. For most of these island populations, the changes in morphology have appeared over about 100–200 generations. It appears likely that these changes have resulted from release of the small Indian mongoose from competition for food, which consists largely of small animals, and an increase in specialization of females for smaller prey and males for larger prey.

Interactions of Predators, Parasites, and Prey

Natural selection favors characteristics of predators and parasites that maximize the fitness of individuals of these species, that is, their contribution to gene pools of subsequent generations. For predators, characteristics of prime importance are morphology and behavior that enable individuals to find, capture, and process prey organisms efficiently. Body size of predators relative to that of their prey, for example, is a feature often subject to strong natural selection.

For parasites and parasitoids, morphology and behavior likewise are important, but physiological characteristics related to virulence—their ability to infect and develop in host species—are also critical. Some fruit flies of the genus *Drosophila*, for example, tend to defend against parasitoid wasps by an immune response that leads to encapsulation of the wasp eggs or larvae (Kraaijeveld and Godfray 1999). The parasitoids themselves counter this response in various ways, including physiological mechanisms and egg placement behavior. Kraaijeveld et al. (2001) showed experimentally that selection can improve the ability of parasitoids to infect *Drosophila* species that defend by encapsulation. In nature, the effectiveness of these responses by parasitoids varies geographically with host species in a complex manner. Nevertheless, it appears that host selection by parasitoids can evolve quickly, given strong selective pressures (Rolff and Kraaijeveld 2001). Distinct host races have been described for several parasitoids of scale insects, for example (Diehl and Bush 1984).

Most predators, vertebrate or invertebrate, tend to be adapted to prey of a particular size. For such predators, especially vertebrates, partitioning of prey sizes is often the evolutionary outcome of food competition. Partitioning is often evident as character displacement when guilds of predator species differing in number of species are compared. Character displacement is the increased difference in quantitative characters of two or more species in areas of sympatry compared to areas of allopatry. For predators, character displacement is usually seen in body size or in size of jaws, teeth, or other elements of the feeding apparatus. In the context of alien species, however, this phenomenon is often seen as character release, a shift in morphology toward an intermediate condition when a species is introduced to an area where it is freed from one or more competitors.

Robinson and Wilson (1994) summarized information on character displacement and release in fish belonging to 52 genera in 17 families, indicating that the phenomena are a frequent response to competition for food. These phenomena are especially common in freshwater faunas of northern North America, suggesting that many of the patterns are postglacial in origin. Dayan and Simberloff (1994) demonstrated that species of mustelid mammals in Britain and Ireland show character displacement in tooth and skull sizes, although the relation of this pattern to prey use is not clear (McDonald 2002). These species are postglacial colonizers of the British Isles. Schluter (2000) summarized information on character displacement for a large number of birds and mammals and a few invertebrates.

In addition to character displacement, predators introduced to new areas may encounter a new spectrum of prey sizes, regardless of whether or nor they have been released from pressure of competitors. Selection may thus favor adjustments of body size or feeding apparatus appropriate to the new range of prey sizes.

Evolutionary Adaptation by Invertebrate Predators and Animal Disease Vectors

Many parasitoid insects have been introduced to North America and other world regions, in almost all cases as potential biological control agents. The target pests themselves are usually alien species. Many introduced parasitoids, however, extend their feeding activity to native species. In Hawaii, for example, more than 32% of 115 parasitoids introduced for biological control have begun to attack hosts other than the target pest. In mainland North America, about 16.3 % of 313 introduced parasitoids have been recorded from native, nontarget species (Hawkins and Marino 1997). At least one parasitoid wasp has shown evolutionary adaptation to conditions of crop and noncrop habitats in which its prey occurs (see chapter 17). Other parasitoid wasps, such as *Aphidius ervi*, which attacks pea aphids (*Acyrthosiphon pisum*) in clover and alfalfa fields in eastern North America, have not. Although individuals of this parasitoid differ genetically in their ability to parasitize pea aphids, no consistent difference in virulence is evident in different crop habitats (Henter 1995; Hufbauer 2001).

As we noted in chapter 3, populations of the Argentine ant (*Linepithema humile*) in North America form supercolonies in which individuals show little or no aggression toward members of different colony units. This appears to be the result of a combination of loss of genetic variability at the time of the colonization event and selection against aggression following establishment in North America (Tsutsui et al. 2003).

Insect vectors of animal disease have invaded many new world regions, and some have shown rapid evolutionary adjustment. The mosquito *Aedes aegypti*, for example, is a vector for the disease agents of both yellow fever and dengue, both viral diseases affecting humans. The mosquito exists as two subspecies, *formosus*, native to tropical forests of Africa, and *aegypti*, now worldwide in tropical environments close to human habitation (Failloux et al. 2002). The *aegypti* form appears to have arisen in North Africa by adaptation of the mosquito to breeding in water storage vessels. This form was spread worldwide in tropical and subtropical areas by commerce between the fifteenth and nineteenth centuries. The forest form, *formosus*, has also been introduced to some islands in the Indian Ocean.

Aedes aegypti aegypti itself shows genetic differentiation in different tropical regions. Populations in South America and Southeast Asia are genetically similar and are the most efficient vectors of the dengue virus (Failloux et al. 2002). South American mosquitoes, however, are effective vectors of the yellow fever virus, whereas Southeast Asian mosquitoes are not. Subspecies *aegypti* in Polynesia is somewhat distinct from the South American and Asian forms of the subspecies, perhaps as the result of a genetic bottleneck at the time of introduction. Subspecies *formosus* on La Réunion Island in the Indian Ocean also differs from populations in African forest areas and is a more efficient vector of dengue than African forest populations. This difference may also have arisen by a founder effect or as an accidental consequence of mosquito control efforts from 1949 to 1953.

Rapid Evolutionary Adaptation by Aquatic Vertebrate Predators

Adaptations for use of prey of a certain size range are common in aquatic vertebrate predators, and many examples of differentiation between sexes or competitor species have been documented (Smith and Skúlason 1996). Although some such differences are the result of phenotypic plasticity, many are genetically based. The genetic basis is often quite simple, at times the result of a single gene. Situations in which rapid evolution of adaptations for altered prey use occurs often involve the invasion of new regions or habitats.

Freshwater fish at northern latitudes in the northern hemisphere present many examples of such divergent evolution, much of which has occurred since retreat of Pleistocene continental glaciers about 15,000 yr ago. These most recent examples are probably replicates of changes following the 20 or so phases of glaciation that occurred over the past 2 million yr. In this most recent postglacial era, colonization of new, biotically impoverished aquatic environments from freshwater refugia or from the ocean has offered many ecological opportunities and has led to some remarkable patterns of adaptive radiation (Robinson and Schluter 2000). Many of these patterns are replicated in different lake and river systems.

Patterns of divergence are most common in larger lakes. The aquatic systems involved possess diverse littoral, benthic, and pelagic environments, where divergent selection is apparently able to overcome the tendency for gene flow to maintain genetically uniform populations.

Races of northern freshwater fish adapted to shallow-water and open-water feeding niches have evolved in 37 species (Robinson and Wilson 1994). Schluter (2000) summarized information on eight sympatric pairs and one trio of fish occupying postglacial lakes in Europe and North America. The ancestors of these species colonized newly formed lakes from refugia south of the glacial front or from the ocean within the past 15,000 yr. In these cases, ecological races of a single species coexist but show genetic divergence and differential ecological specialization. Typically, one form is specialized for feeding on planktonic organisms, the other on benthic organisms. In the case of the trio of divergent forms, one was a plankton-feeder, and the other two were large and small benthic feeders. Several other cases of multiple ecomorphs of individual fish species have been reported but not yet subjected to genetic analysis.

Ecological forms adapted to feeding in different microhabitats and on different prey are common in the arctic char (*Salvelinus alpinus*), a post-glacial colonist of many lakes in Eurasia and North America (Johnson 1980). Typically, a large open-water feeder and a smaller benthic feeder coexist, but occasionally, other forms occur (Griffiths 1994). In Thing-vallavatn Lake, Iceland, for example, four forms can be recognized: small and large benthic, snail-feeding forms that occur in water of different depths, and planktivorous and piscivorous forms that feed in open water (Jonsson et al. 1988; Terje et al. 1992). The four forms all spawn in the littoral zone, where the juveniles live and feed together. The different forms tend to be partially separated in spawning behavior and timing, especially the two benthic forms, which tend to spawn in different months. The degree of genetic difference among these forms is very small, being greatest between the benthic forms. The differentiation of these forms appears to have occurred in sympatry.

A somewhat similar pattern of divergence can be seen for the rainbow smelt (*Osmerus mordax*) in streams and lakes along the Atlantic coast of New England and eastern Canada (Taylor and Bentzen 1993). Typically an anadromous fish that lives in coastal waters and ascends streams to spawn, this species has given rise to lacustrine forms in formerly glaciated regions. Some of these lake populations also exhibit dwarf and normal forms. Similar sets of dwarf and normal populations exist in lakes in Maine, New Brunswick, Nova Scotia, and Quebec. Dwarf smelt exhibit more gill rakers, larger eyes, and shorter upper jaws than normal smelt, correlated with feeding on plankton. Normal smelt feed to a greater extent on small fish. In Lake Utopia, New Brunswick, the dwarf and normal forms spawn in different streams and at different times. Mitochondrial DNA and nuclear minisatellite DNA analyses also indicate that these forms are quite distinct. The pattern of genetic differentiation of dwarf and normal fish in other lakes is less clear. Altogether, the evidence suggests that dwarf and normal fish have evolved independently in the various lakes in which both occur. In cases such as Lake Utopia, these forms appear to be behaving as distinct biological species.

Lake whitefishes (*Coregonus* spp.) have developed up to five ecological races in various northern lakes in Europe and North America. Most frequent are benthic and open-water morphs. These forms differ in various morphological features, including the number and shape of gill rakers, an adaptation for plankton feeding (Lindsey 1981). Many of these forms are genetically distinct and appear to have differentiated in sympatry in individual lakes (Kirkpatrick and Selander 1979; Bodaly et al. 1992). A particularly interesting situation exists in the Allegash River basin of northern Maine (Kirkpatrick and Selander 1979). Here, a dwarf form of the widespread lake whitefish (*Coregonus clupeiformis*) exists alone or together with the normal form of the species in 22 lakes. Ancestral whitefish have colonized this region within the past 12,000 yr, following release from continental glaciation. The dwarf and normal forms are quite distinct in morphology and life history. The dwarf form reaches sexual maturity in 1 or 2 years but rarely lives longer than 4 yr. The normal form does not mature until its fourth year but continues to reproduce annually until a maximum age of about 12 yr. The two forms also differ by several weeks in spawning time. Electrophoretic studies revealed that the two forms differ in frequencies of several genes and suggest that the two forms should be considered sibling species. In all likelihood, the dwarf form is derived from the normal form, although whether differentiation occurred in the same or different lakes is uncertain.

Although much of the differentiation of whitefish has occurred over some unknown length of postglacial time, several cases of recent translocations of these fish show that change can be very rapid (Lindsey 1981). In northern Italy, for example, whitefish did not originally occur in Lake Maggiore. In the late 1860s, two species of *Coregonus* from Lake Constance were translocated to Lake Maggiore. These species differed in the number of gill rakers, but in Lake Maggiore they apparently interbred freely, yielding a form with an intermediate number of gill rakers. Much later, in 1950, a third whitefish was introduced from Lake Neuchâtel. This form initially differed only slightly in gill raker number. Within only a few generations, however, the number of gill rakers of this last form had diverged significantly from that of the fish already present. Several other transplanted whitefish in Europe and North America have also exhibited changes in gill raker characteristics over short intervals (Lindsey 1981). Unfortunately, detailed documentation of the degree of genetic basis for such shifts is lacking, although other studies have shown that gill raker structure has a strong genetic basis.

The pumpkinseed sunfish (*Lepomis gibbosus*) offers one of the best examples of evolutionary change in habitat and resource use (Robinson and Wilson 1996; Robinson et al. 2000). Pumpkinseeds and bluegill sunfish (*Lepomis macrochirus*) coexist in lakes in midwestern North America, but bluegills were originally absent from lakes east of the Appalachians and north of the St. Lawrence River. In lakes where bluegills have been absent, pumpkinseeds exhibit pelagic and littoral ecotypes. The pelagic forms have more slender bodies, smaller pectoral fins, and more closely spaced gill rakers than littoral forms. These characteristics are adaptive in relation to feeding on zooplankton. The littoral forms of the pumpkinseed feed largely on benthic arthropods and mollusks. Bluegills now have been introduced to many lakes where they have recently come into contact with pumpkinseeds. In these lakes, pumpkinseeds have become restricted to the littoral zone and prevented from feeding on zooplankton (Robinson et al. 2000).

In many lakes, bluegill sunfish themselves show pelagic and littoral forms that differ in morphology and behavior (Ehlinger and Wilson 1988). The degree to which these differences have a genetic basis is uncertain.

In other instances, fish have evolved distinct races adapted to freshwater lake and stream habitats in coastal areas released from Pleistocene glaciation (Moodie 1972; Hendry et al. 2002). The threespine stickleback (*Gasterosteus aculeatus*), many populations of which occur in coastal marine waters, has established purely freshwater populations in many locations deglaciated within the past 15,000 yr. These populations have adapted to freshwater habitats in morphology and behavior and in many cases have developed divergent ecotypes (Foster 1995). On coastal islands and the mainland of British Columbia, Canada, pairs of incipient species adapted to lake versus stream or benthic versus open-water habitats have evolved in several locations (McPhail 1994). On Vancouver Island, British Columbia, Canada, for example, sticklebacks from Misty Lake differed in body shape and feeding morphology from sticklebacks in the inflowing stream (Hendry et al. 2002). Lake fish had more slender bodies, interpreted as an adaptation for sustained swimming in large water bodies, and more gill rakers, correlated with planktonic feeding. Fish from the inlet stream, with deeper bodies, were adapted for short swimming bursts, and with fewer gill rakers, for benthic feeding. Reciprocal transplant experiments, in which fish from lake and stream habitats were placed together in cages in the two habitats, showed that each race grew best in its own habitat type (Hendry et al. 2002). Estimates of gene flow among lake and stream populations indicated that genetic interchange was higher between lake and outlet stream fish than between lake and inlet stream fish and that it probably constrained the degree of divergence of the former populations.

In some cases, very rapid evolution of threespine stickleback populations isolated in freshwater areas has been observed. In Bergen, western Norway, a pond was created in 1960 by closing the connection of an inlet to the sea, resulting in its conversion to freshwater. Marine sticklebacks were isolated by the formation of this pond (Klepaker 1993). Three phenotypes of these fish could be recognized in the 1960s, based on the number and arrangement of lateral armor plates: low, partial, and complete. These phenotypes appear to be defined by dominant and recessive alleles of two genes. Sticklebacks in nearby marine waters showed only the complete and partial plate phenotypes, with 98.4% of all fish having the former. In addition, less than 1% showed four, rather than three, dorsal spines. By 1991, 31 yr after isolation, sticklebacks in the pond showed only 85.9% complete plate phenotype, and 12.7% exhibited four dorsal spines. These changes are in the direction of the morphology shown by sticklebacks in other isolated freshwater areas.

Fewer cases are known of rapid evolution in response to biotic conditions by predatory fish introduced to new waters in recent time. Stearns (1983a, 1983b), however, analyzed life history characteristics of mosquitofish (*Gambusia affinis*) that had been introduced to irrigation reservoirs in Hawaii in 1905 for mosquito control. Some of these reservoirs continued to be used for irrigation and experienced fluctuations of water level related to irrigation withdrawals. Others were abandoned, after which water levels remained stable. Studies in 1973 and 1974 showed that several life history parameters varied between reservoirs with fluctuating and nonfluctuating water levels, possibly related to food availability differences (Stearns 1983a). Much of the difference in these parameters was evidently related to short-term changes correlated with water fluctuations.

In 1980, Stearns (1983b) collected fish from reservoirs with stable and fluctuating water levels and propagated them in the laboratory under identical conditions. The life history parameters of laboratory-hatched offspring were then analyzed to determine if genetic differences existed between populations. Fish from reservoirs with stable water levels tended to have smaller offspring than those from fluctuating reservoirs and to be longer lived. The relation of fecundity to body length tended to be negative for fish from stable reservoirs and positive for those from fluctuating reservoirs. Other differences were related to reservoir size, depth, and intensity of fluctuation. Thus, although it is difficult to pinpoint the selective forces operating in these reservoirs, substantial evolutionary change was evident.

Some predatory fish have also made rapid evolutionary adjustments to changes in the predatory regime affecting them. Threespine sticklebacks (*Gasterosteus aculeatus*), native to coastal marine waters, have invaded stream and lagoon environments in many locations and have often become isolated in such environments by natural coastline changes or human modification of the coastline. In these environments, the predation regime on small fish is usually less intense than in the ocean. The threespine stickleback has a series of lateral armor plates varying in number from none to about ten, with most populations showing some variation in number. This characteristic is genetically controlled (Hagen and Gilbertson 1973). Where freshwater habitats have been invaded, the long-term result is usually reduction in the number of armor plates and a shortening of the dorsal spines (Kristjánsson et al. 2002). In many locations these changes have obviously occurred in postglacial time, but the length of isolation involved usually is not precisely known. This pattern of rapid evolution has apparently occurred many times, but these differentiated populations are also prone to extinction because of the transitory nature of the habitats occupied (Bell 2001).

In a fjord in western Iceland, however, a dam was constructed in 1987 to create a lagoon for trout and salmon ranching. The water in this lagoon soon became fresh, so a population of threespine sticklebacks was isolated in a new environment with an altered predation regime. Kristjánsson et al. (2002) examined the sticklebacks isolated in the lagoon in 1999, 12 yr and a maximum of 12 generations after isolation. They found that the fish had shown significant reduction in their armor plates and spine length. Some morphological adaptation to the two major habitats of the lagoon, areas of mud bottom versus lava rock bottom, had also occurred. Although this example does not strictly involve an alien species invasion, the evolutionary dynamics are presumably like those that have occurred in many coastal areas invaded by sticklebacks.

In western Canada, threespine sticklebacks have colonized many coastal streams and lakes in postglacial time, where they experience predation by a diversity of invertebrate and vertebrate predators (Reimchen 1994). The number of lateral plates tends to vary with the type of predator that predominates. Sticklebacks in lakes that lack larger predatory fish but have avian predators tend to possess only three or four plates. Where both predatory fish and birds are present, the number of plates tends to average seven. Threespine sticklebacks often experience seasonally variable intensities of predation by fish, birds, and dragonfly larvae (Reimchen and Nosil 2002). Temporal shifts in selection pressures and morphology associated with these different types of predators can often be recognized. These patterns of shifting selection may help maintain genetic variability in defense morphology in many populations.

At Drizzle Lake in the Queen Charlotte Islands of western Canada, both predatory fish and birds are present, but the seasonal pattern of predation on sticklebacks by these two predator groups varies. Predation by cutthroat trout (*Oncorhynchus clarki*) tends to be concentrated in summer, whereas bird predation can be heavy throughout the year. Only if the lake becomes ice-covered does bird predation cease. Thus, the mean number of lateral armor plates for fish, especially subadults, tends to vary seasonally. When bird predation is heavy, the mean number of plates drops, and when trout predation predominates, it rises. It appears likely that a large number of plates gives protection against fish predators, but it may reduce the ability of sticklebacks to escape diving birds. Clearly, the predation regime can impose strong selection on the number of armor plates over short time periods. Other studies have shown that threespine sticklebacks can respond quickly to change in the predation regime. In northern Russia, for example, Ziuganov (1995) introduced sticklebacks with heavy plating to a freshwater pond that was predator-free. After only eight generations, he found that about 17% of the pond population showed reduced plate numbers.

Another variable feature of stickleback morphology is the presence or absence of a pelvic girdle, which supports ventral spines (Ziuganov and Zotin 1995). In the ninespine stickleback (*Pungitius pungitius*), this structure is present in coastal marine waters and streams with predatory fish but reduced or absent in ponds without such predators. Some of these ponds were isolated about 50 yr earlier by human activities, and it appears that fish lacking pelvic girdles evolved from normal fish during this period. The pelvic fin structures associated with the girdle also function in courtship displays and appear to result in patterns of selective mating among fish with and without these structures. Reimchen (1980) noted similar variation in pelvic girdle and spines, together with its relation to the predation regime, in the threespine stickleback in Canada.

Rapid Evolutionary Adaptation by Terrestrial Vertebrate Predators

Character displacement is frequently observed on oceanic islands where colonizations have brought close competitors together. In a few cases, character displacement has resulted from recent colonization events. Off the northeast coast of New Guinea, a mid-seventeenth century volcanic explosion and caldera collapse created modern Long Island and probably destroyed the biota of other nearby small islands. These islands have since been recolonized by plants and animals, all arrivals being across ocean gaps. Two honeyeaters, insectivorous and nectar-feeding birds, have established populations on the island (Diamond et al. 1989). These closely related species, *Myzomela pammelaena* and *M. schlateri*, occur on many islands of the surrounding ocean but do not occur together except in the Long Island group. Both species appear to be effective colonizers of isolated islands, a species group termed "supertramps" by island biogeographers. On the Long Island group, these species show increased divergence in body size; their weight ratio is 1.52 on Long Island compared to 1.43 in areas where they are not sympatric. Diamond et al. (1989) concluded that the increased size difference evolved after contact on the Long Island group and is probably related to partitioning of insect foods.

Similar rapid evolutionary adjustments to new biotic environments can be seen in mammal invaders of oceanic islands, particularly in body size (Case 1978; Dayan and Simberloff 1998). Yom-Tov et al. (1999) examined relationships between morphology of various rat (kiore, *Rattus exulans*; black rat, *R. rattus*; Norway rat, *R. norvegicus*) and mouse (house mouse, *Mus musculus*) species on Pacific Islands, where these species had all been introduced by humans. They found that the kiore was largest on islands where it was the only species and smallest on islands where all four species were present. The black rat tended to be smaller in body size on islands where both the kiore and the house mouse were present. Norway rats showed no difference in body size depending on the presence or absence of other rodents, but the length of the upper row of molar teeth tended to increase as the number of co-occurring rodents increased. Thus, competitive relationships among these species apparently affected their patterns of evolutionary change.

Several cases of rapid evolution by predatory mammals introduced to or invading new geographical areas have been documented, including the example of the small Indian mongoose discussed at the beginning of the chapter. A similar case involves the shorttail weasel or stoat (*Mustela erminea*). Beginning in 1884, European stoats were introduced to New Zealand from Great Britain in the hope of controlling the European rabbit (*Oryctolagus cuniculus*). They are now distributed throughout the country (King 1991). In New Zealand, the mammalian prey of stoats consists of few small but many large prey, compared to their diet in Britain. Much of their prey consists of European rabbits, European hares (*Lepus europaeus*), brushtail possums (*Trichosurus vulpecula*), and rats (*Rattus* spp.), whereas various species of mice are more important in Britain. This prey shift is correlated with an increase in the body size and skull length of stoats, especially females, in New Zealand. In addition, within New Zealand there is a strong correlation of body weight of stoats with an index of the size of the prey taken in local areas.

In North America, the coyote (*Canis latrans*) may have evolved rapidly in body size as it has spread eastward over the past century. From their original range in the Great Plains, coyotes have spread eastward through southern Canada and the northern United States to occupy most of New England. As we noted in chapter 5, animals in this eastern region tend to be larger and heavier, with males in New Hampshire being about 50% heavier and females 70% heavier than animals in Colorado (Silver and Silver 1969; Thurber and Peterson 1991). In New England, their prey includes adult white-tailed deer (*Odocoileus virginianus*) to a greater extent than in western parts of their range. Larivière and Crête (1993) suggested that the larger size of eastern coyotes is genetically based and either the result of selection for improved ability to hunt larger prey or a favorable consequence of hybridization with the gray wolf (*Canis lupus*) or possibly the red wolf (*C. rufus*).

Recent studies by Paul Wilson (Derr 2002) concluded that eastern gray and red wolves are conspecific and represent an entity that should be called the eastern wolf (*Canis lycaon*). He also concluded that the large-bodied eastern population of the coyote is the result of hybridization between coyotes and the eastern wolf.

The Growing Cast of the Evolutionary Play

Alien predators and parasites are making diverse evolutionary adjustments to their new prey and host environments. Aquatic and terrestrial vertebrates, in particular, have shown patterns of rapid evolution in response to prey size and type. Not to be outdone in this regard, alien agents of plant and animal disease, together with animals that act as their vectors, have begun to participate in the evolutionary play. We shall examine patterns of evolution of these species in the next chapter.

11.

Adaptation of Alien Diseases to Hosts and Vectors

"Migrations of virulent and fungicide-resistant strains in the past two decades have caused a worldwide resurgence of the potato (and tomato) late blight disease. . . . This resurgence supports the view that introduced pathogens and new variants of old ones present a real and immediate threat for plants as well as for animals and humans."

—FRY AND GOODWIN (1997)

The sudden oak death fungus (*Phytophthora ramorum*) was discovered and described in the Netherlands and Germany, where it parasitized *Rhododendron* and *Viburnum* shrubs. In 1995, however, the fungus appeared in central California (Rizzo et al. 2002), where it began to attack and kill a wide variety of broad-leafed trees and shrubs, especially tanoak (*Lithocarpus densiflorus*), various live and deciduous oaks (*Quercus* spp.), and madrone (*Arbutus menziesii*). By summer 2001, the disease had spread along the coastal region from Monterey County to Mendocino County, causing the death of tens of thousands of trees. The range of trees and shrubs affected also widened, and by summer 2002, 17 species had been identified with infections. These included members of five genera of trees belonging to families other than the Fagaceae, to which the oaks belong. The fungus attacks the roots of the species most subject to being killed. California bay laurel (*Umbellularia californica*), in which the leaves, but not the roots, are infected, appears to play a major role in the dispersal of spores of the fungus.

Tanoak, one of the most seriously affected species, is a common understory tree in redwood (*Sequoia sempervirens*) and Douglas-fir (*Pseudotsuga menziesii*) stands in California and may pass the sudden oak death fungus to these species. In 2002, sudden oak death fungus infections were found in young Douglas-firs and redwoods in the wild, and laboratory tests showed that healthy young trees of both species could be infected. These observations raised the fear that the fungus was adapting to two of the most valuable forest trees in North America. In addition, the fungus appears capable of infecting northern red oak (*Quercus rubra*) and pin oak (*Q. palustris*) from eastern North America (Rizzo et al. 2002). Thus, an alien, lethal fungus is spreading and adapting to new hosts at alarming rates. Already devastating to oaks and tanoaks, this evolutionary experiment might change oak-dominated woodlands of the Pacific coast and possibly elsewhere (Gilbert 2002). No one can predict the outcome.

The Evolution of Disease Agents and Their Hosts

All higher plants and animals are host to a variety of microorganisms that may be beneficial, harmless, or pathogenic. Some are organisms that have evolved a mutualistic relationship with their hosts. Others are facultative forms that feed on dead tissues or, in animals, intestinal contents, but can sometimes become pathogenic, as in the case of the human colon bacterium, *Escherichia coli*. Still others are pathogens that are in active coevolution with the host (Levin and Udovic 1977).

The relationship between a pathogen and a particular host is the result of an evolutionary interaction between the defenses of the host and the virulence of the pathogen (see, e.g., Clay and Kover 1996). Natural selection favors an increase in host resistance, on the one hand, and the level of virulence that maximizes the fitness of the pathogen, on the other (Gilbert 2002). In the case of an Australian flax, *Linum marginale*, and its rust pathogen, *Melampsora lini*, for example, the balance between host resistance and rust virulence varies in different populations of the flax (Thrall and Burdon 2003). In the rust, virulence and transmission probability show a strong trade-off. In flax populations most exposed to rust attack, strong rust resistance was favored in the flax plants and high virulence was favored in the rust. In more isolated flax populations, plant resistance was not as highly favored, while high spore production and lower virulence were favored in the rust.

Resulting relationships between a host and an infective agent may vary greatly in their nature. The relationship may be commensal, with neither species harming the other, or even beneficial to one or both species. Most higher plants, for example, possess fungi, known as endophytes, that live within their tissues without causing obvious harm (Palm 2001). This relationship appears to be a balanced antagonism, in which both plant and endophyte have evolved to tolerate each other's offenses (Schulz et al. 1999). Mutualism is a further step in such relationships. The relationship between nitrogen–fixing bacteria and their host plants, for example, is mutualistic, with both members benefiting. The host plant receives fixed nitrogen and the bacteria receive energy-rich photosynthate. Similar relationships occur between many animals and microorganisms. Gut-dwelling endobionts occur in most higher animals, where they may be harmless saprotrophs or mutualists that aid in digestion or produce organic compounds beneficial to their hosts.

Benign or beneficial interactions may be altered, however, when microorganisms that are in evolutionary balance with their native host agents are transported to new areas and introduced to vulnerable new hosts. In the modern world, long-distance transport of microbes is becoming commonplace. The results of such events are some of the most damaging outbreaks of plant and animal diseases (Wingfield et al. 2001).

Chestnut blight (*Cryphonectria parasitica*), a benign fungal associate of Asian relatives of the American chestnut (*Castanea dentata*), is a classic example of the result of introduction of a fungal pathogen to a new geographical area (Liebhold et al. 1996). Chestnut blight is the most destructive tree disease to strike North America. American chestnuts once ranged from Georgia and Alabama north to Maine and west to the Mississippi River. Chestnut was one of the dominant canopy trees in the eastern forests and produced mast that was consumed by many native mammals and birds. It was also one of the most economically important hardwoods, supplying lumber for construction, rot-resistant ties for railroads, and fine wood for manufacture of furniture.

Chestnut blight appeared in New York City prior to 1904, probably entering North America on ornamental Japanese chestnut trees. Once established, it spread rapidly by wind transport of spores and within 20 yr had killed almost all mature chestnut trees in New England. In another 20 yr, it had spread throughout the range of the chestnut. Although the blight kills the aboveground portion of the tree, the roots are resistant. Thus, although adult chestnuts have been eliminated, sprouts continue to be produced by root systems of former trees. These sprouts may grow into small saplings, but they are eventually killed. Loss of the chestnut as a mast-producing canopy tree has altered the ecology of much of the eastern deciduous forest of North America.

As we saw in the introductory example, sudden oak death fungus could cause equal or greater ecological damage than chestnut blight. Other kinds of disease agents can also cause serious impacts on dominant plants. The pine wood nematode (*Bursaphelenchus xylophilus*), introduced to Japan, has become a much more serious pathogen for endemic Japanese pines than for pines from North America, for example (Kiyohara and Bolla 1990).

Many animal diseases have behaved in a similar fashion. A number of forms of the avian malaria pathogen (e.g., *Plasmodium relictum*), for example, infect many species of birds in continental regions of the tropics. These infections are largely benign. In Hawaii, however, avian malaria is highly virulent for native birds and is one of the principal reasons for the disappearance of natives in lowland areas (Van Riper et al. 1986). Whirling disease of salmonid fish is caused by an amoeboid protozoan, *Myxobolus cerebralis*, that probably evolved in Europe (Markiw 1992). The European brown trout (*Salmo trutta*) is relatively resistant to *Myxobolus* but is a carrier that can produce spores that infect tubificid worms, the secondary host of the parasite. *Myxobolus* was introduced to North America in the late 1950s and has had severe impacts on many native species of trout and salmon.

Alien Plant Disease Agents and Their Evolution

Fungi associated with cultivated cereals and other crop plants are notorious both for their ability to track their hosts to new geographical areas and to evolve races that overcome resistant plant varieties. One of the most dramatic examples was the ability of a strain of the blight fungus *Helminthosporium maydis* to infect hybrid maize (*Zea mays*) varieties carrying a particular gene for male sterility. In 1970, this fungal strain caused production losses of maize valued at about $1 billion. Fungi and other pathogens associated with woody plants tend to follow their hosts to new world regions, where they are subject to new evolutionary pressures (Wingfield et al. 2001).

As we saw in chapter 5, strains of individual fungi from different regions have become mixed in areas to which the fungi and their hosts have been introduced. Hybridization of these strains often creates increased genetic diversity and new invasive forms in the fungus population (Brasier 2001). In the case of potato late blight (*Phytophthora infestans*), the Toluca Valley of central Mexico is a center of diversity for the fungus (Flier et al. 2003). Fungal strains differing in genetic structure and interbreeding potential exist in commercial potato fields, in potatoes grown in subsistence farm plots, and in association with wild species of *Solanum*. Although genetic differentiation for these plant hosts exists, measurable gene flow does occur among the fungal strains.

Rapid evolution of many fungal species and their hosts frequently tends to follow a gene-for-gene coevolution involving genes regulating resistance of the host and genes regulating virulence of the pathogen (Bergelson et al. 2001). In most cases, the allele of the host gene for resistance is dominant and the allele for avirulence in the pathogen is dominant, so the combinations in table 11.1 indicate situations in which infection or resistance will be shown. These genes apparently function according to an elicitor-receptor relationship (DeWit 1992). In the pathogen, a gene product, the elicitor, is produced, usually a protein or other organic compound in the pathogen's cell wall. In the plant host, receptor genes code for protein molecules that recognize the elicitor components of the cell wall of the pathogen (Bishop et al. 2000). Recognition leads to the induction of specific defense proteins, such as chitinases that destroy the cell walls of fungi or bacteria. Coevolutionary changes thus involve the ability of the pathogen to change the structure of its surface compounds and the ability of the plant to detect new configurations.

Table 11.1. Gene-for-gene relationships of a host with alleles for resistance (R) or susceptibility (r) and a pathogen with alleles for avirulence (V) or virulence (v). Capital letters indicate allele dominance. Boxes in table body show the combination of host and pathogen genotypes that can occur and whether or not infection is possible. Infection is impossible as long as dominant alleles for resistance (R) and avirulence (V) are combined in host and pathogen.

Pathogen Genotypes	Host Genotypes		
	RR	*Rr*	*rr*
VV	RR + VV	Rr + VV	rr + VV
	Infection prevented	Infection prevented	Infection occurs
Vv	RR + Vv	Rr + Vv	rr + Vv
	Infection prevented	Infection prevented	Infection occurs
vv	RR + vv	Rr + vv	rr + vv
	Infection occurs	Infection occurs	Infection occurs

The molecular structure of chitinases produced by the plant and of chitinase inhibitors produced by the pathogen may also be subject to such selective interaction. Gene-for-gene interactions have been demonstrated for many fungal pathogens, several bacterial and viral pathogens and their hosts, and a few nematodes and insects and their hosts (Thompson 1994). The relationship between the rust, *Melampsora lini*, and its host, *Linum marginale*, discussed earlier, follows this gene-for-gene pattern (Thrall and Burdon 2003).

In other cases, resistance of plants to pathogens has a polygenic basis (Simms 1996). Polygenic systems tend to show continuous variation in degree of resistance by the host to pathogens of a certain degree of pathogenicity. Up to 14 genes with additive effects have been reported in different plants. Resistance of grain plants to several fungi appears to be of this type. Corresponding patterns of virulence of pathogens is poorly understood.

Rust fungi provide some of the most dramatic examples of rapid evolutionary capability. Rust fungi are extraordinarily diverse, consisting of about 5,000 species classified in about 150 genera. Wheat leaf rust (*Puccinia triticina*) and stem rust (*P. graminis*), wheat and barley stripe rust (*P. striiformis*), and oat crown rust (*P. coronata*), together with other cereal grain rusts, have followed their hosts to all parts of the agricultural world. These rusts all show high evolutionary adaptability to grain varieties bearing new patterns of genetic resistance.

Grain rust fungi have very complicated life cycles (Kolmer 1996). The full life cycle of wheat leaf rust, for example, has five stages involving wheat and, in the Old World, a second host plant, meadow rue (*Thalictrum* spp.) (Kolmer and Liu 2000). Diploid teliospores formed on wheat plants in the fall overwinter. These germinate in spring and undergo meiosis, producing haploid basidiospores. Basidiospores engage in a sexual cycle on meadow rue in which different mating types combine and produce aeciospores that contain two haploid nuclei. These spores disperse and infect the primary host, wheat. In wheat, the rust produces masses of urediospores, also containing two haploid nuclei, that can infect other wheat plants in a cycle repeated many times during the growing season. In many areas, including North America, wheat leaf rust does not reproduce sexually but only asexually by means of urediospores. These can be carried by wind over great distances and are responsible for a progression of rust infections that move northward from the southern United States and Mexico into Canada during the spring and summer. In 1981, wind-carried urediospores introduced a virulent strain of *Puccinia triticina* to New

Zealand from somewhere outside the Australasian region (Brown and Hovmøller 2002). At the time, more than 90% of the wheat on the North Island was susceptible to this rust strain.

Wheat stem rust (*Puccinia graminis*) has a similar life cycle, with the usual alternate host being common barberry (*Berberis vulgaris*) in Europe and North America. Some native North American barberries (*Berberis* and *Mahonia* spp.) are occasional alternate hosts. Although the primary host is wheat, varieties of several other small grains, such as barley, oats, and rye, are also susceptible, as is jointed goat grass (*Aegilops cylindrica*), a wild relative of wheat and a common grain field weed. Like wheat leaf rust, stem rust overwinters in southern areas of North America and spreads northward during the growing season for small grains.

Both leaf and stem rusts of wheat have the ability to evolve new virulence races very quickly. The primary strategy for protection of wheat from these rusts has been the breeding of resistant strains of wheat. For wheat leaf rust, about 46 resistance genes, derived from cultivated wheats or their relatives, are now known (Kolmer 2001). These resistance genes tend to correspond to individual virulence genes in the rust. The introduction of a wheat variety with a new resistance gene is typically followed by redevelopment of virulence by the rust within a period of a few years. The origin of increase in virulence appears to be gene mutation during the life cycle phase involving asexual production of urediospores rather than during the sexual phase (Kolmer 2001).

Wheat stem rust, one of the oldest known diseases of cultivated grain, has a similar evolutionary capacity. More than 200 races of this rust are known. New varieties of wheat that are resistant to stem rust are continually under development. As for leaf rust, new races of stem rust can arise quickly, in this case by both mutation and sexual reproduction (Palm 2001).

Stripe rust of wheat and barley (*P. striiformis*) is not known to have an alternate host but does infect many wild native and introduced grasses in North America (Line 2002). This rust, apparently of Asian origin, entered western North America by natural dispersal and infected native grasses prior to European settlement. In the 1800s and early 1900s, it adapted to wheat, barley, and other cultivated grains. Races adapted to cultivated grains are now worldwide in distribution. This rust, although lacking a sexual phase, is highly variable, and many races capable of infecting previously resistant grain varieties have appeared.

Alien rust diseases also infect woody plants. In North America, the most serious rust disease of trees is white pine blister rust (*Cronartium ribi-*

cola). Native to eastern Asia, this disease became established in eastern Europe in the 1800s, apparently by introduction of Asian trees to botanical gardens (Kinloch and Dupper 2002). In Europe, it attacked the eastern white pine (*Pinus strobus*), which is native to North America but had been planted widely. From Europe, it reached North America in about 1900 via importation of white pine seedlings.

The relationship of white pine blister rust virulence to host tree resistance is similar to that of the wheat rusts, except that the host is long-lived (Hoff and McDonald 1993). The rust infects pines by means of spores produced on alternate hosts—currants and gooseberries (*Ribes* spp.). It attacks five-needled pines of the subgenus *Strobus*, to which eastern white pine and several other species belong. The rust probably evolved in eastern Asia, where native members of the subgenus show high resistance to the rust (Liebhold et al. 1996). From there, the rust spread to Europe in the early 1800s and to North America in the early 1900s. Several western pines, especially the whitebark pine (*P. albicaulis*), have been severely affected by this rust (Kinloch et al. 1998; Zeglen 2002).

Evolutionary interaction occurs between white pine blister rust and its hosts. Racial variation exists in the white pine blister rust fungus. At least ten genetic patterns of rust resistance in species of the white pine group have been detected, some of them due to single genes and others to multiple genes. The rust has shown an ability, however, to overcome these resistance systems. In Japan and Canada, strains of the rust differing in their ability to infect secondary host plants have been observed, and infection symptoms on pine hosts also point to the existence of at least four races of the rust (Hoff and McDonald 1993). Rust infections have been observed on several previously resistant forms of western white pine (*Pinus monticola*) and sugar pine (*P. lambertiana*). In 1970, for example, a new rust strain appeared at a site known as Champion Mine in the Umpqua National Forest, Oregon. This strain killed most western white pines at this site, which was previously a site from which resistant tree stock was obtained for propagation. A race of the rust that appeared at Happy Camp, California, in the 1970s also kills formerly resistant sugar pines and has recently begun to spread widely (Kinloch et al. 1998).

Other types of fungi show a similar capacity for rapid evolution. Fungi of the genus *Phytophthora* have followed their hosts to new regions and adopted new hosts. One of the best documented cases in this genus involves *Phytophthora sojae*, a form parasitizing soybean (*Glycine max*) and various species of lupines (*Lupinus* spp.). Thirteen resistance genes are known in soybeans, and many cultivars with one or more of these genes have been produced. Races of *P. sojae* that can overcome these patterns of cultivar resistance arise rapidly, however, and many races of the fungus are known (Forster et al. 1994). More than 200 races of *Phytophthora sojae*, with different combinations of virulence genes, were detected in Ohio soybean fields in the late 1990s, for example (Dorrance et al. 2003). About 20% of these showed combined virulence to ten or more resistance genes in soybean.

In general, for *Phytophthora* fungi, the host-fungus relationship appears to follow a gene-for-gene pattern of resistance and virulence. For the late blight fungus (*P. infestans*), 11 sets of resistance and virulence genes have been discovered in the relationship with plants of the genus *Solanum* (Abu-El Samen et al. 2003a). As we noted in chapter 1, different mating types of the late blight fungus exist. These have the capacity for meiotic recombination, so the spread of a second mating type into areas that formerly possessed only a single mating type threatens to increase the evolutionary potential of the fungus. Genetic forms of the fungus that might have been the result of sexual reproduction were detected in the mid-1990s (Goodwin et al. 1998). In addition, the late blight fungus showed a substantial ability to alter its virulence characteristics during asexual reproduction (Abu-El Samen et al. 2003b).

Many other fungal parasites have shown similar ability to overcome resistance. These include lettuce downy mildew (*Bremia lactucae*), powdery mildew of wheat and barley (*Erysiphe graminis*), barley leaf blotch fungus (*Rhynchosporium secale*), sorghum anthracnose (*Colletotrichum sublinolum*), and rice blast fungus (*Magnaporthe grisea*). Many of these fungi, such as powdery mildew of barley, exhibit different mating types that can allow sexual recombination and promote diversity in virulence patterns (Bousset and de Vallavielle-Pope 2003). Like the situation for the first late blight fungus, these fungi have a substantial evolutionary potential based on the introduction of new strains and complementary mating types to agricultural regions where their various crop hosts are grown. Hybridization among parasitic fungi of the genus *Phytophthora* has given rise to forms adapted to new hosts, as described in chapter 5.

Alien Animal Disease Agents and Their Evolution

Disease agents of animals, particularly viruses, have an enormous capability for rapid evolution. Like plant diseases, these agents are now able to cross geographical barriers in the vehicles of human travel and commerce.

The rabies virus and West Nile virus, disease agents for both animals and humans, are two examples of agents that have invaded new geographical areas and infected new hosts and vectors.

Rabies and related diseases are caused by single-stranded RNA viruses of the genus *Lyssavirus* (Krebs et al. 1995). Rabies in terrestrial mammals, occasionally including humans, is caused by a strain designated Genotype 1. This strain was introduced to Africa and the Americas by infected dogs transported from Europe by early colonists. Because of vaccination programs for domestic animals, however, rabies disease reservoirs in most regions are now in wild mammals.

In North America, raccoons (*Procyon lotor*), foxes (*Vulpes* spp.), skunks (*Mephitis* spp.), and coyotes (*Canis latrans*) are the main terrestrial reservoirs for rabies. These species tend to possess distinct genetic variants of the virus (Krebs et al. 1995). Different variants exist in populations of skunks in north-central and south-central regions of the United States. These strains differ from those in raccoons in eastern states. Strains slightly different from each other are found in foxes in Alaska, Texas, and Arizona. Thus, some evolutionary specialization has occurred since introduction of the virus to North America.

West Nile virus, which appeared in New York City in 1999, is probably also undergoing adaptation to bird species that are vectors for the virus in North America. One of the early signs of the presence of this virus was mortality of large numbers of American crows (*Corvus brachyrhynchos*) and other birds (Rappole et al. 2000). In October 2002, for example, surveys in Lake County, Illinois, where human cases of this viral disease were frequent, revealed greatly reduced populations of crows, jays, and some smaller songbirds (Bonter and Hochachka 2003). In the Old World, heavy mortality of adult birds does not usually accompany outbreaks of West Nile virus infection in humans. North American birds do not appear to be as adapted to the virus as are Old World species. The house sparrow (*Passer domesticus*), an introduced alien native to Europe, may, in fact, be one of the species that has helped disperse the disease because it can carry active virus for a prolonged period (Rappole and Hubálek 2003). Nevertheless, the appearance of the disease in a human resident of Cayman Brac, in the Caribbean Sea, indicates that some long-distance migrant bird is a carrier. Severe declines of wintering North American migrant birds in Costa Rica in winter 2002–03 suggested that these birds may not only have introduced the virus to the neotropics but also suffered heavy mortality (Causey et al. 2003).

Alien Human Diseases and Their Evolution

Vectors and agents of human disease are also subject to rapid evolution in response to many agents of selection. Vectors of disease, ranging from insects to rodents, have evolved resistance to chemical pesticides. Resurgence of human malaria, for example, is due in part to the evolved resistance of *Anopheles* mosquitoes to the insecticide DDT in the 1960s and to pyrethroid insecticides more recently (Hemingway et al. 2002). Disease agents themselves evolve to escape control by modern antibiotics and other drugs. Resistance to the drug chloroquine by three of the four human malaria parasites (*Plasmodium* spp.) has contributed to the resurgence of human malaria (Wellems 2002). The invasion of new geographical areas by strains of many of these disease agents and their vectors is creating opportunities for rapid evolution of new forms of disease.

The influenza virus provides an example of complex, continuing evolution of a disease agent of humans, other mammals, and birds. The original natural reservoir of these viruses is thought to be waterfowl, shorebirds, and gulls. The virus, with an RNA core consisting of ten genes, shows a number of major subtypes that differ in the structure of two surface proteins, hemagglutinin and neuraminidase. Various subtypes based on differences in these proteins have apparently arisen by rapid evolution following the transmission of the virus to other animals, including swine, horses, poultry, and humans.

The influenza virus apparently evolves in two ways. Within each subtype, mutations occur in the hemagglutinin gene, a process known as antigenic drift. These slightly altered forms of the virus enable it to escape strong control by antibodies to former strains of the virus. This requires the creation of new vaccines annually to protect humans. Occasionally, new subtypes that differ to a greater degree in hemagglutinin structure, originating by recombination between different strains in a nonhuman animal host, enter the human population, an event known as antigenic shift. The major human flu pandemics of 1918, 1957, 1968, and 1977 were due to such shifts. The recent year-to-year changes that require new vaccines are the result of antigenic drift.

In 1997, an unusual outbreak of influenza occurred in Hong Kong, killing 6 of the 18 people infected. This virus represented a new subtype that entered the human population from chickens. It possessed a mutant form of a different protein, labeled PB2, which differed in amino acid substitutions at one or two positions (Hatta et al. 2001). This protein is thought to influence the process of virus replication in cells of the host.

Discovery of this form of influenza led public health authorities to order the killing of more than 1 million chickens, perhaps preventing a human pandemic.

The flaviviruses, which include dengue hemorrhagic fever virus, West Nile virus, yellow fever viruses, and several encephalitis viruses, are a highly variable group of about 68 viruses. Many are transmitted by insect vectors.

The virus causing dengue hemorrhagic fever appears to be a relatively recent introduction to human hosts (Twiddy et al. 2003). The dengue flavivirus affects about 50 million people annually in tropical regions, making it the most frequent vector-borne viral disease. The virus has a reservoir in wild primates, and some cases result from transmission of the virus from these primates to humans by *Aedes* mosquitoes native to tropical forest habitats. More frequently, the virus is transmitted from human to human by *Aedes aegypti*, a mosquito that has spread worldwide and typically lives in close association with humans.

Four major strains of the dengue hemorrhagic fever virus exist, designated DEN-1 to DEN-4. These viruses have recently spread widely in tropical and subtropical regions, and the individual strains have become more variable genetically. All four strains of the dengue virus occur in Asia and the New World, but only one has been recorded in Africa (Failloux et al. 2002). Significant evolutionary changes have influenced recent patterns of human disease. The particular variety responsible for explosive outbreaks of dengue in Cuba, Venezuela, and Brazil between 1981 and 1990, for example, appears to have been a newly evolved variant of the DEN-2 virus (Monath 1995). As we noted in chapter 10, strains of the dengue virus show differential association with different forms of the mosquito *Aedes aegypti*.

Molecular genetic studies have now revealed much information about the origin of the dengue virus and its major human disease strains (Twiddy et al. 2003). Based on a molecular clock relationship, these studies suggest that the basic dengue virus originated about 1,115 yr ago. For three of the four strains for which combined human and primate samples were available, the estimated age of divergence ranged from 125 to 320 yr. This would also represent the earliest date for transmission from wild primates to humans. Estimated divergence dates for human-only strains were more recent, ranging from 35 to 215 yr. These dates are considered to be the latest dates for introduction to human hosts from wild primate reservoirs and the approximate dates of epidemic spread within the human population. Thus, the genetic diversification of the dengue virus corresponds closely to the period of rapid growth of human populations, international trade, and urbanization in tropical regions. In fact, the greatest diversification of the virus has occurred within the last century and appears to be continuing at present.

The modern world is ideally suited as an evolutionary stage for viral diseases that are able to move from animal reservoirs to humans. These include the ebola virus of Africa and the SARS (sudden acute respiratory syndrome) corona virus that appeared in China in 2003.

The Responses of Hosts and Vectors

Both plant and animal disease agents are capable of rapid evolution, especially when introduced to new hosts and environments. The spread of such agents to new geographical areas is a major concern for human health, as well as the health of agricultural plants and animals and keystone members of natural ecosystems. As we have indicated several times, however, the relation of disease agents to their hosts is coevolutionary; the host as well as the disease agent is capable of evolution. In the next chapter, we shall examine in more detail the evolutionary responses of plants to alien diseases, as well as to introduced herbivores.

12.

Adaptation of Plants to Alien Herbivores and Diseases

"The ability of a population to respond to phenotypic selection depends on the existence of genetic variation in relevant traits. Genetic variation among host plants may make them differentially preferable to herbivores or influence the ability of the herbivores to use them effectively."

—BYINGTON ET AL. (1994)

The gypsy moth (*Lymantria dispar*) was brought to Massachusetts from France in 1869 to investigate its potential for production of silk. Escaped moths soon created a wild population that caused local outbreaks over a period of years. Beginning in 1905, however, the gypsy moth began to spread westward and southward; it now ranges west to Michigan and south to Virginia. Gypsy moths feed on and defoliate numerous woody plants, with oaks being highly preferred. Repeated defoliation can result in heavy tree mortality and is thus a strong potential selective force.

Byington et al. (1994) examined the variability in growth and mortality of red oak (*Quercus rubra*) seedlings to gypsy moth defoliation. They tested seedlings grown from acorns taken from nine parent trees, none of which had experienced gypsy moth outbreaks. Seedlings were exposed to moth larvae until defoliation was essentially complete. A month later, the seedlings were analyzed. Mortality of defoliated seedlings varied from 0 to 37%. Surviving seedlings varied nearly threefold in the fraction of preexposure foliage that they were able to replace. They also varied in total biomass and portion of biomass allocated to roots at the end of the experiment. Clearly, substantial variation existed among seedlings from different parents, indicating that natural selection based on gypsy moth defoliation might favor rapid development of resistance by red oak.

Mature red oak trees also show substantial differences in constitutive and induced defenses (see below) to gypsy moth feeding (Rossiter et al. 1988). Furthermore, the fecundity and pupal mass of gypsy moths are reduced by high levels of these chemical defenses. Inasmuch as severe, repeated defoliation can kill mature trees, it seems clear that selection for resistance to gypsy moth herbivory is also occurring in mature red oak trees.

Evolutionary Responses by Plants to Herbivory

Native plants are thus very capable of responding to selective pressures introduced by alien herbivores and disease agents (Rausher 2001). This is perhaps not surprising, since in their native region these agents are often associated with related plants that show some resistance to their impacts. General patterns of evolutionary response have in some cases long been known and in others are only now being recognized. The extent of such responses, however, is just beginning to be appreciated.

Plants have three major modes of evolutionary response to herbivory that reduces their reproductive performance (Levin 1976). One response mode is deterrence: the production of constitutive or induced defenses, that is, morphological or chemical traits that prevent or reduce damage by herbivores. Constitutive defenses are those produced by the plant as normal products of growth and development, whereas induced defenses are structural or chemical responses of plants to tissue damage by herbivore feeding. These responses require the allocation of photosynthetic production to defenses rather than to growth and reproduction, so a trade-off between defense and other components of fitness is expected. In one of the best-studied systems, that of wild parsnip (*Pastinaca sativa*) and the parsnip webworm (*Depressaria pastinacella*), chemical defenses and seed production show a negative relationship, indicating that protection against the webworm has a fitness cost (Berenbaum et al. 1986).

The capacity for both constitutive and induced responses is genetically based, but induced defenses require the allocation of resources only if damage occurs. Both constitutive and induced defenses can be modified by natural selection (Agrawal et al. 2002a; Zangerl 2003). Theoretical analyses have shown that induced defenses are probably more difficult for herbivores to overcome (Gardner and Agrawal 2002). This advantage, together with reduced resource allocation needs, contributes to increased plant fitness. The effectiveness of deterrence, either constitutive or induced, can be measured as the reproductive performance of defended plants in the presence of herbivores relative to their performance in the absence of herbivores.

A second defense mode is development of tolerance—mechanisms that compensate for damage caused by herbivory (McNaughton 1983). Mechanisms of compensation include a high intrinsic growth rate, increase in photosynthetic production after herbivory, increased branching or tillering after herbivory, storage of photosynthate in roots or other organs protected from herbivory, and transfer of stored photosynthate to portions of the plant damaged by herbivory (Strauss and Agrawal 1999). In some cases, plants that have been damaged by herbivores experience reduced competition due to herbivore consumption of surrounding vegetation. Thus, selection may favor the ability for rapid use of nutrients made available in a low-competition environment (Westoby 1989). Tolerance, like deterrence, requires investments in structural and physiological mechanisms related to the above processes. For plants emphasizing tolerance, compensation can also be measured as the reduction in reproductive performance of plants exposed to herbivory relative to those protected from herbivory.

Deterrence and tolerance of herbivory are not mutually exclusive strategies, however (Mauricio et al. 1997). Many plant species exhibit genetic variability in traits related both to deterrence and to tolerance. Thus, how selection will act is likely to depend on the precise nature and location of herbivore impact—root or shoot, internal or external, tissue or vascular fluid consumption. The action of natural selection may also be constrained by external factors such as nutrient availability as it relates to compensatory growth and seasonal patterns of availability of pollinators (Stowe et al. 2000).

The degree to which compensation for herbivory on individual plants is possible has been the subject of considerable controversy. This controversy, still active, has centered on whether or not the interaction between an herbivore and a plant can be mutualistic, with the harvest of plant tissue both benefiting the herbivore and increasing the growth or evolutionary fitness of the plant. The hypothesized result of such mutualism is overcompensation, in which the plant realizes greater growth or fitness when grazed or browsed than when protected against herbivory. Many early studies did not strictly address this question or did not consider all aspects of plant growth and reproduction. Belsky (1986) and Belsky et al. (1993) concluded that the evidence for overcompensation in nature was lacking.

More recently, theoretical analyses have suggested that herbivory might alter the architecture of a plant so as to improve its capacity for reproductive success, so the interaction between a plant and herbivore could be mutualistic (Simons and Johnson 1999). In addition, herbivory concentrated on plants of certain size might also select for compensation capability, and in some cases, overcompensation. Thus, overcompensation appears to be possible under various circumstances.

Since the review by Belsky (1986), overcompensation has been demonstrated in some plants, primarily the biennial herbs scarlet gilia (*Ipomopsis aggregata*) (see, e.g., Paige 1992) and field gentian (*Gentianella campestris*) (see, e.g., Lennartsson et al. 1998). In both cases, removal of plant tissue tended to increase the branching pattern of plant growth, resulting in increased numbers of flowering branches and flowers. In the case of field gentian, the timing of plant tissue removal was critical, and the degree of compensation varied from year to year. These studies seemed to indicate that complete compensation or overcompensation can occur under some circumstances, especially for plants that have evolved under a regime of heavy grazing, but also that overcompensation is not a common phenomenon.

A third mode of plant defense is indirect defense, the development of traits that attract enemies of herbivores (Kessler and Baldwin 2002). Indirect defenses include structures such as extrafloral nectaries that attract predatory arthropods, hollow thorns or stems that provide living sites for colonies of such predators, and volatile organic compounds that act as attractants for predators. Plants belonging to at least 66 families produce extrafloral nectaries, which have been shown in several cases to attract predatory arthropods that reduce damage by herbivores. Volatile organic substances are released when plant tissues are damaged by herbivores. These substances, varied in chemical nature, have been shown to attract predators and parasitoids, but the degree to which this mechanism increases plant fitness is still uncertain.

Evolutionary Responses of Herbaceous Plants to Alien Herbivorous Invertebrates

Few studies of the evolutionary response of plants to herbivorous invertebrates have been attempted. The small spring annual, *Arabidopsis thaliana*, native to Europe and Asia, was introduced to eastern North America in the mid-1800s and is now widely distributed. This species has become a model system for studying many aspects of genetics in relation to physiology, plant-microbe relationships, and plant-herbivore interactions. Many of the herbivorous insects with which it now interacts are alien species in either Europe or North America. Many ecotypes of *A. thaliana* have been obtained from locations around the world. The genome of two of the commonly used ecotypes has been sequenced, and it is apparent that great variation exists at the DNA sequence level.

Jander et al. (2001) examined feeding on *A. thaliana* by the cabbage looper (*Trichoplusia ni*), a generalist lepidopteran native to North America but introduced to Europe. They found that ecotypes of *A. thaliana* varied greatly in resistance to the cabbage looper, with some being virtually untouched whereas others were eaten to the ground. Ecotypes from central Asia tended to be highly resistant to cabbage loopers. In addition, some portion of the resistance appeared to be induced, as demonstrated by the loopers' tendency to prefer undamaged leaves over those that had been experimentally damaged. Resistance is apparently controlled by an allele at a locus on Chromosome 1 of *A. thaliana*, but the physiological basis of this resistance is still unknown.

Mauricio and Rausher (1997), also working with *A. thaliana*, examined selection for two constitutive traits of the annual plant. They noted that ecotypes of this plant vary genetically in two characters: concentration of glucosinolates and density of trichomes. Glucosinolates are organic compounds found in many plants of the cabbage family (Brassicaceae). These compounds are unpalatable or toxic to many arthropods and vertebrates. In a field experiment, *A. thaliana* plants from different families were grown in locations where they were exposed to or protected from herbivorous arthropods and fungal pathogens. Results showed that natural selection influenced both defensive characteristics. In plants that were protected from natural enemies, glucosinolate concentration and trichome density tended to decline. In plants exposed to enemies, both constitutive traits were maintained. Thus, it is likely that natural selection acts quickly in natural populations of *A. thaliana* to adjust these defenses to the intensity of influence of natural enemies. This experiment thus strongly supported the concept that constitutive defenses have an appreciable cost.

Similarly, Shonle and Bergelson (2000), working with jimson weed (*Datura stramonium*) in Illinois, found that the concentrations of two alkaloids in leaf tissues were influenced by selection by a combination of specialist and generalist herbivores. This plant, native to Mexico, has apparently spread northward into the United States since European settlement as an agricultural weed. In Illinois, it is attacked by specialist insects associated with it in Mexico and with several generalist insect herbivores, including the Japanese beetle (*Popilia japonica*). Experimental plantings of jimson weed in open field environments showed that herbivory by these insects has a stabilizing influence on the concentration of one alkaloid while tending to reduce the concentration of the second (Shonle and Bergelson 2000).

Evolutionary Responses of Herbaceous Plants to Grazing Animals

The worldwide introduction of domestic grazing animals native to Eurasia has had strong evolutionary impacts on native plants, especially grasses, adapted to other herbivores. In North America, prolonged grazing by various mammals, both native and alien, has been shown to select for low or prostrate ecotypes of many perennial grasses, including species of *Bouteloua* (Smith 1998), *Cenchrus* (McKinney and Fowler 1991), *Schizachryium* (Carman and Briske 1985), *Stipa* (Peterson 1962), and others. Several introduced pasture grasses (Kemp 1937; Hickey 1961) also show ecotypic responses to long-term grazing by livestock. On the other hand, some North American native grasses, including mountain muhly (*Muhlenbergia montana*) and Indian rice grass (*Oryzopsis hymenoides*), show low growth forms that are phenotypic responses to grazing but do not have a genetic basis (Quinn and Miller 1967; Trlica and Orodho 1989).

Detailed studies on a few North American perennial grasses have shown that genetic mechanisms of tolerance are important responses to long-term grazing by introduced livestock animals. Carman and Briske (1985), for example, compared little bluestem (*Schizachryium scoparium*) plants from six sites, three of which had been protected from grazing for many years (56 yr for one site, 128 for two others) and three of which had a long history of grazing by livestock and bison. Plants from these sites were grown under identical greenhouse conditions for 10 months and then subjected to five episodes of clipping at 2-wk intervals, simulating intense grazing. At the time of the first clipping treatment, plants from the areas of long-term grazing had shorter, narrower leaves, and smaller tillers than the plants from ungrazed areas, indicating that genetic differences existed (table 12.1). When clipping was done to reduce the plants to a height of 6 cm, more biomass per tiller was removed from plants from the grazed areas because of their lower overall height. During the clipping episodes, plants from grazed areas produced more new tillers and, at the end of the clipping sequence, showed a greater number of tillers that

Table 12.1. Characteristics of little bluestem (*Schizachyrium scoparium*) plants from three areas in Kansas where plants from grazing exclosures could be compared to those exposed to grazing by domestic animals. Comparisons were of plants grown under identical controlled conditions for 10 months. (Data from Carman and Briske 1985.)

Population	Total plant biomass (mg)	Number of tillers (>6 cm)	Biomass per tiller (mg)	Leaf blade length (cm)
KANSAS STATE UNIVERSITY				
Grazed	707	18.9	46	17.6
Ungrazed	734	14.1	66	18.4
FORT RILEY #1				
Grazed	460	12.6	40	17.1
Ungrazed	961	12.8	87	20.1
FORT RILEY #2				
Grazed	663	15.2	53	18.3
Ungrazed	783	12.8	65	20.3

regrew after being clipped. The weight of leaves per unit area was less for regrowth leaves of plants from the grazed sites.

Thus, little bluestem plants with a long grazing history showed a modified growth form in which a greater proportion of their biomass was close to the ground surface. In addition, in direct response to removal of tissue by grazing, tillering pattern and carbon investment in leaf regrowth were modified.

A second recent study examined the responses of side-oats grama (*Bouteloua curtipendula*), another perennial grass, to livestock grazing (Smith 1998). Smith compared plants from atop a small mesa, inaccessible to large animals, near Tucson, Arizona, with plants from a nearby site that had been grazed regularly since 1900. Plants from both sites were acclimatized to greenhouse conditions for more than a year, during which they were clipped at 6-wk intervals. The plants were then divided into three groups and subjected to clipping at 2-, 4-, or 8-wk intervals for 24 wk. Differences in tillering pattern were apparent. Overall, plants from the regularly grazed area possessed more tillers than those from the ungrazed area at the time of final clipping. Plants from the regularly grazed area also maintained a greater number of tillers relative to the number present at the beginning of the experimental treatments throughout the 4- and 8-

wk clipping sequences. Interestingly, although the leaves of plants from the regularly grazed area were held more toward horizontal under the 8- and 4-wk clipping regimes, those of plants from the ungrazed area were held toward horizontal under the 2-wk clipping regime. Thus, plants from the ungrazed area showed greater plasticity of growth in response to different intensities of grazing.

Nevertheless, both studies (Carman and Briske 1985; Smith 1998) document adaptations and responses that show that tolerance is a major mechanism of adaptation of perennial grasses to grazing. In these responses, however, native North American species are probably not greatly different from Eurasian species. Both of the above studies suggest that perennial grasses tend to possess a range of genotypes that permit many species to adjust to major ecological pressures that characterize the grassland environment, such as grazing, fire, and drought.

Adaptability of perennial grasses to impacts of ungulate grazers is especially evident in the North American Great Plains, where bison (*Bison bison*) and other ungulates were abundant in pre-European time. Evolutionary adaptability in growth form and silicon content of foliage is also shown by various perennial grasses of the Great Plains in response to grazing by prairie dogs (*Cynomys* spp.) (see, e.g., Brizuela et al. 1986; Detling and Painter 1983; Painter et al. 1989; Polley and Detling 1990). In the intermontane region farther west, as well as in the central valley of California, dominant perennials before European settlement were cespitose grasses that were vulnerable not only to grazing but to damage by trampling (Mack and Thompson 1982). Grasslands dominated by cespitose species also occurred in several other world regions, such as New Zealand. In these areas, the introduction of domestic ungulates in large numbers has resulted not in selection for growth forms tolerant of ungulate impacts but instead the extensive replacement of perennial bunchgrasses by alien annual species.

A number of broad-leafed herbaceous plants also show evolutionary adaptation to grazing by livestock. One of the most adaptable species is the ribwort plantain (*Plantago lanceolata*), a species native to Eurasia but now cosmopolitan in distribution. This species exhibits a basal rosette of leaves and a number of naked flowering stalks. In the Netherlands, populations of ribwort plantain in pasture habitats tend to possess shorter leaves, smaller and more numerous flowering stalks, and more vegetative daughter rosettes than plants in ungrazed habitats (Van der Toorn and Van Tienderen 1992). A number of other weedy broad-leafed herbs, such as shepherd's purse (*Capsella bursa-pastoris*), also show similar ecotypic responses to grazing and trampling (see, e.g., Neuffer and Meyer-Wolff 1996).

Evolutionary Responses of Woody Plants to Alien Herbivores

Several alien insects have had enormous impacts on many native North American shrubs and trees. These include Japanese beetles (*Popilia japonica*) as adults on many fruit trees and larvae of the gypsy moth (*Lymantria dispar*) on many species, particularly oaks (*Quercus* spp.) and poplars (*Populus* spp.). Differences in susceptibility to Japanese beetle exist among various taxa and cultivars of birches (*Betula* spp.), elms (*Ulmus* spp.), and various fruit trees (Potter and Held 2002). Several studies have shown that some oaks and poplars vary genetically in vulnerability to gypsy moth herbivory. As we noted at the beginning of the chapter, one of these species is red oak (Byington et al. 1994). Red oak also tends to show local adaptation to site conditions, with the patterns of adaptation conferring resistance to leaf-feeding herbivores (Sork et al. 1993). In experimental studies, seedlings were more resistant to herbivory when grown on the same slope aspect as their parental trees than when transplanted to slopes of differing aspect.

Trembling aspen (*Populus tremuloides*) is one of the poplars frequently attacked by the gypsy moth. Aspen is also subject to outbreaks of native tent caterpillars (*Malacosoma disstria*). Aspen clones show great variation in the concentration of constitutive secondary compounds, particularly phenolic glycosides and condensed tannins (Hemming and Lindroth 1995). The degree of defoliation of different aspen clones during insect outbreaks also varies greatly (Hwang and Lindroth 1997).

Experimental studies (Osier et al. 2000) have shown major differences in survival and growth of gypsy moth caterpillars on different aspen clones. Survival of second-instar caterpillars, for example, varied from about 45 to 95% on 13 clones taken from Wisconsin and Colorado and grown in a common garden. These differences were negatively correlated with the concentrations of phenolic glycosides in the aspen foliage. The aspen clones most resistant to gypsy moth herbivory, and containing the highest concentrations of phenolic glycosides, showed the lowest growth rates. These results suggested that major genetic variation in herbivore resistance exists in aspen and that there is a considerable trade-off between herbivore defense and growth. Comparing the results for gypsy moths with those for native lepidopterans that feed on aspen suggested that gypsy moths were more sensitive to phenolic glycoside defenses than were the native species (Hwang and Lindroth 1998; Osier et al. 2000). Other studies also showed that the chemical variation of aspen tissues had little influence on a nuclear polyhedrosis virus that is a gypsy moth pathogen (Lindroth et al. 1999).

In a similar study, Havill and Raffa (1999) found that clones of various *Populus* hybrids varied genetically in both constitutive and inducible resistance to feeding by gypsy moth larvae. Growth of gypsy moth larvae was 30 times faster on the least resistant clones than on those most resistant, and their consumption of leaf biomass was 250 times greater on the least resistant clones. Inducible resistance of some clones was very strong, whereas other clones showed little or none. The potential for evolutionary response of *Populus* species to gypsy moth defoliation is thus clearly appreciable over the long run.

Despite the massive impact of alien herbivorous vertebrates on woody vegetation in locations such as New Zealand (Campbell 1990), Hawaii (Stone 1985), and the Galapagos Islands (Schofield 1989), clear evidence for evolutionary response by woody plants is still lacking. In New Zealand, where tree fuchsia (*Fuchsia excorticata*) has nearly been eliminated in some areas with introduced brushtail possums (*Trichosurus vulpecula*), but not in other areas with this mammal, a genetic difference in palatability has been postulated (Freeland and Winter 1975). Preliminary studies by Sweetapple and Nugent (1999), however, could not confirm such a difference.

Evolutionary Responses of Plants to Alien Diseases

Trees and shrubs typically show genetic variation in response to alien diseases, even severe diseases such as chestnut blight (*Cryphonectria parasitica*) and Dutch elm disease (*Ophiostoma ulmi*). Various species and varieties of members of the genus *Cornus* also show markedly different patterns of susceptibility to dogwood anthracnose (*Discula destructiva*) (Brown et al. 1996). For species such as the American elm (*Ulmus americana*), individuals showing some resistance have been used as a basis for artificial selection in an effort to create fully resistant varieties. The so-called "liberty elm," for example, is a highly resistant American elm developed in this manner (Smalley et al. 1993).

In California, Monterey pines (*Pinus radiata*) are being attacked by pitch canker (*Fusarium circinatum*), an alien fungal disease that appeared in the state in the 1980s (Gordon et al. 2001). This disease first appeared in the southeastern United States in 1946. It appears to be native to central Mexico and is now affecting various native North American pines in the southeastern United States and in California. Resistant Monterey pines have been identified in some stands that have been affected by the canker disease.

As we noted in chapter 11, the sudden oak death fungus (*Phytophthora ramorum*) appeared in California in 1995. It spread into Oregon in 2001 and has also been found in nurseries and gardens in several European countries. The geographic origin of this fungus, however, still remains unknown. Differential resistance appears to exist to the sudden oak death fungus in coast live oak (*Quercus agrifolia*) along the Pacific coast of North America (Dodd et al. 2002). The distribution of trees with sudden oak death symptoms is patchy where the disease occurs, and the disease itself appears to be absent in many parts of the range of coast live oak. Oak shoots from southern California also appear to show some resistance to experimental infection, compared to those from central and northern California. Genetic variation also appears to exist in susceptibility of California bay laurel (*Umbellularia californica*) to the sudden oak death fungus (Hüberli et al. 2002). This species appears to be a critical vector for the spread of the fungus. Many other trees and shrubs carry mild foliar infections of the fungus, however, so its impacts and evolutionary future are difficult to predict.

Also as noted in chapter 11, several members of the white pine group exhibit genetic variation in resistance to white pine blister rust (*Cronartium ribicola*) (Kinloch and Dupper 2002). These include sugar pine (*Pinus lambertiana*), western white pine (*P. monticola*), southwestern white pine (*P. strobiformis*), and limber pine (*P. flexilis*). The genetic system involves a gene-for-gene relationship between the host tree and the rust. Host trees are homozygous resistant (RR), heterozygous (Rr), or homozygous sensitive (rr). Trees carrying the resistance allele (R) respond to rust infection with a hypersensitive reaction of cells surrounding the infection locus. These cells collapse and die, forming a barrier that prevents spread of the infection (Kinloch 1992). Efforts to breed fully resistant varieties of western pines, based on this resistance gene and other genetic factors, are underway in several laboratories (see, e.g., Bingham 1983).

The selective impacts of blister rust on pines may also influence overall genetic variability of the affected tree species. For western white pine, for example, trees from stands that had been heavily affected by blister rust showed lower genetic polymorphism and heterozygosity than trees in lightly affected stands (Kim et al. 2003). On the other hand, western white pines that survived the blister rust outbreak at the Champion Mine site in Oregon showed a several hundredfold increase in frequency of a gene for blister rust resistance (Kinloch et al. 2003). The selective effect of this rust outbreak was thus enormous.

The incidence of resistance genes to white pine blister rust is unexpectedly high in many populations of several of the pines in western North America, being one, two, or more orders of magnitude greater than expected by mutation alone (Kinloch and Dupper 2002). In sugar pine, the frequency of the resistant gene varies greatly over the range of the species. In much of Oregon, at the northern edge of the range, and in Baja California, Mexico, at the southern edge, incidence is zero. In the southern Sierra Nevada and the Transverse ranges of California, however, the incidence reaches 6.6–8.2%. In most locations, the frequencies of genotypes are those expected under the Hardy-Weinberg equilibrium. In some stands heavily affected by blister rust, however, selection appeared to be acting to increase incidence of the resistance allele above Hardy-Weinberg expectation (Kinloch 1992). In western white pine, a higher general frequency of the resistance gene also exists in the Sierra Nevada of California (Kinloch et al. 2003).

The substantial frequency of resistance among the several pines noted above is difficult to explain. All of these pines, however, occur in environments where singleleaf pinyon (*Pinus monophylla*) and Colorado pinyon (*P. edulis*) occur nearby on drier sites. These pines are often infected by pinyon pine blister rust (*Cronartium occidentale*), a close relative of white pine blister rust. Although this rust does not now attack five-needled western pines, infection can be induced artificially (Kinloch and Dupper 2002). Thus, it appears that the incidence of resistance in western pines may reflect past interaction between these pines and *C. occidentale* or a closely related form of rust, perhaps during the late Pleistocene when sugar pines and singleleaf pinyons grew in closer association.

In the case of the American chestnut, breeding programs have both sought to find resistance within the American chestnut (*Castanea dentata*) and to introduce genetic resistance from Asian relatives that are highly resistant to the disease. Hybridization with the Chinese chestnut (*C. mollisima*) and backcrossing with the American chestnut has resulted in a blight-resistant tree with characteristics close to the American chestnut (Griffin 2000). Recent studies (Rieske et al. 2003) suggested, however, that these chestnut trees may be more susceptible to gypsy moth herbivory than are pure American chestnuts. Efforts have also been made to introduce a strain of the disease fungus with low virulence to surviving

American chestnuts, based on observations in Europe that such strains tended to displace those of high virulence (see, e.g., Grente and Bertthelay-Sauret 1978).

Altogether, these studies demonstrate that plant species tend to show genetic variability to most disease agents, even those that have been introduced to new regions. Strong selection for increased resistance appears likely in most cases and is slowed only by the long generation time of many species of shrubs and trees.

Adaptation by Plants and by Herbivores

Native plants have considerable potential for evolutionary adaptation to introduced herbivores and diseases. For grasses, in particular, rapid evolutionary adjustments can be seen, but for longer lived woody plants, this potential is slow to be realized. As we shall see in the next chapter, adaptation by native herbivores to introduced plants is much more dramatic.

13.

Adaptation of Native Herbivores to Alien Plants

"An ecological genetics approach to the study of herbivorous insects has revealed highly significant genetic variation in characters associated with host plant exploitation. In some cases, as much variability can be seen within single populations as within the species as a whole. In other cases, populations are highly locally adapted to different host plants."

—VIA (1990)

In western Nevada, Edith's checkerspot butterfly (*Euphydryas editha*) occurs in isolated populations where various native plant hosts are available. At Schneider's Meadow in the Sierra Nevadas of Esmeralda County, the native host plant is *Collinsia parviflora*, a member of the figwort family (Scrophulariaceae). With the advent of cattle ranching to the mountain country, ribwort plantain (*Plantago lanceolata*), belonging to the plantain family (Plantaginaceae), became a prominent member of the meadow plant community. This European broad-leafed herb has become almost ubiquitous in meadow and disturbed grassland habitats throughout North America.

At Schneider's Meadow, Edith's checkerspot began to lay eggs on ribwort plantain when it appeared (Thomas et al. 1987). Checkerspots from populations in areas without ribwort plantain, in fact, contain about 10% of individuals that accept ribwort plantain as readily as *Collinsia* (Singer et al. 1993). At Schneider's Meadow, however, the oviposition preference for ribwort plantain increased from less then 10% in 1982 to more than 50%

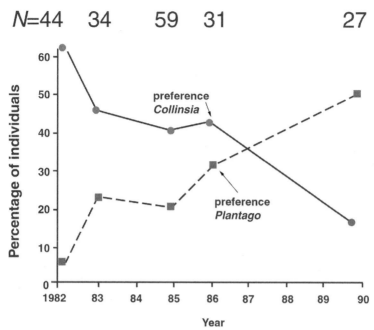

Figure 13.1. Percentage of female Edith's checkerspot butterflies selecting the alien plant *Plantago lanceolata* (■)and the native host plant *Collinsia parviflora* (●) at Schneider's Meadow, Esmeralda County, Nevada, from 1982 through 1990. (Reprinted with permission from M. C. Singer, C. D. Thomas, and C. Parmesan. 1993. Rapid human-induced evolution of insect-host associations. *Nature* 366:681–683. © 1993 Nature Publishing Group.)

in 1990 (fig. 13.1). Greenhouse-reared checkerspots showed this same preference trend, strongly indicating that the preference shift was genetic. In addition, by 1990, individual checkerspots were found that completely rejected their ancestral *Collinsia* host, refusing to oviposit on *Collinsia* even when confined with the plant for several days. In California, populations of Edith's checkerspot in many coastal grassland areas have apparently made a switch to ribwort plantain, as well (Thomas and Singer 1998).

Preferences of female checkerspots for ribwort plantain are also correlated with success of their larvae on this plant. The stronger the preference of the female for ribwort plantain, the faster was the growth of offspring on plantain (Singer et al. 1988). Ribwort plantain, a perennial, remains green throughout the summer, whereas *Collinsia*, an annual, dies by midsummer. Therefore, larval survival is much higher on ribwort plantain (Singer et al. 1994). Thus, preference for an alien plant was coupled with an increased fitness of individual checkerspots selecting this plant. Clearly, an evolutionary shift from a native plant to an alien had occurred.

Host Shifts by Generalist and Specialist Herbivores

The massive introduction of plants to new continents has made a vast number of new hosts available to native herbivores. In California, for example, more than a third of the native butterfly species have been reported to oviposit or feed on alien plants (Graves and Shapiro 2003). We shall examine the accumulation of native herbivores by alien plants in detail in chapter 15.

Herbivores have a wide range of potential tactics that can be used and refined by evolution to permit the use of new host plants (Karban and Agrawal 2002). These include changes in oviposition behavior, morphology, feeding behavior, and physiology by the herbivores themselves. Herbivores can also manipulate the physiology of host plants, as in the induction of gall tissues. Many adjustments to new plant hosts can occur without genetic change, but others can be partly or completely genetic in basis. In fact, genetic variability for host acceptance probably exists in most herbivorous insects (Jaenike 1990).

Generalist herbivores have accepted many alien plants without showing evolutionary shifts. For example, larvae of several of the large Saturniid moths, which use 40 or more genera of food plants, have begun to feed on the alien purple loosestrife (*Lythrum salicaria*) in New York (Barbour and Kiviat 1997). In Arizona, the bruchid seed beetle, *Stator limbatus*, has begun to feed on Texas ebony (*Chloroleucon ebano*), a shrub now widely planted in urban areas, despite the fact that it does not feed on this plant in Texas (Fox and Savalli 2000). Since both the plant and the beetle occur together in Texas, a genetic difference in host plant acceptance between Texas and Arizona beetles seems likely. The valley pocket gopher (*Thomomys bottae*), a generalist feeder on native plants, also uses a wide range of alien grasses and forbs in California coastal grasslands (Hunt 1992) and throughout its range in western North America. Nevertheless, as we have noted, the lag time in utilization of alien plants by native herbivores may be a major factor contributing to the initial success of many invasive alien plants (see chapter 7). For some alien plants, on the other hand, barriers to utilization by native herbivores are very strong. Prickly pear cacti (*Opuntia* spp.), naturalized in parts of Australia and South Africa for 150–250 yr or longer, are still not used by any native tissue-feeding insects (Moran 1980).

Specialist herbivores, primarily insects and other arthropods, have, however, also shown host shifts to many alien plants. Many of the host shifts that were first identified involve the use by native herbivores of introduced crop plants. Recently, several cases have been noted in which native insects have begun to concentrate their feeding on other types of invasive alien plants. A genetic basis for most of these shifts is not yet evident, but for many, the possibility of a genetic basis is being recognized.

Bowers et al. (1992), for example, examined the shift of the Baltimore checkerspot butterfly (*Euphydryas phaeton*), a close relative of Edith's checkerspot, to ribwort plantain in New York State. The native host of the Baltimore checkerspot is turtlehead or balmony (*Chelone glabra*), a member of the family Scrophulariaceae. Ribwort plantain, introduced from Europe in the late 1700s or early 1800s, has become a common weed of disturbed, open habitats in New York. Recently, however, the Baltimore checkerspot has begun to feed on ribwort plantain extensively as a host. Ribwort plantain, belonging to a different plant family than turtlehead, the Plantaginaceae, contains chemicals known as iridoid glycosides that are similar to those present in turtlehead. These chemicals are stored in tissues of the butterfly, making the butterfly unpalatable to vertebrate predators, although butterflies reared on plantain appear to have much lower levels of iridoid glycosides. Some populations of Baltimore checkerspots now reproduce exclusively on ribwort plantain. Laboratory studies of adult and larval preferences (Bowers et al. 1992), however, showed that turtlehead is still preferred and that growth is faster on this native host. Some benefits may exist for butterflies that use plantain, the most likely being escape from parasitoid insects. In addition, abundance of the native host plant, turtlehead, is declining, whereas plantain is flourishing. Thus, although no evidence yet exists for genetic specialization of Baltimore checkerspots for plantain, the potential for such adaptation exists. Several butterflies have also expanded their host use from native legumes to introduced legumes (Barbour and Kiviat 1997). Continued investigation will certainly reveal many more cases of this sort.

In western Europe, a native budworm, *Choristoneura murinana*, attacks silver fir (*Abies alba*) and several other native conifers (Du Merle et al. 1992). With the widespread introduction of exotic conifers from North America, North Africa, and eastern Europe, this lepidopteran species has broadened both its host range and its geographical range. In some cases, these new hosts are more favorable to larval development than silver fir, their original primary host. Thus, the expansion of host and geographic range increases the potential of *Choristoneura* to become a serious forest pest.

Theory relating to patterns of specialization of herbivorous insects has received considerable attention from insect ecologists because of its relevance to pest evolution, and therefore, pest management. Many pest insects exhibit biotypes, which are ecologically or genetically distinct forms adapted to particular hosts (Futuyma and Peterson 1985). To ecologists, biotypes that are genetically distinct are simply ecotypes for which the habitat and food resource are specific plants. Different biotypes may vary, however, in degree of reproductive isolation. Some may be capable of interbreeding freely when they come in contact; others may be reproductively isolated, so they do not come in contact or do not interbreed if they do. Biotypes that show reproductive isolation are effectively distinct species, whether or not they are so classified.

Given that an herbivorous species uses two or more host plants, selection can favor the evolution of distinct biotypes under certain conditions. First, some advantage of specialization for specific plant hosts must exist. That is, adaptation to plant features that influence growth, survivorship, and reproduction must be possible. Second, there must be genetic variability on which selection can act. For many native herbivores, genetic variability may be greater than that for alien herbivores that may have experienced a genetic bottleneck during the introduction process (see chapter 3). Third, the dispersion of plant hosts in space or time must be such that gene flow between populations of the herbivore on different plant hosts does not overwhelm the influence of selection. Plant hosts may differ in the habitats occupied, resulting in reduced movement of individual herbivores between areas with the different hosts. Alternatively, the phenology of flowering or fruiting of the different hosts may be such that individuals of the herbivore become isolated in time. When spatial or temporal isolation is only moderate, a degree of specialization may result, but interbreeding may prevent full specialization of populations for different plant hosts. When isolation is strong, selection may eventually lead to strong reproductive isolation and speciation.

If a new potential host plant becomes intermixed in a plant community with host plants already used by an herbivore, selection may favor expansion of the feeding niche to include the new host plant. Accessory benefits of a host plant shift may involve reduced predation or parasitism by specialist enemies associated with the native host plant.

Evolutionary Adaptation of Native Herbivorous Insects to Introduced Crop Plants

The Colorado potato beetle (*Leptinotarsa decemlineata*) is a native North American insect whose original host appears to have been buffalo bur (*Solanum rostratum*), a spiny broad-leafed herb of the potato family (Solanaceae) occurring from Mexico north into the southwestern United States (Harrison 1987). Buffalo bur itself may have been native to southern Mexico, and, when it was introduced to more northern areas by early Spanish settlers, the beetle may have followed this host plant (Hsiao 1978). In the southwestern United States, the Colorado potato beetle uses other native species of solanaceous plants, such as silver-leaf nightshade (*Solanum eleagnifolium*) and hoe nightshade (*S. sarrachoides*). When the closely related cultivated potato (*Solanum tuberosum*) was introduced to the United States in the early 1800s, it was quickly adopted as a host by the beetle, which acquired its name from the new association. It has also become a serious pest of tomato (*Lycopersicon esculentum*), a member of the same plant family.

The new hosts of the Colorado potato beetle have enabled an enormous expansion of its geographic range. In many areas, the beetle now occurs where its ancestral host plants are absent. Genetically distinct host races have developed on a number of native and cultivated solanaceous plants (Hsiao 1978, 1982). To determine the extent of adaptation to new hosts, Harrison (1987) conducted a series of feeding preference tests with beetles obtained from native hosts in Arizona, potato plants in Alberta, Canada, and tomato plants in Maryland. Beetles from all populations were given the choice of buffalo bur, silver-leaf nightshade, potato, and tomato. Beetles that had developed on native plants in Arizona showed high preference for the two native host plants but low preference for potato and tomato. Beetles from Alberta and Maryland showed high preferences for all plants, both the native host and crop plants. Since the tests were done on newly emerged beetles from laboratory cultures, these results indicated strongly that genetic adjustments had been made by the Alberta and Maryland populations. The change was an expansion of host range, rather than a shift, however, since all beetles retained a high preference for the ancestral hosts.

In another study on the Colorado potato beetle, Horton et al. (1988) examined growth and survival of beetles on buffalo bur, hoe nightshade, and potato in Colorado. Success of the beetle appeared to reflect the local abundance of the three host plants. Where all three were common, performance was best on hoe nightshade. Where only buffalo bur and potato were common, beetles reared on hoe nightshade performed poorly, with mortality of almost 70%. Thus, some genetic differentiation of potato beetle populations for their most common hosts seemed to exist. As we noted in chapter 9, as a result of its expanded geographical distribution, this beetle has adapted genetically to another native solanaceous plant in the eastern United States.

A slightly different situation is illustrated by the shift of the common sulfur butterfly (*Colias philodice*) from native legume plants to alfalfa (*Medicago sativa*). When alfalfa was introduced to Colorado in the late 1800s, the common sulfur began to use it as a host in areas of alfalfa cultivation (Tabashnik 1983a). In localities without alfalfa cultivation, common sulfur butterflies have maintained their traditional host relationships. Studies of preference, larval growth, and survival on native host plants and alfalfa revealed that some divergence of populations in alfalfa-growing and non-alfalfa-growing areas has occurred (Tabashnik 1983b). All populations are able to use both native and crop host plants. Sulfur butterfly larvae from alfalfa areas showed greater survival and faster growth to pupation on alfalfa than on native legume hosts. Larvae from areas without alfalfa showed greater survivorship and heavier pupal weights on native hosts than on alfalfa. Nevertheless, no preference of the alfalfa butterflies for oviposition on alfalfa rather than native hosts was evident (Tabashnik 1983b). Thus, a degree of differentiation in genetic adaptation was evident, but all populations were able to use both ancestral and recently adopted crop host plants.

Perhaps the evolutionary shift that has progressed furthest is that of the apple maggot fly (*Rhagoletis pomonella*) from native hawthorns (*Crataegus* spp.) to introduced apple (*Malus sylvestris*) (Bush 1969; McPheron et al. 1988). This fly may also use dogwood (*Cornus florida*) as a native host (Smith 1988), although these populations may be a distinct species (Feder et al. 1998). The apple maggot fly first began to attack domestic apple trees in the mid-1800s. Studies in the 1980s showed that populations of the fly on hawthorns and apple were genetically differentiated but not completely reproductively isolated (Feder et al. 1988; McPheron et al. 1988). Behavioral differences exist between hawthorn and apple races such that flies from hawthorn populations strongly prefer to lay eggs on hawthorns, whereas flies from apple populations show a slight preference for laying on apple (Prokopy et al. 1988). Extensive sets of field experiments with marked flies from hawthorn and apple populations have supported a genetic basis for host preferences (Feder et al. 1998). The rate of gene flow between these two forms is now estimated to be about 6% annually (Filchak et al. 2000).

Recent studies of apple and hawthorn biotypes of the apple maggot fly in Michigan showed that the seasonal difference in fruiting time, combined with the difference in temperature experienced by larvae in fruit of these trees, forms the selective basis for the strong divergence of biotypes (Feder and Filchak 1999; Filchak et al. 2000). Feeding by the apple biotype was found to begin 3–4 wk earlier than that by the hawthorn biotype. This was correlated with the flies' emergence as adults. Larvae and pupae of the apple biotype also experience warmer temperatures. Filchak et al. (2000) conducted laboratory experiments to determine the genetic basis for biotype differences, using a set of four allozymes the frequencies of which had been correlated with the two biotypes. These experiments showed that allozymes correlated with the apple biotype were favored under warm conditions and those correlated with the hawthorn biotype under cooler conditions. Thus, partial isolation in time, together with selection based on temperature differences existing in the microhabitats of the different plant hosts, was responsible for the divergence of these biotypes.

The apple maggot fly has also adopted sour cherry (*Prunus cerasus*) as a new host (Shervis et al. 1970). Two close relatives of the apple maggot fly, *Rhagoletis fausta*, native to pin cherry (*Prunus pennsylvanica*), and *Rhagoletis cingulata*, native to black cherry (*Prunus serotina*), have also shifted to sour cherry (Feder 1995). These forms also showed some evidence of development of distinct host races on this new host species (Diehl and Bush 1984).

Members of the genus *Rhagoletis* seem particularly prone to evolving new host relationships. In Chile, another maggot fly, *Rhagoletis conversa*, uses tomatillo (*Solanum tomatillo*) as its native host. A host race has evolved on black nightshade (*S. nigrum*), an alien plant native to Europe (Diehl and Bush 1984).

Evolutionary Shifts of Native Herbivorous Insects to Introduced Noncrop Plants

Several well-documented examples of shifts of native herbivores to noncrop plants are now available. The case involving Edith's checkerspot, discussed at the beginning of the chapter, is one. Many other native insects have shown similar evolutionary shifts.

The most complex, well-documented example is provided by the soapberry bug (*Jadera haematoloma*), a true bug (Order Hemiptera) whose native North American hosts are the soapberry tree (*Sapindus saponaria*) in the south-central United States and the balloon vine (*Cardiospermum corindum*) in southern Florida (Carroll and Dingle 1996). The soapberry bug feeds on the seeds of these plants by using a tubular beak to pierce the fruit wall and gain access to the seeds, which are then liquified and sucked out. The bug's beak length must thus be adapted to the thickness of the fruit wall. The average beak lengths of soapberry bugs living on the balloon vine are significantly longer than those living on the soapberry tree, corresponding to the balloon vine's larger, thicker walled fruits (table 13.1).

Several exotic plants of the family Sapindaceae have been introduced to the southern United States, and soapberry bugs have adopted them as hosts (Carroll and Dingle 1996). The small-fruited flamegold tree (*Koelreuteria elegans*) has been introduced to peninsular Florida, near the region where the native host plant is the balloon vine. A clear pattern of evolutionary adaptation to this new introduced host is evident (table 13.1). Soapberry bugs feeding on the flamegold tree have evolved beaks more than 25% shorter than those feeding on balloon vines (Carroll and Boyd

Table 13.1. Fruit radius of native and alien plants of the family Sapindaceae, together with beak lengths of soapberry bugs feeding on these hosts. (Data from Carroll and Dingle 1996.)

Host plant	Status	Fruit radius (mm)	Beak length (mm)
FLORIDA			
Balloon vine (*Cardiospermum corindum*)	Native	11.92	9.32
Flamegold tree (*Koelreuteria elegans*)	Alien	2.82	6.93
SOUTH-CENTRAL UNITED STATES			
Soapberry tree (*Sapindus saponaria*)	Native	6.05	6.68
Goldenrain tree (*Koelreuteria paniculata*)	Alien	7.09	7.23
Heartseed vine (*Cardiospermum halicacabum*)	Alien	8.54	7.80

1992). A second species, the goldenrain tree (*Koelreuteria paniculata*), has been introduced farther north, where the native host is the soapberry tree. Soapberry bugs feeding on this tree now have beaks averaging about 8% longer than those feeding on the soapberry tree. Another alien plant, the heartseed vine (*Cardiospermum halicacabum*), has also been introduced to areas where the native plant host is the soapberry tree. Its fruits are still larger, and soapberry bugs feeding on this plant exhibit beaks averaging almost 17% longer than those on the soapberry tree. Laboratory experiments have shown that beak length has a genetic basis (Carroll and Dingle 1996). Thus, the shift to new plant hosts has been accompanied by rapid evolutionary adjustment of beak length to fruit wall thickness.

Additional studies of soapberry bugs on the native balloon vine and the alien small-fruited flamegold tree have shown that fecundity and juvenile survivorship are now greater for each population on its own plant host (Carroll et al. 1998). Furthermore, soapberry bugs living on the flamegold tree mature more rapidly and lay twice the number of eggs as those reared on the balloon vine (Carroll et al. 2001). Although the eggs laid by soapberry bugs on flamegold trees are smaller than those of ancestral bugs living on balloon vine, they achieve a much greater lifetime reproductive effort on this host than do ancestral bugs on the balloon vine. Thus, physiological adjustments as well as morphological changes, have occurred in the evolutionary shift of soapberry bugs to their new hosts. These adjustments have occurred over a period of about 100 generations.

Further studies have revealed still other life history adjustments by soapberry bugs on balloon vine and flamegold tree (Carroll et al. 2003a). These are related to the seasonal pattern of seed production and availability of the two host plants. Balloon vines tend to produce small seed crops at various times throughout the year, with considerable variability and asynchrony from plant to plant. Soapberry bugs are thus able to move from plant to plant and to remain active throughout the year. Flamegold trees simultaneously produce larger crops of seeds in late November and December, with seeds persisting only until March. On flamegold trees, soapberry bugs are forced to enter a diapause for much of the year because of seed unavailability.

Because of these striking differences in seed production by the native balloon vine and introduced flamegold tree, Carroll et al. (2003a) investigated reproductive patterns of soapberry bugs on the two hosts. On both hosts, long-winged females, capable of flight, and flightless, short-winged female morphs existed in about the same frequencies. The short-winged morphs essentially lacked flight muscles and were capable of egg production earlier than long-winged morphs. On the flamegold tree, however, about half of the long-winged morphs also lacked flight muscles and thus were flightless. These individuals were also able to produce eggs earlier than long-winged bugs that were able to fly. Thus, selection apparently favored the maintenance of more individuals capable of flight in balloon vine areas, where flight was advantageous to enable bugs to locate new seed-producing plants throughout the year. In areas of flamegold trees, selection favored early egg production during the short period of the year when seeds were available.

A third example of a shift of native herbivores to noncrop plants involves the western anise swallowtail butterfly (*Papilio zelicaon*), which uses 40 or more native species of plants of the carrot family (Apiaceae) and the rue family (Rutaceae) (Thompson 1993). In California, this butterfly has begun to use fennel (*Foeniculum vulgare*), an invasive alien plant of the carrot family that is abundant in many locations. Populations on native plant hosts produce only a single brood each year, since these plants are available for only a short period. Populations feeding on fennel, however, produce two or more broods annually, since this coarse weed remains green throughout the summer.

Thompson (1993) conducted oviposition preference tests, using laboratory-reared butterflies obtained from a population near Sacramento, California, that was using fennel as its host plant. These tests compared egg laying on fennel with egg laying on two locally available native host plants and a third plant used as a host by related swallowtail species. All groups of butterflies tested deposited eggs on fennel and the two native host plants. Overall, however, a significant preference for fennel was shown at the expense of one of the native food plants. In this case, therefore, only a slight evolutionary adjustment had been made to the new alien host, in spite of its availability in California for perhaps 50–100 yr.

Besides use of several fruit crop trees discussed above, flies of the genus *Rhagoletis* have adapted to alien honeysuckle (*Lonicera*) species in the northeastern United States (Schwarz et al., submitted). In this case, the population appears to be a hybrid of the native blueberry (*R. mendax*) and snowberry maggot (*R. zephyria*) flies. This new form of *Rhagoletis* appears to be widely distributed in regions where alien hosts occur and has apparently arisen within the last 250 yr.

Native herbivorous insects have also shifted to introduced aquatic plants. The weevil *Euhrychiopsis lecontei*, native to the northern water milfoil (*Myriophyllum sibericum*), has shifted its feeding activity to include the Eurasian water milfoil (*M. spicatum*). The Eurasian water milfoil has become a troublesome weed in fresh and estuarine waters throughout much of North America. The weevil has been shown experimentally to cause substantial damage to Eurasian water milfoil and also to be the likely cause of declines of this plant in nature (Newman and Biesboer 2000). Newman et al. (1997) found that development time of the weevil was 1–3 days shorter on the Eurasian plant than on the native water milfoil. Progeny of mothers reared on Eurasian water milfoil also tended to show better survival on Eurasian water milfoil than on the native plant. Weevils exposed to the Eurasian plant developed a strong preference for it. More recent studies (Solarz and Newman 2001) suggested that biotypes of weevils adapted to northern and Eurasian water milfoil species exist, but whether host conditioning, genetic specialization, or both are involved in biotype differentiation is still uncertain. Thus, this weevil appears to be adapting to new hosts, and some degree of evolutionary adaptation might be occurring.

Utilization of Alien Plants by Other Animals

Pocket gophers (family Geomyidae) are among the most variable groups of mammals in body size, color, and morphology. For the pocket gophers of the genus *Thomomys* in western North America, literally hundreds of subspecies have been described. Modern genetic analyses have tended to show that many of these do not have an evolutionary basis but simply reflect direct environmental influences on growth and development. Nevertheless, that their fossorial lifestyle makes them more susceptible than many other animals to geographic isolation by physical barriers such as rivers and mountain systems favors their evolutionary divergence.

Along the eastern slope of the Sierra Nevada in California, Patton and Brylski (1987) examined populations of the valley pocket gopher (*Thomomys bottae*) living in Joshua Tree and Pinyon-Juniper woodland, on the one hand, and nearby in irrigated alfalfa (*Medicago sativa*) fields, on the other. The alfalfa field animals were heavier in weight and larger in skull measurements than those from the native woodlands. Males from alfalfa fields were more than 90% heavier and had skulls more than 55% longer than woodland males. Females showed smaller differences: weights 23% greater and skulls only about 14% longer. Animals from the two populations showed no differences in the shape of the skull, however, suggesting that the differences were largely, if not entirely, due to better nutrition in the alfalfa field habitat.

The alfalfa field and native woodland populations also differed strikingly in life history features (Patton and Brylski 1987). Alfalfa field populations were more than 16-fold denser than those in native woodland. The sex ratio was more heavily biased toward females in the alfalfa field habitat than in native woodland. Alfalfa field females became sexually mature and bred in their birth season, whereas native woodland females did not breed until their second year. Litter size was larger and the breeding season longer in the alfalfa field habitat because of irrigation and greatly increased food availability. The result of early breeding by alfalfa habitat females was that their growth in size slowed when they reached sexual maturity and allocated metabolic resources to reproduction. Males in the alfalfa field population did not breed in their birth season. They continued to grow, leading to a larger sexual dimorphism in body size than was the case in the native woodland animals. These habitat-related ecological differences could result in patterns of mate competition, so the original body-size differences could become stabilized by sexual selection (Patton and Smith 1990). Such a difference would be especially likely if gene flow between the two populations would be interrupted. Whether or not genetic differentiation of these two types of pocket gopher populations has occurred is still uncertain.

Other Evolutionary Considerations

Many native herbivores have thus begun to feed on alien plants that have appeared in their environment. The use of alien plants is frequent for herbivores that have a wide native host range, but many specialist herbivores have also shifted to alien species that are closely related to their native hosts. As we saw earlier, oviposition by arthropods on alien plants that possess secondary chemicals similar to those of their native hosts also leads to their use by native species. The results of these shifts are quite variable. Some shifts lead to evolutionary specialization for the new hosts. In other cases, however, larval development may not always be possible on the new host (see, e.g., Chew 1977), and the alien species may thus become a threat to populations of the native herbivore by attracting individuals to plants on which reproduction fails (see chapter 16).

The successful utilization of alien plant species, however, may lead to the formation of new genetic races or even species (Futuyma and Peterson 1985). Speciation is possible if spatial separation due to different host use results in reduced gene flow, if individuals tend to remain on the host on which they developed and mate there, or if selection related to performance on the different hosts is able to reinforce genetic mechanisms of host preference and host-specific mating patterns. Later, in chapter 19, we shall consider speciation in detail.

Alien Opportunities Versus Alien Challenges

Alien plants constitute underused resources for many native herbivores, and thus it is not surprising that they become incorporated in the diets of generalist and even specialist animals. The massive introduction of alien species to new regions presents not only these sorts of opportunities for native animals but also presents challenges from alien predators, parasites, and disease agents. In the next chapter, we shall examine the adaptation of animals to these alien challenges.

14.

Adaptation of Animals to Alien Predators, Parasites, and Disease Agents

"Everything else being equal, there is an advantage to parasites that carry virulent alleles, as these parasites are able to infect a broader spectrum of hosts than parasites carrying avirulent alleles. Similarly, there is an advantage to hosts that carry resistant alleles, as these hosts are able to resist infection from a broader array of parasites than hosts carrying susceptible alleles."

—AGRAWAL AND LIVELY 2002.

The brown trout (*Salmo trutta*), native to Europe, was introduced to many rivers in New Zealand beginning in the late 1860s and now occurs in most streams and lakes throughout the country. This fish has greatly affected the distribution of native fish belonging to the genus Galaxiids in many streams. Galaxiids and brown trout rarely occur together at the same location. In most cases, galaxiids prosper only in waters inaccessible to brown trout. In the Taieri River system of the South Island, for example, galaxiids occur only in stream headwaters above waterfalls that are high enough to prevent access by brown trout (Townsend 1996).

Brown trout and galaxiids differ in feeding behavior. Trout are daytime feeders that forage in the water column and locate prey primarily by vision. Galaxiids are nocturnal substrate feeders that rely primarily on mechanical stimuli for prey recognition. Larvae of the mayfly *Nesameletus ornatus* are an important prey of both fish in the Taieri River. Where only galaxiids occur, mayfly nymphs are active on rock surfaces both day and night and also drift in the water column. In brown trout waters, however, the mayflies mostly remain beneath rocks during the day and usually only forage on exposed surfaces and drift in the water column at night (McIntosh and Townsend 1994). These nocturnal patterns of behavior were retained when mayflies from brown trout streams were tested in experimental streams without fish or with galaxiids. Other stream invertebrates may also have experienced similar evolutionary shifts (Townsend 2003). Thus, in a little more than a century, brown trout predation has led to evolutionary shifts in activity patterns of at least one native New Zealand invertebrate.

Exploiters and the Exploited: The Red Queen Hypothesis

Introduction of alien predators, parasites, or disease agents often creates abruptly new relationships between these types of organisms and their prey or hosts. In evolutionary terms, the exploitation of one species by an organism of a higher trophic level tends to follow the Red Queen Hypothesis (Van Valen 1973). This hypothesis, named for a character in Lewis Carroll's book *Through the Looking Glass*, states that the members of an exploitation interaction tend to establish an evolutionary stand-off, in which improvements in exploitation ability by the one member are matched by improvements in defense by the other. Or, as the Red Queen put it, "Now, here, you see, it takes all the running you can do just to stay in the same place."

The introduction of alien predators, parasites, or disease agents may create a situation in which native prey or host species are subjected to new, more intense patterns of exploitation. The same can be true when alien prey or host species are confronted with alien enemies that they have not previously encountered. In some cases, these new interactions may lead to extirpation or extinction of the prey or host (see chapter 16). In other cases, they may lead to rapid evolutionary adjustments by the prey or host to the new selective pressures.

Evolutionary Adaptation to Predators and Parasitoids by Native Invertebrates

Several good examples of evolutionary adaptation by native invertebrate prey species to alien predators are available. The European green crab (*Carcinus maenas*) was introduced to the North American east coast in the early 1800s, and has now spread along the coast from New Jersey to Nova

Scotia. This crab is a voracious predator on gastropod molluscs. The native dog whelk (*Nucella lapillus*) was one of the common prey species encountered as the green crab spread north from the area of Cape Cod, Massachusetts. Vermeij (1982) examined collections of dog whelks collected before and after the arrival of the green crab from Massachusetts to Nova Scotia. He noted that the frequency of repaired injuries to the shells of whelks increased from 2.5% before the green crab's arrival to 4.4% afterward. Predation attempts on dog whelks had thus increased substantially following appearance of the green crab. Furthermore, Vermeij found that the thickness of the lip of the whelk shell and the height of the shell spire were significantly greater in shell samples taken after the arrival of the crab than before its arrival. Today, populations of dog whelks in areas with green crabs possess more slender, heavier shells with a smaller aperture and thicker outer lip than do populations in areas were green crabs are absent. Shell shape in dog whelks has been shown to be under a strong degree of genetic control (Funasaki et al. 1988).

Even more striking is the change in spire height and shell thickness of *Littorina obtusata* in most locations in northern New England after the arrival of the European green crab in about 1900 (Seeley 1986). *Littorina* snails collected in 1982–1984 on the coast of Maine had much broader shells and lower spires than those collected in the late 1800s. Shell thickness was also much greater in the 1980s. Experiments in which snails with shells of the two types were exposed to green crabs in natural habitats showed that predation was much higher on the tall-spired, thin-shelled animals. Laboratory tests also showed that green crabs could crush shells of the vulnerable snails in less than a minute, but were successful in crushing only a small percentage of the more resistant snails.

Seeley (1986) interpreted the change in shell morphology of *Littorina obtusata* as direct natural selection on shell shape. More recently, Trussell and Nicklin (2002) showed that change in shell shape in the presence of the European green crab is an induced response. *Littorina* reared in the presence of crabs show thickened shells, and when *Littorina* injured or killed by green crabs are also present, induced thickening is accentuated. Nevertheless, the strength of the induction response was apparently the object of natural selection. In the northern Gulf of Maine, the green crab has been present only about 50 yr, compared to about 100 yr in the southern Gulf of Maine. *Littorina* in the southern Gulf of Maine produced thicker and heavier shells than those in the north, even in the absence of induction cues. *Littorina* in the northern Gulf of Maine showed variability in the shell thickness response to simple presence of crabs two to three times as great as *Littorina* in the southern Gulf. This suggests that in the northern Gulf, where green crab populations are smaller and of more recent arrival, crab predation has not exerted as consistent a selective force as in the southern Gulf. The evolutionary response of *Littorina* to the alien green crab is thus surprisingly complex in nature (Trussell and Etter 2001).

In freshwater environments, the introduction of alien fish has led to evolutionary changes in the behavior of several invertebrates, as noted in the introductory example. A number of aquatic insects, especially mayfly larvae, drift-feed in the water column, probably enabling them to capture certain algal foods that are not readily available in benthic situations. While they are drifting, they are at increased risk of predation, especially during the day when many insectivorous fish forage in the water column. Thus, in streams where insect-feeding fish are present, drift-feeding by invertebrates tends to be nocturnal. When insect-feeding fish are absent, drift-feeding tends to occur both at night and during the day. In most cases, differences in the pattern of drift-feeding appear to be genetic (Flecker 1992). In some cases, mayflies from streams without fish may shift from day-and-night drift-feeding to nocturnal feeding when transplanted to streams with trout (Cowan and Peckarsky 1994).

In Venezuela, Flecker (1992) investigated mayfly drift-feeding in streams with various numbers of fish that feed on drifting invertebrates. He noted a very strong positive relationship between the diversity and abundance of insectivorous fish and the tendency of mayflies to drift-feed at night. In low-elevation streams with up to 20 species of insectivorous fish, the abundance of drifting mayflies at night was 100 or more times that during the day. In high-elevation streams that originally lacked any insectivorous fish, he found that in streams still lacking such fish mayflies drift-fed both day and night. In streams to which rainbow trout (*Oncorynchus mykiss*) had been introduced within the preceding 60 yr, however, mayflies showed a stronger tendency to drift-feed at night.

In the North American Great Lakes, the rapidly changing biotic structure resulting from numerous introductions has probably had more evolutionary impacts than are yet recognized. Wells (1970) noted that following introduction of the alewife (*Alosa pseudoharengus*), which feeds largely on zooplankton, many declines occurred in populations of cladocerans and copepods. In the case of the cladoceran *Daphnia retrocurva*, however, a reduction in body size at which individuals matured was observed. Before the alewife became common, the smallest mature females were 1.26 mm in length. Alewives appeared in the lake in 1949 but were still rare in

1954. By the early 1960s, they had become abundant. By 1966, the smallest mature *Daphnia retrocurva* was 1.05 mm in length. This cladoceran reproduces parthenogenetically for most of the year, and clones vary in body size. Thus, it appears that alewife predation was selecting for small, early maturing clones.

In Belgium, another cladoceran, *Daphnia magna*, was found to show rapid evolutionary changes in vertical migration behavior, and possible in morphology, to changing predation patterns due to the introduction of plankton-feeding fish to a small pond (Cousyn et al. 2001). The pond, constructed in 1970, acquired a natural population of *Daphnia magna*. For the first 3 yr, only benthic-feeding fish were stocked. Then, for about a decade, planktivorous fish were stocked in large numbers. Finally, after the mid-1980s, stocking was gradually reduced and finally stopped in 1993. Thus, the predation regime on *Daphnia* changed from light to heavy and then back to light over about 23 yr. Cousyn and his coinvestigators were able to recover resting eggs of *Daphnia* from sediment deposits dating from these three periods, and because these eggs are very long-lived, establish laboratory populations of parthenogenetic offspring derived from individual eggs.

The vertical migration behavior of *Daphnia magna* from the three periods of different predation intensity showed marked differences when tests were conducted in water containing chemical signals produced by fish. Most *Daphnia* from the period of heavy predation by plankton-feeding fish migrated downward in the water column in response to light, whereas almost all of those from periods of low predation intensity did not. These differences were quite significant, and clearly genetic in their basis. In addition, the size of the resting eggs produced by animals during the period of heavy predation was smaller than those of animals from periods of low predation, a difference that probably also had a genetic basis. Frequencies of microsatellite alleles, considered to be neutral in terms of selection by predators, for animals through the three predation periods showed no change, indicating that factors such as genetic drift could not account for the genetic changes. Thus, evolutionary changes had occurred in *Daphnia magna* over periods of only about 7–10 yr as predation intensity at first increased and then decreased.

Another good example of response by a native invertebrate comes from New Zealand, where many alien predators have been introduced. Wetas (Orthoptera: Stenopalmatidae) are large, flightless cricket-like animals that occur in forest habitats in New Zealand. Introduced mammalian predators that feed on wetas include black rats (*Rattus rattus*), kiores (*Rat-*

tus exulans), hedgehogs (*Erinaceus europaeus*), stoats (*Mustela erminea*), and feral cats (*Felis catus*). These predators have eliminated ground-dwelling wetas on mainland areas and near-shore islands, but a number of primarily tree-dwelling wetas (*Hemideina* spp.) have survived both on the mainland and on islands that have few or no introduced predators (Moller 1985). On islands with mammalian predators, wetas are strongly arboreal, whereas on islands without such predators they are commonly seen on the ground. In areas with mammalian predators, they also shelter in tree holes with constricted openings that prevent predator access, whereas on predator-free islands they commonly shelter in more open sites. These behavioral tendencies are apparently genetic, as they are maintained by animals in the laboratory (Rafanut 1995).

Native parasitoids have in several cases expanded their host use to include introduced host species. The native North American braconid wasp *Macrocentrus ancylivorous*, for example, has expanded its parasitism to include the oriental fruit moth (*Grapholita molesta*), an alien orchard pest. Parasitoid insects are also among the species most frequently introduced for biological control of invertebrate pests, as we noted in chapter 10. In at least one case, involving pea aphids and an introduced parasitoid (Hufbauer 2001), the aphid hosts have shown evolutionary adaptation. We shall examine this case in detail in chapter 17.

Evolutionary Adaptation to Predators by Native Vertebrates

The bullfrog (*Rana catesbeiana*), native to eastern North America, has been introduced to many areas of western North America, where it has become a serious predator of many native amphibians and reptiles (Cox 1999). Both adult bullfrogs and large tadpoles are predators on the tadpoles of other frogs. In California and Oregon, the red-legged frog (*Rana aurora*) has been extirpated in many locations by bullfrog predation.

In Oregon, bullfrogs were introduced in the early 1930s and have invaded many, but not all, habitats occupied by red-legged frogs. Kiesecker and Blaustein (1997) examined the behavior and survival of red-legged frogs from populations that coexisted with bullfrogs versus those from locations without bullfrogs. Red-legged frogs show antipredator behavior, typically hiding or a reduction of activity, in response to chemical cues of predators such as fish. When red-legged frog tadpoles were exposed to chemical cues of bullfrogs, individuals from populations that coexisted with bullfrogs showed strong antipredator responses, whereas those from

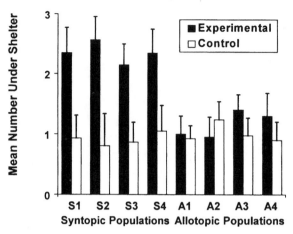

Figure 14.1. Mean number of red-legged frog (*Rana aurora*) tadpoles from populations existing with (syntopic) and without (allotopic) bullfrogs (*Rana catesbeiana*) seeking shelter when exposed versus not exposed to chemical cues of larval bullfrogs. Each test involved 10 tadpoles. One standard error is indicated by the error bars (Reprinted with permission from J. M. Kiesecker and A. R. Blaustein. 1997. Population differences in responses of red-legged frogs (*Rana aurora*) to introduced bullfrogs. *Ecology* 78:1752–1760. © 1997 Ecological Society of America.)

populations without bullfrogs did not (fig. 14.1). Experimental predation experiments were also conducted in the laboratory and in pens located in natural waters. In the laboratory, survival of red-legged frog tadpoles over 3 days was 87.7% for individuals from populations with bullfrogs and 64.7% for those from sites without bullfrogs. For tests lasting 8 days in natural waters, the difference was much greater; 90.7% of tadpoles from populations with bullfrogs survived, whereas only 43.5% of those from sites without bullfrogs survived. Kiesecker and Blaustein (1997) concluded that the differences shown by red-legged frog tadpoles had at least some genetic basis, since all of the test animals were obtained as prehatching embryos.

Fish faced with introduced predators show several examples of rapid evolution of antipredator behavior. Perhaps the most detailed studies of evolutionary change in response to predation have been carried out with the guppy (*Poecilia reticulata*) in Trinidad. Although the field situation in Trinidad does not really involve introduced species that are alien to the island, stream areas exist in which guppy populations are exposed to and protected from various predatory fish. These situations have permitted the experimental study of evolution in populations of guppies to which predatory fish were introduced. Guppies from stream areas with high versus low predation regimes show differences in many characteristics, including coloration, behavior, life history pattern, and response to predators (see, e.g., Magurran et al. 1992). Experimental manipulation of the predation regime for guppies showed that shifts in various life history patterns could be induced in 30–60 generations, corresponding to about 11 yr (Reznick et al. 1999).

In one of the most interesting sets of experiments, O'Steen et al. (2002) examined the escape behavior in guppies from field populations that differed naturally in presence or absence of predatory fish, as well as populations that were created in 1976 and 1981 by introduction of guppies or their predators to new stream areas. For example, in the Arima Valley of northern Trinidad, the pike cichlid (*Crenicichla alta*), a major guppy predator, was introduced to a stream section from which it had been absent. Guppies were also introduced from stream sections with pike cichlids to areas without this predator. In 1996 and 1997, 26–36 generations after these introductions, tests of survival of guppies from low and high predation stream areas were conducted in artificial ponds containing pike cichlids. In each case, guppies from areas of low predation showed significantly lower survival than those from high predation areas (table 14.1). Guppies transplanted from areas without pike cichlids to areas with this predator had gained in survival ability. Guppies transplanted from

Table 14.1. Survival of guppies from populations of natural high and low predation regimes and from populations of high and low predation intensity created by transplanting guppies or their pike cichlid predator. Survival is the mean number of individuals surviving out of six individuals per test group. (Data from O'Steen et al. 2002.)

SOURCE POPULATIONS		MEAN NUMBER OF SURVIVORS		
High predation source	*Low predation source*	*High predation survivors*	*Low predation survivors*	*Significance level*
Aripo Valley (natural)	Aripo Valley (natural)	5.0 +/- 0.8	1.1 +/- 0.6	0.0001
Aripo Valley (introduced)	Aripo Valley (natural)	3.5 +/- 1.4	2.3 +/- 1.0	0.005
Aripo Valley (natural)	Aripo Valley (introduced)	4.3 +/- 1.3	2.0 +/- 0.9	0.0006
El Cedro Valley (natural)	El Cedro Valley (introduced)	4.1 +/- 1.3	2.4 +/- 1.2	0.003

areas with pike cichlids to areas without this predator had declined in survival ability.

In addition to the tests with wild-caught guppies, O'Steen et al. (2002) reared guppies from the natural and introduced high and low predation stream situations in the laboratory for two generations. The second-generation guppies were then tested to determine if their survival abilities when exposed to pike cichlids were retained. In all tests, guppies from high predation stream areas, regardless of whether they were natural or introduced, survived better than guppies from low predation sources. These results clearly show that natural selection modified genetically based traits related to predator avoidance within relatively few generations.

Introduced predatory fish may also have secondary impacts on native predatory species through food competition. The fish fauna of the North American Great Lakes was altered enormously by the invasion of predatory fish such as the sea lamprey (*Petromyzon marinus*), alewife (*Alosa pseudoharengus*), and rainbow smelt (*Osmerus mordax*) (Cox 1999). The lamprey, a predator on large fish, decimated populations of large predatory fish, driving some species to extinction. The alewife and smelt, both plankton feeders, competed with other native fish for small prey.

One of the native fish to survive the impacts of these introductions is the bloater (*Coregonus hoyi*). The larvae of bloaters feed on small zooplankton in pelagic waters, but shift to benthic feeding on larger invertebrates as they mature. Following the explosion of alewife populations in the 1960s, a major shift in feeding pattern occurred (Crowder and Crawford 1984). By 1979 and 1980, sampling of bloater populations showed that they had shifted from small zooplankton to larger benthic prey about 2 yr earlier than before the alewife explosion. Analysis of foraging behavior of bloaters showed that they were more efficient at harvesting benthic prey than are alewives (Crowder and Binkowski 1983).

In addition, within less than 20 yr, a morphological shift in the feeding apparatus of bloaters occurred. By 1979, the number of gill rakers of adult bloaters had declined by about 15% (Crowder 1984). These structures serve as filters that retain particles in the digestive tract, preventing their passage into the gill chamber and eventually the outside water. This shift was correlated with the earlier switch to larger benthic prey. The most likely reason for the shift is competition for small zooplankton with the alewife.

Fewer examples of such evolutionary responses exist for terrestrial vertebrates. The spread of the brown-headed cowbird (*Molothrus ater*) to virtually all temperate areas of North America from its original range in the

Great Plains has exposed many new populations of songbirds to nest parasitism by cowbirds. In southern California, the cowbird first appeared as a breeding species in about 1920. Cowbird nest parasitism is now a major cause of nest failure for the California gnatcatcher (*Polioptila californica*). Analysis of clutch completion dates for California gnatcatchers from 1880 through 1959 showed that since 1920 a significant shift toward earlier clutch completion has occurred (Patten and Campbell 1998). The mean date of clutch completion between 1920 and 1959 was 9 days earlier than for the period prior to 1920. Egg laying by cowbirds tends to be concentrated in late spring and early summer. It is likely that other songbirds have made similar adjustments to cowbird parasitism.

In Hawaii, another bird, the i'iwi (*Vestiaria coccinea*) has apparently undergone a reduction in bill length correlated with the considerable decline in plants of the genus *Lobelia* (Smith et al. 1995). The long, curved bill of the i'iwi was adapted to the tubular corollas of lobelias, which provided the birds with abundant nectar. Most of the low-elevation native forest has disappeared and introduced ungulates have decimated lobelia populations in the understory of the remaining forest at higher elevations (Scott et al.1986). As a result, the i'iwi has shifted much of its feeding to the ohia tree (*Metrosideros polymorpha*), which has flowers lacking a corolla and accessible to short-billed birds. In this case, the evolutionary response of the i'iwi is an indirect effect of the impact of alien animals on native plants.

Adaptation of Native Animals to Introduced Diseases

Alien diseases often impose very strong selective pressures on native animals, and many examples now exist of evolutionary adaptation to alien diseases. The whirling disease parasite (*Myxobolus cerebralis*), native to Eurasia, was introduced to North America in the late 1950s. This parasite has a life history alternating between two hosts, salmonid fish and tubificid worms. Spores from dead fish enter the stream water and are ingested by tubifex worms (*Tubifex* spp.), small annelid worms that live in muddy stream bottoms. Clusters of a new spore stage develop in the worms. These clusters have hooks that enable them to attach to the gills or other internal surfaces of fish. The spores then enter the circulatory system of the fish. The parasite attacks developing cartilage tissues of young fish, eventually disrupting tissues associated with the cranial balance organs. As a result, the fish swims erratically and has difficulty in feeding and avoiding predators. Severe infections cause high rates of mortality of young fish. Brown trout (*Salmo trutta*), native to Europe, are carriers of the disease, but rarely suffer serious effects. Some native North American salmonids, especially the rainbow trout (*Oncorhynchus mykiss*), are severely infected, especially in some parts of the Rocky Mountain region.

Many species of trout and salmon can be infected by the whirling disease parasite, but different species and subspecies show varying degrees of susceptibility to infection. Among cutthroat trout (*Oncorhynchus clarki*) subspecies, for example, the subspecies *O. c. utah* from Bear Lake, on the border of Utah and Idaho, shows lower susceptibility to infection than other subspecies (Wagner et al. 2002). Fry of this form of the cutthroat trout tend to grow rapidly in length and to switch from feeding on plankton to feeding on other fish earlier in life than do other forms of cutthroat trout. The reasons for this difference are unclear.

In North America, some evidence of evolutionary adaptation exists for both tubifex worms and rainbow trout. One *Tubifex* lineage from Ontario, Canada, for example, appears to be highly resistant to infection by *Myxobolus* (Beauchamp et al. 2001). This lineage, however, may really be one of several cryptic species of *Tubifex* that cannot be distinguished by morphology. More recently, Beauchamp et al. (forthcoming) found that in Colorado two *Tubifex* lineages appeared to consist of individuals largely resistant to infection and two others to contain both resistant and susceptible individuals. Thus, a considerable potential for evolutionary adjustment by *Tubifex* forms to *Myxobolus* appears to exist.

Rainbow trout imported into Germany about 120 yr ago recently were found to show resistance to whirling disease (El-Matbouli et al. 2002). Development of this resistance was presumed to be the result of growth and reproduction of rainbow trout under conditions of continuous exposure to the parasite in hatcheries that use river water and mud-bottomed rearing ponds. Laboratory tests of the ability of rainbow trout from North America and Germany to resist infection by *Myxobolus* were conducted by Hedrick et al. (2002). These tests showed that trout from Germany were much more resistant than any North American strain that has been tested.

Avian malaria, caused by the blood parasite *Plasmodium relictum*, was brought to Hawaii by the introduction of alien birds and the mosquito *Culex quinquefasciatus*, which serves as a vector (van Riper et al. 1986). Native Hawaiian songbirds initially lacked resistance to avian malaria, which has evidently contributed substantially to their decline. Most native land birds no longer occur at lower elevations to which *Culex* mosquitoes and the malaria parasite are restricted (Jarvi et al. 2001).

A few populations of native songbirds do survive, however, at low elevations (Shehata et al. 2001). One of these is the O'ahu 'amakihi (*Hemignathus flavus*), which occurs at the Lyon Arboretum, where it is in close association with many alien birds, mosquito vectors, and the *Plasmodium* parasite. Closely related 'amakihi species on other islands are often infected by *Plasmodium* and suffer lower survival rates than infected species of alien birds. Using molecular genetic techniques, Shehata et al. (2001) examined native and introduced birds at the Lyon Arboretum for a gene specific to the malaria parasite as an indication of active infection. Of 13 species of alien birds examined, 11 showed some malaria infections, the average incidence being about 11.5%. None of 42 individuals of the 'amakihi showed infections. Thus, the O'ahu 'amakihis have apparently evolved some mechanism of resistance to avian malaria. The resistance of O'ahu 'amakihis has probably evolved over some 125–170 generations, depending on the exact time that both the mosquito vector and the disease agent became established. Resistance in such cases can be expected to appear in 5–50 generations (Dobson and May 1986), so this case is well within expectation. A more limited degree of resistance also seems to exist for the Hawai'i 'amakihi (*Hemignathus virens*) (Jarvi et al. 2001).

Another example of adaptation by native organisms to alien diseases involves plague (*Yersinia pestis*), a bacterial disease of mammals, including humans. It is known from more than 200 mammal species (Biggins and Kosoy 2001). Plague can be transmitted from one animal feeding on another or by bites of fleas carried by infected animals. The plague bacterium apparently evolved in Central Asia some time within the past 20,000 yr and was introduced to North America and many other parts of the world by infected rats transported by ocean ships. That plague is a newcomer to North America is evident from its relative homogeneity and the absence of strains adapted to specific animals.

North American mammals now show varying degrees of sensitivity to plague. The primary hosts of plague are rodents, both in Asia and North America. Most North American carnivores appear to be resistant to the effects of plague. Rodents, on the other hand, vary greatly in resistance, most being highly susceptible. Populations of prairie dogs (*Cynomys* spp.), in particular, appear to be highly susceptible to plague, and local populations have been extirpated by plague outbreaks. A few rodent species show high resistance, apparently in some measure in response to whether or not the disease has recently affected their populations.

Clear evidence that evolutionary resistance is fostered by exposure to plague exists for at least some species (Biggins and Kosoy 2001). Offspring of grasshopper mice (*Onychomys leucogaster*) from Colorado populations that had experienced a plague outbreak showed 75% survival when infected with plague, whereas individuals from an Oklahoma population that had been plague-free showed only 27% survival (Thomas et al. 1988). Similarly, California ground squirrels (*Spermophilus beecheyi*) from an area with a plague history showed 67% survival compared to 39% survival for animals from a plague-free area (Meyer 1942).

Adaptation of Animals to Alien Ecosystem Engineers

Ecosystem engineers are species that exert a dominating influence on the physical or structural environment in an ecosystem. The beaver (*Castor canadensis*) is such a species. By their cutting of woody plants and damming of streams, beavers are capable of transforming a shaded forest stream environment into one of open ponds, marshes, and shrublands.

In New England, where the beaver was extirpated from most areas following European settlement, it is now reinvading many areas. Although not an alien species in the strict sense, the ecosystem impacts of beaver activity are substantial, and the reinvasion of the species is influencing the evolution of at least one species, the wood frog (*Rana sylvatica*). Skelly and Freidenberg (2000) have examined the thermal biology of wood frogs in forested wetlands and in beaver wetlands in Connecticut. The beaver wetlands were created by reinvasion of beavers about 36 yr before. These wetlands constitute a much warmer aquatic environment for egg and tadpole development than do forested wetland areas. When eggs from forested and beaver wetlands were incubated under conditions of the forest environment, the development of eggs of the forest animals was faster. On the other hand, tests of tolerance of high water temperatures showed that tadpoles from beaver wetlands tolerated significantly warmer conditions. The critical upper temperature for tadpoles from the beaver wetlands was 0.4°C higher than that for tadpoles from the forest wetlands. Skelly (2004) has shown that compensatory microevolutionary adjustments can be made by populations of the wood frog to differing thermal environments separated by tens to hundreds of meters. These adjustments are rapid and appear to be made within a time frame measured in decades. Thus, the extirpation and reinvasion of the beaver have both led to changes in the thermal biology of the wood frog, as in all probability have landscape changes directly caused by human settlement.

Potential for Evolutionary Adaptation to Aliens

In the last three chapters, we have seen that native species, or in some cases, established alien species, have a considerable capacity for evolutionary adaptation to invading species that offer opportunities for exploitation or challenges to survival. Recent alien invaders, some of which flourish because they have been freed from their enemies at home, begin almost immediately to accumulate predators, including herbivores in the case of alien plants, and parasites. How this accumulation of predators and parasites proceeds determines the potential for evolutionary integration of an alien into its new biotic community. We shall examine the pattern of accumulation of species in the next chapter.

15.

Accumulation of Herbivores, Predators, and Parasites by Alien Species

"New invaders may also act as foci for the assembly of native species that can use them as resources. If the invasion is successful, a new invader-centered species assemblage will be generated, and the food web complexity of the local community will be increased."

—CORNELL AND HAWKINS (1993)

In 1967, 10 trees of sawtooth oak (*Quercus acutissima*) and 20 of Japanese chestnut (*Castanea crenata*) were planted in an open field at Tall Timbers Research Station, near Tallahassee, Florida. Although these species had been imported to North America in the late 1800s, none were present in the vicinity of the Tall Timbers site. In 1980 and 1981, Auerbach and Simberloff (1988) censused leaf-mining insects on four trees of each species, as well as on a series of native water oaks (*Quercus nigra*) in the same general location.

The censuses produced 17 species of leaf-miners on both the water oak and sawtooth oak and 15 species on the Japanese chestnut. All of the leaf-miners found on the alien trees were found on water oaks or were known from other oak species present at Tall Timbers. Two of the species found on sawtooth oak and four of the species on Japanese chestnut, however, apparently did not complete their development and emerge as adults. This suggested that they were not fully adapted to the physiology of these tree species. The percentage of all leaf-miners that completed development and emerged was smallest, 7.3%, for water oak. Emergence percentages of leaf-miners were 14.4 for sawtooth oak and 26.8 for Japanese chestnut. This suggested that the introduced trees were very favorable hosts for some of the miners. Thus, both alien trees had acquired a rich fauna of leaf-mining insects in only 13–14 yr. The species with close relatives in nearby forests, the sawtooth oak, appeared to have gained more leaf-miners than the Japanese chestnut, which lacked nearby congeners. Some combination of nutritional factors, together with parasitism and predation patterns, seemed to be responsible for the greater overall emergence success of leaf miners on the alien trees.

This study (Auerbach and Simberloff 1988) showed that colonization of newly introduced plants by herbivorous arthropods can be very fast and that the taxonomic similarity of new plant species to natives is an influential factor in this colonization process. Furthermore, it appeared that the physiological condition of successful plant colonists might facilitate the success of some of these arthropods.

Biotic Responses to Alien Species

As we saw in chapter 7, newly colonizing alien plants and animals are often free of many of the enemies that attack them in their native region. For at least some species, this release is a major factor in their becoming highly invasive. Very few aliens, however, remain free from attack by native herbivores, predators, or parasites for very long. The pattern of interaction that develops between alien species and these new enemies can lead to patterns of rapid evolution in both alien and native species, as we have also seen. The potential for such evolution depends on the number of native colonists and the speed with which they begin to colonize and interact with aliens.

Factors Influencing Accumulation of Species by Alien Plants

In almost all cases, introduced plants sooner or later become the object of exploitation by native herbivores and parasites. Acquisition of such enemies tends to follow an asymptotic curve, being rapid at first and slowing as an equilibrium relationship is approached (Bernays and Graham 1988). Generalist species are the first to use new aliens, with their diversity reaching a plateau in as little as 100 yr. Colonization of new aliens by feeding specialists, on the other hand, may take as much as 10,000 yr.

The pattern of accumulation differs for various kinds of aliens and is influenced by characteristics of the native community and its environment (Kogan 1991). At first, this accumulation reflects two relationships: the similarity of the alien species to native host species and the lack of evolved defenses of aliens to natives that begin to exploit them. In particular, the presence of plants closely related to a newly arrived alien is a strong determinant of the speed and diversity of an alien plant's colonization by herbivores (Connor et al. 1980). Over time, however, additional natives may evolve to use the aliens, while the aliens evolve ways to repel their exploiters.

Accumulation of Herbivorous Arthropods by Crop Plants

Crop plants introduced to new regions are often quick to accumulate herbivorous arthropods from the native fauna. Three major factors seem to determine the speed and magnitude of recruitment of herbivores by introduced crop plants (Kogan 1991). First, the diversity of generalist herbivores and specialist herbivores associated with related plants or plants with similar patterns of secondary chemical defenses defines the potential reservoir of herbivores that might be recruited. Second, the degree to which the phenology of the crop corresponds to the seasonal life history patterns of herbivores influences those that are most likely to begin to use the new plant host. Third, the strength of herbivore defenses of the crop plant influences the success of herbivores that attempt to use the plant. In some cases, crop plant species have been bred to reduce the content of defensive chemicals, which can be distasteful to humans. Of course, all of these relationships are subject to evolutionary modification.

Several extensive studies have been done of the accumulation of herbivorous arthropods by introduced agricultural crops. Some of these have focused on specific crops, others on crops in specific regions.

Some of the most interesting studies have compared the diversity of herbivorous arthropods on a single crop in different world regions. One of the most comprehensive studies is for sugar cane (*Saccharum officinarum*) by Strong et al. (1977). These authors compiled data for 75 world regions to which sugar cane had been introduced, and for which the number of arthropod pests, the area of cane in cultivation, and often the date of introduction were available. Some 1,645 arthropod pests were identified. More than 58% of these were recorded from a single location and another 9.5% from only two locations. Thus, at least two-thirds, and probably much more, of the pests were recruited from the local native faunas of the regions of introduction.

For sugar cane, one might expect that the length of time since introduction would be one of the most significant determinants of the number of pest arthropods encountered. The dates of introduction, for example, varied from 500 B.C. to 1840 A.D. No relationship with time could be shown, however, but a strong correlation existed between pest arthropod diversity and the area of sugar cane under cultivation at present (fig. 15.1). In this case, accumulation of species seems to have been influenced by the ecological setting of the region. This setting, which influenced the extent of cultivation that was practical, also supplied arthropods in more or less proportional numbers. These arthropods seem to have colonized sugar cane in a relatively short time, reaching a numerical plateau set by the ecological features of the region.

A second study, of the herbivorous insects associated with cacao (*Theobroma cacao*) in different world regions, showed a similar pattern (Strong 1974a). Of 1,905 insects, more than 80% occurred in only one cacao-growing region. Again, the diversity of insects was closely correlated with the area of cacao under cultivation. This relationship apparently developed

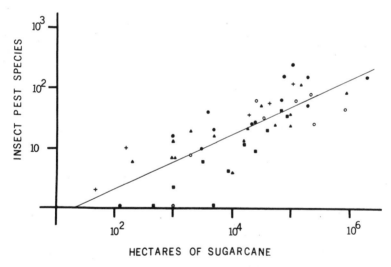

Fig. 15.1. The number of herbivorous arthropods associated with sugar cane in different world regions in relation to the area of sugar cane under cultivation. Symbols: ○ - continental Americas, ● - Asia, ▲ - West Indies, ■ - Europe and Africa, + - Oceania. (Reprinted with permission from D. R. Strong, E. D. McCoy, and J. R. Ray. 1977. Time and the number of herbivore species: The pests of sugar cane. *Ecology* 58:167–175. © 1977 Ecological Society of America.)

quickly as native species colonized cacao after its introduction (Strong 1979). Similar observations have been made for the insect pests associated with rubber trees (*Hevea brasiliensis*) in various tropical areas (Strong et al. 1977).

Legume crops belonging to at least 225 genera have been introduced throughout the world. The soybean (*Glycine max*), for example, has been introduced from its native region of northeastern China to all continents with agriculture within the past 100–200 yr. In general, soybeans, as well as many other crop legumes, lack highly specialized herbivorous arthropods in the regions to which they have been introduced (Kogan 1991). Instead, they are colonized by generalist species, mostly from faunas of the regions of introduction. About 77% of the herbivorous arthropods associated with soybeans occur in only one of the six continental areas where this crop is now grown, and more than 90% occur in only one or two regions.

In North and South America, the arthropod herbivores of soybean are dominated by three major groups of species (Kogan 1991). Among herbivorous lepidopteran, coleopteran, and hemipteran insect pests, 14 of the 22 most important species are generalists and five others are insects specialized for the legume subfamily to which soybean belongs. Entire groups of insects that are important feeders on soybean in China are absent in North and South America. These include aphids, stem-boring flies, and seed-feeding lepidopterans.

Still other studies have examined the accumulation of herbivorous arthropods by various introduced plants in a particular region. The most comprehensive study of this sort (Andow and Imura 1994) was for herbivorous insects of crop plants introduced to Japan. Andow and Imura examined 23 crop species and a fauna of 498 herbivorous arthropods, 462 of which were native and 36 exotic. Time since crop plant introduction was not related to current richness of all herbivorous arthropods, but area of crop under cultivation showed a weak positive relationship to richness, as noted earlier for sugar cane and cacao. When arthropods that were specialized for feeding on plants of only one family were considered, however, time since crop plant introduction did show a positive relation with arthropod diversity. This result suggests that native arthropods specialized for members of a particular plant family tend to adapt evolutionarily to introduced crop plants through time. One major implication of this observation is that recently introduced crop plants are likely to acquire such specialist herbivores from the native fauna through future time.

Andow and Imura (1994) were also able to sort out native and introduced arthropod herbivores. They found that alien herbivorous arthropods tended to be generalists. These arthropods also showed no change in range of crop plants they used through time. Thus, the primary evolutionary process at the community level in Japan was the gradual adaptation of native herbivores to use introduced plants of families to which they were already specialized.

Accumulation of Herbivorous Arthropods by Noncrop Plants

Both woody and herbaceous plants introduced to new continental areas accumulate herbivorous insects rapidly. Several studies have examined the frequency of insects and other organisms associated with tree species in the British Isles. Southwood (1961) examined the numbers of herbivorous insects on British trees in relation to their postglacial appearance and abundance and compared numbers of insects on trees in Britain with those in other areas. He found a strong positive relationship between numbers of insects and the frequency of Quaternary fossil remains of the species, a measure that he considered to combine postglacial length of presence and general abundance of the various native species. He also noted that most species introduced since Roman times supported fewer herbivorous insect species. The maple, *Acer pseudoplatanus*, introduced about 1250 A.D., supported only 15 insect species, whereas the native maple, *A. campestre*, supported 26 species. The insect fauna of the introduced oak, *Quercus ilex*, introduced about 1580 A.D., consisted of only 2 species, whereas native oaks, *Q. robur* and *Q. petraea*, supported 284 species.

Southwood (1961) also called attention to the fact that species of spruce (*Picea abies*), larch (*Larix decidua*), and fir (*Abies* spp.), all introduced to the British Isles within the last 500 yr, supported many fewer herbivorous insects in Britain than in Russia. He suggested that this difference was largely related to the much more extensive distribution of these species on the continent, as well as on their longer postglacial presence.

Strong (1974b, 1974c) reexamined Southwood's (1961) data, pointing out that the relationship of number of insect species with the Quaternary age-abundance estimates implied that the number of species associated with each tree would continue to increase indefinitely. Strong used estimates of the present areal range of the various tree species in Britain and found that a very strong relationship existed between number of insect species and the range of the tree species in square kilometers. Based on the results of multivariate analyses incorporating both range area and Quaternary age-abundance, he argued that range area accounted for essentially all of the variability. He therefore concluded that length of postglacial presence had little to do with insect species richness and that faunas in equilibrium with each tree species developed within a few hundred years and were related primarily to distributional area.

Birks (1980) noted that the Quaternary age-abundance data used by Southwood (1961) and Strong (1974b) were crude, and presented estimates of the time of appearance of tree species in Britain based on radiocarbon dates for postglacial pollen profiles and other dateable fossils. He found that significant correlations existed for numbers of insects and time that various tree species had been present, with the correlation being strongest for angiosperms. He also emphasized that correlation does not prove causation and suggested that evolutionary time might have been more important than Strong (1974b, 1974c) inferred. Nevertheless, these analyses do suggest that area is probably an important factor and that British trees probably accumulate many herbivorous insects soon after they invade. The analyses of insect diversity unfortunately do not distinguish generalist versus specialist species for the tree taxa.

Kennedy and Southwood (1984) reexamined a refined data set on insects associated with British trees. Using stepwise multiple regression techniques, these authors confirmed the importance of an index of area and abundance as the strongest indicator of number of insect species associated with each tree. However, they also found that the time data used by Birks (1980) remained a significant variable in multivariate analyses including area and abundance. In addition, they found that the number of close relatives a tree species had in Britain had a positive influence on the number of associated insects. Thus, this series of studies over more than 20 yr showed that both abundance and evolutionary time seem to influence the diversity of insect herbivores that an introduced tree acquires.

Strong and Levin (1975) examined the richness of parasitic fungal species for British trees, including natives and those introduced in recent historical time. They also found that species richness was closely related to distributional area. The slope of the relationship of number of species to area was much lower for fungi than that for herbivorous insects, presumably reflecting the fact that fungi exhibit a much greater dispersal ability than insects. Fungal species thus appear to have attained the equilibrium diversity expected by species-area relations within a few hundred years of introduction of their hosts.

Many other studies have focused on the arthropods associated with alien plants, usually invasive weeds, in a particular region compared to their native area. These studies have shown that the species that first colonize alien plants tend to be feeding generalists. The rate of accumulation of herbivorous arthropods varies greatly. For some time after plant introduction, the diversity of herbivorous arthropods tends to be lower than for the plant in its native region, especially if the plant lacks close relatives in the new region. In general, alien herbaceous plants accumulate new herbivores faster than woody plants. In a few cases, introduced herbaceous species may host more herbivorous arthropods than close native relatives (see, e.g., Frenzel et al. 2000).

The herbivores of thistles alien to North America have been a popular object of study, usually in relation to a search for potential biocontrol species. The phytophagous insects associated with milk thistle (*Silybum marianum*) and Italian thistle (*Carduus pycnocephalus*) in southern California are numerous but consist mostly of polyphagous species that feed on the foliage of these plants (Goeden 1971, 1974). In Eurasia, however, many insect species that feed internally, and thus are much more destructive to these plants, are known. Species of this type, of course, are the ones most often sought for classical biological control. Similar observations have been made for Russian thistle (*Salsola tragus*) and purple loosestrife (*Lythrum salicaria*) in North America (Goeden and Ricker 1968; Diehl et al. 1997).

For Italian thistle, Goeden (1974), for example, compared the insects associated with the plant in southern California with those associated with it in southern Europe. This species first appeared in California in the early 1930s. Slightly more than 40 species of insects belonging to 7 orders and 28 families were recorded on Italian thistle in southern California. Only about 15 of these were reproducing on the plant. In southern Europe, more than 80 species belonging to 8 orders and 31 families were recorded. At least 33 of these were reproducing on the plant. Thus, in the 30–40 or so years that Italian thistle had been present in California, it had accumulated about half the total species that were present in Europe. The low representation of reproducing species in California supports the hypothesis that many of the first colonizers are generalists.

Another thistle of European origin, Canada thistle (*Cirsium arvense*), arrived in North America in the 1700s (Moore 1975). This species has occupied North America much longer than the Italian thistle and is much more widespread. In Europe, at least 86 species of insects are found on Canada thistle, and in Canada, some 84 species are known to feed on this species, many of them reproducing within plant organs rather than feeding on foliage. Thus, the richness of the insect fauna on this species in Canada approaches that in Europe.

In spite of the rapid accumulation of pests by many introduced species, the time to fully exploit hosts is often much longer (Strong 1979). Kogan (1981), for example, found that in Asia, the native home of soybean (*Glycine max*), the phytophagous arthropods of this plant feed in ways that include all those used by soybean arthropods in North America as well as several additional modes.

Several good examples are available of alien plants that native phytophages have not fully exploited. Scotch broom (*Cytisus scoparius*), introduced to North America from the British Isles, is a highly invasive shrub in the Pacific Northwest. In Britain, this shrub hosts a rich assemblage of specialist herbivores, including 23 species of insects that feed on the plant's pods and seeds. A survey in 1963 (Waloff 1966) recorded only 17 species of herbivorous insects on Scotch broom at sites in California and British Columbia. No pod or seed feeders were recorded at these North American sites. The lack of seed- and pod-feeders on Scotch broom in California and British Columbia (Waloff 1966) shows that North American insects have not yet exploited this plant to the degree that British insects have. Memmott et al. (2000) examined Scotch broom in New Zealand and Australia and compared the invertebrate fauna to broom in France and England, where the species is native. Specialist phytophages were also deficient in New Zealand and Australia, especially those feeding on flowers and seeds.

Yellow starthistle (*Centaurea solsticialis*), native to Eurasia, is an invasive rangeland weed that was introduced to North America in the early or mid-1800s. It is now present on more than 3 million ha in the northern intermontane region of North America. In Idaho, a survey of the insect fauna associated with the plant revealed numerous species that used nectar or pollen but only eight native insects that fed on the foliage of the plant (Johnson et al. 1992). Only two of these were regularly present. In contrast, in southern Europe, Clement (1990) found 42 species of herbivorous insects feeding on yellow starthistle. At least 18 of these species were specialists for yellow starthistle or close plant relatives. Similar observations were made by Wolfe (2002) for white campion (*Silene latifolia*), a widespread noxious weed native to Europe.

The colonization of alien plants by native herbivores is clearly influenced by the taxonomic relatedness of alien plants with native plants. This is shown by the speed at which sawtooth oak was colonized by leaf-mining insects at Tall Timbers Research Station in Florida. In England, the lepidopteran herbivore faunas of two trees, one an oak (*Quercus cerris*) and the second a maple (*Acer pseudoplatanus*), that had been introduced to England in the late 1600s or early 1700s were examined by Yela and Lawton (1997). These trees had accumulated faunas comparable to members of the same genera that occurred at the study site and had been present in England for thousands of years. *Acer pseudoplatanus* has a very close native relative in *A. campestre*, which may account for the high number of insect colonists (Frenzel et al. 2000). *Quercus cerris* belongs to the same genus as the native *Q. robur*, a tree that harbors an abundant fauna of herbivorous insects. A third alien plant, *Rhododendron ponticum*, which was introduced in 1763 and has no native congeners in England, had a lepidopteran fauna much less diverse than the oak and maple aliens.

The introduction of various species of oaks (*Quercus*) to different world regions has shown clearly how the presence and absence of close relatives influences colonization by herbivores (Connor et al. 1980). Sawtooth oak (*Q. acutissima*), native to eastern Asia, has acquired a fauna of leaf-mining insects comparable to that of native oaks since its introduction to North America in 1862. This oak, belonging to the same subgenus as North American white oaks, has several close North American relatives. Japanese blue oak (*Q. glauca*), on the other hand, lacks close subgeneric relatives. Although it was introduced to North America in 1865, it has accumulated few if any leaf miners. Several species of European, North American, and Asian oaks have been introduced to Australia and New Zealand at various times, for some species as early as 1820. Oaks are not native to these regions, although the plant family, Fagaceae, represented by southern hemisphere beeches (*Nothofagus* spp.), is present. Although in their native regions, oak species tend to possess 15–24 or more species of leaf mining insects, oaks in Australia and New Zealand were found to almost completely lack such species.

Brazilian pepper (*Schinus terebinthifolius*), a major invasive tree in Florida, is an example of a plant lacking close relatives in North America. Brazilian pepper was introduced to the United States in about 1840 but was popularized as an ornamental plant in the 1920s. Surveys of the insect fauna of Brazilian pepper revealed a fauna of 115 species in Florida (Cassani 1986; Cassani et al. 1989). Of these, 46 were phytophagous species, but none of them appeared to cause serious damage to the tree. The insect fauna associated with the tree in Brazil is at least 200 species (Medal et al. 1999). A similar situation prevails for the Australian paperbark (*Melaleuca quinquenervia*), another invasive alien tree in Florida. In Australia, more than 450 species of herbivorous insects are known to feed on the species, but only a few native insects attack the tree in Florida (Simberloff et al. 1997). In Australia, these herbivores substantially reduce the growth of paperbarks (Balciunas and Burrows 1993).

Alien plants belonging to families that are not represented in the region of introduction are especially impoverished in native herbivore colonizers. *Opuntia* cacti introduced to South Africa, for example, have not acquired any native herbivorous arthropods even after 250 yr (Moran 1980). American mangrove (*Rhizophora mangle*), introduced to Hawaii in 1902, lacks lepidopteran herbivores there, although several such species attack the plant in Florida (Connor et al. 1980). Trees of the genera *Eucalyptus* and *Casuarina* introduced into various world regions from their home in Australasia likewise have very depauperate faunas of herbivorous arthropods (see, e.g., Ohmart and Edwards 1991). About 90 species of woody plants of the genus *Eucalyptus* have been introduced into North America (Paine and Millar 2002), beginning in the 1800s. Until recently, these plants were almost completely free of herbivorous insects and plant diseases. Few native insects have proven able to feed on eucalypts, and only since 1984 have pest insects invaded from Australia. About 15 species have now become established in California.

Accumulation of Predators and Parasitoids by Alien Animals

Introduced arthropods also tend to acquire predators and parasites from the native fauna of the new region. Several studies have been made of the acquisition of parasitoids by alien arthropods. Parasitoids, like herbivorous arthropods, vary from being highly host-specific to having a very wide host range. Species of parasitoids that are closely adapted to host physiology, so that the host continues to be active and feed for some time, tend to be more host-specific (Askew and Shaw 1986).

The speed with which parasitoids can become associated with new alien hosts is illustrated by a study of two recently introduced leaf-mining moth species in England (Godfray et al. 1995). These moths, belonging to the genus *Phyllonorycter*, were native to continental Europe. One species, first noted in 1989, attacked garden shrubs of the genus *Pyracantha*, itself an alien plant. The second, seen first in 1990, attacked species of sycamore or plane tree (*Platanus* spp.). Data on the parasitoids associated with these moths were collected from 1991 to 1993, just a few years after they had been first noted. The parasitoids associated with these species were compared to those known for 35 other species of *Phyllonorycter* native to England and associated with 32 different host plants.

Each of the two newly colonizing species of *Phyllonorycter* was found to support 16 species of parasitoids, a diversity that was essentially equal to that shown by native moth species. Furthermore, the parasitoids associated with these colonist moths did not show a greater proportion of generalists. One of the parasitoids associated with the species mining leaves of *Platanus*, in fact, was a specialist on this host moth. It was discovered during this study and very likely immigrated to England at the same time as its host. The suite of parasitoids associated with the new hosts was not predictable from the pattern of parasitism of native moths and their plant hosts. Thus, a normal number of parasitoids became associated with the two colonist moths in only a few years. The rapidity with which these associations developed was certainly aided by the proximity of England to the continental source area for the two moth species, and by the fact that many moth congeners and their associated parasitoids already existed in England.

For alien insect herbivores, the *Phyllonorycter* example is probably somewhat extreme, and the accumulation of parasitoids is usually not as fast nor as full. For a set of 87 herbivorous insects, for example, Cornell and Hawkins (1993) compared the number of insect parasitoids that had been recorded in areas where they were native and in areas to which they had been introduced. For most of these species, the time since introduction was known and varied from 1 to 155 yr. Analysis of these data showed, first, that in areas of introduction, the herbivore species had accumulated fewer parasitoids, about 4.0, than they possessed in their native regions, about 7.7. The number of parasitoids per herbivore in the native region, however, was positively related to that in the region of introduction. That is, herbivores with many parasitoids in their native region tended to have many in the region to which they were introduced, and vice versa. The intensity of parasitism was also higher in most cases in the native region of herbivores.

Many herbivorous arthropods apparently present a substantial challenge to exploitation by native parasitoids, however, and the natives may require evolutionary adjustments in seasonal activity pattern, behavior, or ecology to attack the new hosts. Evidence of this is the fact that the number of parasitoids accumulated by an herbivore in its region of introduction showed a slightly positive relationship with time since introduction (Cornell and Hawkins 1993). Variability in this relationship was great, however, with some herbivores accumulating parasitoid complexes as great as those in their native region in only 10 yr and others not even after 140 yr. Nevertheless, it appears that accumulation of parasitoids had not reached a plateau in the case of these herbivorous insects by 155 yr after introduction.

Only a few studies on accumulation of parasites by introduced vertebrates are available. In North America, the house sparrow (*Passer domesticus*), first introduced in 1852 or 1853, has accumulated about 33 species of mites, ticks, fleas, and parasitic flies, compared to 69 species known in Europe (Brown and Wilson 1975). Of these 33, 18 are species not known from the Old World. In North America, European starlings *Sturnus vulgaris*, introduced in 1890, have only 22 species of parasitic worms, whereas 70 have been recorded in Europe (Hair and Forrester 1970). Of the 22 North American species, 8 are not recorded from Europe. Thus, in a century to a century and a half, these species have not accumulated numbers of parasites equal to those they possess in Europe.

Although no comprehensive analysis is available, many insects introduced as biocontrol agents for herbivorous pests are themselves highly vulnerable to hyperparasitism (McEvoy and Coombs 2000). The frequency with which hyperparasites become associated with newly introduced parasitoids could thus influence the effectiveness of biocontrol efforts.

Thus, it appears that colonization of newly introduced host species by native herbivores, predators, and parasites may follow a pattern similar to the colonization of small, defaunated mangrove islands in Florida, as studied by Simberloff and Wilson (1969, 1970) and Wilson (1969). Like a defaunated island, a newly introduced host may rapidly accumulate many opportunistic species that eventually reach a maximum richness corresponding to a "noninteractive species equilibrium." Ecological interactions among these species and later colonizers then may lead to the loss of some of the original colonists, producing an "assortative equilibrium" that may be less diverse. Still later, in the case of new host species, evolutionary adjustments may lead to a still different equilibrium richness of species exploiting the host.

The Worst Case Scenario

The interactions of introduced and native species can thus be complex. Introduced plants acquire a fauna of both native and alien herbivores, and these, in turn, a series of predators and parasites of varied origins. As these species interact, some may be extirpated or driven to extinction. The risk of extinction of native species by introduced aliens is, in fact, enormous. We shall examine this threat in detail in the next chapter.

Part IV.

Global Evolutionary Consequences of Alien Invasions

The worldwide introduction of species to new geographical areas is influencing global biodiversity in a number of major ways. Native floras and faunas are being altered permanently by the massive introduction of alien species, so much so that invasion biologists speak of the result as "biotic homogenization." Evolutionary interactions of alien and native species are permanently altering these member species, as well as the communities they form.

Introduced species are one of the main causes of increase in rates of extirpation and extinction of native species, especially in insular environments such as oceanic islands and freshwater lakes and streams. In chapter 16, we shall examine the kinds of alien impacts that cause extirpations and extinctions. The deliberate introduction of alien species for biological control represents a special issue in alien biology. In chapter 17, we shall examine the controversy relating to the possible role of deliberately introduced biocontrol species in extirpation and extinction.

On the other hand, diversity in many ecological systems is being increased by the addition of new species. In chapter 18, we shall examine how the negative impacts of some of these new species are mitigated and how they become integrated into these systems. In addition, interactions of aliens and natives may result in the origin of new species, thus offsetting to a degree the impacts of aliens as agents of extinction. In chapter 19, we shall consider the role of alien introductions in increasing the rate of speciation.

Finally, in chapter 20, we shall examine how alien introductions interact with other aspects of global change, particularly climatic change, to create permanently altered biotic communities. The changes that are now under way in ecosystems throughout the world's lands, freshwaters, and oceans demand new strategies for conservation that recognize the dangers and benefits presented by the capacity of alien and native species to evolve.

16.

Alien Species as Agents of Extirpation and Extinction

"Through gains of exotic species and losses of native ones, the total number of species world-wide has declined and faunas and floras are losing their regional distinction."

—LOCKWOOD ET AL. (2000)

The White Mountains of Arizona hold the headwater streams of several branches of the Salt, Gila, and Little Colorado rivers. These streams were originally occupied by the Apache trout (*Oncorhynchus apache*). Some of these streams were first stocked with cutthroat trout (*O. clarki*) in the late 1800s, and many were repeatedly stocked with cutthroat, rainbow (*O. mykiss*), brook (*Salvelinus fontinalis*), and brown trout (*Salmo trutta*) through the mid- and late 1900s (Carmichael et al. 1993). The uniqueness of the Apache trout was recognized in the 1960s, although the species was not formally described until 1972. Since the 1960s, efforts have been made to protect White Mountain streams and stock them with hatchery-reared Apache trout. By then, however, it was apparent that the native Apache trout population had been severely affected by competition with brown and brook trout and hybridization with cutthroat and rainbow trout.

Studies were undertaken in 1987–1989 to determine the genetic status of trout in the White Mountain area, using allozyme electrophoresis. A series of genetic markers for Apache, cutthroat, and rainbow trout were identified, enabling all possible genetic intergrades among these species to be distinguished. Out of 31 populations sampled, only 11 contained pure

Apache trout. Hybrids with cutthroats were found at 20 sites, hybrids with rainbows at 16 sites, and hybrids with both aliens at 2 sites. Altogether, more than 60% of the fish examined were hybrids. This analysis reveals the extent to which careless introduction of alien fish can destroy the genetic uniqueness of native species and highlights the complexity of efforts that will be required to prevent the genetic extinction of this federal endangered species.

Extinction, Extirpation, and Endangerment

Extinction is the disappearance of species due to demographic failure—mortality that exceeds reproduction until the last individual dies—or genetic swamping—the loss of genetic identity due to interbreeding with other species. Extirpation is simply the local extinction of part of an overall population of a species. Endangerment is the existence of conditions that have not only reduced the population of a species to a critical level, but also, if continued, are likely to lead to extinction. Extinction and extirpation of populations are natural evolutionary events, but they have been magnified in severity one thousandfold by human influences.

The impacts of introduced alien species are the most rapidly growing cause of extinction and extirpation of endemic, native species. Alien species can cause extinction through predation, competition, or disease. Introgressive hybridization, the interbreeding of two or more species to produce fertile offspring, can also lead to the disappearance of species as distinct entities. Reid and Miller (1989) attributed 20–42% of all historic extinctions of mammals, birds, reptiles, and fish to introductions of alien species. Wilcove et al. (1998) judged that alien introductions were a significant factor in 47% of vertebrates and 27% of invertebrates that are now imperiled in the United States (table 16.1).

Species of insular environments, including oceanic islands, lakes, and streams, are particularly vulnerable to extinction. According to the World Conservation Monitoring Centre (1992), 100% of reptile extinctions, 90% of bird extinctions, 79% of mollusc extinctions, and 59% of mammal extinctions have been of island species. More than 36% of all historical extinctions of plants and animals have been of island species (Reid and Miller 1989). A large fraction of these extinctions has been due to the introduction of alien species. For birds, King (1980) estimated that more than 49% of extinctions on oceanic islands were due to predation, competition, or genetic swamping.

As the global impact of human activities has grown, however, the pre-

Table 16.1. Percentages of native species in the United States threatened by various major impacts. (Data from Wilcove et al. 1998.)

	Habitat degradation	Alien species	Pollution	Overexploitation	Disease
All species (1880)	85	49	24	17	3
Vertebrates (494)	92	47	46	27	11
Invertebrates (331)	87	27	45	23	0
Plants (1055)	81	57	7	10	1
Mainland (641)	90	30	12	13	1
Hawaii (414)	66	99	0	6	0
Birds (98)	90	69	22	33	37
Mainland (56)	88	48	38	39	4
Hawaii (42)	93	98	2	24	81

dominance of extinctions among island species now may be declining. Lomolino and Channell (1995) noted that the rate of extinction of continental mammals per unit time has risen until it almost equals that for islands. Relative to habitat area or number of species, on the other hand, mammal extinctions are still higher on islands.

Extinction and Extirpation due to Predation and Herbivory

The role of alien species in extinction on islands has a long history. Numerous native birds on Pacific islands, including Hawaii, were driven to extinction by predation by dogs, pigs, and rats, together with human hunting, following the arrival of Polynesian colonists (Olson and James 1984; Steadman 1995). In Hawaii alone, about 60 species became extinct during the Polynesian period. These included flightless species of geese, ibis, and rails, as well as flying members of several other families. Many of these species were probably easy prey because of the previous absence of terrestrial predators. In New Zealand, the kiore (*Rattus exulans*) introduced by Polynesian colonists, has probably been responsible for extirpation of tuataras (*Sphenodon* spp.), lizards, frogs, and large terrestrial orthopterans on the mainland and some offshore islands.

More recently, predation and destruction of vegetation following the introduction of goats, pigs, dogs, cats, rats, mongooses, and other mammals to oceanic islands has also been the cause of numerous extinctions of plants and animals. Numerous island plants have been driven to extinction by habitat conversion and the impacts of introduced mammals. In the Hawaiian Islands, for example, 80–90 species of plants have become extinct and about 270 additional species are threatened or endangered (F. Kraus, personal communication). Many island reptiles have been driven to extinction by introduced predators (Honegger 1980; Case and Bolger 1991). In particular, the Indian mongoose (*Herpestes auropunctatus*), which has been introduced to many Pacific and West Indian islands, has extirpated many snakes and lizards. Cats have had a serious impact on arboreal lizards on which mongooses cannot prey.

A striking example of how an alien species can lead to extirpation of prey species is provided by the brown tree snake (*Boiga irregularis*), introduced to the island of Guam in about 1950 (Rodda et al. 1999). This nocturnal predator, native to northern Australia, New Guinea, and neighboring Pacific islands, is active in both terrestrial and arboreal habitats. No such predator existed on Guam, so native species were naive prey for the brown tree snake. Predation by the brown tree snake has been implicated as the principal cause of extirpation of nine species of forest birds, three seabirds, and between three and five lizards.

In addition to the impacts of predatory mammals introduced by Polynesians to Pacific islands, including the Hawaiian Islands, invertebrate predators are taking a toll on native species. Hawaiian tree snails of the genus *Achatinella* originally included 41 species that evolved on the island of Oahu. Although reduced in numbers by the effects of habitat destruction and predation by mammals, the final blow was the introduction of a predatory rosy wolfsnail (*Euglandina rosea*) in 1958 as a hoped-for biological control of the alien giant African snail (*Achatina fulica*). The giant African snail survives, but more than half of the *Achatinella* snails are now extinct, and the remaining species are declining (Hadfield 1993). On Kauai, many endemic snails of the family Amastridae have disappeared due to predation by *Euglandina* (Civeyrel and Simberloff 1996). *Euglandina* also feeds on native aquatic snails in Hawaii and may be contributing to their decline (Kinzie 1992). The rosy wolfsnail has been introduced to other Pacific islands, including American Samoa, where its impact on native land snails is also severe (Cowie and Cook 2001), and French Polynesia, where many land snail extinctions have occurred (Civeyrel and Simberloff 1996). On the French Polynesian island of Raiatea, 33 species of *Partula* have become extinct, and on Moorea, 7 species have been lost (Coote and Loève 2003). In Hawaii, introduced insects, particularly the

Argentine ant, also are exerting severe pressures on native arthropods of many sorts (Cole et al. 1992).

Insular aquatic environments are also likely to experience extinctions due to introduced predators. Many native species of fish have become extinct due to the impacts of alien fish invaders or introductions (Miller et al. 1989). In North America, 27 species and 13 subspecies of fish have become extinct over the past 115 yr. Direct impacts of alien fish contributed to about 68% of these extinctions. Predation by species such as the sea lamprey (*Petromyzon marinus*) and largemouth bass (*Micropterus salmoides*) were implicated in the extinction of several species. In at least one case, that of the landlocked Miller Lake lamprey (*Lampetra minima*) in Klamath County, Oregon, extinction was an indirect effect of the introduction of alien fish. The species was deliberately poisoned because it parasitized trout introduced to the lake.

Predatory fish of several species have been introduced to lakes throughout the world in the name of improved sportfishing. In North America, for example, these introductions have reduced or extirpated native populations of many amphibians (Hecnar and M'Closkey 1997) and minnows of the family Cyprinidae (Whittier et al. 1997). Similar effects have been noted in Europe (Brönmark and Edenhamn 1994). Mosquitofish (*Gambusia affinis* and related species) have been introduced widely for the biological control of mosquitoes. In California (Gamradt and Kats 1996) and Australia (Komack and Crossland 2000), they have contributed to the decline of native amphibians by predation on eggs and larvae. On Oahu, Hawaii, *Gambusia affinis* and *Poecilia reticulata*, members of the same fish family, have caused the extirpation of native damselflies in streams to which these fish have been introduced (Englund 1999). Alien crayfish also prey on native amphibian larvae in California (Gamradt et al. 1997).

Some amphibians can be serious predators when introduced outside their native range. Bullfrogs (*Rana catesbeiana*), as well as other ranid frogs, have been introduced to various parts of western North America. These introductions have contributed to the extirpation or endangerment of several fish, amphibians, and reptiles (Cox 1999). In Australia, the cane toad (*Bufo marinus*), introduced in 1935 for biological control, is of concern because of its toxicity to native amphibians and fish that prey on its eggs, tadpoles, and young (Crossland and Alford 1998).

The introduction of the Nile perch (*Lates nilotica*) to Lake Victoria, East Africa, in the 1950s has probably had a greater impact than any other single species introduction to an aquatic ecosystem. Lake Victoria had an endemic fauna of more than 500 species of cichlid fish (Seehausen et al. 1997b). Direct and indirect effects of the Nile perch have contributed to the loss of many of these species. During the 1980s, about 200 of these species disappeared, apparently due to predation by Nile perch. These species lived mostly in the offshore and deep waters. The lake has experienced severe eutrophication due to accelerated nutrient inputs and predation by Nile perch on herbivorous and detritus-feeding fish. Massive growths of another alien, the water hyacinth (*Eichhornia crassipes*), have also changed the ecology of the shallower waters. These and other factors have contributed to further loss of species from the littoral zone. In turn, eutrophication, increased turbidity, and reduced visibility appear to interfere with color vision of many cichlids (Seehausen et al. 1997a). The result is reduced sexual selection, incorrect mate choice, and breakdown of reproductive isolation, leading to loss of species diversity. Other fish, including ten species of native catfish, have also been affected, and at least one species has become extinct (Goudswaard and Witte 1997). The Lake Victoria ecosystem is still undergoing rapid change, and the fate of its endemic fish fauna is still uncertain.

Alien animals have had much less impact on native plants and animals in continental areas than in insular environments. Several forest insects, including the gypsy moth (*Lymantria dispar*) and the adelgid scale insects (*Adelges* spp.), have caused local extirpation of sensitive forest tree species in many areas in eastern North America (Liebhold et al. 1996). Feral domestic cats (*Felis catus*) and red foxes (*Vulpes vulpes*) have been introduced or become established in many continental areas, where they prey on native animals. In Australia, these predators have certainly contributed to the decline of some endemic mammals, but whether or not they have caused extinctions is uncertain (Burbridge and McKenzie 1989). Although cats were introduced in the early 1800s and had almost completely colonized the continent by 1890, it is unlikely that they played a substantial role in extinction of native vertebrates (Abbott 2002).

Extinction and Extirpation due to Interspecific Competition

Invasive aliens can cause the extinction and extirpation of native species through competition, again largely in insular environments such as oceanic islands and fresh waters. Plants as well as animals are contributing to these losses in some cases.

The massive transformation of native vegetation by human activity and the introduction of exotic plants has placed many endemic plants at risk on many oceanic islands. In the Hawaiian Islands, for example, somewhere between 460 and 690 species of introduced plants have become established in the wild (Mueller-Dombois and Loope 1990). The resultant vegetational changes, together with other anthropogenic pressures, have driven about 177 native plants to extinction. With extinction of these plants, many endemic arthropods are likely also to have become extinct.

Individual island invaders can sometimes present major threats to native plants. In Tahiti, for example, 40–50 of the island's 212 endemic plant species are considered to be threatened by the spread of the South American shrub, *Miconia calvescens* (Meyer and Florence 1996). This plant, introduced in 1937 as an ornamental, has spread into the mountain forests, where it forms nearly pure stands over about two-thirds of the land area of the island. At least one endemic plant is believed extinct and 15 others critically endangered as a result.

Alien aquatic animals present competitive challenges to the survival of native species. Among invertebrates, for example, introduced crayfish have become serious threats to native crayfish in both Europe and North America (Lodge et al. 2000). Only five native crayfish occur in Europe, but four alien species have been introduced from North America and one from Australia. These aliens, and crayfish diseases introduced with them, have displaced European natives in thousands of locations.

North America has about 75% of the world's freshwater crayfish fauna, about 333 species in all. Many of these species are threatened by a variety of factors, including the spread of species to new waters by fishermen using them as bait. Many of these North American species are quite localized in distribution, however, and are thus at risk from the widespread introduction of nonindigenous species. One of the most frequently introduced crayfish, *Orconectes rusticus*, has extirpated native crayfish in many locations in the midwestern United States (Perry et al. 2002).

North America also has the world's richest fauna of freshwater mussels, some 296 species (Perry et al. 2002). Alien molluscs, particularly the zebra mussel (*Dreissena polymorpha*) and its close relative, the quagga mussel (*D. bugensis*), pose a serious threat to many native mussels, especially large mussels of the family Unionidae (Strayer 1999). The most direct impacts on unionids are through fouling, that is, growth of zebra and quagga mussels on unionid shells. In the Rideau River in eastern Ontario, Canada, for example, fouling by zebra mussels led to the extirpation of three formerly abundant unionids between 1993 and 2000 (Martel et al.

2001). In Lake St. Clair, between Lakes Huron and Erie, it appears that all native freshwater mussels were extirpated by 1997 (Nalepa et al. 2001).

Because of the enormous densities reached by *Dreissena* species, they also reduce the abundance of particulate foods required by both unionids and other smaller clams (Strayer 1999). The Asian clam (*Corbicula fluminea*) may also be a food competitor for native mussels in some situations.

Among aquatic vertebrates, competition has figured in the extinction of several North American fish (Miller et al. 1989). Impacts of alien species, often a combination of predation, competition, and hybridization, are implicated in 68% of the 40 species or subspecies of fish that have disappeared.

Among terrestrial vertebrates in continental areas, displacement of the red squirrel (*Sciurus vulgaris*) by the gray squirrel (*Sciurus carolinensis*) in Britain is one of the few examples that may be due to competition (Usher et al. 1992). Beginning in 1876, gray squirrels were introduced to various parks and estates on many occasions. Grays have replaced reds, especially in broad-leaved forests, in much of England and Wales and are still spreading in Scotland. The range of the gray squirrel is now about twice that of the red squirrel. Recently, the possibility was suggested that a viral disease introduced with the gray squirrel has contributed to decline of red squirrel populations (Tompkins et al. 2003). The barred owl (*Strix varia*) of eastern North America has expanded its range into the Pacific Northwest, perhaps as a result of human impacts on the landscapes of the upper Great Plains. This species may be displacing the ecologically similar and endangered spotted owl (*Strix occidentalis*) in some areas (Kelly et al. 2003).

Extinctions and Extirpations due to Disease Agents

Alien disease agents have had a major impact on tree species in North America. Perhaps the most destructive forest disease on record is the chestnut blight (*Cryphonectria parasitica*), which caused the virtual elimination of the American chestnut (*Castanea dentata*) as an ecologically important tree of the eastern deciduous forests. Early in the 1900s, this disease, a fungal canker, was introduced to New York State on Asian chestnut trees planted as ornamentals. The fungal hyphae spread through the phloem and xylem tissues, girdling and eventually killing the tree (Liebhold et al. 1996). From New York, the fungus spread rapidly and in about 40 yr had killed mature chestnut trees through the species' range, which extended from Maine to Georgia and west to the Mississippi River. Although the blight kills the aboveground parts of the tree, the roots often survive and produce sprouts. The sprouts survive for a number of years , until they are attacked and killed. Thus, the American chestnut is not extinct, but it is no longer an ecologically significant species of the eastern forests. Other tree species have filled the gap left by the death of the chestnut. The loss of this species, which was the most important mast-producing tree of the deciduous forest, probably had a major impact on forest birds and mammals (Campbell and Schlarbaum 1994).

Several other tree diseases, including white pine blister rust (*Cronartium ribicola*), Dutch elm disease (*Ophiostoma ulmi*; see chapter 5), dogwood anthracnose (*Discula destructiva*), and sudden oak death canker (*Phytophthora ramorum*), also are potential agents of extirpation of native trees. Recent reports indicate that sudden oak death canker also affects several other woody plants of the North American Pacific coast, including the coast redwood (*Sequoia sempervirens*).

Alien diseases are increasing contributors to extirpation of populations of animals. Crayfish plague, a fungal disease endemic to North America, has played a major role in the decline of native crayfish in Europe (Lodge et al. 2000).

Avian pox and avian malaria, brought to Hawaii by the introduction of alien birds, are now one of the major threats to the remaining endemic birds. Avian malaria resulted from the introduction both of alien mosquito vectors and birds carrying the malaria parasites (Scott and Sincock 1985; van Riper et al. 1986; Warner 1968). More recently, toxoplasmosis, a disease caused by a parasitic protozoan (*Toxoplasma gondii*), has been found in the 'alala or Hawaiian crow (*Corvus hawaiiensis*), one of the most endangered birds in the world (Work et al. 2000). The definitive host and primary reservoir of this disease in the wild is the feral domestic cat. The 'alala has been the object of a major reintroduction effort with captive-bred birds. The eradication of the feral cat population being nearly impossible, this disease poses a very serious problem for 'alala recovery.

Extinction and Extirpation due to Hybridization

Hybridization with alien species is a threat to a number of plants ranging from grasses and broad-leaved herbs to woody shrubs and trees (Levin et al. 1996; Daehler and Carino 2001). Simulation models of the hybridization process indicate that it can lead to extinction of native species by aliens in five or fewer generations (Wolf et al. 2001). A current example is *Lantana depressa*, a member of the verbena family, which is distributed throughout peninsular Florida. This diploid species has come into close contact with *L.*

camara, a widely planted, exotic tetraploid species. Hybrids between the two produce triploid progeny that spread vigorously through the natural habitat of *L. depressa* (Sanders 1987). It appears likely that in time these hybrids will completely displace diploid populations of *L. depressa*.

Several freshwater mussels and crayfish in North America are also suffering from hybridization because of the introduction of species to waters to which they are alien. Hybridization has been documented between several species of the genus *Orconectes*, thus complicating the already serious problem of competitive displacement of locally endemic crayfish described earlier (Perry et al. 2001b). Several cases of interspecific hybridization between mussels also have been documented, and the decline of two related species in the Susquehanna River has been attributed to hybridization (Perry et al. 2002). Hybridization is probably much more widespread than yet recognized among freshwater invertebrates.

In New Zealand, introduction of the common blue butterfly (*Zizina labradus*) from Australia has led to the genetic extinction of the southern blue butterfly (*Z. oxyleyi*) by hybridization (Barlow and Goldson 2002).

About 38% of the fish extinctions in North America within recorded history (Miller et al. 1989) were judged to have been caused in some measure by introgressive hybridization. These include the extinctions of at least two subspecies of cutthroat trout (*Oncorhynchus clarki*) and two locally endemic species of *Gambusia* that hybridized with the widely introduced *Gambusia affinis*.

Isolated populations of fish in springs and headwater streams are at high risk from hybridization. Often these forms are closely related to more widespread forms from which they have diverged because of their isolation. In Texas, for example, the Leon Springs pupfish (*Cyprinodon bovinus*) occurs in a small, spring-fed tributary of the Pecos River. Recent examination of these field populations revealed that hybridization has occurred with the more widespread sheepshead minnow (*Cyprinodon variegatus*), which was introduced to its habitat (Echelle and Echelle 1997). All field populations of this endemic are affected, but fortunately, a pure captive population exists. In a related case, the Pecos pupfish (*Cyprinodon pecosensis*), which occupies the main portion of the Pecos River in Texas and New Mexico, has suffered introgression from the sheepshead minnow over about 300 km of the river in Texas (Wilde and Echelle 1997). Both of these cases of introduction of sheepshead minnows to waters with related species are probably the result of the common use of sheepshead minnows as bait fish.

A special circumstance involves hatchery and wild salmon in the North Atlantic and North Pacific. In Norway, for example, Atlantic salmon (*Salmo salar*) farmed for seven generations differed significantly in morphology, behavior, growth, and life history features from the native fish from which they were derived (Fleming and Einum 1997). The changes, adaptive to the aquacultural environment, can be transmitted to wild populations through the escape of farmed animals. Interbreeding with wild salmon may thus reduce the fitness of wild salmon and hasten the extinction of wild populations. In Ireland, studies suggested that interbreeding of farmed and native salmon would lead to an increase in age of maturity in native populations, which might be maladaptive for salmon runs in shallow streams (McGinnity et al. 1997).

Mammals and birds are in a few cases placed at risk of extinction through hybridization. In Scotland, for example, sika deer (*Cervus nippon*) introduced from Japan more than 100 yr ago are interbreeding with the native red deer (*Cervus elaphus*). The zone of interbreeding covers an area about 350 km from the point of introduction of the sika deer and does not appear to have stabilized (Abernethy 1994). Thus, the Scottish red deer population at large may be at risk from genetic introgression.

The North American ruddy duck (*Oxyura jamaicensis*) was introduced to England in 1949 and has established a large population, which has recently invaded continental Europe. A small population of a close relative, the white-headed duck (*O. leucocephala*), has survived in southern Spain. Ruddy ducks have appeared in Spain, and some hybridization has been observed (Rhymer and Simberloff 1996). The Spanish population of the white-headed duck is small and isolated from the only other population of the species in central Asia. In this case, hybridization is a distinct threat to survival of the white-headed duck.

Mallards have hybridized with other members of the genus *Anas* in Florida, Hawaii, and New Zealand to an extent that threatens the genetic extinction of local forms (Rhymer and Simberloff 1996). In eastern North America, hybridization between mallard (*Anas platyrhynchos*) and black (*A. rubripes*) ducks may be contributing to the gradual decline of the latter species. A 1991 study in New Brunswick, for example, found that 14% of pairs were of mixed composition (D'Eon et al. 1994).

The European quail (*Coturnix coturnix*) is a widespread, migratory European bird that winters partly in southern Spain and North Africa and partly in the sub-Saharan Sahel. Domesticated Japanese quail (*Coturnix japonica*), selected by animal breeders for lack of migration, have been stocked for hunting in countries around the Mediterranean Sea. These two species easily interbreed (Deregnaucourt et al. 2002), which could lead to detrimental genetic pollution of the migratory birds native to

Europe. The trans–Saharan migratory population of the European quail, in particular, has declined in abundance in recent decades, and behavioral evidence for hybridization in field populations exists in France and Spain.

Interaction of Competition and Hybridization

Interspecific hybridization is clearly becoming a more frequent component of the impact of alien species. Many of the related species being brought together evolved their differences in geographic isolation, under conditions in which reproductive isolation was not a significant target of selection.

Huxel (1999) examined the interaction of competition and hybridization for simple two-species evolutionary systems. When competition acts alone, the outcome depends on the fitness differential between the species and the rate of immigration. If the fitness advantage of the alien is small and its immigration rate low, the likelihood of the alien succeeding is small. On the other hand, an alien species with greater relative fitness or a high rate of immigration is likely to displace its native competitor. A high rate of immigration, even when the alien had lower relative fitness, also can enable the alien to displace its native competitor.

With introgressive hybridization and competition, the outcome also depends on the fitness of hybrid genotypes. If hybrids are not favored or are disadvantaged, the outcome is similar to that without hybridization. If hybrid individuals have a fitness disadvantage, however, the displacement of the native is speeded. If hybrid individuals show greater fitness, or hybrid vigor, the complete displacement of the pure native species is prevented unless the invasion rate of the alien is very high. This last case corresponds to genetic assimilation, in which the native effectively becomes extinct by being absorbed into the gene pool of the alien. This appears to be the case in Trout Lake, Wisconsin, where the introduced *Orconectes rusticus* both competes with and interbreeds with the native *O. propinquus* (Perry et al. 2001a). The hybrids between the two appear to be competitively superior to both parents but equivalent in fecundity. The outcome thus is likely to be a population morphologically much like *O. rusticus* but with a component of genes from *O. propinquus*. Both competition and hybridization may be responsible for the replacement of native North American subspecies of red foxes (*Vulpes vulpes*) by European red foxes introduced to eastern North America beginning in the 1700s (Kamler and Ballard 2002).

Good Intentions and Extinction Risks

Biological invasions have become a major cause of extinction, extirpation, and genetic modification, especially in insular environments. A category of alien species that we have not yet considered includes biological control agents that are introduced not only deliberately, but also because of the likelihood that they will greatly reduce the population of a target species. In the next chapter, we shall turn our attention to these species and the evolutionary issues they present.

17.

Evolutionary Ecology of Alien Biological Control Agents

"Another pervasive problem engendered by the fact that biological-control agents are alive is that they evolve."

—SIMBERLOFF AND STILING (1996)

Common St. John's wort (*Hypericum perforatum*) is a European broad-leaved herb that was introduced into eastern North America in the late 1700s. It ultimately reached the western United States and Canada, where, because of its toxicity to livestock, it became a noxious weed over millions of hectares. It also became a noxious weed in Australia, where one of the earliest successful biological control campaigns was carried out on it, using three foliage-feeding beetles. Prior to their release, Australian scientists had tested the beetles for their ability to feed on plants of some 35 families. The tests included several species of *Hypericum*, on which some of the beetles survived and reproduced. Additional testing was done by American scientists, although none was done with species of *Hypericum*. Canadian scientists also tested the feeding preferences of the beetles and found that species of *Hypericum* were accepted as food plants. Despite the evidence that the beetles could feed on various species of *Hypericum*, all three beetles were approved and released in Canada and the United States in the late 1940s (Harris 1988).

One of the beetles, *Chrysolina quadrigemina*, proved to be an effective control agent for common St. John's wort. In 1975, however, *C. quadrigemina* was found to be attacking an introduced horticultural plant, creeping

St. John's wort or Aaron's beard (*Hypericum calycinum*). Reproductive success of *C. quadrigemina* was much greater on creeping St. John's wort than on common St. John's wort, so in a short time a strain of this beetle adapted to this host evolved (Harris 1988). *C. quadrigemina* has also been observed to attack a native plant known as goldwire (*Hypericum concinnum*). Two other biological control insects introduced for common St. John's wort have also been found to attack goldwire. This case demonstrates that biological control agents have the potential to shift to nontarget hosts and eventually to evolve forms specific to these hosts.

Biological Control with Introduced Enemies

Biological control involves a variety of strategies, including the augmentation of existing natural enemies of pest species, the release of sterilized insects to interfere with reproduction of field populations of the same species, and the use of various microbial agents dispersed in the manner of chemical pesticides. Traditional biological control, however, involves the introduction of predators, parasites, or pathogens that are hoped to reduce the population of a pest to a level at which it does not cause economic damage. Classic biological control uses one or more species that were associated with an alien pest in its native region—the hope being that it will reduce the pest as much as, or more than, it did in its native situation. A potential biocontrol agent, introduced without its own predators, parasites, or diseases, might be expected to be more effective than it was in its native area.

Many biocontrol efforts, however, involve new associations between potential biocontrol species and pests (Hokkanen and Pimentel 1989). Myxomatosis, the disease introduced to Australia as a biocontrol agent for European rabbits (*Oryctolagus cuniculus*), for example, is a disease of New World cottontail rabbits (*Sylvilagus* spp.). Cottontails are only mildly affected by the disease, whereas it was initially highly lethal to European rabbits. Some biocontrol scientists believe that new associations like this offer the greatest potential for effective control of pests.

In either case, introducing species for biocontrol purposes carries several risks. In some cases, biocontrol species can use nontarget species closely related to the target species. In other cases, variation in host preference may exist in the introduction stock, particularly if the introduced organisms come from different geographical areas where host differences exist. In still other cases, an evolutionary change may enable an introduced biocontrol agent to use nontarget hosts. In such cases, biocontrol species may cause economic damage, reduce populations of nontarget hosts, or even lead to the extinction of nontarget species.

An additional little-recognized possibility is that the introduced biocontrol agent may carry other organisms that may have unexpected impacts of their own (Slippers et al. 2001). For example, a wood wasp (*Sirex noctilio*) associated with northern hemisphere pines was accidentally introduced to New Zealand and Australia and has subsequently spread to South America and South Africa. This wood wasp has a symbiotic relationship with white rot fungus (*Amylostereum areolatum*), a destructive agent in plantations of exotic pines. A nematode (*Deladenus siricidicola*) that sterilizes the eggs of the wasp was introduced to Australia as a biological control agent for the wasp. Subsequently, this nematode was introduced to South Africa and South America from Australia. The introduced nematode, which also feeds on the fungus, carried a distinct strain of the fungus, which has now become established in the introduction areas (Slippers et al. 2002).

An initially effective biocontrol species may select for resistance on the part of the host, just as the use of chemical pesticides has selected for resistance by many pest species. Biological control programs have tended to ignore this possibility, largely because few instances of this have yet been noted. Holt and Hochberg (1997), however, have suggested that apparent stability of biological control relationships is real, especially for biocontrol predators and parasitoids. The low frequency of evolved resistance to such agents may be due to lack of genetic variability by the host, factors that offset the influence of selection by the control agent, or the coevolutionary dynamics that tend to balance agent effectiveness and host resistance.

Ecological Host Shifts by Biological Control Agents

Species introduced for biological control may expand or shift their feeding activity to nontarget hosts (Louda et al. 2003b). Although such shifts may occur without genetic changes in the biocontrol species, in time, selection may lead to adaptation to a widened range of hosts or to specialization for nontarget species. Serious impacts on nontarget species may occur if high populations of the biocontrol agent shift from the target host to other hosts, even species of low preference (Lynch et al. 2002). In extreme cases, this may lead to extinction of nontarget species (see chapter 16).

Many such host shifts have been documented. In some cases, the host

Table 17.1. Biological agents introduced to control target plants and their use of nontarget plant species in the United States and the Caribbean region in relation to presence or absence of congeners. (Data from Pemberton 2000.)

	TARGET PLANTS WITH CONGENERS			TARGET PLANTS LACKING CONGENERS		
	Total BC agents released	Agents adopting nontarget plants	Total nontarget plants attacked	Total BC agents released	Agents adopting nontarget plants	Total nontarget plants attacked
U.S. Mainland and Caribbean	56	10	37	12	0	0
Hawaii	5	4	3	49	1	1

shift is incidental, resulting from high populations of the biocontrol species on the target host that cause individuals to move to other species on which they cannot complete their life cycle (Blossey et al. 2001). In many other cases, the shift is to plants or animals on which the biocontrol species can reproduce. For the United States mainland, Hawaii, and the Caribbean region, Pemberton (2000) listed 15 species of herbivorous biocontrol insects that have extended their feeding habits to 41 species of native plants; in almost all cases, the extension species were close relatives of the target plant (table 17.1). The plants involved included shrubs, cacti, broad-leaved herbs, and flatsedges (*Cyperus* spp.). McFadyen (1998) and Dennill et al. (1993) noted additional examples from other world regions.

Similar shifts have occurred for biocontrol agents of animal pests. For parasitoids introduced to North America for control of insect pests, Hawkins and Marino (1997) found that 51 (16.3%) of the 313 introduced species were recorded from nontarget hosts. For Hawaii, 37 (32.2%) of 115 parasitoid species were noted to use nontarget hosts (Funasaki et al. 1988). In some cases, a single biocontrol parasitoid can attack many nontarget species. The parasitoid fly *Compsilura concinnata* was introduced for biological control of gypsy moth (*Lymantria dispar*) from 1906 through 1986 (Boettner et al. 2000). This parasitoid attacks many nontarget host moths in New England, including several Saturniid silk moths, the populations of which have declined substantially or been extirpated in some areas. In particular, wild populations of one silk moth, *Hemileuca maia*, a species listed as threatened in Massachusetts, were found to be severely affected by the parasitoid fly. In New Zealand, an introduced parasitoid was found to attack 13 species of nontarget beetles (Samways 1997).

One of the most extensive examples of biocontrol agents attacking nontarget animal species involved parasitoids introduced to the Hawaiian Islands for control of lepidopteran pests. On the island of Kauai, Hawaii, 122 species of wasp and fly parasitoids have been introduced over the past century (Henneman and Memmott 2001). These parasitoids have attacked many native species of moths, even in the remote highland forests. Of more than 200 parasitoid individuals reared from caterpillars collected in the Alakai Swamp wilderness preserve, 83% were species deliberately introduced for biological control and an additional 14% were alien species that were not deliberately introduced. The overall incidence of parasitism of native moth caterpillars was estimated at 19–22%. Since the parasitoids involved have been present in Kauai for many years, these moth species are probably not endangered. Whether or not other species of native moths have become extinct because of parasitism by alien parasitoids is not known. In other parts of the Hawaiian Islands, biological control introductions are considered to be responsible for extinctions of at least 15 native moth species (Howarth and Ransey 1991). Fortunately, some distinctive groups of native moths, including forms that are uniquely carnivorous, have not been attacked by alien parasitoids.

Only a few true predators have been introduced for biological control, but almost all use nontarget species, in some cases to a greater extent than target species. Mosquitofish (*Gambusia* spp.), widely introduced for mosquito control, prey on many other small aquatic vertebrates (McEvoy 1996). The cane toad (*Bufo marinus*), privately introduced to Australia (Samways 1997), has proven to be a serious predator on many native fish and amphibians. The impacts of introduced mongooses on oceanic islands were discussed in chapter 16.

A recent example that has been studied in detail illustrates the risks of introduction of herbivorous insects for the control of problem plants. Musk thistle (*Carduus nutans*) is one of the troublesome Eurasian thistles that have been introduced to North America. It is now known from almost all of the contiguous United States. After screening for its ability to use various native North American thistles, a weevil (*Rhinocyllus conicus*) was judged to be a potentially effective biological control agent for musk thistle and one that would probably not attack native thistles of the genus *Cirsium* to a significant degree. Beginning in the early 1970s, *R. conicus* was released in various areas where major infestations of musk thistle occurred.

By the late 1980s, however, *R. conicus* had begun to attack many native thistles (Louda et al. 1997; Louda 1998). In 1993, for example, it was attacking native thistles in Colorado, Nebraska, and South Dakota, including the Platte thistle (*Cirsium canescens*), an untroublesome species endemic to sand prairies of the upper Great Plains. Reproduction by this thistle is limited by a number of native insects, so the addition of a seed predator such as *R. conicus* presents a serious threat to its survival. A close relative of the Platte thistle, pitcher's thistle (*C. pitcheri*), a sand-habitat species of the Great Lakes region, is a federally listed endangered species, so the potential exists for extinction of one or more distinctive native plants due to the utilization of native thistles by *R. conicus*. Numerous other native *Cirsium* thistles in the western United States have been attacked by this weevil, with populations on these species increasing through time (Louda and Arnett 2000; Pemberton 2000).

Another seed-head weevil, *Larinus planus*, has also attacked native North American thistles (Louda and O'Brien 2001). This weevil, screened for its potential as a biological control for Canada thistle (*Cirsium arvense*), was found to attack several other European species of thistles of the genus *Cirsium* and was considered inappropriate for introduction to North America. In the 1960s and early 1970s, however, *L. planus* was discovered in the wild in New York State and Maryland. It was then screened further for its ability to attack Canada thistle and native North American thistles of the genus *Cirsium*. These tests seemed to show that development was poor on native thistles, and *L. planus* was therefore distributed in Canada and the United States. In 1999, Louda and O'Brien (2002) discovered that it was attacking native wavyleaf thistle, *Cirsium undulatum*, in Colorado. Infestations on this native thistle were, in fact, heavier than on Canada thistle in the same area. *L. planus* has recently been found attacking several native thistles in Oregon (Louda et al. 2003b).

A similar case involves the cinnabar moth (*Tyria jacobaeae*), introduced for control of the tansy ragwort (*Senecio jacobeae*). Tansy ragwort, native to Eurasia, is a rangeland weed that is highly toxic to livestock. It is a major problem species in the Pacific Northwest and the Canadian Maritimes. Larvae of the cinnabar moth feed on the foliage of tansy ragwort, giving a moderate degree of control. The genus *Senecio* is represented by numerous native species in North America, and the cinnabar moth has begun to use some of these (Diehl and McEvoy 1990). In Oregon, for example, it commonly feeds on *Senecio triangularis*, especially where this species grows in close association with tansy ragwort. Growth is somewhat slower on *S. triangularis*, and the pupae are lighter in weight than on tansy ragwort.

Still another case involves the moth *Cactoblastis cactorum*, which has been introduced in various regions for control of invasive species of prickly pear cactus (*Opuntia* spp.). This moth, introduced to the West Indies, dispersed by natural means to the Florida Keys in 1989. There, it began to attack several native *Opuntia* species (Samways 1997). By 2002, *Cactoblastis* had spread in coastal areas throughout the Florida peninsula, west to St. George Island in the Florida Panhandle, and north to near Charleston, South Carolina (Hight et al. 2002). It is unlikely that spread of this insect can be prevented to areas of the western United States and Mexico, where numerous species of *Opuntia*, both wild and cultivated, exist. Clearly, many biocontrol arthropods have a considerable dispersal capacity that must be considered when introductions are made.

In a few cases, biocontrol herbivores have extended their feeding to plants distantly related to their target species. The lace bug (*Teleonemia scrupulosa*) has been introduced in many countries as a biocontrol for lantana (*Lantana camara*), a plant of the family Verbenaceae that is a troublesome weed in tropical regions. In East Africa, the lace bug was found to attack one variety of cultivated sesame (*Sesamum indicum*) belonging to a different family, Pedaliaceae (Harris 1988; Hokkanen and Pimentel 1989). In Hawaii, this same bug has also been found to attack a small native tree known as naio (*Myoporum sandwicense*), a member of the family Myoporaceae. Another case involves a weevil (*Neochetina eichhorniae*) introduced for control of water hyacinth (*Eichhornia crassipes*) in the southern United States. This weevil has been found to attack plants of at least two other families (Harris 1988).

Host shifts by introduced predators and parasites have led to negative impacts on native species, as well as on some other biocontrol species. Introductions of vertebrate predators, such as mosquitofish (*Gambusia* spp.), the small Indian mongoose (*Herpestes javanicus*), and the cane toad (*Bufo marinus*) for control of various pests have led to severe impacts on native freshwater and terrestrial vertebrates. Introduction of parasitic insects and predatory molluscs to Hawaii and other Pacific islands has caused the endangerment or extinction of many native arthropods and molluscs. We have examined these cases in detail in chapter 16.

Alien biocontrol species can create impacts throughout the food web in which target or nontarget hosts are enmeshed. On Platte thistle (*Cirsium canescens*), the weevil *Rhinocyllus conicus*, for example, may negatively influence populations of other thistle insects that attack other, weedier thistles later in the summer (Louda and Arnett 2000). One species of introduced parasitoid has also caused an indirect negative effect by hyperparasitism of another parasitoid that had been introduced for biological control (Flanders 1943).

Evolutionary Adaptation by Biological Control Species

In a few instances, herbivorous alien arthropods introduced for biocontrol have adapted evolutionarily to nontarget plants, as we noted in the introductory example. Such examples are still uncommon, and some entomologists (see, e.g., van Klinken and Edwards 2002) have argued that only the potential for altered frequency of use of existing hosts needs to be considered in risk assessment of introduction of a biocontrol species. According to them, fundamental shifts in host range are very unlikely and do not need to be considered. Nevertheless, considering the patterns of adaptation shown by similar native arthropods to alien plants (chapter 13), the potential for such adaptation seems appreciable. That biotypes specific to related host species are known for some biocontrol agents (see, e.g., Hoffmann et al. 2002) indicates that evolutionary adaptation to related hosts can occur.

Alien biocontrol species have also shown evolutionary adaptation to conditions of their new habitat. Studies of a nonnative parasitoid and its prey show that rapid evolution can occur in relation to habitat conditions. In North America, the small cabbage white butterfly (*Pieris rapae*), itself an alien introduced from Europe, is parasitized by a wasp (*Cotesia glomerata*) that was introduced from Europe in the late 1800s as a potential biological control agent. In North America, the butterfly feeds on a variety of plants of the Brassicaceae, both native and introduced. Some of these plants, such as cabbage (*Brassica oleracea*), are cultivated in monoculture, whereas others grow wild as individuals or small clusters in diverse stands of herbaceous vegetation. Van Nouhuys and Via (1999) examined the behavior of *Cotesia* wasps from cabbage fields and wild vegetation under laboratory conditions. Wasps from the two habitats differed in behavior in test situations simulating cabbage fields. Wasps from the wild vegetation switched locations more often than wasps from cabbage fields, suggesting that cabbage-field wasps had evolved to be more sedentary because suitable host plants for their butterfly prey were close together. Furthermore, Van Nouhuys and Via (1999) were able to show that these differences had a genetic basis.

In Australia, the moth *Cactoblastis cactorum* was introduced from Argentina in 1925 as a biological control agent for prickly pear cacti (*Opuntia* spp.). This moth typically has two generations per year in Argentina and exhibits this pattern in Queensland and New South Wales, where it has become very widely established. Sometime between 1945 and 1955, it appeared near Melbourne, Victoria, an area of cooler climate. The population here has only one generation annually and produces eggs that hatch in less than half the time as eggs in New South Wales and Queensland. Allozyme studies also revealed that Victoria moths show significant differences in allele frequencies at several loci. Thus, in about 100 generations or fewer, the moth has made substantial adjustment to climatic conditions (Murray 1982).

Few cases of evolutionary adaptation of introduced biocontrol insects to new hosts have been documented, aside from the example cited at the beginning of this chapter. Arnett and Louda (2002) tested the host plant preferences of *Rhinocyllus conicus* for musk thistle (*Carduus nutans*) and various native thistles after about 28 generations had elapsed since introduction of the beetle for musk thistle biocontrol. They found no evidence of a preference shift. In the Old World, however, this beetle is known to have biotypes adapted to several thistle species of different genera (Zwölfer and Preiss 1983). The beetles introduced to North America included two of these forms (Goeden et al. 1985).

An interesting case of evolutionary adaptation by an introduced biocontrol insect to a target host was documented by Messenger and van den Bosch (1971). A parasitic wasp, *Bathyplectes curculionis*, introduced for control of alfalfa weevils of the genus *Hypera*, was initially only weakly effective against the Egyptian alfalfa weevil, *H. brunneipennis*, because larval weevils killed 35–40% of the wasps eggs by an immune response. Fifteen years after the wasp's introduction, however, it had largely overcome the weevil's immune response, and egg mortality had dropped to only 5%.

Microorganisms introduced for biological control have shown evolutionary adaptation to their target hosts. Channer and Gowen (1992), for example, examined patterns of infection of nematodes of the genus *Meloidogyne* by the obligate bacterial parasite *Pasturella penetrans*. They found that populations of both organisms tended to be genetically heterogeneous. For the bacterial parasite, which produces spores that attach to the nematode host, experiments showed that culturing the bacterium on one nematode biotyps increased the effectiveness of spore attachment to that biotype and reduced its effectiveness for other biotypes.

Perhaps the best-studied case of evolutionary change involving microorganisms is that of the myxoma virus (*Leporipoxvirus* spp.). Rapid evolutionary adaptation by the virus was expressed as a reduction in virulence following its introduction to Australia for biological control of the European rabbit (*Oryctolagus cuniculus*). The myxoma virus, an endemic disease of cottontail rabbits (genus *Sylvilagus*) in South America, had been investigated for nearly 30 yr as a possible biological control for the European rabbit (Richardson 2001), a major alien pest in Australia. In 1950, before final authorization for release, the virus escaped from trials in field pen populations in New South Wales, infecting wild populations. Spreading from this area, and from deliberate releases in other locations, the virus became introduced to rabbit populations throughout Australia. The virus strain was highly virulent, typically killing more than 99% of rabbits in pen trials and more than 90% in its initial spread through field populations.

Very soon after the first epizootics of myxomatosis, less virulent strains of the myxoma virus appeared independently in many locations (Richardson 2001). Reduction in virulence was progressive and was documented by laboratory tests of rabbits from populations never exposed to the virus. By 1956–57, viral strains that killed less than 50% of rabbits were common in the field. The initial, highly virulent strain was displaced almost completely by strains of lesser virulence.

Interestingly, a second viral disease, rabbit hemorrhagic disease (RHD) was introduced in 1995 to mainland Australian populations of rabbits (Hayes and Richardson 2001). In a fashion very similar to the escape of the myxoma virus, the RHD virus escaped from a field test on an island off the eastern coast of Australia. It has now spread to rabbit populations throughout Australia.

Evolutionary Counteradaptation of Hosts to Biological Control Agents

Target plants of biological control have shown indications of evolution of resistance to control agents. Substantial variability in target plant susceptibility to introduced biocontrol herbivores has been observed with several species. In North America, a number of insects have been introduced for control of leafy spurge (*Euphorbia esula*), a major rangeland weed. Six species of root-feeding weevils (*Aphthona* spp.) have been introduced to various parts of the northern Great Plains (Lym and Carlson 2002). Leafy spurge populations in North America, however, consist of diverse genetic strains introduced from different parts of Eurasia. These strains show major differences in susceptibility to *Aphthona* weevils. As a genetically variable, outcrossing species, leafy spurge has a high potential for evolutionary response to biocontrol species.

In North America, common St. John's wort (*Hypericum perforatum*) was the object of one of the earliest classical biological control programs. This plant, a toxic, alien rangeland weed, was controlled in the western United States by a leaf beetle, *Chrysolina quadrigemina*. After this system had been in operation for about 54 yr, Maron and Luke (2000) examined the effectiveness of the beetle in suppressing St. John's wort. Field populations of St. John's wort in the western United States were more tolerant of herbivory than St. John's wort plants in either the midwestern United States, where the beetle is absent, or in Europe, where St. John's wort is native. Genetic analyses suggested that selection had favored increased tolerance by St. John's wort to this biocontrol agent.

A similar case in Australia involves common St. John's wort and a mite (*Aculus hyperici*) introduced in 1991 for biological control. This mite is one of six biocontrol species that have been established in the hope of achieving control of this rangeland weed (Mayo and Roush 1997). Introductions of the mite succeeded in some locations and failed in others (Jupp et al. 1997). Four morphologically distinct forms of St. John's wort are known in Australia, and it appears that these forms are differentially susceptible to the mite.

Another Australian case involves rush skeletonweed (*Chondrilla juncea*) and a rust (*Puccinia chondrillina*) introduced as a biocontrol (Burdon et al. 1981). The rust was effective in controlling one of the three forms of rush skeletonweed, but the remaining two resistant forms quickly invaded areas where the susceptible form had been eliminated.

Several cases of evolutionary resistance of target animals of biocontrol agents have also been reported. The parasitoid wasp *Aphidius ervi* was introduced to the northeastern United States in 1959 as a biological control for the pea aphid (*Acyrthosiphon pisum*), an alien pest of alfalfa (*Medicago sativa*), red clover (*Trifolium pratense*), and other legumes. The introduced wasps, originating from alfalfa fields in France, have spread and become a successful control agent for pea aphids throughout much of North America.

The genetic structure of populations of pea aphids and parasitoid wasps has been the focus of ongoing studies by several investigators (see, e.g., Henter and Via 1995; Via 1999; Hufbauer and Via 1999). These studies revealed that aphids in alfalfa fields suffer less parasitism than those in red clover, with the difference being a greater physiological resistance to parasitism in alfalfa aphids. This difference cannot be explained by nutritional or secondary chemical differences related to the two crops and thus appears to be genetic. Genetic variability in resistance to parasitoids is abundant in the alfalfa populations but undetectable in those in red clover. Lack of genetic variability may thus constrain the evolution of resistance in the clover aphids.

Other cases involve microorganisms, including the example of myxomatosis and rabbits in Australia. Paralleling the evolution of reduced virulence in the myxoma virus in Australia, described earlier, European rabbits rapidly evolved increased resistance following the spread of the virus through field populations (Richardson 2001). By 7 yr after the initial infection of field populations, more than 10% of rabbits from field populations survived infection by the original highly virulent strain that killed more than 99% of laboratory animals that had not previously been exposed to the virus. By the late 1970s, the survival rate of animals from field populations had risen to about 40%.

In the example involving the *Pasturella* bacterium and nematodes discussed earlier, another consequence of the interaction of these organisms was that infections by *Pasturella* tended to select for resistant forms of *Meloidogyne* (Channer and Gowen 1992).

Precautions for Introductions of Biocontrol Species

Predicting the ultimate consequences of introducing biocontrol species to new regions is much more difficult than has been believed (Louda et al. 2003a). Although awareness of many potential problems with introduction of species for biological control has improved, many releases of species have inadequate justification. A recent example is the introduction of parasitoids for control of the brown citrus aphid (*Toxoptera citricida*) in Florida (Michaud 2002). In this case, no evidence exists that the two introduced parasitoid species exert control over the brown citrus aphid in other regions of the world.

The first goal of research must be to show that the introduced biological control agent will not itself cause damage. This is especially true for agents that attack plants, since many problem weeds have nonweedy, or even highly beneficial, relatives. In many cases, impacts on such relatives do not become evident until 5–10 yr after a biocontrol agent has been introduced (McEvoy 1996). Improved testing of host specificity is thus essential. A fly under consideration for use as a biological control of yellow starthistle (*Centaurea solsticialis*), for example, was found to have become established, presumably accidentally, and to attack one variety of safflower (*Carthamus tinctorius*), a major crop in California (Balciunas and Villegas 2001). Although it appeared that the risk of serious side effects on most safflower is at present small, the argument that a slight evolutionary shift in preference might make the entire safflower crop sensitive is difficult to refute.

Greater consideration must also be given to the potential for geographic and habitat spread of biocontrol agents once they are introduced. Not only must the potential for natural dispersal be fully considered, as indicated by the invasion of Florida by *Cactoblastis cactorum*, the potential for distribution by unauthorized sale and exchange of the biocontrol agent must be taken into account. Sales and exchanges via the Internet have now become a major but poorly regulated means of dispersal of organisms (Kay and Hoyle 2001).

Fuller consideration of the potential community effects of biocontrol species is also needed. Any biological agent that has a strong impact on its target host is likely to influence other species that are part of the host's food web.

Finally, although the evolutionary potential of biocontrol species has been shown in only a few instances, this potential needs greater consideration. At the very least, evaluation of genetic variability related to host use and the response of laboratory populations to artificial selection for adaptation to potential nontarget hosts needs to be conducted. Monitoring of the genetic responses of introduced agents that have begun to use nontarget hosts clearly deserves much increased effort.

Biological Control and Coevolution

Thus, we see that biological control species and the target species with which they interact are capable of rapid evolution. These evolutionary adjustments are some of the first stages of the coevolutionary adaptation of new community members to each other. We have seen that alien species of all types, both inadvertently and deliberately introduced, begin to make evolutionary adjustments to the new biotic and abiotic conditions they encounter. In the next chapter, we shall examine longer term patterns of coevolution and integration of alien species into the biotic community.

18.

Counteradaptation and Integration into the Biotic Community

"The history of evolution and biodiversity is fundamentally a history of the evolution of species interactions. . . . The more we learn about the diversity of life and the structure of genomes, the more it appears that much of the evolution of biodiversity is about the manipulation of other species—to gain resources and, in turn, to avoid being manipulated.

—THOMPSON (1999c)

The zebra mussel (*Dreissena polymorpha*) appeared in Lake St. Clair, between Lakes Erie and Huron, in 1986. Since then, it has spread throughout the North American Great Lakes and many other lakes and rivers in the eastern part of the continent. By 1989, zebra mussels had apparently colonized the northern shore of Lake Erie from Long Point eastward. The closely related quagga mussel (*D. bugensis*) appeared in this area somewhat later. When invasion of these mussels was recognized, an extensive sampling program for mussels was initiated because of the ecological richness of the bay area inside Long Point, Ontario, and its importance as a stopover area for migratory waterfowl (Petrie and Knapton 1999).

The first mussel sampling in 1991 revealed that almost 27% of sampling stations were occupied by mussels and that Long Point Bay held an estimated biomass of about 1,189 tons of mussels. By 1992, mussels occurred at 80% of sites, and the bay's biomass had grown to 4,536 tons. Beginning in 1992, stomach analyses of ducks killed by hunters were added to the sampling program. Three duck species were found to feed heavily on mussels: lesser scaup (*Aythya affinis*), greater scaup (*A. marila*), and bufflehead (*Bucephala albeola*).

Beginning in 1993 and continuing through 1995, the abundance of mussels in Long Point Bay declined, dropping to a biomass of only 758 tons in 1995. The abundance of the three major duck predators on mussels grew correspondingly over the sampling period. In 1986, prior to the mussel invasion, waterfowl days spent in Long Point Bay for the two scaup species combined were 38,500 and for the bufflehead 4,700. By 1997, waterfowl days for scaup had grown to 3.5 million and for bufflehead to 67,000. From 1993 through 1995, when mussels were declining, the three duck species were estimated to have consumed a minimum of 39–46% of the mussel biomass annually.

Ecological and Evolutionary Responses to Invasive Aliens

The above example shows a strong ecological response to invading zebra and quagga mussels in only one location. Nevertheless, it emphasizes the fact that the native biotic community does respond to an invasive alien in a fashion that tends to integrate it into the food web. The aquatic ecosystem of Long Point Bay probably will never return to its pre-mussel state, but a new state, in which the mussel population is intimately linked with native species by ecological and evolutionary adjustments, will eventually develop.

Over evolutionary time, invasive species tend to become integrated into the new biotic community in such a way that their initial impacts are softened. Integration occurs through the processes of coevolution and counteradaptation. Coevolution is the mutual evolutionary adaptation of two or more species to each other: herbivore with plant, predator with prey, and parasite with host. These evolutionary sequences eventually may lead to patterns of mutual benefit for the interacting species. Counteradaptation is a related concept and refers to the total of evolutionary adjustments by members of the native community to the new invader. These adjustments may involve improved defenses, refined competitive capabilities, or adaptations for exploiting the new community member. As we have seen, the invading species is also evolving adjustments to the physical and biotic conditions it encounters.

The sum total of these biotic adjustments constitutes the organization that exists in biotic communities. Major questions in evolutionary ecology concern the importance of coevolution and counteradaptation in communities and the time scale on which they develop and change. The degree of biotic organization varies greatly, tending to be low in communities of habitats that exhibit extreme physical conditions or frequent disturbance and substantial in communities of habitats that are equitable and stable.

Ecological Adjustments

Ecological adjustments tend to precede evolutionary adjustments. Many plants, for example, show induced responses to herbivory, such as altered growth form or production of deterrent chemicals (Agrawal 1998). Thus, native plants may respond quickly to introduced herbivores. As we have seen (chapter 15), introduced plants typically acquire native herbivores and introduced animals a set of native predators and parasites. Zebra mussels are beginning to show ecological pressure from a variety of predators, as indicated by the example at the beginning of this chapter. Many native fish, including freshwater drum (*Aplodinotus grunniens*), redear sunfish (*Lepomis microlophus*), pumpkinseed (*Lepomis gibbosus*), copper redhorse (*Moxostoma hubbsi*), and river redhorse (*Moxostoma carinatum*), have teeth and chewing pads that enable them to crush and eat zebra mussels (French 1993). The freshwater drum now feeds heavily on zebra mussels in Lake Erie (Morrison et al. 1997). In Arkansas, blue catfish (*Ictalurus furcatus*) feed heavily on zebra mussels for part of the year, apparently swallowing them whole (Magoulick and Lewis 2002). Other native fish, as well as the introduced common carp (*Cyprinus carpio*), also consume zebra and quagga mussels to some degree.

Zebra mussels have also been colonized by freshwater sponges in many locations. Heavy growth of such sponges on the shells of mussels has significant negative impacts on growth and survival of zebra mussels (Ricciardi et al. 1995; Lauer and Spacie 2000). A few native North American trematodes also have been found to infect zebra mussels (Molloy et al. 1997), although the diversity of parasites in North America is far below that in the Old World.

A similar example is provided by the imported fire ant (*Solenopsis invicta*), which has dramatically affected populations of native ants and other arthropods (Gotelli and Arnett 2000). In a 1987 study in Texas, Porter and Savignano (1990) found that the fire ant had reduced native ant diversity by 50% and had reduced the abundance of many other arthropods. Morrison (2002) repeated the study in 1999. He found that native ant diversity and abundance had recovered to pre-fire ant levels. Numbers of both species and individuals of other arthropod groups were also higher in fire ant sites in 1999 than in 1987. The fire ant itself was still abundant, but not as numerous as in 1987. One factor responsible for the recovery of native ants and other arthropods was postulated to be acquisition of natural enemies. In particular, a microsporidian parasite of fire ants, *Thelohania solenopsae*, was found at the study site. This parasite has been shown to reduce fire ant populations in their native region in South America.

For many strongly invasive species, however, ecological responses alone are likely to be delayed or inadequate. These may lead to a "boom and bust" pattern of population behavior by the introduced species, in which its population grows rapidly to a very high level and then declines as its food resource is overexploited (Williamson 1996). Herbivores introduced to predator-free islands often show this pattern, which may cause the species to fall to a very low population or even become extinct. On St. Matthew Island, in the Bering Sea, for example, a population of reindeer (*Rangifer tarandus*) grew from 29 individuals in 1944 to an estimated 6,000 in 1963 (Klein 1968). In the winter of 1963–64, all but 50 animals, all females, died of starvation, so the population essentially fell to extinction. Similar patterns of population growth and crash have been observed for reindeer on several other arctic islands.

Other invasive species may experience ecological responses that are negligible or even beneficial. Plants such as salt cedar (*Tamarix* spp.) and Russian olive (*Eleagnus angustifolia*) receive little negative ecological response and are used to a degree by native animal species such as birds and mammals. Russian olive is, in fact, actively dispersed by birds that feed on its fruits. Other interactions between invasive species and natives may in some instances become mutualistic. In the western United States, native animals such as the giant kangaroo rat (*Dipodomys ingens*) and the valley pocket gopher (*Thomomys bottae*) feed heavily on alien annual plants and, at the same time, create soil disturbances favoring the growth of these species (Cox 1999).

Ecological relationships thus both influence and are influenced by the establishment of alien species that reach new areas by dispersal or human introduction. These interactions are capable of sorting alien species and creating an initial degree of community organization. For vertebrate animals, interspecific competition can be a significant sorting factor for establishment of alien species that reach an area. The role of competition among alien species can be evaluated, at least roughly, by examining the interactions of vertebrates introduced to island archipelagos such as Hawaii (Moulton and Pimm 1983). More species of songbirds have been introduced to Hawaii than to any other location in the world. On the six main islands of Hawaii, 47 species of songbirds were introduced between 1871 and 1960 to one or more islands, for a total of 145 introductions. These species have largely occupied the disturbed urban and agricultural habitats that predominate at lower elevations, although some do invade native forest and other natural communities.

About 36% of the songbirds (passerines and members of the pigeon order) introduced to Hawaii failed after several to many years (Moulton and Pimm 1983). Nevertheless, 9–20 species of aliens have survived, creating a community of largely alien species in the Hawaiian lowlands. For the islands of Oahu, Kauai, Maui, and Hawaii, the number of surviving species of alien birds has apparently reached a plateau. For Molokai and Lanai, such a plateau is not yet evident. Between 7 and 15 extinctions were noted on the four islands on which the number of extant species reached a plateau. As the number of established alien species increased, so did the rate of extinction of species that had managed to prosper for some time. In fact, the extinction rate for the archipelago as a whole increased at a significantly faster rate than the increase in number of species, strongly indicating that interactions among species were contributing to the extinctions. In several cases, the establishment of an ecologically similar species was associated with the extinction of a previously established species. Thus, on four of the islands, an equilibrium number of species appeared to have become established, such that the establishment of new species tended to be balanced by the extinction of previously established species.

The success of introduced birds in Hawaii also relates to their apparent competitive relationship with other introduced species (Moulton 1985). Although the size and shape of the beak are far from giving a complete picture of the pattern of food resource use by a bird, major differences are usually related to feeding ecology. In some 18 cases, congeneric songbirds were introduced to the main islands of Hawaii in such a fashion that two species were present in similar habitat at the same time (Moulton 1985). In three cases, neither species survived, and in nine cases, one of the two failed to survive. The six pairs that did survive on average showed more that twice the percentage difference in bill length as did the members of pairs for which only one member survived. In turn, members of pairs in which one member survived showed greater percentage difference in bill lengths than did members of pairs both of which failed to survive. More detailed analyses of morphological difference among introduced birds on Hawaii and other oceanic islands further supported the conclusion that differentiation of feeding ecology is prerequisite to survival (Moulton and Pimm 1987; Lockwood et al. 1993, 1996).

Short-term Evolutionary Responses

As we have seen, many recent invaders trigger rapid evolutionary responses, as well as ecological responses, by native species (chapters 12, 13, and 14). Areas where this occurs are termed evolutionary hot spots (Parchman and Benkman 2002) and show that evolutionary adjustments may begin quickly but continue for long periods of evolutionary time. In spite of many years of presence, however, some invasive species and the natives with which they interact in other locations show little coevolutionary adjustment, in a sense representing evolutionary cold spots. Thus, on a geographic scale, a mosaic of coevolved relationships, varying in the species involved and in the strength of the interaction, is expected (Thompson 1999c).

Examples of how invading species can adapt to new biotic environments are also provided by species that have colonized regions released from the most recent phase of Pleistocene glaciation. Parchman and Benkman (2002), for example, showed that coevolution has occurred between black spruce (*Picea mariana*) and red crossbills (*Loxia curvirostra*) in Newfoundland, Canada, following release of this island from glaciation about 9,000 yr ago. These two species colonized Newfoundland, but the red squirrel (*Tamiasciurus hudsonicus*), a major predator on black spruce seeds, did not. Under these circumstances, black spruce reduced cone defenses that functioned against red squirrels and increased those that functioned against crossbills. In Newfoundland, black spruce cones exhibited greater numbers of seeds and a higher ratio of seed mass to cone mass than in mainland Canada, evidently as a result of reduced red squirrel predation. In contrast, cone scales were thicker and the force required to pry them open to expose the seeds was greater than in mainland Canada, correlated with high seed predation by crossbills. The crossbill itself showed a larger, deeper bill than crossbills of mainland Canada and was considered to be a distinct subspecies (*Loxia curvirostra percna*). Unfortunately, this crossbill race declined to extinction following the introduction of red squirrels to Newfoundland in 1963.

The pattern of coevolution of red crossbills and conifers in Newfoundland is similar to that in the Cypress Hills, on the border of British

Columbia and Alberta, Canada (Benkman 1999). Red squirrels were absent from this hill area until their introduction in 1950. Red crossbills probably colonized the Cypress Hills within the past 6,800 yr. The population of red crossbills there evolved larger, deeper bills, while the lodgepole pines (*Pinus murrayana*) evolved larger cones with more seeds and thicker distal scales. Again, the red crossbill population apparently became extinct following introduction of red squirrels. This pattern of coevolution is also evident in other isolated mountain ranges in Idaho and Montana (Benkman et al. 2003).

A more complex example of the organization of an animal group invading an area in post-glacial time, for the most part, is provided by the land birds of Tasmania (Keast 1970). Located about 225 km south of the state of Victoria, Australia, Tasmania is an island about 66,560 km^2 in area. During the last Pleistocene glaciation, about 2,000 km^2 of the island were covered by glacial ice and the climate was very severe. Timberline lowered in elevation to about 90–115 m, and bird habitats were much less diverse than those at present. Because of lowered sea level, however, Tasmania possessed a land connection with mainland Australia. Some bird species that colonized Tasmania before the last glacial period may have survived throughout glaciation. At the end of the glacial period, about 12,000 yr ago, however, the land connection was broken and warming conditions brought rapid habitat change that made Tasmania favorable for colonization by many new species. Nevertheless, in spite of the current wide range of bird habitats, the land bird fauna is impoverished compared to adjacent mainland Australia. Only 43 species of small passerine birds occur in Tasmania, compared to 89 in southern Victoria.

This less diverse land bird fauna of Tasmania, however, shows many ecological and evolutionary adjustments to the modern environment (Keast 1970). Tasmania, for example, has only two common species of owls, which are conspecific with two of the six owl species that occur in southern Victoria. The body sizes of the Tasmanian owls differ from those of birds in Victoria. The smaller Tasmanian species is reduced in body size, whereas the larger species has become still larger and shows greater sexual dimorphism in body size, compared to the same two species in Victoria. These differences are presumed to reflect the altered way that the Tasmanian species partition prey by body size.

The passerine birds of Tasmania show many differences in habitat relations, feeding behavior, and morphology, as well (Keast 1970). Several species occupy a greater range of habitats and show more diverse feeding patterns than equivalent species in Victoria. The pink robin (*Petroica rodinogaster*) of Tasmania combines the feeding behaviors of two robin species in Victoria, foraging on the ground, in tree canopies, and by hawking insects in the air. Only two species of canopy-feeding, insectivorous thornbills (*Acanthiza* spp.) are present in Tasmania, compared to four species in southern Victoria. Two of the Victoria species are specialist canopy feeders. In Tasmania, the two species of thornbills that are present have expanded their feeding activity into the canopy zone.

Changes in tarsus length and in bill shape and length are shown by many of the passerine birds in Tasmania that have shifted their feeding behavior relative to equivalent species in Victoria (Keast 1970). True trunk-foraging species of sittellas (*Neositta* spp.) and tree-creepers (*Climacteris* spp.), widespread in mainland Australia, are absent from Tasmania. Several birds from groups that are not trunk-foragers on the mainland have moved into this niche in Tasmania. These species tend to have longer bills, which are more effective for probing crevices, than their mainland relatives. Other species, such as the pink robin, that have expanded ground foraging activity show a lengthened tarsus.

In addition to these adaptive shifts in habitat use, foraging behavior, and morphology by many species, double invasions of Tasmania from mainland Australia have occurred in two bird genera. These invasions have given rise to sibling species of foliage-gleaning insectivores, which are among the groups most poorly represented in Tasmanian forests (Keast 1970). Thus, by a combination of speciation, habitat and foraging shifts, and evolutionary adjustments, the bird fauna of Tasmania has achieved a high degree of integration over the past few thousand years.

Long-term Evolutionary Integration

One of the most interesting examples of a geologically recent plant invader of North America is the creosote bush (*Larrea tridentata*), which is the dominant woody shrub of the Sonoran, Mojave, and Chihuahuan deserts. The genus *Larrea* is of South American origin, and four species of this genus now occur in Argentina. These species include *L. divaricata*, a sister species of *L. tridentata* (Hunter et al. 2001). Several other genera closely related to *Larrea* also occur in South America. It is generally agreed that *L. tridentata* reached North America by long-distance dispersal, probably as seeds carried by migratory birds (Wells and Hunziker 1976) during a period of climatic aridity corresponding to glacial periods in the northern hemisphere. These periods of aridity may have allowed the South American *L. divaricata* to spread farther north than its current northernmost locality in southern Peru. The gap between desert areas in North and South America at this time may have been as short as 2,000 km.

The oldest fossil record of *L. tridentata* in North America is 18,700 yr BP, based on material from a fossil packrat midden near the head of the Gulf of California (Van Devender 1990). This date, together with speculation about Pleistocene glacial climate changes, has led some workers to speculate that the ancestor of *L. tridentata* arrived in North America within the last 1.5 million yr (Hunter et al. 2001).

Fingerprinting analysis of chloroplast and ribosomal DNA from the five species of *Larrea* and members of related South American genera, however, suggested an earlier divergence of *L. divaricata* and *L. tridentata* (Lia et al. 2001). This analysis suggested that these two species diverged between 8.4 and 4.2 million yr ago, the most likely factor initiating divergence being the dispersal of ancestral *L. tridentata* into North America. Whether this dispersal occurred by a single long-distance transport of seeds or by the stepping-stone occupation of dry habitats in northern South America and Central America is still uncertain.

In North America, *L. tridentata* has evolved three races differing in chromosome number (Hunter et al. 2001). Plants of the Chihuahuan Desert are diploid, with a chromosome number identical to that of *L. divaricata* in Argentina. Plants of the Sonoran Desert are tetraploid, and those of the Mojave Desert hexaploid. These races follow a climatic gradient of increasing summer heat and aridity from southeast to northwest. Although the ploidy races are morphologically indistinguishable, it is presumed that the ploidy levels correspond to some physiological adaptation to this climatic gradient. Thus, following invasion of North America, *L. tridentata* has undergone substantial evolution.

In addition, *L. tridentata* has established coevolved relationships with many insects. Some 30 species of insects of 5 orders are associated with North American creosote bush (Schultz et al. 1977). Many of these are restricted to creosote bush, suggesting a long period of coevolution. The biochemical distinctiveness of creosote bush suggests that herbivorous insects in North America were not likely preadapted to use this plant immediately after its arrival, and that this fauna has been accumulated gradually over several million years.

The ability to determine the degree of genetic differentiation among species and relate differences to evolutionary time by means of molecular clock relationships gives us an improved ability to understand patterns of invasion and adaptation. This relationship, coupled with information on geological history, is enabling evolutionary ecologists to piece together the history of invasion and differentiation of species in many locations. One of the best-studied cases involves land birds in the Lesser Antilles.

The island of Barbados probably appeared about 700,000 yr ago by geological uplift. This island, with 11 species of land birds and one recently extinct species, has the most depauperate fauna of any of the larger islands of the Lesser Antilles. None of the land birds is considered endemic, even at the subspecific level. Since Barbados has never been connected to any other island or to South America, its bird fauna has arrived by over-water dispersal. The nearest islands, about 175 km to the west, are St. Vincent and St. Lucia. Volcanic in origin, these islands are 20–30 million yr older than Barbados.

Lovette et al. (1999) examined mitochondrial DNA (mtDNA) variability of eight bird species present on Barbados, St. Vincent, and St. Lucia. Two species, the black-faced grassquit (*Tiaris bicolor*) and the common ground dove (*Columbina passerina*), were not only common South American mainland birds but also showed very little divergence among the three islands. Thus, it appears that they colonized Barbados from either St. Vincent and/or St. Lucia quite recently. A second pair, the Caribbean elaenia (*Elaenia martinica*) and the Lesser Antillean bullfinch (*Loxigilla noctis*), are both endemic species of Caribbean islands. The degree of mtDNA differentiation was about the same between all three pair combinations of islands, suggesting that these species colonized all three islands at about the same time, but earlier than the grassquit and ground dove. A third pair, the black-whiskered vireo (*Vireo altiloquus*) and the bananaquit (*Coereba flaveola*), showed strong mtDNA differentiation between St. Lucia and St. Vincent, but only moderate differentiation between St. Lucia and Barbados. These species may have colonized Barbados from St. Lucia at about the time that the elaenia and bullfinch arrived. Finally, a fourth pair, the Antillean crested hummingbird (*Orthorhynchus cristatus*) and the Carib grackle (*Quiscalus lugubris*), showed little differentiation between St. Lucia and St. Vincent but substantial differentiation between Barbados and these other islands. Based on the molecular clock relationship of about 2% divergence per million years (Lovette et al. 1999), the maximum divergence that might be expected for birds on Barbados, assuming that they came from St. Vincent or St. Lucia, is about 1.4%. The hummingbird, differing on Barbados by 1.1–1.2% from St. Vincent and St. Lucia, respectively, may thus have been a very early invader. The grackle, differing by 3.4% from both other islands, is likely to have colonized Barbados from a source area other than St. Vincent or St. Lucia. The mtDNA profiles of

Barbados grackles showed strong similarity to those of Trinidad, a more distant but still reasonable source area.

Thus, Barbados has received its fauna at various times and from different sources. It is an incomplete fauna, lacking at least ten species present on St. Vincent and St. Lucia for which habitat seemingly suitable is present. No resident hawk is present on Barbados, for example. Thus, although the species present on Barbados have differentiated, presumably in an adaptive manner, the set of species present is far from a fully integrated tropical land bird fauna.

On an even longer time scale, the insular nature of the Lesser Antilles has resulted in a land bird fauna that is still not in equilibrium in an evolutionary sense. Based on mtDNA fingerprinting of 37 of the 65 land birds of the Lesser Antilles and their nearest relatives in South America or the Greater Antilles, this fauna began to invade only about 7.5–10.0 million yr ago (Ricklefs and Bermingham 2001). Modeling of the rates of colonization and extinction that best account for the pattern of genetic divergences of these 37 species suggested that over this period of faunal accumulation no significant rate of general extinction has prevailed. Rather, the pattern suggested that at about 550,000–750,000 yr ago, either a mass extinction of more than 90% of the extant lineages occurred or the rate of colonization increased about 13-fold to a new level that has continued until recent time. The timing of the extinction event or colonization change corresponds roughly to the beginning of Pleistocene glaciation, when drier climates may have modified habitat conditions and lowered sea levels increased land areas and connected some islands that are now separated.

This general analysis suggested that for insular areas such as the Lesser Antilles, truly equilibrium conditions for an overall bird fauna are unlikely ever to develop. On the other hand, it confirmed that older taxa have much more restricted island and habitat distributions, indicative of substantial evolutionary adjustment to island environments (Ricklefs and Bermingham 1999). These adjustments are evidently influenced not only by general habitat conditions but also by interactions with other species of birds, including later arrivals, and also with biotic agents such as parasites (Apanius et al. 2000). Thus, on a time scale of several million years, integration of invading species is evident, even though the overall biota is still not at equilibrium.

That the bird faunas of older West Indian islands are well integrated, as suggested by the studies of Tasmanian birds described earlier, is shown by comparative ecological and morphological analyses (Cox and Ricklefs

Table 18.1. Characteristics of bird faunas of five tropical regions based on standardized counts in nine matching habitat types. Density and morphological space indexes refer to the overall bird fauna. The nearest neighbor index is the mean of values for eight habitats.

Locality	Total species in counts	Density index[1]	Morphological space index[2]	Mean nearest neighbor index[2]
Panama	135	15.3	5.90	0.19
Trinidad	108	17.0	6.37	0.19
Jamaica	55	24.5	5.07	0.18
St. Lucia	34	23.3	5.69	0.26
St. Kitts	20	19.8	3.41	0.29

[1] See Cox and Ricklefs (1977).
[2] See Travis and Ricklefs (1983).

1977; Travis and Ricklefs 1983). Data were first collected on the diversity and abundance of species across nine habitat types in central Panama, Trinidad, Jamaica, St. Lucia, and St. Kitts. These locations included a continental area and West Indian islands with progressively smaller land bird faunas (table 18.1). The number of bird species encountered in the various habitats varied almost sevenfold, being greatest in Panama and least in St. Kitts. Nevertheless, indices of total bird density showed that increased abundance of individual species compensated fully, or even overcompensated, for the reduction in number of species (Cox and Ricklefs 1977).

Analyses of the morphology of passerine species in the Panama-to-St. Kitts study were carried out by Travis and Ricklefs (1983). Data were obtained on eight measurements: body length; wing, tail, tarsus, and middle toe lengths; and beak length, width, and depth. Multivariate analyses were carried out to determine the overall degree of difference among species in various communities and the five localities. For the five localities, the combined mensural characteristics occupied almost the same total morphological space (table 18.1). St. Kitts, with the fewest species, was somewhat of an exception, with the space occupied being substantially less. The average multivariate distance between species was greater for the bird communities of St. Lucia and St. Kitts than for communities of the larger islands and Panama. For the community types in a given location, the average multivariate distance between species tended to be very similar. Evidence was thus strong that ecological interactions among species were setting some limits to coexistence, especially in the small islands where density overcompensation appeared to exist.

Studies of the evolutionary history of land birds in the West Indies support the concept of the taxon cycle, in which taxa invade and expand through new geographical areas, undergo evolutionary modification, and eventually become adapted to specialized or restricted habitats (Wilson 1961; Ricklefs and Cox 1972; Ricklefs and Bermingham 2002). Taxa late in this sequence may also undergo secondary or repeated expansions. In the West Indian land bird fauna, the youngest colonizing lineages of the Lesser Antilles appear to have entered the islands from historical time to 750,000 yr BP (Ricklefs and Bermingham 2002). Many other lineages entered between 750,000 and 10 million yr BP. The oldest colonist may date from 9 to 12 million yr BP. Secondary expansions of taxa within the Lesser Antilles appear to have occurred 6.5–8.6 million yr BP or more recently. Taxon cycles are most easily recognized in insular regions, but also occur in continental taxa (Cox 1985).

Taxon cycles are postulated to be driven by the changing coevolutionary balance between a taxon and its competitors, predators, and parasites (Ricklefs and Cox 1972). Invading species succeed in large measure by virtue of their escape from such biotic constraints. In time, pressure from counteradaptation by members of the native biota and by later invaders forces the invading taxon to adapt to local conditions and may cause the extinction of some local populations.

Host-parasite coevolutionary interactions may play a significant role in the taxon cycle process (Apanius et al. 2000; Ricklefs and Bermingham 2002). In Lesser Antillean land birds, for example, the relationship of host species and malaria parasites tends to coevolve independently on different islands (Fallon et al. 2003). These patterns seem to reflect interactions between parasite virulence and host resistance mediated by mutation-driven evolutionary change.

Coevolution and Biodiversity

Processes of integration of invading species into new biotic assemblages lead not only to coevolutionary specialization, but often to speciation. Counteracting the tendency of alien species to cause the extinction of native species with which they interact is the potential for origin of new species in the longer term. In the next chapter, we shall examine the extent to which speciation is stimulated as the result of alien invasions.

19.

Dispersing Aliens and Speciation

"Under the biological species concept, taxa that are fully reproductively isolated are called separate species, and identifying the conditions under which reproductive isolation will (or will not) evolve to completion is therefore crucial to understanding speciation."

—VIA (1999)

Three herbaceous composites of the genus *Tragopogon* have been widely introduced and naturalized in North America from Europe: salsify (*T. porrifolius*), yellow salsify (*T. dubius*), and yellow goat's beard (*T. pratensis*). In eastern Washington State, these species became established, usually in waste areas in towns, between 1916 and 1930. Marion Owenby, a botanist at Washington State University (then known as State College of Washington), was aware of these plants and their hybrids, which comprised all three pair combinations of the species. These hybrids were common, but sterile. In 1949, however, he detected colonies of two forms that were similar to hybrids but were larger, coarser, and produced fertile seeds (Owenby 1950). One form, found in two colonies in Pullman and Palouse, Washington, was similar to the hybrid of *dubius* and *porrifolius*. The second, also found in two colonies in Moscow, Idaho, was similar to the hybrid of *dubius* and *pratensis*. On examination, these two forms turned out to be tetraploid in chromosome number (n = 12) rather than diploid (n = 6) as in the naturalized species and their hybrids. Since these tetraploid colonies were flourishing and not backcrossing with other tragopogons, Owenby concluded that they were new, reproductively isolated species, arising by the doubling of chromosome number in some of

258

the hybrid forms. This doubling made possible a normal process of meiosis and thus restored fertility to the offspring. He named the *dubius* × *porrifolius* form *T. mirus* ("remarkable") and the *dubius* × *pratensis* form *miscellus* ("mixed").

In 1990, Novak et al. (1991b) surveyed the distribution of the *Tragopogon* species in Washington and Idaho and pulled together other information that had accumulated since 1949. Both *T. mirus* and *T. miscellus* had been subsequently discovered in northern Arizona and *T. miscellus* in Montana and Wyoming. In eastern Washington and northern Idaho, however, they found that both new tetraploid species had spread considerably and appeared in new localities within a five-county area. *T. miscellus*, in fact, was more abundant than *T. porrifolius* and *T. pratensis*. The distribution of both tetraploid species suggested that they had arisen on multiple occasions. The number and widely scattered localities at which *T. mirus* was found in particular suggested that the spread of this species was largely the product of multiple origins, rather than long-distance seed dispersal. Finally, Novak et al. (1991b) discovered hybrids between *T. mirus* and *T. miscellus*, raising the possibility that a still different, octoploid species might arise in the future.

Thus, the introduction of three European species to new environments in North America has enabled the origin of two new plant species, with a potential for others.

Setting the Stage for Speciation

In the evolutionary long run, the introduction of species to new geographical areas, where they are isolated from interbreeding with their ancestors, will frequently result in these separate ancestral forms becoming differentiated into new species. At some future time, perhaps in thousands or millions of years from now, the speciation pulse now beginning might compensate for the extinctions that are presently resulting from alien introductions. The new *Tragopogon* species are an indication that this process is beginning and that the bringing together of alien species in a new environment can facilitate hybridization and the origin of reproductively isolated species by polyploidy. As we shall see, however, simply introducing species to new abiotic and biotic environments can lead to selection that ultimately results in speciation.

For flowering plants, the incidence of speciation by mechanisms involving polyploidy is estimated to be between 2 and 4% (Otto and Whitton 2000). Cases of rapid speciation, however, frequently involve hybridization, polyploidy, or both. Polyploidy can be the result in an increase in the number of sets of chromosomes in individuals of one species, a process termed autopolyploidy, or an increase in the number of chromosome sets in individuals produced by interspecific hybridization, a process termed allopolyploidy. For polyploids to be fertile, an even number of sets of chromosomes must usually exist, so that chromosome pairing in meiosis is possible. Triploid forms resulting from autopolyploidy or allopolyploidy are usually sterile. Homoploid hybrid speciation involves the hybridization of species with the same chromosome number, leading to a form that is distinct and has strong reproductive isolation without the occurrence of polyploidy (Rieseberg 1997; Rieseberg et al. 2003). Speciation can also result from the appearance of a genetic characteristic that leads to reproductive isolation between sets of individuals in a formerly fully interbreeding population.

For animals, various processes may lead to rapid speciation. Polyploidy is less common in animals but occurs in many molluscs, crustaceans, insects, fish, amphibians, and a few higher vertebrates. Many of the polyploid forms do not reproduce sexually, so forms different in chromosome number are essentially reproductively isolated. For animals, however, speciation results more often by divergent natural selection. Allopatric and, possibly, sympatric speciation have apparently resulted in the recent origin of hundreds of species of cichlid fishes in East African lakes such as Lake Malawi (Owen et al. 1990) and Lake Victoria (Seehausen and Van Alphen 1999). The Lake Victoria basin is inferred to have completely dried out in the Late Pleistocene, so the endemic species of cichlids have apparently arisen within the past 12,000 yr (Johnson et al. 1996). The precise mechanisms involved in these remarkable radiations are still somewhat unclear but may include disruptive sexual selection, as well as selection for adaptation to diverse habitats. Seehausen et al. (2003) showed that the ancestors of this species flock were members of the genus *Thoracochromis* of the Congo and Nile river systems and that much of the genetic diversity that permitted rapid speciation in Lake Victoria probably arose much earlier. Extensive hybridization and genetic introgression likely occurred among species colonizing the reformed Lake Victoria. In any case, the evidence is now strong that unusual biogeographic events, such as the massive introduction of species to new geographic areas, can lead quickly to the origin of new species.

Darwin's finches, confined to the Galapagos Islands and Cocos Island, 720 km to the north, are another group of rapidly evolving species (Petren et al. 1999). Differentiation of populations into reproductively isolated daughter species is promoted by geographical isolation and divergent selection on different islands of the archipelago. These finches are traditionally considered to comprise 6 genera and 14 species. Selection has favored divergence in feeding behavior and morphology in these birds. Recent studies show, however, that the six species of ground finches (*Geospiza* spp.) and the five tree finches (*Camarhynchus* spp.) are subject to frequent hybridization and are still incompletely differentiated. Their status is perhaps best characterized as an adaptive radiation in progress (Sato et al. 1999; Zink 2002).

Speciation in Plants

Allopolyploidy is a frequent mechanism of origin of new plant species, and several cases involving alien species have been documented. The *Tragopogon* example described at the beginning of the chapter stands as one of the best examples of rapid speciation by hybridization and allopolyploidy. As we noted in chapter 5, the origin of *Spartina anglica* on the coast of England occurred by essentially the same mechanism. By a somewhat more complicated process, a new species of groundsel (*Senecio*) originated by hybridization and doubling of the hybrid chromosome number, as discussed below.

Autopolyploidy also leads to speciation of plant populations invading new regions. The groundnut (*Apios americana*) is a plant native to eastern North America. Populations in the southern United States are diploid in chromosome number and reproduce sexually. Farther north, those in areas covered by Wisconsin glaciation are triploid and reproduce vegetatively. Triploid forms, differing in flower color, appear to have arisen both east and west of the Appalachian Mountains and invaded glaciated regions after glacial retreat (Joly and Bruneau 2002). Although diploid and triploid forms are not classified as separate species, they are reproductively isolated.

A similar example involves *Tolmiea menziesii*, an herbaceous plant of the saxifrage family (Saxifragaceae). Two chromosomal races of *Tolmiea menziesii* are known, a diploid with 14 chromosomes and a tetraploid with 28 (Soltis and Rieseberg 1986). These races are morphologically identical, although the tetraploid tends to be more robust in growth form. The tetraploid occurs on Wisconsin glaciated areas from southern Alaska southward to central Oregon, whereas the diploid occurs in unglaciated areas from central Oregon south into northern California. Tetraploids show much higher levels of heterozygosity than diploids (Soltis and Soltis

1989), a fact perhaps related to their success in colonizing northern areas in postglacial time.

Homoploid hybrid speciation has been implicated in the origin of species following invasion of new regions by ancestral species. One of the most interesting examples of apparent homoploid hybrid speciation involves sunflowers of the genus *Helianthus*. The common sunflower (*H. annuus*) and the prairie sunflower (*H. petiolaris*), both annuals, were once thought to have been restricted to largely nonoverlapping ranges in the Great Plains (Heiser 1947). They are now sympatric over much of central North America and occasionally interbreed, creating hybrid swarms containing F_1 hybrids and individuals resulting from backcrosses.

More interestingly, Rieseberg (1991) concluded that three highly localized species of *Helianthus* have resulted from hybridization of the common and prairie sunflowers. Although these forms may not be good examples of hybridization resulting from recent introductions of the parental species to new regions, they clearly illustrate how homoploid hybrid speciation can occur. These two parental species differ in at least 10 chromosomal translocations and inversions. In each of the derived species, hybridization was followed by some reorganization of the genome, leading to a form that is self-fertile, distinctive in morphology, phytochemistry, and habitat, and strongly reproductively isolated from both parents. Based on microsatellite differences, these daughter species appeared to be at least 60,000 yr old (Rieseberg et al. 2003). Thus, they may have arisen by hybridization during previous periods of climate favorable to spread of the parent species into areas of the southwestern United States. Two of the species, *H. anomalus* and *H. deserticola*, are restricted to sand dune habitats in different locations. The third, *H. paradoxus*, is restricted to brackish or saline marshes (Welch and Rieseberg 2002). For *H. anomalus*, Rieseberg et al. (1995) were able to map the pattern of chromosomal reorganization in relation to the chromosome structure of the parent species. Hybridization involving introduced common sunflowers and other native species of *Helianthus* has also resulted in the origin of weedy subspecies or populations.

The genetic mechanisms that have enabled the puzzle sunflower (*Helianthus paradoxus*) to succeed in a saline marsh environment unsuitable for either parent have been explored (Lexer et al. 2003a, 2003b). The puzzle sunflower has from 5- to 14-fold greater salt tolerance than its parents and exhibits more succulent leaves, as do many salt marsh plants. When grown under irrigation by water of high salinity, puzzle sunflower showed greater survivorship and maintained greater root biomass than its

Table 19.1. Mean survivorship and root biomass of puzzle sunflower (*Helianthus paradoxus*) and its parent species, *H. annuus* and *H. petiolaris*, under irrigation by water of different salinities. (Data from Welch and Rieseberg 2002.)

	Salinity*	Helianthus annuus	Helianthus paradoxus	Helianthus petiolaris
Survivorship (%)	0	100	100	100
	100	75	100	33
	200	42	83	8
Root Biomass (g)	0	2.3	1.2	0.4
	100	0.4	0.7	0.05
	200	0.05	0.2	0.003

*mmol/L NaCl

parents (table 19.1). Field studies with puzzle sunflower and both parents in a saline habitat in New Mexico showed that natural selection favored leaf succulence, high calcium uptake, and reduced uptake of sodium and related cations (Lexer et al. 2003a). Laboratory analysis of the genetic basis of these traits, and their relation to survivorship, showed that the hybrid puzzle sunflower has achieved a recombination of traits fixed for opposite influences in its parents (Lexer et al. 2003b).

Another example of speciation resulting from an alien introduction involves the white cattail (*Typha glauca*), which appears to be a stabilized hybrid between the native North American broadleaf cattail (*T. latifolia*) and the introduced narrowleaf cattail (*T. angustifolia*) (Kuehn et al. 1999).

R. J. Abbott (1992) investigated the origin and spread of the Oxford ragwort (*Senecio squalidus*). This species apparently originated by homoploid hybridization on Mt. Etna, Italy. It occurs in an altitudinal range of 1,000–1,800 m, which lies between the elevations of its two parental species. Introduced to Oxford, England, in the 1800s, isolated from its parents, it spread along the expanding railway network and has become widely established as an alien of homoploid hybrid origin (Abbott 1992).

Following its spread in Britain, Oxford ragwort has interbred with common groundsel (*Senecio vulgaris*), with remarkable evolutionary results (Abbott 1992). Oxford ragwort, with a diploid chromosome number of 20, and common groundsel, with a diploid number of 40, have hybridized, yielding offspring with a diploid chromosome number of 30. This form has backcrossed to common groundsel, giving rise to what is considered variety *hibernicus* of common groundsel, with a diploid number of 40. The hybrid has also experienced chromosome doubling, giving rise to a new groundsel, *S. cambrensis*, with a diploid chromosome number of 60 (Ashton and Abbott 1992).

Speciation can also occur without hybridization. New species of plants may arise by evolutionary change in a single parent species, without alteration of chromosome number. Divergence of allopatric populations due to selection for different characteristics is perhaps the most frequent pattern of speciation. Such change can also occur in sympatry. Smooth cordgrass (*Spartina alterniflora*), native to the eastern coast of North America, was introduced to San Francisco Bay in the 1970s (Daehler et al. 1999). This species has spread aggressively in the upper intertidal zone of the bay area. In 1991, a dwarf form of cordgrass, reaching only about one-fifth the height of typical smooth cordgrass, was found in several locations. The dwarf form appears to be identical to smooth cordgrass in chromosome number and genomic DNA markers. Thus, it may be interpreted most conservatively as a dwarf ecotype of smooth cordgrass. Its distinctive growth form, lack of plants of intermediate stature, and restriction to a higher tidal zone than typical smooth cordgrass suggest that it might represent a distinct species.

Recent speciation may also be occurring in green algae of the genus *Caulerpa*. Two forms of *Caulerpa* have long been present in the eastern Mediterranean Sea. One, *C. racemosa* var. *turbinata*, has been known since the mid-1920s, and the second, *C. racemosa* var. *lamourouxii*, appeared in the 1950s. Both, restricted to relatively warm waters, are noninvasive and were probably introduced in the ballast water of cargo ships (Verlaque et al. 2000). Beginning in 1984, however, an invasive form, *Caulerpa taxifolia*, appeared and has spread rapidly throughout the Mediterranean Sea, including the colder waters of the western basin. This form has subsequently colonized coastal waters in southern California and along the coast of Australia near Sydney (Meusnier et al. 2002). This invasive form reproduces vegetatively to produce dense mats over submerged substrates, crowding out other organisms.

The origin of this invasive form in the Mediterranean has been the object of speculation. It was once believed to be a hybrid between *Caulerpa racemosa* var. *turbinata* and an unknown tropical form of *Caulerpa* (Durand et al. 2002), but it now seems certain that it originated in aquarium culture in Monaco and was carelessly released into ocean waters (Meusnier et al. 2002). Recent analyses of nuclear and chloroplast DNA of the various forms of *Caulerpa*, however, indicated that the invasive form is native to coastal areas of northern Queensland, Australia. This form apparently spread into more temperate waters near Brisbane, Australia, from which it was taken to aquarium culture in Monaco.

Thus, adaptation to colder waters has occurred in *Caulerpa taxifolia*, enabling its success in the Mediterranean (Meusnier et al. 2002). These colder water strains are more robust in growth form than those in northern Queensland. Furthermore, distinct coastal and reef ecotypes of *Caulerpa taxifolia* have been recognized. This species appears to be a complex of genetically differentiating forms that probably represent sibling species.

Speciation in Animals

Polyploidy is frequent in animal species of arctic environments that have been recolonized since the last glacial retreat. Polyploid species of the cladocerans *Daphnia* and *Bosmina* are confined to the arctic, where they reproduce parthenogenetically (Beeton and Hebert 1988). During periods of maximum glacial advance, populations of these species may have been confined to isolated refugia south of the glacial front. As these populations expanded during glacial retreat, secondary contacts between them may have led to allopolyploidy. Polyploidy may be advantageous in the arctic because of developmental advantages (Adamowicz et al. 2002). The polyploid forms of these species, many of which are likely of recent origin, are genetically isolated from their diploid ancestors.

Recent speciation has been documented for animals, as well, including many instances involving alien species. Native animals may undergo sympatric speciation when alien plants provide suitable resources and a mechanism for reproductive separation of portions of a parental population (Via 2001). Often this appears to occur because the alien plants have a different reproductive phenology than that of native plants. Perhaps the best-documented example involves the maggot flies (*Rhagoletis* spp.) described in chapter 13. Biotypes of these flies on introduced apple and cherry trees are almost completely isolated from their ancestral forms on native trees, thus representing incipient species. Two-spotted spider mites (*Tetranychus urticae*) also tend to form genetically distinct host races adapted to the secondary chemistry or defensive morphology of the host plants (Agrawal et al. 2002b), as we noted in chapter 9. Adaptation to different hosts often involves fitness tradeoffs, that is, adaptation to a new host results in reduced fitness on the old host.

Another well-documented example of this sort involves the pea aphid

(*Acyrthosiphon pisum*), which was introduced to North America from Europe in the late 1800s (Via 1999). In North America, the pea aphid is considered a pest of alfalfa (*Medicago sativa*) and red clover (*Trifolium pratense*). Via (1999) showed that populations of aphids on these two forage plants are genetically divergent and that gene flow between them is reduced. She concluded that incipient barriers to successful interbreeding exist and that alfalfa and red clover biotypes of pea aphids are on the road to becoming reproductively isolated species.

Divergence of host-related populations of crop insect pests is probably not unusual. In France, for example, the European corn borer (*Ostrinia nubilalis*) has evolved host races on mugwort (*Artemisia vulgaris*), a wild plant, and maize (*Zea mays*), a crop plant native to the Americas (Martel et al. 2003). The frequency of interbreeding between the two forms appears to be less than 1%. Several factors apparently contribute to the strong genetic isolation of the two forms (Thomas et al. 2003). Populations on mugwort complete their larval development and emerge about 10 days earlier than those on maize, so the chances of mating between the two forms are greatly reduced. Sex pheromones produced by the two races also differ, reinforcing the tendency for mating of individuals of the same race. Selection for populations on maize also appears to be related to an enemy-free environment. A parasitoid wasp usually kills more than 50% of corn borer larvae overwintering on mugwort but does not attack larvae overwintering on maize plants.

Over the longer term, good evidence exists for full speciation by these sorts of processes. When Polynesian colonists reached Hawaii in about 400 CE, they brought with them a variety of food plants, including banana (*Musa paradisiaca*) and coconut palm (*Cocos nucifera*). Zimmerman (1960) noted that since the arrival of these plants, five species of moths of the genus *Hedylepta* have evolved to use banana and one to use coconut palm. This genus of moths includes 23 species endemic to Hawaii; the remaining 17 species feed primarily on various monocot plants. The ancestral form of *Hedylepta* apparently used a native Hawaiian palm of the genus *Pritchardia*.

Animals occupying insular environments of relatively recent origin or recent colonization demonstrate that speciation can easily occur within a few thousand years. Many examples of this process have been documented for fish in lakes and coastal lagoons in regions covered by the last Pleistocene glaciers (Schluter 1997, 2000). Many of these lakes contain pairs or trios of closely related species that show character displacement in feeding morphology (Schluter and McPhail 1992, 1993). Many sets of species differ in the number of gill rakers; those with the larger number are plankton feeders and those with the smaller number are benthic feeders. Recent invasions of freshwater rivers, lakes, and impoundments by many marine organisms have set the stage for evolutionary adaptation and speciation (Lee and Bell 1999).

In Tasmania, Australia, populations of *Galaxias truttaceus* have become isolated in lakes that have been separated from streams in the last 3,000–7,000 years (Ovenden and White 1990). The stream *Galaxias* are anadromous, spawning in autumn and spending 3 months at sea before returning to streams. The lake *Galaxias* spawn in spring and are thus isolated in space and time from their stream relatives. Although not the result of recent invasion of new environments in the strict sense, silverside fish (*Odontesthes* spp.) in coastal waters of southern Brazil show similar patterns of rapid speciation (Beheregaray et al. 2002).

The threespine stickleback (*Gasterosteus aculeatus*), a widespread marine and anadromous fish of the northern hemisphere, has invaded postglacial freshwater environments in many locations. Many of these invasions have given rise to incipient species that have differentiated in sympatry or parapatry (McKinnon and Rundle 2002). For example, Schluter and McPhail (1992) examined the pattern of distribution and divergence of marine and freshwater sticklebacks in coastal British Columbia, Canada. The marine form (*Gasterosteus aculeatus*) occurs in estuarine habitats. Since the end of Pleistocene glaciation, about 13,000 yr ago, this marine form has colonized many rivers and lakes. Many of the lakes became separated from the ocean about 12,500 yr ago, but some may have been reconnected for a period about 11,000 yr ago. In five lakes on islands in the Strait of Georgia, two sympatric forms of sticklebacks exist, apparently reflecting invasions dating from these two periods. These forms are best regarded as separate species, as they are strongly reproductively isolated, the incidence of hybrid individuals being only about 1%. In addition, they are divergent in morphology and feeding ecology, with one form being specialized for planktonic and one for benthic feeding.

Anadromous and freshwater forms of the threespine stickleback occur in many, perhaps hundreds, of streams and rivers that have become available only in postglacial times (McKinnon and Rundle 2002). In some river systems, differentiated lake and stream forms exist. The differentiated forms of these fish typically differ in multiple traits and appear to be the result of divergent selection, rather than of genetic drift or founder effects.

Most also show some degree of hybridization as well as a strong degree of assortative mating because of differences in habitat preferences or habitat-related courtship traits.

Incipient speciation is likely in several other taxa of northern fish (Schluter 1996). In the case of rainbow smelt (*Osmerus mordax*) in Lake Saint-Jean, Ontario, Canada, dwarf and normal forms coexist and use the same spawning areas in two inflowing rivers (Saint-Laurent et al. 2003). Smelt populations in Lake Saint-Jean probably date from between 8,700 and 10,300 yr ago. Genetic analyses revealed that fish spawning in the two inflowing rivers were distinct and that within each river population dwarf and normal forms existed. The dwarf forms grow more slowly, reach maturity more quickly, and reproduce once at maturity. The normal form grows faster, matures more slowly, and reproduces repeatedly. Dwarf fish possess more closely spaced gill rakers, suggesting a greater tendency to feed on plankton in open water. No evidence was found that these forms resulted from separate invasions of Lake Saint-Jean by smelt. Thus, divergent selection, strong enough to outweigh gene flow between dwarf and normal forms, was apparently responsible for differentiation of the two forms.

The development of reproductive isolation between different populations of colonizing species can begin very soon after colonization. Hendry et al. (2000) documented incipient speciation between populations of sockeye salmon (*Oncorhynchus nerka*) breeding in different locations within the Lake Washington watershed, Washington State. Sockeye salmon were extirpated in this watershed by anthropogenic impacts in the early 1900s. Successful reintroductions were made between 1937 and 1945 using hatchery-propagated juveniles originally obtained from Baker Lake, Washington. These introductions resulted in a large population that breeds in the Cedar River, which flows into the southern end of Lake Washington. In 1957, a small population breeding at Pleasure Point, on the eastern shore of Lake Washington, was discovered. The Cedar River sockeyes spawn in gravel beds in flowing water that varies substantially in temperature from fall through spring, whereas the Pleasure Point fish spawn in quiet-water gravel beds in which little change in temperature occurs seasonally.

Comparisons of the fish were made at these two breeding sites in 1992, a maximum of 56 yr or 13 fish generations after the original introductions to the Lake Washington watershed (Hendry et al. 2000; Hendry 2001). By examining otoliths, calcareous structures of the inner ear, the site at which individual fish were hatched could be determined because the incubation temperature creates distinctive otolith patterns. By this method, fish resident at the two breeding sites could be distinguished from new immigrants from the opposite site. Resident fish at the two breeding sites differed significantly in morphology in ways that correlated with characteristics of the two habitats. Males had shallower bodies in the river population, as expected for fish adapted for maximum swimming efficiency. Females in the river population were larger bodied, which enables them to spawn at greater depths in the river gravel, reducing the chance that the eggs will be lost by scouring by the flowing water. Differences were also found in features adapting the fry to the different temperature regimes of the two sites. All of these differences are known to have a strong genetic basis in salmon. Furthermore, the differentiation of the Pleasure Point population occurred in spite of an immigration rate of about 39%, indicating that gene flow into the Pleasure Point population was much less. Thus, although full reproductive isolation had not yet been achieved, selection was favoring reduced interbreeding.

Animals that have colonized oceanic islands or other islands of recent origin also show many instances of incipient speciation. On the island of Madeira, located in the Atlantic 600 km west of North Africa, the house mouse (*Mus musculus*) was introduced by humans, either via early Portuguese ships that carried them to the islands or by Viking visitors as early as the ninth century (Gündüz et al. 2001). In either case, within a few hundred years, six distinct chromosomal races have evolved in coastal valleys separated by mountain barriers that reach from the interior highlands to the coast (Britton-Davidian et al. 2000). Owing to chromosomal fusions, these races possess reduced chromosome numbers relative to mainland European mice. Formation of fertile hybrids among these races appears to be impossible, so they are reproductively isolated and constitute sibling species. Mitochondrial DNA analyses suggest that the Madeiran mice are most similar to present-day populations in northern Europe, an observation consistent with an introduction by Viking ships (Gündüz et al. 2001).

Speciation and Extinction: Long-term Prospects

The earth is experiencing an anthropogenic mass extinction of species comparable in magnitude to the catastrophic mass extinctions of past geological times. As many authors have shown, these extinctions reflect combined impacts of several types of human activity, especially habitat destruction, exploitation of plant and animal populations, and introduction of alien species (Cox 1999). For most groups of organisms, extinctions have been concentrated in insular environments, including islands and freshwater lakes and streams. Evidence from past extinction episodes suggests that diversity does not rebound quickly in geological time (Kirchner and Weil 2000). The marine fossil record, for example, shows that rates of origin of species are correlated with extinction rates about 10 million yr earlier. Recovery of diversity appears to be a complex process of adaptive radiation that is in some degree self-reinforcing. This implies that the current extinction episode will require millions of years for recovery of biodiversity, even with the increased rate of speciation that may result from introductions of organisms to new geographical areas.

The long-term impact of the massive introduction of species to new biogeographic regions, given the roles both of speciation and extinction, may not itself cause an overall reduction of the diversity of species, regionally or globally (Rosenzweig 2001). In the short run, introductions are likely to increase local species diversity, at least in continental regions, since extinctions triggered by the impacts of aliens are often slow. Numbers of naturalized plants, especially, have far exceeded the number of alien-caused plant extinctions (Sax et al. 2002). On oceanic islands, extinctions tend to occur more quickly, and the evolutionary time required for speciation to offset extinction may be much longer than in continental regions.

Over the long term, biotic relaxation is expected to occur where species diversity has been raised above a level set by environmental conditions that influence the rate of natural invasion, speciation, and extinction for the geographical region. Biotic relaxation is simply the decline in diversity due to an excess of extinctions over appearance of new species by invasion and speciation. Relaxation has been demonstrated in the biotas of oceanic islands formed by rising postglacial sea levels. In the Gulf of California, for example, Wilcox (1978) showed that islands formed in this manner held more lizard species than could be maintained and that the longer the island has been isolated, the fewer species remained.

In small areas of habitat that become isolated, relaxation can occur very quickly. Barro Colorado Island, Panama, was formed by the flooding of Gatun Lake in 1913. On this island of tropical forest, 15.6 km^2 in size, more than 27% of the original breeding bird species were lost by the early 1980s (Karr 1982). In cases such as this, many of the losses are due to stochastic fluctuations in environmental conditions or population demography that result in total mortality or reproductive failure of small populations.

In the changing world, areas of natural habitat are declining in size and becoming highly fragmented, so their effective areas may be overstocked with species, both locally and for the region as a whole. Thus, eventual declines in number of species are expected due both to the direct effects of alien species on native species and to biotic relaxation in communities that have become reduced to small remnants.

New Species, New Biotic Communities, and New Ecosystems

Alien species exhibit all stages of speciation, from daughter forms that show full reproductive isolation to those that are only partially isolated and show very early degrees of divergence. These daughter populations are contributing to the evolution of biotic communities that differ not only in their composition of old and new species but also in the ways in which they interact with their physical environment. Entire ecosystems have become permanently altered by the incorporation of aliens and by the evolutionary processes that have been set in motion. In addition, these processes are being played out in an environment of global change. We shall consider some of the implications of the evolutionary biology of alien species in this context in our final chapter.

20.
Permanently Altered Biotic Communities

"As we continue to manipulate biodiversity, our experience so far with the evolution of virulence in diseases, short-term effectiveness of resistant crop varieties, and rapid evolution of interactions within natural communities suggests that the health and welfare of human societies will demand an increased understanding of the ongoing evolutionary dynamics of species interactions."

—THOMPSON (1999c)

In the early 1900s, the southern flanks of the Alps in southern Switzerland and northern Italy were dominated by temperate deciduous forests of oaks, chestnut, linden, and ash, growing under a strongly seasonal climate. Many human influences have affected these original forests, including tree harvesting and planting, domestic animal grazing, modification of the fire regime, and introduction of exotic plants, all of which have changed over time. Added to these factors, however, is a changing climate, especially during the last three decades of the twentieth century. Low winter temperatures, especially those below freezing, have become much less frequent, and the length of the growing season has increased. These climatic changes have favored broad-leaved evergreen woody species over deciduous species (Walther 2002).

Nonindigenous evergreen plants from several world regions have invaded the forests of this region of the Alps (Walther 2000). More than a dozen invaders are involved. Some, such as the European laurel (*Laurus nobilis*), have simply migrated north from Mediterranean Italy. Another, cherry laurel (*Prunus laurocerasus*) comes from the Middle East. North America has contributed holly-leaved barberry (*Mahonia aquifolium*). Several species are native to eastern Asia: Nepal camphor tree (*Cinnamomum glanduliferum*), silverberry (*Eleagnus pungens*), glossy privet (*Ligustrum lucidum*), windmill palm (*Trachycarpus fortunei*), and several species of cotoneasters (*Cotoneaster* spp.) and honeysuckles (*Lonicera* spp.). This invasion has created a new forest type, which will provide a habitat for many exotic animals and microorganisms, and a new evolutionary stage for both native and exotic species.

The developmental trajectory of ecosystems is thus being altered permanently by alien invasions coupled with global climate change. The species composition of many communities has been altered by intercontinental and interoceanic invasions of aliens that have become established so extensively that their eradication is impossible. Global climate change has now shifted climatic zones so that species from locations within continents and oceans are invading new areas (Root and Schneider 2002; Beaugrand et al. 2002). The ecological and evolutionary adjustments by both alien and native species mean that maintaining or restoring the original community composition of many areas is impossible.

Under the influence of global change, the question of what species are truly alien becomes nebulous because range expansions within continental areas by many species involve hundreds of kilometers. Numerous species are invading new regions, both through human-assisted introduction and by natural dispersal. These changes, and their evolutionary consequences, pose major issues for environmental management.

Changing Communities and Ecosystems

The numbers of alien species that are established in many ecosystems has stimulated the origin of a new measure in community structure—xenodiversity: the richness of a community or biota in alien species. In many environments, xenodiversity equals or exceeds the diversity of native species. Alien species, together with changing distributions and abundances of native species in response to global change, are altering the structure of all types of communities: terrestrial, freshwater, and marine.

Xenodiversity is evident at the community level, as well. New community types, created by alien invasions of native assemblages, have become established over wide areas in North America and many other parts of the world (Cox 1999). In North America, for example, invasive trees such as casuarinas (*Casuarina* spp.), Australian paperbark (*Melaleuca quinquenervia*), Brazilian pepper (*Schinus terebinthefolius*), and others have established woodland communities in areas of former coastal strand and marsh in Florida. Along the Gulf Coast of the United States, Chinese tallow (*Sapium sebiferum*) is converting coastal prairie to alien woodland (Bruce et al. 1995). Riparian woodlands in the western United States have been transformed by invasions of salt cedars (*Tamarix* spp.), Russian olive (*Eleagnus angustifolia*), and several other alien trees that are gradually displacing native trees and shrubs. Intermontane grasslands and shrub steppes of the western United States and Canada are being invaded or almost completely displaced by annual brome grasses (*Bromus* spp.) and broadleaved herbaceous knapweeds and starthistles (*Centaurea* spp.). Alien annual and perennial grasses are invading warm deserts, where they are introducing fire to vegetation types that rarely burned. Native strand communities of the Pacific coast are becoming dominated by European beachgrass (*Aimophila arenaria*).

Elsewhere in the world, similar community transformations also are occurring, as we saw in the example opening this chapter. Many other examples can be cited. In Australia, Monterey pine (*Pinus radiata*) is invading native eucalyptus woodland from adjacent pine plantations (Burdon and Chilvers 1977). Australian eucalypts (*Eucalyptus* spp.) have become established in many locations around the world, creating woodland communities in former grasslands and shrublands. North American and European pines (*Pinus* spp.) and Australian acacias (*Acacia* spp.) and needlebushes (*Hakea* spp.) are threatening the fynbos shrublands of South Africa.

Aquatic ecosystems, both freshwater and marine, are being altered as well. Deliberate and accidental introduction of nonindigenous species, especially fish and molluscs, is one of the major threats to native biodiversity in freshwater lakes (Lodge 2001). The North American Great Lakes, for example, are now home to more than 139 alien plants and animals. The Baltic Sea is now home to 100 or more alien species, derived from all continents except Antarctica (Leppäkoski and Olenin 2001; Leppäkoski et al. 2002). In Pearl Harbor, Hawaii, alien species dominate the biota (Englund 2002). A recent survey documented 191 alien aquatic species derived from all parts of the world.

Not only is the composition of these biotic communities altered, the pattern of ecosystem function is transformed as well. Thus, native species are not only faced with new biotic challenges of competition, predation, and disease, but also with changes in physical and chemical conditions, resource availabilities, and disturbance regimes. The evolutionary stage for both native and alien species has been largely rebuilt.

Alien Species, Biotic Homogenization, and Invasional Meltdown

As alien species invade and alter native communities, endemic native species disappear and the communities of similar climatic zones in different world regions become homogenized. The number of successful alien species is strongly correlated with the number of native species whose existence is threatened (McKinney and Lockwood 2001). In the short run, as alien species become naturalized, the richness of species, especially of plants, tends to increase (Sax et al. 2002). In Hawaii, for example, the native flora consists of 1,294 species, 71 of which are now extinct. About 1,090 species have become naturalized in Hawaii, however, so the flora has nearly doubled in number of species. For vertebrate animals on islands, on the other hand, establishment of alien species and extinction of native species tend to balance each other very closely. In Hawaii, 64 bird species have become extinct since humans arrived, whereas 55 species have become naturalized.

The extent of homogenization in some types of ecosystems is often not at all obvious. In stream faunas of mountainous regions, for example, human land use and, increasingly, global climate change, tend to promote the spread of downstream organisms into higher elevation, upstream areas (Scott and Helfman 2001). Downstream faunas tend to comprise generalist and alien species, so their spread is often accompanied by extirpation of species endemic to highland areas.

The disruption of native communities by alien invaders has a distinctly ominous potential: the process tends to exhibit positive feedback. Simberloff and Von Holle (1999) coined the term "invasional meltdown" for such a process. Simply stated, invasional meltdown means that successful invaders facilitate the invasion of still other alien species. This might occur because aliens disrupt the structure or function of the ecosystem so as to create conditions favoring invasion by other species, including other aliens. It might also occur because aliens create conditions or constitute resources that specifically favor other aliens.

The precise nature of synergistic effects has been documented by two recent analyses. Simberloff and Von Holle (1999) examined a large number of articles in journals of ecology and conservation biology to determine the frequency of positive interactions among introduced species. Out of 190 interactions that could be categorized, 10 were mutually beneficial (mutualistic), 12 were beneficial to one species and harmless to the other (commensal), 156 were beneficial to one and harmful to the other (exploitative), and only 12 were harmful to both species (antagonistic). Although this was not a rigorous statistical test of facilitation, it showed that interactions that benefited one or both alien species were very frequent.

Ricciardi (2001) performed a more rigorous test for aquatic species introduced to the North American Great Lakes. Reviewing articles dealing with the 162 alien species now known from the lakes, he identified 101 interspecific interactions that could be categorized. Of these, 17 were either mutualistic or commensal, 73 were exploitative, and only 11 were antagonistic or amensal (detrimental to one but harmless to the other). Of the exploitative interactions, more than one-third were instances in which a later invader exploited a previously established alien. Ricciardi (2001) found, furthermore, that the number of invaders per decade had increased in a straight-line manner with time since the early 1800s. Thus, invaders tended to show a degree of synergism, although whether this effect was stronger than for relations among native species was still not clear.

Global Climate Change and Alien Invasions

The magnitude of worldwide invasion of alien species is itself a phenomenon unique in the history of life on earth. Superimposed on rapid spread of species to new geographical areas, however, is global climate change, a phenomenon also occurring at an unprecedented rate. Global climate change is both directly and indirectly promoting alien invasions and their evolutionary consequences.

Little doubt now exists that the global environment is changing. Global change involves several components. Global climatic warming, as a consequence of increasing concentrations of carbon dioxide and other anthropogenic greenhouse gases, is the primary driver of climate change. The overall climate of the earth has warmed by about 0.6°C during the past century, with the increase being much greater at high than at low latitudes (Walther et al. 2002). Other components of global change include the fertilization effect of increased atmospheric carbon dioxide; increases in ultraviolet radiation due to weakening of the stratospheric ozone layer; discharges of acids, oxides, heavy metals, and other products of fossil fuel combustion; environmental pollution by industrial and agricultural chemicals; and increased mobilization of bioactive elements such as mercury, selenium, and many others. Stratospheric depletion of ozone over the south polar region may also be a major contributor to altered atmospheric circulation and surface warming of the Antarctic Peninsula and southern oceans (Thompson and Solomon 2002). The chemistry of the earth's air, waters, and soils has thus been altered in many ways.

In terrestrial ecosystems, global climate change is expressed as altered annual regimes of temperature and precipitation, longer growing seasons at high latitudes, reduced snow cover at high latitudes and altitudes, reduced cloud cover in the humid tropics, and increasing incidence of severe weather events. Patterns of change are complex, however, and major regional differences exist in the magnitude and direction of changes. Nevertheless, several general patterns are evident. Satellite data show that the growing season at latitudes between 45° and 70°N has lengthened by about 18 days in Eurasia and 12 days in North America over the past 20 yr (Peñuelas and Filella 2001; Lucht et al. 2002). Terrestrial snow and ice cover has declined about 10% since 1960. These changes translate into an increase of about 6% in total terrestrial net primary production between 1980 and 2000 (Nemani et al. 2003). Ecosystems in the humid tropics and higher latitudes of the northern hemisphere showed the greatest increases.

Freshwater ecosystems, especially at higher latitudes, are also beginning to experience altered seasonal temperature regimes (Schindler 1988). The ice-free season is lengthening, water levels are dropping, the surface water temperatures are increasing, and the thermocline is deepening. Surface water inflows are likely to decrease, together with inflow of dissolved materials. Acid deposition and increased ultraviolet radiation are additional impacts of particular importance in freshwaters.

Marine ecosystems are experiencing global change. In the southern oceans, both surface and subsurface waters to a depth of 1,100 meters have warmed significantly over the past 50 yr (Gille 2002). In tropical oceans, surface waters have warmed by about 1–2°C over the past century. Thermal expansion of warmed surface water, together with melting land and sea ice, is leading to rising sea level. In the North Atlantic, release of freshwater by melting of sea ice and terrestrial ice caps may alter ocean currents that bring warm water to the coast of northwestern Europe (Stevens 1999). In the Pacific Ocean, oceanic circulation and water temperature changes beginning in the mid-1970s have affected major oceanic regions both north and south of the equator (Hayward 1997). In the California Current, for example, warmer water has been associated with a large decline in zooplankton and seabirds (Veit et al. 1997).

From the arctic to the tropics, climatic change has already affected the distribution and phenology of many species and communities (Peñuelas et al. 2002; Walther et al. 2002). Comparison of aerial photos taken in

1948–50 with photos taken in 1999–2000 on the north slope of Alaska, for example, show substantial expansion of the range of several deciduous shrubs and white spruce (*Picea glauca*) (Sturm et al. 2001). Even in deserts, terrestrial ecosystems are responding to global change. In southeastern Arizona, for example, increased winter rainfall since 1977 is associated with major increases in shrub density and cover on a long-term study area (Brown et al. 1997).

Numerous changes in the phenology of plant species appear to result from these global changes. In parts of the temperate zone, many plants have shown earlier leafing and flowering in spring (Fitter and Fitter 2002). Some of the best long-term observations of phenological change for plants come from southern Wisconsin. Leopold and Jones (1947) compared the timing of seasonal events in 1935–45 with those observed by William Trelease at a nearby location in 1881–85. In general, spring events occurred 2 wk earlier in 1935–45 than in the late 1800s. Bradley et al. (1999) extended the comparison to 1998. Of 55 spring events that could be compared to those in the 1930s and 1940s, 18 were up to 2 wk earlier in 1998. Another 20 events showed no significant change, indicating that relationships involving various components of the ecosystem were not occurring in parallel.

Terrestrial animals have also shown changes in seasonal activity patterns. Many migratory birds have appeared earlier in the season in Europe and North America, although in a few cases migration has been delayed. Many short-, medium-, and long-distance migrants showed earlier migration schedules in western Europe, apparently in close response to stronger influence of the North Atlantic Oscillation (Hüppop and Hüppop 2002). In New York and Massachusetts, short-distance migrants showed spring arrival dates averaging 13 days earlier and long-distance migrants 4 days earlier in 1951–93 compared to 1903–50 (Butler 2003). Changes in community composition have occurred among land birds (Lemoine and Böhning-Gaese 2003). In the Lake Constance region of central Europe, long-distance migrant species have declined while short-distance migrants and resident species have increased in abundance as winter temperatures have become milder. In California, many butterfly species of the Central Valley show earlier spring flights, in many cases by more than 3 wk (Forister and Shapiro 2003). In the United Kingdom, numerous butterflies have emerged and amphibians have begun to breed earlier in the year (Beebee 2002; Root et al. 2003).

Range shifts by plant and animal species also appear to be resulting from climatic change. Meta-analysis of long-term studies of geographic and phenological shifts by plant and animal species showed that more than 80% of the species involved have extended their temporal or spatial activities in the direction expected by known physiological limitations (Root et al. 2003). In the temperate zone and subarctic, various species of plants and animals have extended their ranges to higher elevations and higher latitudes. Butterflies, in particular, have proven to be sensitive indicators of shifts in climatic zones. In a study of range limits of 35 species of nonmigratory butterflies in Europe and North America, Parmesan et al. (1999) found that 22 species extended their ranges northward by 35–240 km during the twentieth century. Only one species had expanded southward to a significant degree. In western North America, where temperature isotherms have shifted north about 105 km, the mean latitude of populations of Edith's checkerspot (*Euphydryas editha*) has shifted northward 92 km (Parmesan 1996). The sachem skipper (*Atalopedes campestris*) has spread northward in the Pacific states by about 700 km over the past 35 yr (Crozier 2002). This butterfly, a member of a tropical genus, is intolerant of severe winter cold, so warming of winter temperature has probably contributed to its expansion into Oregon and Washington State. In southeastern Arizona, several formerly common animal species disappeared and one new rodent species appeared (Brown et al. 1997).

In some mountainous areas, plant species have moved upward in elevation as the climate has warmed. In the Scandes Mountains of Sweden, for example, the limits of several species of evergreen and deciduous trees and shrubs have risen by 120–375 m (Kullman 2002). In Austria, Grabherr et al. (1994) collected data on increased elevational limits of nine plant species. In this region, the increase in temperature has been about 0.7°C over the past 70–100 yr. This change should correspond to an increase of 8–10 m per decade in climate zones. Plant distribution limits, however, increased much less, with the maximum approaching 4 m per decade. Clearly, even over short distances, plant migration is lagging behind the rate of climate change.

Warm-water marine invertebrates and fish have expanded their ranges northward in Europe and North America. In the North Atlantic, for example, marine copepod assemblages typical of warmer waters have spread northward more than 10° of latitude (Beaugrand et al. 2002).

Climatic change thus is shifting the location of climatic zones to which many species are adapted, as well as creating new climatic patterns. At a given location, conditions change so that some species native to that region are likely to disappear and others, native to adjacent regions, are likely to invade. Under this scenario, the distinction between natives and aliens becomes blurred. Many temperate zone species will likely spread to areas much farther north, and desert species into areas that are becoming warmer and drier.

Because climatic zones are likely to shift faster than long-lived species can track through reproduction and dispersal, communities in disequilibrium may result, with conditions that indirectly favor weedy species, many of which are likely to be aliens. Dispersal is hindered, as well, by the high degree of fragmentation of many natural habitats due to human land use. In Britain, for example, an analysis of changes in distribution of 46 species of butterflies that reach their northern limits within the islands showed that most had declined over the past 30 yr despite the expansion of areas of favorable climate (Warren et al. 2001). Those species that did expand as expected were mostly habitat generalists.

Habitat fragmentation can seriously impede plant migration. In Belgium, where forest habitat is highly fragmented, Honnay et al. (2002) examined the colonization of suitable new forest patches by forest plant species. The average distance from source to target patches in the area studied was 210 m. The required migration rates of these species under projected climate change are 3–5 km per year (Davis and Shaw 2001). The rates observed in the Belgian study were only a few meters per year, and some species showed essentially no ability to colonize new patches over a period of about 40 yr. Interestingly, migration rates were highest for plant species dispersed by birds and mammals and lowest for those dispersed by wind.

Whether or not invasive species will benefit more than noninvasive species by global change is uncertain (Dukes 2000). Many invasive plants show considerable growth stimulation by elevated carbon dioxide and increased nitrogen availability, but their responses do not appear to be greater than those of related noninvasive species. Nevertheless, other characteristics of many invasive species, particularly the dispersal capability and opportunistic response to disturbance, means that they are well adapted to changing and fragmented habitats (Dukes and Mooney 1999; Barrett 2000). In Sweden, several nonnative trees, including Norway maple (*Acer platanoides*), Swiss stone pine (*Pinus cembra*), and lodgepole pine (*Pinus contorta*), have spread upward to near the treeline formed by native species (Kullman 2002).

Many invasive animal species are likely to invade new areas where climate has warmed. In North America, several widely introduced warm-water fish, including largemouth bass (*Micropterus salmoides*), bluegill sunfish (*Lepomis macrochirus*), and green sunfish (*Lepomis cyanellus*), are likely to spread into higher latitudes and altitudes (Eaton and Scheller 1996). At the same time, at high latitudes, many cold-adapted aquatic species may disappear as freshwater ecosystems warm and are invaded by such species (Lodge 2001).

Global Change, Shifting Ranges, and Accelerated Evolution

Alien invasions have led to evolutionary responses of both aliens and the native species with which they interact, as we have seen in detail. Global climatic change is now modifying the ecological theater in which these evolutionary processes are playing out. Both native and alien species are now influenced by the selective pressures of global change. The increasing husbandry of transgenic plants and animals is a wild card that will certainly have increasing evolutionary consequences.

Most analyses of the possible response of biotas to climatic change have considered either the need or the potential for species to track the climatic zones to which they are adapted by dispersal and colonization of areas that become suitable. Typically, such analyses have assumed genetic uniformity of species in question and landscape conditions permissive to dispersal mechanisms. Malcolm et al. (2002) modeled the migration rates required by member species of various biomes to keep pace with the shifts of climatic zones resulting from a doubling of carbon dioxide over the next 100 yr. This analysis showed that required rates were much higher than those calculated for species that moved northward rapidly during the last glacial retreat in the northern hemisphere. Required rates were highest for arctic and temperate biomes, where global warming is predicted to be greatest. Not surprisingly, incorporation of migration barriers, such as water areas for terrestrial communities, increased the migration rates required to keep pace with climate change. Other modeling efforts suggest that the effect of reducing the latitudinal gradient of temperature will be to increase the rapidity of northward invasions (García-Ramos and Rodríguez 2002).

Few studies have been attempted of the capability of plant species for dispersal into new areas of favorable habitat such as those created by climate change. Many of the available studies deal with invasive plant species, which show migration rates of several to many kilometers per year (Malcolm et al. 2002). Among animals, birds and mammals expanding into new regions may show very high migration rates. The range of the coyote (*Canis latrans*) spread eastward in North America at a rate in excess of 20 km per year between 1900 and 1990 (Malcolm et al. 2002).

Analyses of the abilities of plants and animals to shift their ranges to keep pace with changing climates have given little consideration to intraspecific genetic adaptation (Davis and Shaw 2001). Most widely distributed plants and animals show some degree of genetic adaptation to local environmental conditions. In particular, plant species that have undergone altitudinal or latitudinal migrations following retreat of the last continental glaciers show various patterns of genetic variability and ecotypic adaptation (see, e.g., Cwynar and MacDonald 1987). Some species, for example, show a decline in variability from southern areas close to their interglacial refugia to northern areas, where sequential founder effects have caused progressive loss of alleles. Others, such as Scotch pine (*Pinus sylvestris*), which followed retreating glaciers northward in Europe, now show ecotypic adaptation to local temperature and photoperiod conditions. The same is true of several North American trees and shrubs.

Inouye et al. (2000) documented an example of the origin of new climatic and phenological conditions to which existing species do not appear to be well adapted. At the Rocky Mountain Biological Laboratory in Gothic, Colorado, warmer spring temperatures appear to be coupled with increased winter snowfall in a manner that has kept the time of disappearance of the winter snowpack essentially constant. In response to warmer temperatures, however, American robins (*Turdus migratorius*) are appearing about 2 wk earlier than in the early 1980s, and yellow-bellied marmots (*Marmota flaviventris*) are emerging from hibernation about 38 days earlier than in the mid-1970s. These species, and presumably other migrants and hibernators, are thus experiencing a much longer period of spring snowpack at the beginning of their summer breeding season. This represents a new combination of environmental conditions to which they may not be fully adapted.

Although attention has been concentrated on the abilities of native species to respond to climatic change, invasive alien species possess the same opportunities. As we have seen, many of these species possess high evolutionary adaptability and respond to resources made available by environmental disruption. The spread of invasive tree species into high mountain zones made favorable by climatic warming in Sweden demonstrates that alien plants are taking advantage of such opportunities (Kullman 2002). Several alien trees that are widespread in the Mediterranean region of the Old World have shown earlier flowering by 14–24 days (Peñuelas et al. 2002).

Analysis of the harmful alien plants and animals that have invaded the United States indicates that about 48% are likely to expand their ranges northward in response to climatic warming (Zavaleta and Royval 2002). An increase of mean annual temperature of 1°C, for example, is projected to enable the imported red fire ant (*Solenopsis wagneri*) to expand its range by more than 23%, including much of the states of Virginia and Tennessee. Drier and warmer conditions would allow salt cedar (*Tamarix* spp.) to spread into many areas now too humid for the species. Similar predictions of expansion of alien species have been formulated in Europe, Australia, New Zealand, and other areas. Similarly, several tropical diseases of humans are likely to expand into presently temperate regions.

Evolutionary Adaptation to Changing Global Climate

Several studies have shown rapid evolution in characteristics of insects whose ranges are spreading northward in response to climatic warming. In chapter 2, we examined evolutionary changes related to increased dispersal capabilities of such forms. In southern England, several insects have shown substantial range expansions correlated with climatic warming (Thomas et al. 2001). One of these, the brown argus butterfly (*Aricia agestis*), has also shown a host plant shift correlated with host plant availabilities in areas into which it has spread. In newly colonized areas, it has shifted its preference more strongly to a wild geranium (*Geranium molle*) that is more widespread in the invaded areas. Preference for this species by the progeny of butterflies taken from invaded areas and reared in captivity shows that this shift has a genetic basis.

In Europe, strong evidence also exists for evolutionary responses of several migratory birds to changing climate. The blackcap (*Sylvia atricapilla*), one of the Old World warblers, wintered almost exclusively in the Mediterranean region prior to the 1950s. Since then, a large wintering population has developed in England (Berthold 1995). These birds come from central Europe and have been shown experimentally to possess a genetically based migratory orientation pattern that enables them to migrate west-northwest to their wintering area in England. Other land birds, such as the serin (*Serinus serinus*), have expanded their ranges northward and modified their migration patterns, so populations that were once completely migratory are now partial migrants (Berthold 1999). Berthold (2001) showed that the change from a fully migratory to a permanent resident songbird can occur within 25 generations. Thus, many of the recent changes in ranges and migratory times of birds probably have an evolutionary basis. Selection for earlier breeding has also contributed to the advancement of egg laying by more than 1 wk during the past 20 yr in The Netherlands (Coppack and Both 2002).

Other signs of evolutionary adaptation to climatic change are now being seen. In Israel, for example, where minimum summer temperatures have increased more than 1°C during the last half of the twentieth century, Yom-Tov (2001) showed that the body mass of several resident birds has decreased. Jarvinen (1994) found an increase in egg volume of the pied flycatcher (*Ficedula hypoleuca*) in northern Finland from 1975 to 1993 and attributed the change to the warming temperatures in this region. For plants, Beering and Kelly (1997) noted increases in stomatal density for herbaceous species of temperate forest over 70–200 yr. Although the degree of genetic control is uncertain for some of these changes, it is clear that global climate change will favor many physiological adjustments of species within their present ranges.

Adaptive shifts in the ranges of species, whether they be native or alien, in response to changing climate in many cases thus require evolutionary adjustments as well as successful dispersal capabilities. Furthermore, populations at the expanding edge of the range of a species may possess greater variability than those at the receding edge (Davis and Shaw 2001). Expanding edge populations receive pollen and seeds from populations away from the expanding edge but adapted to conditions ahead of the expansion front (fig. 20.1). Populations at the receding edge depend only on their own genetic variability to adapt to changing climate and are more likely to fail and become extirpated.

Conservation in an Era of Rapid Evolution

This constellation of new relationships demands a new view of biotic communities and their management. Many intercontinental aliens are so fully integrated into ecosystems that their eradication is impossible, or even undesirable. The majority of these are not invasive and are not ecologically disruptive. Some are beneficial through their roles in nutrient cycling, biocontrol, and mutualistic interactions with native species. Thus, in practice, we must assess the ecological and evolutionary processes

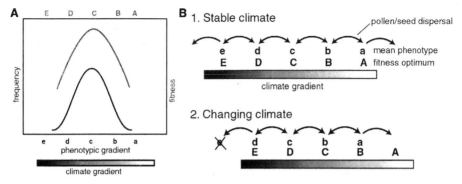

Figure 20.1. Adaptation by a species with a range expanding into a region of favorable climate and withdrawing from a region of unfavorable climate. (A) Curves of phenotype frequencies (lower curve and lowercase letters) and fitness (upper curve and capital letters) for a population occupying a portion of a climate gradient. The highest frequency of phenotypes and optimal fitness coincide at c and C. (B) As the climate gradient shifts, pollen and seed dispersal may help enable the species to keep up with the shift in the fitness optimum at the advancing edge, but without an evolutionary shift in the fitness optimum, the population cannot maintain itself in areas where the climate has become unfavorable. (Reprinted with permission from M. B. Davis and R. G. Shaw. 2001. Range shifts and adaptive responses to quaternary climate change. *Science* 292:673–679. © 2001 AAAS.)

involving both native and alien species and evaluate their influence on community function.

Biotic communities that are changing in composition require that a distinction be made between intracontinental and intercontinental aliens. Serious threats are posed to many native species by the continuing invasion of species from other continents. To fail to restrict these invasions is obviously counter to conservation goals. In the modern world, however, complete suppression of intercontinental invasions is impossible, so we must recognize these invasions as part of global change. On the other hand, we must recognize that the ranges of many species are shifting within continents due to the effects of global change and direct human modification of the environment. To treat such species as aliens as they extend their ranges into areas that have become favorable as a result of climatic change is also counter to the goal of conservation.

The dynamic nature of biotic communities in a changing world means that conservation efforts must be flexible and in tune with biogeographic and evolutionary realities. To protect threatened and endangered species under changing environmental conditions, management must maximize the ability of these species to adjust their geographic ranges as conditions demand and to adapt to new biotic and abiotic challenges by evolution. The best protection that we can give species unique to our land, freshwater, and ocean areas is the potential to adapt by evolution and dispersal to conditions of a rapidly changing environment.

Literature Cited

Abbott, R. J. 1992. Plant invasions, interspecific hybridization and the evolution of new plant taxa. *Trends in Ecology and Evolution* 7:401–405.

Abbott, I. 2002. Origin and spread of the cat, *Felis catus*, on mainland Australia, with a discussion of the magnitude of its early impact on native fauna. *Wildlife Research* 29:51–74.

Abernethy, K. 1994. The establishment of a hybrid zone between red and sika deer (genus *Cervus*). *Molecular Ecology* 3:551–562.

Able, K. P., and J. R. Belthoff. 1998. Rapid 'evolution' of migratory behaviour in the introduced house finch of eastern North America. *Proceedings of the Royal Society of London B* 265:2063–2071.

Abu-El Samen, F. M., G. A. Secor, and N. C. Gudmestad. 2003a. Variability in virulence among asexual progenies of *Phytophthora infestans*. *Phytopathology* 93:293–304.

Abu-El Samen, F. M., G. A. Secor, and N. C. Gudmestad. 2003b. Genetic variation among asexual progeny of *Phytophthora infestans* detected with RAPD and AFLP markers. *Plant Pathology* 52:314–325.

Adamowicz, S. J., T. R. Gregory, M. C. Marinone, and P. D. N. Hebert. 2002. New insights into the distribution of polyploid *Daphnia*: the Holarctic revisited and Argentina explored. *Molecular Ecology* 11:1209–1217.

Adams, M. J., C. A. Pearl, and R. B. Bury. 2003. Indirect facilitation of an anuran invasion by non-native fishes. *Ecology Letters* 6:343–351.

Adler, G. H., and R. Levins. 1994. The island syndrome in rodent populations. *Quarterly Review of Biology* 69:473–490.

Agrawal, A. A. 1998. Induced responses to herbivory and increased plant performance. *Science* 279:1201–1202.

Agrawal, A. A. 2000. Host-range evolution: adaptation and trade-offs in fitness of mites on alternate hosts. *Ecology* 81:500–508.

Agrawal, A. A., and C. M. Lively. 2002. Infection genetics: gene-for-gene versus matching-alleles models and all points in between. *Evolutionary Ecology Research* 4:79–90.

Agrawal, A. A., J. K. Conner, M. T. J. Johnson, and R. Wallsgrove. 2002a. Ecological genetics of an induced plant defense against herbivores: additive genetic variance and costs of phenotypic plasticity. *Evolution* 56:2206–2213.

Agrawal, A. A., F. Vala, and M. W. Sabelis. 2002b. Induction of preference and performance after acclimation to novel hosts in a phytophagous spider mite: adaptive plasticity? *American Naturalist* 159:553–565.

Ainouche, M. L., R. J. Bayer, J.-P. Gourret, A. Defontaine, and M.-T. Misset. 1999. The allotetraploid invasive weed *Bromus hordaceus* L. (Poaceae): genetic diversity, origin and molecular evolution. *Folia Geobotanica* 34:405–419.

Albert, M. E., C. M. D'Antonio, and K. A. Schierenbeck. 1997. Hybridization and introgression in *Carpobrotus* spp. (Aizoaceae) in California. I. Morphological evidence. *American Journal of Botany* 84:896–904.

Allen, P. S., and S. E. Meyer. 2002. Ecology and ecological genetics of seed dormancy in downy brome. *Weed Science* 50:241–247.

Allendorf, F. W. 1986. Genetic drift and the loss of alleles versus heterozyosity. *Zoo Biology* 5:181–190.

Alroy, J. 2001. A multispecies overkill simulation of the end-Pleistocene megafaunal mass extinction. *Science* 292:1893–1896.

Alstad, D. N., and D. A. Andow. 1995. Managing the evolution of insect resistance to transgenic plants. *Science* 268:1894–1896.

Amsellem, L., J-L. Noyer, and M. Hossaert-McKey. 2001. Evidence for a switch in the reproductive biology of *Rubus alceifolius* (Rosaceae) towards apomixis, between its native range and its area of introduction. *American Journal of Botany* 88:2243–2251.

Andersone, Ž, V. Lucchini, E. Randi, and J. Ozoliš. 2002. Hybridisation between wolves and dogs in Latvia as documented using mitochondrial and microsatellite DNA markers. *Mammalian Biology* 67:79–90.

Andow, D. A., and O. Imura. 1994. Specialization of phytophagous arthropod communities on introduced plants. *Ecology* 75:296–300.

Anttilla, C. K., C. C. Daehler, N. E. Rank, and D. R. Strong. 1998. Greater male fitness of a rare invader (*Spartina alterniflora*, Poaceae) threatens a common native (*Spartina foliosa*) with hybridization. *American Journal of Botany* 85:1597–1601.

Anttilla, C. K., R. A. King, C. Ferris, D. R. Ayres, and D. R. Strong. 2000. Reciprocal hybrid formation of *Spartina* in San Francisco Bay. *Molecular Ecology* 9:765–770.

Apanius, V., N. Yorinks, E. Bermingham, and R. E. Ricklefs. 2000. Island and taxon effects in parasitism and resistance of Lesser Antillean birds. *Ecology* 81:1959–1969.

Arias, D. M., and L. H. Rieseberg. 1994. Gene flow between cultivated and wild sunflower. *Theoretical and Applied Genetics* 89:665–660.

Arnett, A. E., and S. M. Louda. 2002. Re-test of *Rhinocyllus conicus* host specificity, and the prediction of ecological risk in biological control. *Biological Conservation* 106:251–257.

Arriola, P. E., and N. C. Ellstrand. 1996. Crop-to-weed gene flow in the genus *Sorghum* (Poaceae): spontaneous interspecific hybridization between johnsongrass, *Sorghum halepense*, and crop sorghum, *S. bicolor*. *American Journal of Botany* 83:1153–1160.

Ashton, P. A., and R. J. Abbott. 1992. Multiple origins and genetic diversity in the newly arisen allopolyploid species, *Senecio cambrensis* Rosser (Compositae). *Heredity* 68:25–32.

Askew, R. R., and M. R. Shaw. 1986. Parasitoid communities: their size, structure, and development. pp. 225–264, *in* J. K. Waage and D. Greathead (Eds.), *Insect parasitoids.* London: Academic Press.

Auclair, J. L. 1978. Biotypes of the pea aphid, *Acyrthosiphon pisum*, in relation to host plants and chemically defined diets. *Entomologia Experimentalis et Applicata* 24:12–16.

Auerbach, M., and D. Simberloff. 1988. Rapid leaf-miner colonization of introduced trees and shifts in sources of herbivore mortality. *Oikos* 52:41–50.

Badyaev, A. V., and G. E. Hill. 2000. The evolution of sexual dimorphism in the house finch. I. Population divergence in morphological covariance structure. *Evolution* 54:1784–1794.

Badyaev, A. V., and T. E. Martin. 2000. Sexual dimorphism in relation to current selection in the House Finch. *Evolution* 54:987–997.

Badyaev, A. V., G. E. Hill, A. M. Stoehr, P. M. Nolan, and K. J. McGraw. 2000. The evolution of sexual size dimorphism in the House Finch. II. Population divergence in relation to local selection. *Evolution* 54:2134–2144.

Bailey, J. P. 1999. The Japanese knotweed invasion of Europe; the potential for further evolution in non-native regions. pp. 27–37, *in* E. Yano, K. Matsuo, M. Syiyomi, and D. A. Andow (Eds.), *Biological invasions of ecosystems by pests and beneficial organisms.* Tsukuba, Japan: Institute of Agro-Environmental Sciences.

Bais, H. P., T. S. Walker, F. R. Stermitz, R. A. Hufbauer, and J. M. Vivanco. 2002. Enantiomeric-dependent phytotoxic antimicrobial activity of ($\pm$)-catechin. A rhizosecreted racemic mixture from spotted knapweed. *Plant Physiology* 128:1173–1179.

Bais, H. P., R. Vepachedu, S. Gilroy, R. M. Callaway, and J. M. Vivanco. 2003. Allelopathy and exotic plant invasion: from molecules and genes to species interactions. *Science* 301: 1377–1380.

Baker, H. G. 1974. The evolution of weeds. *Annual Review of Ecology and Systematics* 5:1–24.

Baker, A. J., and A. Moeed. 1979. Evolution in the introduced New Zealand populations of the common myna, *Acridotheres tristis. Canadian Journal of Zoology* 57:570–584.

Baker, A. J., and A. Moeed. 1987. Rapid genetic differentiation and founder effect in colonizing populations of common mynas (*Acridotheres tristis*). *Evolution* 41:525–538.

Baker, A. J., M. K. Peck, and M. A. Goldsmith. 1990. Genetic and morphometric differentiation of introduced populations of common chaffinches (*Fringilla coelebs*) in New Zealand. *Condor* 92:76–88.

Balciunas, J. K., and D. W. Burrows. 1993. The rapid suppression of the growth of *Melaleuca quinquenervia* saplings in Australia by insects. *Journal of Aquatic Plant Management* 31:265–270.

Balciunas, J. K., and B. Villegas. 2001. Unintentionally released *Chaetorellia succinea* (Diptera: Tephritidae): is this natural enemy of yellow starthistle a threat to safflower growers? *Environmental Entomology* 30:953–963.

Baranchikov, Y. N. 1997. Siberian forest insects: ready for exports. *in* K. O. Britton (Ed.), *Proceedings of the Exotic Pests of Eastern Forests Conference*. Nashville, Tenn.: USDA Forest Service and Tennessee Exotic Plant Council. (http://www.invasive.org/symposium/baranchi.html).

Barber, S. 1999. Transgenic plants: field testing and commercialisation including a consideration of novel herbicide resistant oilseed rape (*Brassica napus* L.). *British Crop Protection Council Symposium Proceedings* 72:3–11.

Barbour, J. G., and E. Kiviat. 1997. Introduced purple loosestrife as host of native Saturniidae (Lepidoptera). *The Great Lakes Entomologist* 30:115–122.

Barlow, N. D., and S. L. Goldson. 2002. Alien invertebrates in New Zealand. pp. 195–216, *in* D. Pimentel (Ed.), *Biological invasions: economic and environmental costs of alien plant, animal, and microbe species*. Boca Raton, Fla.: CRC Press.

Barrett, S. C. H. 1983. Crop mimicry in weeds. *Economic Botany* 37:255–282.

Barrett, S. C. H. 2000. Microevolutionary influences of global changes on plant invasions. pp. 115–139, *in* H. A. Mooney and R. J. Hobbs (Eds.), *Invasive species in a changing world*. Washington, D.C.: Island Press.

Bartlett, E., S. J. Novak, and R. N. Mack. 2002. Genetic variation in *Bromus tectorum* (Poaceae): differentiation in the eastern United States. *American Journal of Botany* 89:602–612.

Bartsch, D., and N. C. Ellstrand. 1999. Genetic evidence for the origin of California wild beets (genus *Beta*). *Theoretical and Applied Genetics* 99:1120–1130.

Bartsch, D., M. Lehnen, J. Clegg, M. Pohl-Orf, I. Schuphan, and N. C. Ellstrand. 1999. Impact of gene flow from cultivated beet on genetic diversity of wild sea beet populations. *Molecular Ecology* 8:1733–1741.

Bartsch, D., U. Brand, C. Morak, M. Pohl-Orf, I. Schuphan, and N. C. Ellstrand. 2001. Biosafety of hybrids between transgenic virus-resistant sugar beet and Swiss chard. *Ecological Applications* 11:142–147.

Bastrop, R., K. Jürss, and C. Sturmbauer. 1998. Cryptic species in a marine polychaete and their independent introduction from North America to Europe. *Molecular Biology and Evolution* 15:97–103.

Baumel, A., M. L. Ainouche, R. J. Bayer, A. K. Ainouche, and M. T. Misset. 2002a. Molecular phylogeny of hybridizing species from the genus *Spartina* Schreb. (Poaceae). *Molecular Phylogenetics and Evolution* 22:303–314.

Baumel, A., M. Ainouche, R. J. Bayer, R. Kalendar, and A. H. Schulman. 2002b. Retrotransposons and genomic stability in populations of the young allopolyploid species *Spartina anglica* C. E. Hubbard (Poaceae). *Molecular Biology and Evolution* 19:1218–1227.

Beauchamp, K. A., R. D. Kathman, T. S. McDowell, and R. P. Hedrick. 2001. Molecular phylogeny of tubificid oligochaetes with special emphasis on *Tubifex tubifex* (Tubificidae). *Molecular Phylogenetics and Evolution* 19:216–224.

Beauchamp, K. A., M. Gay, G. O. Kelley, M. El-Matbouli, R. D. Kathman, R. B. Nehring, and R. P. Hedrick. 2002. Prevalence and susceptibility of infection to *Myxobolus cerebralis* and genetic differences among populations of *Tubifex tubifex*. *Diseases of Aquatic Organisms* 51:113–121.

Beaugrand, G., P. C. Reid, F. Ibañez, J. A. Lindley, and M. Edwards. 2002. Reorganization of North Atlantic marine copepod biodiversity and climate. *Science* 296:1692–1694.

Beaumont, M., E. M. Barratt, D. Gottelli, A. C. Kitchener, M. J. Daniels, J. K. Pritchard, and M. W. Bruford. 2001. Genetic diversity and introgression in the Scottish wildcat. *Molecular Ecology* 10:319–336.

Beebee, T. J. C. 2002. Amphibian phenology and climate change. *Conservation Biology* 16:1454.

Beering, D. J., and C. K. Kelly. 1997. Stomatal density responses of temperate woodland plants over the past seven decades of CO_2 increase: a comparison of Salisbury (1927) and contemporary data. *American Journal of Botany* 84:1572–1583.

Beeton, M. J., and P. D. N. Hebert. 1988. Geographical parthenogenesis and polyploidy in *Daphnia pulex*. *American Naturalist* 132:837–845.

Beheregaray, L. B., P. Sunnucks, and D. A. Briscoe. 2002. A rapid fish radiation associated with the last sea-level changes in southern Brazil: the silverside *Odontesthes perugiae* complex. *Proceedings of the Royal Society of London B* 269:65–73.

Bell, M. 2001. Lateral plate evolution in the threespine stickleback: getting nowhere fast. *Genetica* 112–113:445–461.

Belsky, A. J. 1986. Does herbivory benefit plants? A review of the evidence. *American Naturalist* 127:870–892.

Belsky, A. J., W. P. Carson, C. J. Jensen, and G. Fox. 1993. Overcompensation by plants: herbivore optimization or red herring? *Evolutionary Ecology* 7:109–121.

Benkman, C. W. 1999. The selection mosaic and diversifying coevolution between crossbills and lodgepole pine. *American Naturalist* 153:S75–S91.

Benkman, C. W., T. L. Parchman, A. Favis, and A. M. Siepielski. 2003. Reciprocal selection causes a coevolutionary arms race between crossbills and lodgepole pine. *American Naturalist* 162:182–194.

Berenbaum, M. R., and A. R. Zangerl. 1998. Chemical phenotype matching between a plant and its insect herbivore. *Proceedings of the National Academy of Sciences USA* 95:13743–13748.

Berenbaum, M. R., A. R. Zangerl, and J. K. Nitao. 1986. Constraints on chemical coevolution: wild parsnips and the parsnip webworm. *Evolution* 40:1215–1228.

Berg, D. J., D. W. Garton, H. J. MacIsaac, V. E. Panov, and I. V. Telesh. 2002. Changes in genetic structure of North American *Bythotrephes* populations following invasion from Lake Ladoga, Russia. *Freshwater Biology* 47:275–282.

Bergelson, J., and C. B. Purrington. 2002. Factors affecting the spread of resistant *Arabidopsis thaliana* populations. pp. 17–31, *in* D. K. Letourneau and B. E. Burrows (Eds.), *Genetically engineered organisms: assessing environmental and human health effects.* Boca Raton, Fla.: CRC Press.

Bergelson, J., M. Kreitman, E. A. Stahl, and D. Tian. 2001. Evolutionary dynamics of plant R-genes. *Science* 292:2281–2285.

Berger, J. 1998. Future prey: some consequences of the loss and restoration of large carnivores. pp. 80–100, *in* T. M. Caro (Ed.), *Behavioral ecology and conservation biology.* New York: Oxford University Press.

Beringer, J. E. 2000. Releasing genetically modified organisms: will any harm outweigh any advantage? *Journal of Applied Ecology* 37:207–214.

Bernays, E. A., and D. J. Funk. 2000. Electrical penetration graph analysis reveals population variation of host-plant probing behaviors within the aphid species *Uroleucon ambrosiae*. *Entomologia Experimentalis et Applicata* 97:183–191.

Bernays, E., and M. Graham. 1988. On the evolution of host specificity in phytophagous arthropods. *Ecology* 69:886–892.

Berthold, P. 1995. Microevolution of migratory behaviour illustrated by the Black-cap *Sylvia atricapilla*: 1993 Witherby lecture. *Bird Study* 42:89–100.

Berthold, P. 1999. Towards a comprehensive theory for the evolution, control and adaptability of avian migration. *Ostrich* 70:1–11.

Berthold, P. 2001. *Bird migration: a general survey*, 2nd ed. Oxford, England: Oxford University Press.

Bertolino, S., and P. Genovesi. 2003. Spread and attempted eradication of the grey squirrel (*Sciurus carolinensis*) in Italy, and consequences for the red squirrel (*Sciurus vulgaris*) in Eurasia. *Biological Conservation* 109:351–358.

Biggins, D. E., and M. Y. Kosoy. 2001. Influences of introduced plague on North American mammals: implications from ecology of plague in Asia. *Journal of Mammalogy* 82:906–916.

Bingham, R. T. 1983. *Blister rust resistant western white pine for the Inland Empire: the story of the first 25 years of the research and development program*. USDA Forest Service, General Technical Report INT-146. Ogden, Utah: Intermountain Forest and Range Experiment Station.

Birks, H. J. B. 1980. British trees and insects: a test of the time hypothesis over the last 13,000 years. *American Naturalist* 115:600–605.

Birungi, J., and L. E. Munstermann. 2002. Genetic structure of *Aedes albopictus* (Diptera: Culicidae) populations based on mitochondrial ND5 sequences: evidence for an independent invasion into Brazil and United States. *Annals of the Entomological Society of America* 95:125–132.

Bishop, J. G., A. M. Dean, and T. Mitchell-Olds. 2000. Rapid evolution in plant chitinases: molecular targets of selection in plant-pathogen coevolution. *Proceedings of the National Academy of Sciences USA* 97:5322–5327.

Black, W. C., A. J. Ferrari, K. S. Rai, and D. Sprenger. 1988a. Breeding structure of a colonizing species: *Aedes albopictus* (Skuse) in the United States. *Heredity* 60:173–181.

Black, W. C., W. A. Hawley, K. S. Rai, and G. B. Craig. 1988b. Breeding structure of a colonizing species: *Aedes albopictus* (Skuse) in peninsular Malaysia and Borneo. *Heredity* 61:439–446.

Blair, A. C., and L. M. Wolfe. Forthcoming. The evolution of a high performance invasive phenotype: an experimental study with a perennial plant. *Proceedings of the Royal Society of London B*.

Bleeker, W. 2003. Hybridization and *Rorippa austriaca* (Brassicaceae) invasion in Germany. *Molecular Ecology* 12:1831–1841.

Blem, C. R. 1974. Geographic variation of thermal conductance in the house sparrow (*Passer domesticus*). *Comparative Physiology and Biochemistry* 47A:101–108.

Blondel, J. 2000. Evolution and ecology of birds on islands: trends and prospects. *Vie et Milieu* 50:205–220.

Blossey, B., and R. Nötzold. 1995. Evolution of increased competitive ability in invasive nonindigenous plants: A hypothesis. *Journal of Ecology* 83:887–889.

Blossey, B., R. Casagrande, L. Tewksbury, D. A. Landis, R. N. Wiedenmann, and D. R. Ellis. 2001. Nontarget feeding of leaf-beetles introduced to control purple loosestrife (*Lythrum salicaria* L.). *Natural Areas Journal* 21:368–377.

Blumstein, D. T. 2002. Moving to suburbia: ontogenetic and evolutionary consequences of life on predator-free islands. *Journal of Biogeography* 29:685–692.

Bodaly, R. A., J. W. Clayton, C. C. Lindsey, and J. Vuorinen. 1992. Evolution of the lake whitefish (*Coregonus clupeaformis*) in North America during the Pleistocene: genetic differentiation between sympatric populations. *Canadian Journal of Fisheries and Aquatic Sciences* 49:769–779.

Boettner, G. H., J. S. Elkington, and C. J. Boettner. 2000. Effects of a biological control introduction on three nontarget native species of Saturniid moths. *Conservation Biology* 14:1798–1806.

Bonter, D. N., and W. M. Hochachka. 2003. Taking count in the wake of West Nile Virus. *Birdscope* 17(2):1,14–15.

Boudry, P., M. Mörchen, P. Saumitou-Laprade, P. Vernet, and H. Van Dijk. 1993. The origin and evolution of weed beets: consequences for the breeding and release of herbicide-resistant transgenic sugar beets. *Theoretical and Applied Genetics* 87:471–478.

Bousset, L., and C. de Vallavielle-Pope. 2003. Effect of sexual recombination on pathotype frequencies in barley powdery mildew populations of artificially inoculated field plots. *European Journal of Plant Pathology* 109:13–24.

Bowers, M. D., N. E. Stamp, and S. K. Collinge. 1992. Early stage of host range expansion by a specialist herbivore, *Euphydryas phaeton* (Nymphalidae). *Ecology* 73:526–536.

Bradley, N., C. Leopold, J. Ross, and W. Huffaker. 1999. Phenological changes reflect climate change in Wisconsin. *Proceedings of the National Academy of Sciences USA* 96:9701–9704.

Brasier, C. M. 2001. Rapid evolution of introduced plant pathogens via interspecific hybridization. *BioScience* 51:123–133.

Brasier, C. M., and K. W. Buck. 2001. Rapid evolutionary changes in a globally invading fungal pathogen (Dutch elm disease). *Biological Invasions* 3:223–233.

Brasier, C. M., D. Cooke, and J. M. Duncan. 1999. Origin of a new *Phytophthora* pathogen through interspecific hybridization. *Proceedings of the National Academy of Sciences USA* 96:5878–5883.

Britton-Davidian, J., J. Catalan, M. G. Ramalhinho, G. Ganem, J.-C. Auffray, R. Capela, M. Biscoito, J. B. Searle, and M. L. Mathias. 2000. Rapid chromosomal evolution in island mice. *Nature* 403:158.

Brizuela, M. A., J. K. Detling, and M. S. Cid. 1986. Silicon concentration of grasses growing in sites with different grazing histories. *Ecology* 67:1098–1101.

Brönmark, C., and P. Edenhamn. 1994. Does the presence of fish affect the distribution of tree frogs (*Hyla arborea*)? *Conservation Biology* 8:841–845.

Brown, J. K. M., and M. S. Hovmøller. 2002. Aerial dispersal of pathogens on the global and continental scales and its impact on plant disease. *Science* 297: 537–541.

Brown, A. H. D., and D. R. Marshall. 1981. Evolutionary changes accompanying colonization in plants. pp. 351–363, *in* G. G. T. Scudder and J. L. Reveal (Eds.), *Evolution Today, Proceedings of the Second International Congress of Systematic and Evolutionary Biology.* Pittsburgh, Pa.: Carnegie-Mellon University.

Brown, N. S., and G. I. Wilson. 1975. A comparison of the ectoparasites of the house sparrow (*Passer domesticus*) from North America and Europe. *American Midland Naturalist* 94:154–165.

Brown, D. A., M. T. Windham, and R. N. Trigiano. 1996. Resistance to dogwood anthracnose among *Cornus* species. *Journal of Arboriculture* 22:83–86.

Brown, J. H., T. J. Valone, and C. G. Curtin. 1997. Reorganization of an arid ecosystem in response to recent climate change. *Proceedings of the National Academy of Sciences USA* 94:9729–9733.

Bruce, K. A., G. N. Cameron, and P. A. Harcombe. 1995. Initiation of a new woodland type on the Texas coastal prairie by the Chinese tallow tree (*Sapium sebiferum* (L.) Roxb.). *Bulletin of the Torrey Botanical Club* 122:215–225.

Burbridge, A. A., and N. L. McKenzie. 1989. Patterns in the modern decline of Western Australia's vertebrate fauna: causes and conservation implications. *Biological Conservation* 50:143–198.

Burdon, J. J., and G. A. Chilvers. 1977. Preliminary studies on a native Australian eucalypt forest invaded by exotic pines. *Oecologia* 31:1–12.

Burdon, J. J., R. H. Groves, and J. M. Cullen. 1981. The impact of biological control on the distribution and abundance of *Chondrilla juncea* in south-eastern Australia. *Journal of Applied Ecology* 18:957–966.

Burke, J. M., K. A. Gardner, and L. H. Rieseberg. 2002. The potential for gene flow between cultivated and wild sunflower (*Helianthus annuus*) in the United States. *American Journal of Botany* 89:1550–1552.

Bush, G. L. 1969. Sympatric host race formation and speciation in frugivorous flies of the genus *Rhagoletis* (Diptera: Tephritidae). *Evolution* 23:237–251.

Buth, D. G., and R. W. Murphy. 1999. The use of isozyme characters in systematic studies. *Biochemial Systematics and Ecology* 27:117–129.

Butler, C. J. 2003. The disproportionate effect of global warming on the arrival dates of short-distance migratory birds in North America. *Ibis* 145:484–495.

Byers, J. E. 2002. Impact of non-indigenous species on natives enhanced by anthropogenic alteration of selection regimes. *Oikos* 97:449–458.

Byers, J. E., and E. G. Noonberg. 2003. Scale dependent effects of biotic resistance to biological invasion. *Ecology* 84:1428–1433.

Byington, T. S., K. W. Gottschalk, and J. B. McGraw. 1994. Within-population variation in response of red oak seedlings to herbivory by gypsy moth larvae. *American Midland Naturalist* 132:328–339.

Cabe, P. R. 1998. The effects of founding bottlenecks on genetic variation in the European starling (*Sturnus vulgaris*) in North America. *Heredity* 80:519–525.

Callaway, R. M., and E. T. Aschehoug. 2000. Invasive plants versus their new and old neighbors: a mechanism for exotic invasion. *Science* 290:521–523.

Campbell, D. J. 1990. Changes in structure and composition of a New Zealand lowland forest inhabited by brushtail possums. *Pacific Science* 44:277–296.

Campbell, F. T., and S. E. Schlarbaum. 1994. *Fading forests: North American trees and the threat of exotic pests.* New York: Natural Resources Defense Council.

Cardé, R. T. 1983. The role of pheromones in reproductive isolation and speciation of insects. *in* M. D. Huettel (Ed.), *Evolutionary genetics of invertebrate behavior.* New York: Plenum.

Cardé, R. T., W. L. Roelofs, R. G. Harrison, A. T. Vawter, P. F. Brussard, A. Mutuura, and E. Munroe. 1978. European corn borer: pheromone polymorphism or sibling species? *Science* 199:555–556.

Carey, J. R. 1996. The incipient Mediterranean fruit fly population in California: implications for invasion biology. *Ecology* 77:1690–1697.

Carino, D. A., and C. C. Daehler. 2002. Can inconspicuous legumes facilitate alien grass invasions? Partridge peas and fountain grass in Hawai'i. *Ecography* 25:33–41.

Carman, J. G., and D. D. Briske. 1985. Morphologic and allozyme variation between long-term grazed and non-grazed populations of the bunchgrass *Schizachryium scoparium* var. *frequens. Oecologia* 66:331–337.

Carmichael, G. J., J. N. Hanson, M. E. Schmidt, and D. C. Morizot. 1993. Introgression among Apache, cutthroat, and rainbow trout in Arizona. *Transactions of the American Fisheries Society* 122:121–130.

Carroll, S. P., and C. Boyd. 1992. Host race radiation in the soapberry bug: natural history, with the history. *Evolution* 46:1052–1069.

Carroll, S. P., and H. Dingle. 1996. The biology of post-invasion events. *Biological Conservation* 78:207–214.

Carroll, S. P., S. P. Klassen, and H. Dingle. 1998. Rapidly evolving adaptations to host ecology and nutrition in the soapberry bug. *Evolutionary Ecology* 12:955–968.

Carroll, S. P., H. Dingle, T. R. Famula, and C. W. Fox. 2001. Genetic architecture of adaptive differentiation in evolving host races of the soapberry bug, *Jadera haematoloma. Genetica* 112–113:257–272.

Carroll, S. P., M. Marler, R. Winchell, and H. Dingle. 2003a. Evolution of cryptic flight morph and life history differences during host race radiation in the soapberry bug, *Jadera haematoloma* Herrich-Schaeffer (Hemipteda: Rhopalidae). *Annals of the Entomological Society of America* 96:135–143.

Carroll, S. P., H. Dingle, and T. R. Famula. 2003b. Rapid appearance of epistasis during adaptive divergence following colonization. *Proceedings of the Royal Society of London B* (Supplement) 270:S80–S83.

Case, T. J. 1978. A general explanation for insular body size trends in terrestrial vertebrates. *Ecology* 59:1–18.

Case, T. J., and D. T. Bolger. 1991. The role of introduced species in shaping the distribution and abundance of island reptiles. *Evolutionary Ecology* 5:272–290.

Cassani, J. R. 1986. Arthropods on Brazilian peppertree, *Schinus terebinthefolius* (Anacardiaceae) in south Florida. *Florida Entomologist* 69: 184–196.

Cassani, J. R., D. R. Maloney, D. H. Habeck, and F. D. Bennett. 1989. New insect records on Brazilian peppertree, *Schinus terebinthefolius* in south Florida. *Florida Entomologist* 72:714–716.

Cassey, P. 2002. Life history and ecology influences establishment success of introduced land birds. *Biological Journal of the Linnean Society* 76:465–480.

Causey, D., J. Trimble, W. Hallwachs, D. Brooks, and D. Janzen. 2003. Migratory birds and the spread of West Nile. *Science* 299:821.

Channer, A. G. de R., and S. R. Gowen. 1992. Selection for increased host resistance and increased pathogen specificity in the *Meloidogyne-Pasteuria penetrans* interaction. *Fundamental and Applied Nematology* 15:331–339.

Chapman, F. A. 1992. *Culture of hybrid tilapia: a reference profile.* Department of Fisheries and Aquatic Sciences, Florida Cooperative Extension Service, Institute of Food and Agricultural Sciences, University of Florida. Circular 1051.

Charalambidou, I., and L. Santamaría. 2002. Waterbirds as endozoochorous dispersers of aquatic organisms: a review of experimental evidence. *Acta Oecologica* 23:165–176.

Chew, F. S. 1977. The effects of introduced mustards (Cruciferae) on some native North American cabbage butterflies (Lepidoptera: Pieridae). *Atala* 5(2):13–19.

Civeyrel, L., and D. Simberloff. 1996. A tale of two snails: is the cure worse than the disease. *Biodiversity and Conservation* 5:1231–1252.

Claridge, M. F., and J. den Hollander. 1980. The "biotypes" of the rice brown leafhopper, *Nilaparvata lugens. Entomologia Experimentalis et Applicata* 27:23–30.

Clarke, K. E., B. P. Oldroyd, J. Javier, G. Quezada-Euán, and T. E. Rinderer. 2001. Origin of honeybees (*Apis mellifera* L.) from the Yucatan peninsula inferred from mitochondrial DNA analysis. *Molecular Ecology* 10:1347–1355.

Clausen, P., B. A. Nolet, A. D. Fox, and M. Klaassen. 2002. Long-distance endozoochorous dispersal of submerged macrophyte seeds by waterbirds in northern Europe—a critical review of possibilities and limitations. *Acta Oecologica* 23:191–203.

Clay, K. and P. Kover. 1996. Evolution and stasis in plant-pathogen associations. *Ecology* 77:997–1003.

Clegg, M. T., and R. W. Allard. 1972. Patterns of genetic differentiation in the slender wild oat species *Avena barbata. Proceedings of the National Academy of Science USA* 69:1820–1824.

Clegg, S. M., S. M. Degnan, J. Kikkawa, A. Estoup, and I. P. F. Owens. 2002. Genetic consequences of sequential founder events by an island-colonizing bird. *Proceedings of the National Academy of Sciences USA* 99:8127–8132.

Clement, S. L. 1990. Insect natural enemies of yellow starthistle in southern Europe and the selection of candidate biological control agents. *Environmental Entomology* 19:1882–1888.

Cocks, P. S., and J. R. Phillips. 1979. Evolution of subterranean clover in South Australia. I. The strains and their distribution. *Australian Journal of Agricultural Research* 30:1035–1052.

Cody, M. L., and J. Overton. 1996. Short-term evolution of reduced dispersal in island plant populations. *Journal of Ecology* 84:53–61.

Cole, F. R., A. C. Medeiros, L. L. Loope, and W. W. Zuehlke. 1992. Effects of the Argentine ant on arthropod fauna of Hawaiian high-elevation shrubland. *Ecology* 73:1313–1322.

Collins, T. M., J. C. Trexler, L. G. Nico, and T. A. Rawlings. 2002. Genetic diversity in a morphologically conservative invasive taxon: multiple introductions of swamp eels to the southeastern United States. *Conservation Biology* 16:1024–1035.

Conant, S. 1988. Saving endangered species by translocation. *BioScience* 38:254–257.

Connell, J. H. 1978. Diversity in tropical rain forests and coral reefs. *Science* 199:1302–1310.

Connor, E. F., S. H. Faeth, D. Simberloff, and P. A. Opler. 1980. Taxonomic isolation and the accumulation of herbivorous insects: A comparison of introduced and native trees. *Ecological Entomology* 5:205–211.

Coote, T., and E. Loève. 2003. From 61 species to five: endemic tree snails of the Society Islands fall prey to an ill-judged biological control program. *Oryx* 37:91–96.

Coppack, T., and C. Both. 2002. Predicting life-cycle adaptation of migratory birds to global climate change. *Ardea* 90:369–378.

Cornell, H. V., and B. A. Hawkins. 1993. Accumulation of native parasitoid species on introduced herbivores: A comparison of hosts as natives and hosts as invaders. *American Naturalist* 141:847–865.

Cornell, H. V., and B. A. Hawkins. 2003. Herbivore responses to plant secondary compounds: A test of phytochemical coevolution theory. *American Naturalist* 161:507–522.

Costa-Pierce, B. A., and R. W. Doyle. 1997. Genetic identification and status of tilapia regional strains in southern California. pp. 1–17, *in* B. A. Costa-Pierce and J. E. Rakocy (Eds.), *Tilapia aquaculture in the Americas*, vol. 1. Baton Rouge, La.: World Aquaculture Society.

Courtenay, W. R., Jr., D. A. Hensley, J. N. Taylor, and J. A. McCann. 1984. Distribution of exotic fishes in the continental United States. pp. 41–77, *in* W. R. Courtenay Jr. and J. R. Stauffer Jr. (Eds.), *Distribution, biology, and management of exotic fishes*. Baltimore, Md.: Johns Hopkins University Press.

Cousyn, C., L. De Meester, J. K. Colbourne, L. Brendonck, D. Verschuren, and F. Volckaert. 2001. Rapid, local adaptation of zooplankton behavior to changes in predation pressure in the absence of neutral genetic changes. *Proceedings of the National Academy of Sciences USA* 98:6256–6260.

Cowan, C. A., and B. L. Peckarsky. 1994. Diel feeding and positioning of a grazing mayfly nymph in a trout stream and a fishless stream. *Canadian Journal of Fisheries and Aquatic Sciences* 51:450–459.

Cowie, R. H., and R. P. Cook. 2001. Extinction or survival: partulid tree snails in American Samoa. *Biodiversity and Conservation* 10:143–159.

Cox, G. W. 1985. The evolution of avian migration systems between temperate and tropical regions of the New World. *American Naturalist* 126:451–474.

Cox, G. W. 1999. *Alien species in North America and Hawaii: impacts on natural ecosystems*. Washington, D. C.: Island Press.

Cox, G. W., and R. E. Ricklefs. 1977. Species diversity and ecological release in Caribbean land bird faunas. *Oikos* 28:113–122.

Crawley, M. J. 1987. What makes a community invasible? pp. 429–453, *in* A. J. Gray,

M. J. Crawley, and P. J. Edwards (Eds.), *Colonization, succession, and stability.* Oxford, England: Blackwell.

Crawley, M. J., S. L. Brown, R. S. Hails, D. D. Kohn, and M. Rees. 2001. Transgenic crops in natural habitats. *Nature* 409:682–683.

Cremer, K. 1999. Willow management for Australian rivers. *Natural Resource Management*, Special Issue, pp. 2–22.

Cristescu, M. E. A., P. D. N. Hebert, J. D. S. Witt, H. J. MacIsaac, and I. A. Grigorovich. 2001. An invasion history for *Cercopagis pengoi* based on mitochondrial gene sequences. *Limnology and Oceanography* 46:224–229.

Crooks, J. A., and M. E. Soulé. 1999. Lag times in population explosions of invasive species: causes and implications. pp. 103–125, *in* O. T. Sandlund, P. J. Schei, and Å. Viken (Eds.), *Invasive species and biodiversity management.* Dordrecht, The Netherlands: Kluwer Academic Publishers.

Crossland, M. R., and R. A. Alford. 1998. Evaluarion of the toxicity of eggs, hatchlings and tadpoles of the introduced toad *Bufo marinus* (Anura: Bufonidae) to native Australian aquatic predators. *Australian Journal of Ecology* 23:129–137.

Crossman, E. J. 1984. Introduction of exotic fishes into Canada. pp. 78–101, *in* W. R. Courtenay Jr. and J. R. Stauffer Jr. (Eds.), *Distribution, biology, and management of exotic fishes.* Baltimore, Md.: Johns Hopkins University Press.

Crowder, L. B. 1984. Character displacement and habitat shift in a native cisco in southeastern Lake Michigan: evidence for competition? *Copeia* 1984:878–883.

Crowder, L. B., and F. P. Binkowski. 1983. Foraging behaviors and the interaction of alewife, *Alosa pseudoharengus*, and bloater, *Coregonus hoyi. Environmental Biology of Fishes* 8:105–113.

Crowder, L. B., and H. L. Crawford. 1984. Ecological shifts in resource use by bloaters in Lake Michigan. *Transactions of the American Fisheries Society* 113:694–700.

Crozier, L. 2002. Climate change and its effect on species range boundaries: a case study of the sachem skipper butterfly, *Atalopedes campestris.* pp. 57–91, *in* S. H. Schneider and T. L. Root (Eds.), *Wildlife response to climate change.* Washington, D.C.: Island Press.

Cwynar, L. C., and G. M. MacDonald. 1987. Geographical variation of lodgepole pine in relation to population history. *Ecology* 68:791–802.

Daehler, C. C. 1998. The taxonomic distribution of invasive angiosperm plants: ecological insights and comparison to agricultural weeds. *Biological Conservation* 84:167–180.

Daehler, C. C. 1999. Inbreeding depression in smooth cordgrass (*Spartina alterniflora*, Poaceae) invading San Francisco Bay. *American Journal of Botany* 86:131–139.

Daehler, C. C. 2001. Darwin's naturalization hypothesis revisited. *American Naturalist* 158:324–330.

Daehler, C. C., and D. A. Carino. 2001. Hybridization between native and alien plants and its consequences. pp. 81–102, *in* J. L. Lockwood and M. L. McKinney (Eds.), *Biotic homogenization.* New York: Kluwer Academic/Plenum Publishers.

Daehler, C. C., and D. R. Strong. 1997a. Hybridization between introduced smooth cordgrass (*Spartina alterniflora*; Poaceae) and native California cordgrass (*S. foliosa*) in San Francisco Bay, California, USA. *American Journal of Botany* 84:607–611.

Daehler, C. C., and D. R. Strong. 1997b. Reduced herbivore resistance in introduced smooth cordgrass (*Spartina alterniflora*) after a century of herbivore-free growth. *Oecologia* 110:99–108.

Daehler, C. C., C. K. Anttila, D. R. Ayres, D. R. Strong, and J. P. Bailey. 1999. Evolution of a new ecotype of *Spartina alterniflora* (Poaceae) in San Francisco Bay, California, USA. *American Journal of Botany* 86:543–546.

Dale, P. J., B. Clarke, and E. M. G. Fontes. 2002. Potential for the environmental impact of transgenic crops. *Nature Biotechnology* 20:567–574.

Davis, M. A., and M. Pelsor. 2001. Experimental support for a resource-based mechanistic model of invasibility. *Ecology Letters* 4:421–428.

Davis, M. B., and R. G. Shaw. 2001. Range shifts and adaptive responses to quaternary climate change. *Science* 292:673–679.

Davis, M. A., J. P. Grime, and K. Thompson. 2000. Fluctuating resources in plant communities: a general theory of invasibility. *Journal of Ecology* 88:528–534.

Dayan, T., and D. Simberloff. 1994. Character displacement, sexual dimorphism, and morphological variation among British and Irish mustelids. *Ecology* 75:1063–1073.

Dayan, T., and D. Simberloff. 1998. Size patterns among competitors: ecological character displacement and character release in mammals, with special reference to island populations. *Mammal Review* 28:99–124.

Del Pozo, A., C. Ovalle, J. Aronson, and J. Avedaño. 2002. Ecotypic differentiation in *Medicago polymorpha* L. along an environmental gradient in central Chile. I. Phenology, biomass production and reproductive patterns. *Plant Ecology* 159:119–130.

DeMelo, R., and P. D. N. Hebert. 1994. Allozyme variation and species diversity in North American Bosminidae. *Canadian Journal of Fisheries and Aquatic Sciences* 51:873–880.

Dennill, G. G., D. Donnelly, and S. L. Chown. 1993. Expansion of host range of a biocontrol agent *Trichilogaster acaciaelongifoliae* (Pteromalidae) released against the weed *Acacia longifolia* in South Africa. *Agriculture, Ecosystems, & Environment* 43:1–10.

D'Eon, R. G., N. R. Seymour, and A. H. Boer. 1994. Black duck-mallard behavioural interactions in relation to hybridization. *Canadian Journal of Zoology* 72:1517–1521.

Deregnaucourt, S., J-C. Guyomarc'h, and N. J. Aebischer. 2002. Hybridization between European quail *Coturnix coturnix* and Japanese quail *Coturnix japonica*. *Ardea* 90:15–21.

Derr, M. 2002. Crossbreeding to save species and create new ones. *New York Times*, 9 July, Section F, p. 3.

Desplanque, B., N. Hautekèete, and H. van Dijk. 2002. Transgenic weed beets: possible, probable, avoidable? *Journal of Applied Ecology* 39:561–571.

Detling, J. K., and E. L. Painter. 1983. Defoliation responses of western wheat grass populations with diverse histories of prairie dog grazing. *Oecologia* 57:65–71.

DeWit, P. J. G. M. 1992. Molecular characterization for gene-for-gene systems in plant-fungus interactions and the application of avirulence genes in control of plant pathogens. *Annual Review of Phytopathology* 30:391–418.

Diamond, J., S. L. Pimm, M. E. Gilpin, and M. LeCroy. 1989. Rapid evolution of character displacement in myzomelid honeyeaters. *American Naturalist* 134:675–708.

Dieckmann, U., B. O'Hara, and W. Weisser. 1999. The evolutionary ecology of dispersal. *Trends in Ecology and Evolution* 14:88–90.

Diehl, S. R., and G. L. Bush. 1984. An evolutionary and applied perspective of insect biotypes. *Annual Review of Entomology* 29:471–504.

Diehl, J. W., and P. B. McEvoy. 1990. Impact of the cinnabar moth, *Tyria jacobeae*, on *Senecio triangularis*, a non-target native plant in Oregon. pp. 119–126, *in* E. S. Delfosse (Ed.), *Proceedings 7th International Symposium on Biological Control of Weeds*. Melbourne, Australia: CSIRO.

Diehl, J. K., N. J. Holliday, C. J. Lindren, and R. E. Roughley. 1997. Insects associated with purple loosestrife, *Lythrum salicaria* L., in southern Manitoba. *The Canadian Entomologist* 129:937–948.

Dillon, A. K., and C. A. Stepien. 2001. Genetic and biogeographic relationships of the invasive round (*Nesogobius melanostomus*) and tubenose (*Proterorhinus marmoratus*) gobies in the Great Lakes versus Eurasian populations. *Journal of Great Lakes Research* 27:267–280.

Dobson, A. P. 1988. Restoring island ecosystems: the potential of parasites to control introduced mammals. *Conservation Biology* 2:31–39.

Dobson, A. P., and R. M. May. 1986. Patterns of invasions by pathogens and parasites. pp. 58–75, *in* H. A. Mooney and J. A. Drake (Eds.), *Ecology of biological invasions of North America and Hawaii*. New York: Springer-Verlag.

Dodd, R. S., D. Hüberli, V. Douhovnikoff, T. Harnik, Z. Afzal-Rafii, and M. Garbelotto. 2002. Towards a model of the genetic architecture of *Phytophthora ramorum* susceptibility in coast live oak. Presented at the American Phytopathological Society *Sudden Oak Death Symposium*, December 15–18, 2002. Monterey, California.

Donald, W. W. 1994. The biology of Canada thistle (*Cirsium arvense*). *Reviews in Weed Science* 6:77–101.

Dorrance, A. E., S. A. McClure, and A. deSilva. 2003. Pathogenic diversity of *Phytophthora sojae* in Ohio soybean fields. *Plant Disease* 87:139–146.

Downie, D. A. 2002. Locating the sources of an invasive pest, grape phylloxera, using a mitochondrial DNA gene genealogy. *Molecular Ecology* 11:2013–2026.

Doyle, J. D., G. Stotsky, G. McClung, and C. W. Hendricks. 1995. Effects of genetically engineered micro-organisms on microbial populations and processes in natural habitats. *Advances in Applied Microbiology* 40:237–287.

Dukes, J. S. 2000. Will the increasing atmospheric CO_2 concentration affect the success of invasive species? pp. 95–113, *in* H. A. Mooney and R. J. Hobbs (Eds.), *Invasive species in a changing world*. Washington, D.C.: Island Press.

Dukes, J. S. 2001. Biodiversity and invasibility in grassland microcosms. *Oecologia* 126:563–568.

Dukes, J. S. 2002. Species composition and diversity affect grassland susceptibility and response to invasion. *Ecological Applications* 12:602–617.

Dukes, J. S. and H. A. Mooney. 1999. Does global change increase the success of biological invaders? *Trends in Ecology and Evolution* 14:135–139.

Du Merle, P., S. Brunet, and J.-F. Cornic. 1992. Polyphagous potentialities of *Choristoneura murinana* (Hb.) (Lep., Tortricidae): a "monophagous" folivore extending its host range. *Journal of Applied Entomology* 113:18–40.

Durand, C., M. Manuel, C. F. Boudouresque, A. Meinesz, M. Verlaque, and Y. Le Parco. 2002. Molecular data suggest a hybrid origin for the invasive *Caulerpa racemosa* (Caulerpales, Chlorophyta) in the Mediterranean Sea. *Journal of Evolutionary Biology* 15:122–133.

Dushoff, J., and G. Dwyer. 2001. Evaluating the risks of engineered viruses: modeling pathogen competition. *Ecological Applications* 11:1602–1609.

Dutton, A., H. Klein, J. Romeis, and F. Bigler. 2002. Uptake of Bt-toxin by herbivores feeding on transgenic maize and consequences for the predator *Chrysoperla carnea*. *Ecological Entomology* 27:441–447.

Eaton, J. G., and R. M. Scheller. 1996. Effects of climatic warming on fish thermal habitat in streams of the United States. *Limnology and Oceanography* 41:1109–1115.

Echelle, A. A., and A. F. Echelle. 1997. Genetic introgression of endemic taxa by non-natives: a case study involving Leon Springs pupfish and sheepshead minnow. *Conservation Biology* 11:153–161.

Ehlinger, T. J., and D. S. Wilson. 1988. Complex foraging polymorphism in bluegill sunfish. *Proceedings of the National Academy of Sciences USA* 85:1878–1882.

Ehrlich, P. R. 1986. Which animals will invade? pp. 79–95, *in* H. A. Mooney and J. A. Drake (Eds.), *Ecology of biological invasions of North America and Hawaii*. New York: Springer-Verlag.

Elderkin, C. L., P. L. Klerks, and E. Theriot. 2001. Shifts in allele and genotype frequencies in zebra mussels, *Dreissena polymorpha*, along the latitudinal gradient formed by the Mississippi River. *Journal of the North American Benthological Society* 20:595–605.

Ellstrand, N. C. 2001. When transgenes wander, should we worry? *Plant Physiology* 125:1543–1545.

Ellstrand, N. C., and C. A. Hoffman. 1990. Hybridization as an avenue of escape for engineered genes. *BioScience* 40:438–442.

Ellstrand, N. C., and K. A. Schierenbeck. 2000. Hybridization as a stimulus for the evolution of invasiveness in plants? *Proceedings of the National Academy of Sciences* 97:7043–7050.

Ellstrand, N. C., H. C. Prentice, and J. F. Hancock. 1999. Gene flow and introgression from domesticated plants into their wild relatives. *Annual Review of Ecology and Systematics* 30:539–563.

El-Matbouli, M., R. Hoffmann, and M. P. Küppers. 2002. Identification of a whirling disease resistant strain of rainbow trout in Germany. Presented at the *2002 Whirling Disease Symposium*. Denver, Colo.

Elton, C. S. 1958. *The ecology of invasions by animals and plants.* London, England: Methuen and Co.

Englund, R. A. 1999. The impacts of introduced poeciliid fish and Odonata on the endemic *Megalagrion* (Odonata) damselflies of Oahu Island, Hawaii. *Journal of Insect Conservation* 3:225–243.

Englund, R. A. 2002. The loss of native biodiversity and continuing nonindigenous species introductions in freshwater, estuarine, and wetland communities of Pearl Harbor, Oahu, Hawaiian Islands. *Estuaries* 25:418–430.

Epifanio, J. M., M. Hooe, D. H. Buck, and D. P. Philipp. 1999. Reproductive success and assortative mating among *Pomoxis* species and their hybrids. *Transactions of the American Fisheries Society* 128:104–120.

Ewel, J. J., D. J. O'Dowd, J. Bergelson, C. C. Daehler, C. M. D'Antonio, L. D. Gómez, D. R. Gordon et al.. 1999. Deliberate introductions of species: research needs. *BioScience* 49:619–630.

Failloux, A.-B., M. Vazeille, and F. Rodhain. 2002. Geographic genetic variation in populations of the dengue virus vector *Aedes aegypti*. *Journal of Molecular Evolution* 55:653–663.

Fallon, S. M.., E. Bermingham, and R. E. Ricklefs. 2003. Island and taxon effects in parasitism revisited: avian malaria in the Lesser Antilles. *Evolution* 57:605–615.

Feder, J. L. 1995. The effects of parasitoids on sympatric host races of *Rhagoletis pomonella* (Diptera: Tephritidae). *Ecology* 76:801–813.

Feder, J. L., and K. E. Filchak. 1999. It's about time: the evidence for host plant-mediated selection in the apple maggot fly, *Rhagoletis pomonella*, and its implications for fitness trade-offs in phytophagous insects. *Entomologia Experimentalis et Applicata* 91:211–225.

Feder, J. L., C. A. Chilcote, and G. L. Bush. 1988. Genetic differentiation between sympatric host races of the apple maggot fly *Rhagoletis pomonella*. *Nature* 336:61–64.

Feder, J. L., S. H. Berlocher, and S. B. Opp. 1998. Sympatric host-race formation and speciation in *Rhagoletis* (Diptera: Tephritidae): a tale of two species for Charles D. pp. 408–441, *in* S. Mopper and S. Y. Strauss (Eds.), *Genetic structure and local adaptation in natural insect populations.* New York: Chapman and Hall.

Filchak, K. E., J. B. Roethele, and J. L. Feder. 2000. Natural selection and sympatric divergence in the apple maggot *Rhagoletis pomonella*. *Nature* 407:739–742.

Fitter, A. H., and R. S. R. Fitter. 2002. Rapid changes in flowering time in British plants. *Science* 296:1689–1691.

Flanders, S. E. 1943. Indirect hyperparasitism and observations on three species of indirect hyperparasites. *Journal of Economic Entomology* 36:921–926.

Flecker, A. S. 1992. Fish predation and the evolution of invertebrate drift periodicity: evidence from neotropical streams. *Ecology* 73:438–448.

Fleischer, R. C., and R. F. Johnston. 1982. Natural selection on body size and proportions in house sparrows. *Nature* 298:747–749.

Fleischer, R. C., R. N. Williams, and A. J. Baker. 1991. Genetic variation within and among populations of the common myna (*Acridotheres tristis*) in Hawaii. *Journal of Heredity* 82:205–208.

Fleming, I. A., and S. Einum. 1997. Experimental tests of genetic divergence of farmed from wild Atlantic salmon during domestication. *ICES Journal of Marine Science* 54:1051–1063.

Flier, W. G., N. J. Grünwald, L. P. N. M. Kroon, A. K. Sturbaum, T. B. M. van den Bosch, E. Garay-Serrano, H. Loyaza-Saldaña, W. E. Fry, and L. J. Turkjensteen. 2003. The population structure of *Phytophthora infestans* from the Toluca Valley of central Mexico suggests genetic differentiation between populations from cultivated potato and wild *Solanum* spp. *Phytopathology* 93:382–390.

Forister, M. L., and A. M. Shapiro. 2003. Climatic trends and advancing spring flight of butterflies in lowland California. *Global Change Biology* 9:1130–1135.

Fornwalt, P. J., M. R. Kaufmann, L. S. Huckaby, J. M. Stoker, and T. J. Stohlgren. 2003. Non-native plant invasions in managed and protected ponderosa pine/Douglas-fir forests of the Colorado front range. *Forest Ecology and Management* 177:515–527.

Forster, H., B. M. Tyler, and M. D. Coffey. 1994. *Phytophthora sojae* races have arisen by clonal evolution and by rare outcrosses. *Molecular Plant-Microbe Interactions* 7:780–791.

Foster, S. A. 1995. Understanding the evolution of behavior in threespine stickleback: the value of geographic variation. *Behaviour* 132:1107–1129.

Foster, B. L., V. H. Smith, T. L. Dickson, and T. Hildebrand. 2002. Invasibility and compositional stability in a grassland community: relationships to diversity and extrinsic factors. *Oikos* 99:300–307.

Fox, C. W., and U. M. Savalli. 2000. Maternal effects mediate host expansion in a seed-feeding beetle. *Ecology* 81:3–7.

Freeland, W. J., and J. W. Winter. 1975. Evolutionary consequences of eating: *Trichosurus vulpecula* (Marsupalia) and the genus *Eucalyptus*. *Journal of Chemical Ecology* 1:439–455.

French, J. R. P., III. 1993. How well can fishes prey on zebra mussels in eastern North America? *Fisheries* 18(6):13–19.

Frenzel, M., M. Brändle, and B. Roland. 2000. The colonization of alien plants by native phytophagous insects. pp. 223–225, *in* P. S. White, L. Mucina, J. Leps, and E. Van der Maarel (Eds.) *Proceedings of the 41st IAVS Symposium*. Uppsala, Sweden: Opulus Press.

Frey, P., M. Gatineau, F. Martin, and J. Pinon. 1999. Molecular studies of the poplar rust *Melampsora medusae-populina*, and interspecific hybrid between *M. larici-populina* and *M. medusae*. p. 34, *Proceedings of the International Poplar Symposium II*, September 13–17, 1999. International Union of Forestry Research Orginizations Orleans, France.

Fry, J. D. 1989. Evolutionary adaptation to host plants in a laboratory population of the phytophagous mite *Tetranychus urticae* Koch. *Oecologia* 81:559–565.

Fry, W. E., and S. B. Goodwin. 1997. Resurgence of the Irish potato famine fungus. *BioScience* 47:363–371.

Funasaki, G. Y., P.-O. Lai, L. M. Nakahara, J. W. Beardsley, and A. K. Ota. 1988. A review of biological control introductions in Hawaii: 1890–1985. *Proceedings of the Hawaiian Entomological Society* 28:105–160.

Funk, D. J., and E. A. Bernays. 2001. Geographic variation in host specificity reveals host range evolution in *Uroleucon ambrosiae* aphids. *Ecology* 82:726–739.

Furnier, G. R., A. M. Stolz, R. M. Mustaphi, and M. E. Ostry. 1999. Genetic evidence that butternut canker was recently introduced into North America. *Canadian Journal of Botany* 77:783–785.

Futuyma, D. J. 2000. Potential evolution of host range in herbivorous insects. pp. 42–53, *in* R. Van Driesche, T. A. Heard, A. S. McClay, and R. Reardon (Eds.), *Proceedings of Session: Host Specificity testing of exotic arthropod biological control agents— the biological basis for improvement in safety.* USDA Forest Service, Publication no. FHTET-99-1, August 2000.

Futuyma, D. J., and S. C. Peterson. 1985. Genetic variation in the use of resources by insects. *Annual Review of Entomology* 30:217–238.

Gallagher, K. G., K. A. Schierenbeck, and C. M. D'Antonio. 1997. Hybridization and introgression in *Carpobrotus* spp. (Aizoaceae) in California. II. Allozyme evidence. *American Journal of Botany* 84:905–911.

Gamradt, S. C., and L. B. Kats. 1996. Effect of introduced crayfish and mosquitofish on California newts. *Conservation Biology* 10:1155–1162.

Gamradt, S. C., L. B. Kats, and C. Anzalone. 1997. Aggression by non-native crayfish deters breeding in California newts. *Conservation Biology* 11:793–796.

Garbutt, K., and J. R. Whitcombe. 1986. The inheritance of seed dormancy in *Sinapis arvensis. Heredity* 56:25–31.

García-Ramos, G., and D. Rodríguez. 2002. Evolutionary speed of species invasions. *Evolution* 56:661–668.

Gardner, S. N., and A. A. Agrawal. 2002. Induced plant defence and the evolution of counter-defenses in herbivores. *Evolutionary Ecology Research* 4:1131–1151.

Gaskin, J. F., and B. A. Schall. 2002. Hybrid *Tamarix* widespread in U.S. invasion and undetected in native Asian range. *Proceedings of the National Academy of Sciences USA* 99:11256–11259.

Gasparich, G. E., J. G. Silva, H.-Y. Han, B. A. McPheron, G. J. Steck, and W. S. Sheppard. 1997. Population genetic structure of Mediterranean fruit fly (Diptera: Tephritidae) and implications for worldwide colonization patterns. *Annals of the Entomological Society of America* 90:790–797.

Geller, J. B., E. D. Walton, E. D. Grosholz, and G. M. Ruiz. 1997. Cryptic invasions of the crab *Carcinus* detected by molecular phylogeography. *Molecular Ecology* 6:901–906.

Gil-ad, N. L., and A. A. Reznicek. 1997. Evidence for hybridization of two Old World *Rhamnus* species—*R. cathartica* and *R. utilis* (Rhamnaceae)—in the New World. *Rhodora* 99:1–22.

Gilbert, G. S. 2002. Evolutionary ecology of plant diseases in natural ecosystems. *Annual Review of Phytopathology* 40:13–43.

Gilchrist, G. W., R. B. Huey, and L. Serra. 2001. Rapid evolution of wing size clines in *Drosophila subobscura. Genetica* 112–113:273–286.

Gille, S. T. 2002. Warming of the southern ocean since the 1950s. *Science* 295:1275–1277.

Glover, T. J., J. K. Knodel, P. S. Robbins, C. J. Eckenrode, and W. L. Roelofs. 1991.

Gene flow among three races of European corn borers (Coleoptera: Pyralidae) in New York State. *Environmental Entomology* 20:1356–1362.

Godfray, H. C. J., D. J. L. Agassiz, D. R. Nash, and J. H. Lawton. 1995. The recruitment of parasitoid species to two invading herbivores. *Journal of Animal Ecology* 64:393–402.

Goeden, R. D. 1971. The phytophagous insect fauna of milk thistle in southern California. *Economic Entomology* 64:1101–1104.

Goeden, R. D. 1974. Comparative survey of the phytophagous insect faunas of Italian thistle, *Carduus pycnocephalus*, in southern California and southern Europe relative to biological weed control. *Environmental Entomology* 3:464–474.

Goeden, R. D., and D. W. Ricker. 1968. The phytophagous insect fauna of Russian thistle (*Salsola kali* var. *tenuifolia*) in southern California. *Annals of the Entomological Society of America* 61:67–72.

Goeden, R. D., D. W. Ricker, and B. A. Hawkins. 1985. Ethological and genetic differences among three biotypes of *Rhinocyllus conicus* (Coeloptera: Curculionidae) introduced into North America for the biological control of asteraceous thistles. pp. 181–189, *in* E. S. Delfosse (Ed.), *Proceedings of the VI International Symposium on Biological Control of Weeds.* Ottawa, Canada: Agriculture Canada.

Goergen, E., and C. C. Daehler. 2001a. Reproductive ecology of a native Hawaiian grass (*Heteropogon contortus*; Poaceae) versus its invasive alien competitor (*Pennisetum setaceum*; Poaceae). *International Journal of Plant Science* 162:317–326.

Goergen, E., and C. C. Daehler. 2001b. Inflorescence damage by insects and fungi in native pili grass (*Heteropogon contortus*) versus alien fountain grass (*Pennisetum setaceum*) in Hawai'i. *Pacific Science* 55:129–136.

Goodwin, B. J., A. J. McAllister, and L. Fahrig. 1999. Predicting invasiveness of plant species based on biological information. *Conservation Biology* 13:422–426.

Goodwin, S. B., C. D. Smart, R. W. Sandrock, K. L. Deahl, Z. K. Punja, and W. E. Fry. 1998. Genetic change within popoulations of *Phytophthora infestans* in the United States and Canada during 1994 to 1996: role of migration and recombination. *Phytopathology* 88:939–949.

Gordon, T. R., A. J. Storer, and D. L. Wood. 2001. The pitch canker epidemic in California. *Plant Disease* 85:1128–1139.

Goslee, S. C., D. P. C. Peters, and K. G. Beck. 2001. Modeling invasive weeds in grasslands: the role of allelopathy in *Acroptilon repens* invasion. *Ecological Modeling* 139:31–45.

Gotelli, N. J., and A. E. Arnett. 2000. Biogeographic effects of red fire ant invasion. *Ecology Letters* 3:257–261.

Gottelli, D., C. Sillero-Zubiri, G. D. Applebaum, M. S. Roy, D. J. Girman, J. Garcia-Moreno, E. A. Ostrander, and R. K. Wayne. 1994. Molecular genetics of the most endangered canid: the Ethiopian wolf (*Canis simiensis*). *Molecular Ecology* 3:301–312.

Goudswaard, K., and F. Witte. 1997. The catfish fauna of Lake Victoria after the Nile perch upsurge. *Environmental Biology of Fishes* 49:21–43.

Gould, F. 1979. Rapid host range evolution in a population of the phytophagous mite *Tetranychus urticae* Koch. *Evolution* 33:791–802.

Gould, F. 1991. The evolutionary potential of crop pests. *American Scientist* 79:496–507.

Grabherr, G., M. Gottfried, and H. Pauli. 1994. Climate effects on mountain plants. *Nature* 369:448.

Grant, V. 1981. *Plant speciation*, 2nd ed. New York: Columbia University Press.

Gratton, C., and S. C. Welter. 1999. Does "enemy-free space" exist? Experimental host shifts of an herbivorous fly. *Ecology* 80:773–785.

Graves, S. D., and A. M. Shapiro. 2003. Exotics as host plants of the California butterfly fauna. *Biological Conservation* 110:413–433.

Gray, A. J. 1986. Do invading species have definable genetic characteristics? *Philosophical Transactions of the Royal Society of London B* 314:655–674.

Gray, A. J., D. F. Marshall, and A. F. Raybould. 1991. A century of evolution in *Spartina anglica*. *Advances in Ecological Research* 21:1–62.

Greenberg, N., R. L. Garthwaite, and D. C. Potts. 1996. Allozyme and morphological evidence for a newly introduced species of *Aurelia* in San Francisco Bay, California. *Marine Biology* 125:401–410.

Greene A. E., and R. F. Allison. 1994. Recombination between viral RNA and transgenic plant transcripts. *Science* 263:1423–1425.

Grente, J., and S. Berthelay-Sauret. 1978. Biological control of chestnut blight in France. pp. 30–34, *in* W. L. MacDonald, F. C. Cech, J. Luchock, and C. Smith (Eds.), *Proceedings of the American Chestnut Symposium*. Morgantown, W.Va.: West Virginia University.

Griffin, G. J. 2000. Blight control and restoration of the American chestnut. *Journal of Forestry* 98:22–27.

Griffiths, D. 1994. The size structure of lacustrine arctic charr (Pisces: Salmonidae) populations. *Biological Journal of the Linnaean Society* 51:337–357.

Groot, A. T., and M. Dicke. 2002. Insect-resistant transgenic plants in a multi-trophic context. *The Plant Journal* 31:387–406.

Grotkopp, E., M.. Rejmánek, and T. L. Rost. 2002. Toward a causal explanation of plant invasiveness: seedling growth and life-history strategies of 29 pine (*Pinus*) species. *American Naturalist* 159:396–419.

Guadagnuolo, R., D. Savona-Bianchi, and F. Felber. 2001. Gene flow from wheat (*Triticum aestivum* L.) to jointed goatgrass (*Aegilops cylindrica* Host.), as revealed by RAPD and microsatellite markers. *Theoretical and Applied Genetics* 103:1–8.

Gündüz, I., J.-C. Auffray, J. Britton-Davidian, J. Catalan, G. Ganem, M. G. Ramalhinho, M. L. Mathias, and J. B. Searle. 2001. Molecular studies on the colonization of the Madeiran archipelago by house mice. *Molecular Ecology* 10:2023–2029.

Gustine, D. L., P. W. Voigt, E. C. Brummer, and Y. A. Papadopoulos. 2002. Genetic Variation of RAPD markers for North American white clover collections and cultivars. *Crop Science* 42:343–347.

Hadfield, M. G., S. E. Miller, and A. H. Carwile. 1993. The decimation of endemic Hawai'ian tree snails by alien predators. *American Zoologist* 33:610–622.

Hagen, D. W., and L. G. Gilbertson. 1973. The genetics of plate morphs in freshwater threespine sticklebacks. *Heredity* 31:75–84.

Hair, J. D., and D. J. Forrester. 1970. The helminth parasites of the starling (*Sturnus vulgaris*). *American Midland Naturalist* 83:555–564.

Hall, H. G., and M. A. McMichael. 2001. Frequencies of restriction fragment-length polymorphisms indicate that neotropical honey bee (Hymenoptera: Apidae) populations have African and west European origins. *Annals of the Entomological Society of America* 94:670–676.

Hänfling, B., G. R. Carvalho, and R. Brandl. 2002. Mt-DNA sequences and possible invasion pathways of the Chinese mitten crab. *Marine Ecology Progress Series* 238:307–310.

Hansen, M. H. 2002. Estimating the long-term effects of stocking domesticated trout into wild brown trout (*Salmo trutta*) populations: an approach using microsatellite DNA analysis of historical and contemporary samples. *Molecular Ecology* 11:1003–1015.

Hansen, L. B., H. R. Siegismund, and R. B. Jorgensen. 2001. Introgression between oilseed rape (*Brassica napus* L.) and its weedy relative *B. rapa* L. in a natural population. *Genetic Resources and Crop Evolution* 48:621–627.

Hare, J. D. 1983. Seasonal variation in plant-insect associations: utilization of *Solanum dulcamara* by *Leptinotarsa decemlineata*. *Ecology* 64:345–361.

Hare, J. D., and G. G. Kennedy. 1986. Genetic variation in plant-insect associations: survival of *Leptinotarsa decemlineata* populations on *Solanum carolinense*. *Evolution* 40:1031–1043.

Harrington, R. A., B. J. Brown, and P. B. Reich. 1989. Ecophysiology of exotic and native shrubs in southern Wisconsin. I. Relationship of leaf characteristics, resource availability, and phenology to seasonal patterns of carbon gain. *Oecologia* 80:356–367.

Harris, P. 1988. Environmental impact of weed-control insects. *BioScience* 38:542–548.

Harrison, G. D. 1987. Host-plant discrimination and evolution of feeding preference in the Colorado potato beetle *Leptinotarsa decemlineata*. *Physiological Entomology* 12:407–415.

Hatta, M., P. Gao, P. Halfmann, and Y. Kawaoka. 2001. Molecular basis for high virulence of Hong Kong H5N1 influenza A viruses. *Science* 293:1840–1842.

Havel, J. E., J. K. Colbourne, and P. D. N. Hebert. 2000. Reconstructing the history of intercontinental dispersal in *Daphnia lumholtzi* by use of genetic markers. *Limnology and Oceanography* 45:1414–1419.

Havill, N. P., and K. F. Raffa. 1999. Effects of eliciting treatment and genotypic variation on induced resistance in *Populus*: Impacts on gypsy moth development and feeding behavior. *Oecologia* 120: 295–303.

Hawkins, B. A., and P. C. Marino. 1997. The colonization of native phytophagous insects in North America by exotic parasitoids. *Oecologia* 112:566–571.

Hayes, R. A., and B. J. Richardson. 2001. Biological control of the rabbit in Australia: lessons not learned? *Trends in Microbiology* 9:459–460.

Haynes, S., M. Jaarola, and J. B. Searle. 2003. Phylogeography of the common vole (*Microtus arvalis*) with particular emphasis on the colonization of the Orkney archipelago. *Molecular Ecology* 12:951–956.

Hayward, T. L. 1997. Pacific Ocean climate change: atmospheric forcing, ocean circulation and ecosystem response. *Trends in Ecology and Evolution* 12:150–154.

Heap, I. M. 1997. The occurrence of herbicide-resistant weeds worldwide. *Pesticide Science* 51:235–243.

Heath, D. D., J. W. Heath, C. A. Bryden, R. M. Johnson, and C. W. Fox. 2003. Rapid evolution of egg size in captive salmon. *Science* 299:1738–1740.

Hebert, P. D. N., and M. E. A. Cristescu. 2002. Genetic perspectives on invasions: the case of the Cladocera. *Canadian Journal of Fisheries and Aquatic Sciences* 59:1229–1234.

Hecnar, S. J., and R. T. M'Closkey. 1997. The effects of predatory fish on amphibian species richness and distribution. *Biological Conservation* 79:123–131.

Hedrick, R. P., T. S. McDowell, G. D. Marty, G. Fosgate, K. Mukkatira, and K. Myklebust. 2002. Comparative susceptibility of two strains of rainbow trout: one from Germany with suspected resistance to *Myxobolus cerebralis*, the cause of salmonid whirling disease. Presented at the *2002 Whirling Disease Symposium*, February 2002. Denver, Colo.

Heiser, C. B., Jr. 1947. Hybridization between the sunflower species *Helianthus annuus* and *H. petiolaris*. *Evolution* 1:249–262.

Hemming, J. D. C., and R. L. Lindroth. 1995. Intraspecific variation in aspen phytochemistry: effects on performance of gypsy moths and forest tent caterpillars. *Oecologia* 103:79–88.

Hemingway, J., L. Field, and J. Vontas. 2002. An overview of insecticide resistance. *Science* 298:96–97.

Hendry, A. P. 2001. Adaptive divergence and the evolution of reproductive isolation in the wild: an empirical demonstration using introduced sockeye salmon. *Genetica* 112:515–534.

Hendry, A. P., E. B. Taylor, and J. D. McPhail. 2002. Adaptive divergence and the balance between selection and gene flow: lake and stream stickleback in the Misty system. *Evolution* 56:1199–1216.

Hendry, A. P., J. K. Wenberg, P. Bentzen, E. C. Volk, and T. P. Quinn. 2000. Rapid evolution of reproductive isolation in the wild: evidence from introduced salmon. *Science* 290:516–518.

Henneman, M., and J. Memmott. 2001. Infiltration of a Hawaiian community by introduced biological control agents. *Science* 293:1314–1316.

Henter, H. J. 1995. The potential for coevolution in a host-parasitoid system. II. Genetic variation within a population of wasps in the ability to parasitize an aphid host. *Evolution* 49:439–445.

Henter, H. J., and S. Via. 1995. The potential for coevolution in a host-parasitoid system. I. Genetic variation within an aphid population in susceptibility to a parasitic wasp. *Evolution* 49:427–438.

Hickey, W. C., Jr. 1961. Growth form of crested wheatgrass as affected by site and grazing. *Ecology* 42:173–176.

Hight, S. D., J. E. Carpenter, K. A. Bloem, S. Bloem, R. W. Pemberton, and P. Stiling. 2002. Expanding geographical range of *Cactoblastis cactorum* (Lepidoptera: Pyralidae) in North America. *Florida Entomologist* 85:527–529.

Hilbeck, A. 2001. Implications of transgenic, insecticidal plants for insect and plant biodiversity. *Perspectives in Plant Ecology, Evolution, and Systematics* 4:43–61.

Hill, J. K., C. D. Thomas, and D. S. Blakely. 1999. Evolution of flight morphology in a butterfly that has recently expanded its geographic range. *Oecologia* 121:165–170.

Hillis, D. M., C. Moritz, and B. K. Mable (Eds.). 1996. *Molecular systematics*, 2nd ed. Sunderland, Mass.: Sinauer.

Hoff, R. J., and G. I. McDonald. 1993. Variation in virulence of white pine blister rust. *European Journal of Forest Pathology* 23:103–109.

Hoffman T., C. Golz, and O. Schneider. 1994. Foreign DNA sequences are received by a wild-type strain of *Aspergillus niger* after co-culture with transgenic higher plants. *Current Genetics* 27:70–76.

Hoffmann, J. H, F. A. C. Impson, and C. R. Volchansky. 2002. Biological control of cactus weeds: implications of hybridization between control agent biotypes. *Journal of Applied Ecology* 39:900–908.

Hokkanen, H. M. T., and D. Pimentel. 1989. New associations in biological control: theory and practice. *The Canadian Entomologist* 121:829–840.

Holdaway, R. N., and C. Jacomb. 2000. Rapid extinction of the moas (Aves: Dinornithiformes): model, test, and implications. *Science* 287:2250–2254.

Holland, B. S. 2000. Genetics of marine bioinvasions. *Hydrobiologia* 420:63–71.

Holland, B. S. 2001. Invasion without a bottleneck: microsatellite variation in natural and invasive populations of the brown mussel *Perna perna* (L). *Marine Biotechnology* 3:407–415.

Holmes, T. M., and E. R. Ingham. 1995. The effects of genetically engineered microorganisms on soil foodwebs. *Supplement to Bulletin of the Ecological Society of America 75/2. Abstracts of the 79th Annual ESA Meeting: Science and Public Policy.* Ecological Society of America: Washington, D.C.

Holsinger, K. E. 1988. Inbreeding depression doesn't matter: the genetic basis of mating-system evolution. *Evolution* 42:1235–1244.

Holt, R. D., and M. E. Hochberg. 1997. When is biological control evolutionarily stable (or is it)? *Ecology* 78:1673–1683.

Holway, D. A., L. Lach, A. V. Suarez, N. D. Tsutsui, and T. J. Case. 2002. The causes and consequences of ant invasions. *Annual Review of Ecology and Systematics* 33:181–233.

Honegger, R. E. 1980. List of amphibians and reptiles either known or thought to have become extinct since 1600. *Biological Conservation* 19:141–158.

Honnay, O., K. Verheyen, J. Butaye, H. Jacquemyn, B. Bossuyt, and M. Hermy. 2002. Possible effects of habitat fragmentation and climate change on the range of forest plant species. *Ecology Letters* 5:525–530.

Horton, D. R., J. L. Capinera, and P. L. Chapman. 1988. Local differences in host use by two populations of the Colorado potato beetle. *Ecology* 69:823–831.

Howarth, F. G., and G. W. Ramsay. 1991. The conservation of island insects and their habitats. pp. 71–107, *in* N. M. Collins and J. A. Thomas (Eds.), *The conservation of insects and their habitats.* San Diego, Calif.: Academic Press.

Hsaio, T. H. 1978. Host plant adaptations among geographic populations of the Colorado potato beetle. *Entomologia Experimentalis et Applicata* 24:237–247.

Hsaio, T. H. 1982. Geographic variation and host plant adaptation of the Colorado potato beetle. pp. 315–324, *in* J. H. Visser and A. K. Minks (Eds.), *Proceedings of the Fifth International Symposium on Host-Plant Relationships.* Wageningen, The Netherlands: Pudoc.

Hüberli, D., W. Van Sant, S. Swain, J. Davidson, and M. Garbelotto. 2002. Resistance of *Umbellularia californica* (Bay laurel) to *Phytophthora ramorum.* Presented at the American Phytopathological Society *Sudden Oak Death Science Symposium.* December 15–18. Monterey, California.

Hudon, M., and E. J. LeRoux. 1986. Biology and population dynamics of the European corn borer (*Ostrinia nubilalis*) with special reference to sweet corn in Quebec. I. Systematics, morphology, geographical distribution, host range, and economic importance. *Phytoprotection* 67:39–54.

Huey, R. B., G. W. Gilchrist, M. L. Carson, D. Berrigan, and L. Serra. 2000. Rapid evolution of a geographic cline in size in an introduced fly. *Science* 287:308–309.

Hufbauer, R. A. 2001. Pea aphid-parasitoid interactions: have parasitoids adapted to differential resistance? *Ecology* 82:717–725.

Hufbauer, R. A., and S. Via. 1999. Evolution of an aphid-parasitoid interaction: variation in resistance to parasitism among aphid populations specialized on different plants. *Evolution* 53:1435–1445.

Hume, L., and P. B. Cavers. 1982. Geographic variation in a widespread perennial weed, *Rumex crispus.* The relative amounts of genetic and environmentally induced variation among populations. *Canadian Journal of Botany* 60:1928–1937.

Hunt, J. 1992. Feeding ecology of valley pocket gophers (*Thomomys bottae sanctidiegi*) on a California coastal grassland. *American Midland Naturalist* 127:41–51.

Hunter, K. L., J. H. Betancourt, B. R. Riddle, T. R. Van Devender, K. L. Cole, and W. G. Spaulding. 2001. Ploidy race distributions since the Last Glacial Maximun in the North American desert shrub, *Larrea tridentata. Global Ecology and Biogeography* 10:521–533.

Hüppop, O. and K. Hüppop. 2002. North Atlantic Oscillation and timing of spring migration in birds. *Proceedings of the Royal Society of London B* 270:233–240.

Huxel, G. R. 1999. Rapid displacement of native species by invasive species: effects of hybridization. *Biological Conservation* 89:143–152.

Hwang, S.-Y., and R. L. Lindroth. 1997. Clonal variation in foliar chemistry of aspen: effects on gypsy moths and forest tent caterpillars. *Oecologia* 111:99–108.

Hwang, S.-Y., and R. L. Lindroth. 1998. Consequences of clonal variation in aspen phytochemistry for late season folivores. *Ecoscience* 5:508–516.

Inouye, D. W., B. Barr, K. B. Armitage, and B. D. Inouye. 2000. Climate change is affecting altitudinal migrants and hibernating species. *Proceedings of the National Academy of Sciences USA* 97:1630–1633.

Ivie, M. A. 2001. On the geographic origin of the wheat stem sawfly (Hymenoptera: Cephidae): a new hypothesis of introduction from northeastern Asia. *American Entomologist* 47:84–97.

Jackman, T. R. 1998. Molecular and historical evidence for the introduction of clouded salamanders (genus *Aneides*) to Vancouver Island, British Columbia, Canada, from California. *Canadian Journal of Zoology* 76:1570–1580.

Jaenike, J. 1990. Host specialization in phytophagous insects. *Annual Review of Ecology and Systematics* 21:243–273.

Jain, S. K., and P. S. Martins. 1979. Ecological genetics of the colonizing ability of rose clover (*Trifolium hirtum* All.). *American Journal of Botany* 66:361–366.

Jander, G., J. Cui, B. Nhan, N. E. Pierce, and F. M. Ausubel. 2001. The TASTY locus on chromosome 1 of *Arabidopsis* affects feeding of the insect herbivore *Trichoplusia ni*. *Plant Physiology* 126:890–898.

Jarvi, S. I., C. T. Atkinson, and R. C. Fleischer. 2001. Immunogenetics and resistance to avian malaria in Hawaiian honeycreepers (Drepaniidae). *Studies in Avian Biology* No. 22:254–263.

Jarvinen, A. 1994. Global warming and egg size of birds. *Ecography* 17:108–110.

Jesse, L. C. H., and J. J. Obrycki. 2000. Field deposition of Bt transgenic corn pollen: lethal effects on the monarch butterfly. *Oecologia* 125:241–248.

Johnson, L. 1980. The arctic charr. pp. 15–98, *in* E. K. Balon (Ed.), *Charrs, salmonid fishes of the genus* Salvelinus. The Hague, Netherlands: W. Junk.

Johnson, R. F., and W. J. Klitz. 1977. Variation and evolution in a granivorous bird: the house sparrow. pp. 15–51, *in* J. Pinowski and S. C. Kendeigh (Eds.), *Granivorous birds in ecosystems*. London, England: Cambridge University Press.

Johnson, J. B., J. P. McCaffrey, and F. W. Merickel. 1992. Endemic phytophagous insects associated with yellow starthistle in northern Idaho. *Pan-Pacific Entomologist* 68(3):169–173.

Johnson, T. C., C. A. Scholz, M. R. Talbot, K. Kelts, R. D. Ricketts, G. Ngobi, K. Beuning, I. Ssemmanda, and J. W. McGill. 1996. *Late Pleistocene desiccation of Lake Victoria and rapid evolution of cichlid fishes*. Science 273:1091–1093.

Johnston, R. F., and R. C. Fleischer. 1981. Overwinter mortality and sexual size dimorphism in the house sparrow. *Auk* 98:503–511.

Johnston, R. F., and R. K. Selander. 1964. House sparrows: rapid evolution of races in North America. *Science* 144:548–550.

Joly, S., and A. Bruneau. 2002. Multiple origins of autopolyploidy in *Apios americana* (Leguminosae: Papilionoidae) as revealed by genealogical analysis of the H3-D histone gene. Presented at the *Botany 2002 Conference*. Madison, Wisc.

Jones, E. T. 1938. Infestation of grasses of the genus *Aegilops* by the Hessian fly. *Journal of Economic Entomology* 31:333–337.

Jones, E. T. 1939. Grasses of the tribe Hordeae as hosts of the Hessian fly. *Journal of Economic Entomology* 32:505–510.

Jones, R. W. 2001. Evolution of the host plant associations of the *Anthonomus grandis* species group (Coleoptera: Curculionidae): phylogenetic tests of various hypotheses. *Annals of the Entomological Society of America* 94:51–58.

Jonsson, B., S. Skúlason, S. S. Snorrason, O. T. Sandlund, H. J. Malmquist, P. M. Jónasson, R. Gydemo, and T. Lindem. 1988. Life history variation of polymorphic Arctic Charr (*Salvelinus alpinus*) in Thingvallavatn, Iceland. *Canadian Journal of Fisheries and Aquatic Sciences* 45:1537–1547.

Jørgensen, R. B. 1999. Gene flow from oilseed rape (*Brassica napus*) to related species. *British Crop Protection Council Symposium Proceedings* No. 72:117–123.

Jørgensen, R.B., B. Andersen, L. Landbo, and T. R. Mikkelsen. 1998. Spontaneous hybridisation between oilseed rape (*Brassica napus*) and weedy relatives. *Acta Horticulturae* 407:193–200.

Jules, E. S., M. J. Kauffman, W. D. Ritts, and A. L. Carroll. 2002. Spread of an invasive pathogen over a variable landscape: a nonnative root rot on Port Orford cedar. *Ecology* 83:3167–3181.

Jupp, P. W., D. T. Briese, and J.M. Cullen. 1997. Evidence for resistance in *Hypericum perforatum* to a biological control agent, the eriophyid mite *Aculus hyperici. Plant Protection Quarterly* 12:67–70.

Kamler, J. F., and W. B. Ballard. 2002. A review of native and nonnative red foxes in North America. *Wildlife Society Bulletin* 30:370–379.

Karban, R., and A. A. Agrawal. 2002. Herbivore offense. *Annual Review of Ecology and Systematics* 33:641–664.

Karr, J. R. 1982. Avian extinction on Barro Colorado Island, Panama: a reassessment. *American Naturalist* 119:220–239.

Kay, S. H., and S. T. Hoyle. 2001. Mail order, the Internet, and invasive aquatic weeds. *Journal of Aquatic Plant Management* 39:88–91.

Keane, R. M., and M. J. Crawley. 2002. Exotic plant invasions and the enemy release hypothesis. *Trends in Ecology and Evolution* 17:164–170.

Keast, A. 1970. Adaptive evolution and shifts in niche occupation in island birds. *Biotropica* 2:61–75.

Kelly, E. G., E. D. Forsman, and R. G. Anthony. 2003. Are Barred Owls displacing Spotted Owls? *Condor* 105:45–53.

Kemp, W. B. 1937. Natural selection within plant species as exemplified in a permanent pasture. *Journal of Heredity* 28:329–333.

Kendeigh, S. C., and C. R. Blem. 1974. Metabolic adaptation to local climate in birds. *Comparative Biochemistry and Physiology* 48A:175–187.

Kennedy, C. E. J., and T. R. E. Southwood. 1984. The number of species of insects associated with British trees: a re-analysis. *Journal of Animal Ecology* 53:455–478.

Kennedy, T. A., S. Naeem, K. M. Howe, J. M. H. Koops, D. Tilman, and P. Reich. 2002. Biodiversity as a barrier to ecological invasion. *Nature* 417:636–638.

Kessler, A., and I. T. Baldwin. 2002. Plant responses to insect herbivory: the emerging molecular analysis. *Annual Review of Plant Biology* 53:299–328.

Kiesecker, J. M., and A. R. Blaustein. 1997. Population differences in responses of red-legged frogs (*Rana aurora*) to introduced bullfrogs. *Ecology* 78:1752–1760.

Kim, M.-S., S. J. Brunsfeld, G. I. McDonald, and N. B. Klopfenstein. 2003. Effect of white pine blister rust (*Cronartium ribicola*) and rust-resistance breeding on genetic variation in western white pine (*Pinus monticola*). *Theoretical and Applied Genetics* 106:1004–1010.

King, W. B. 1980. Ecological basis of extinction in birds. pp. 905–911, *in* R. Nohring (Ed.) *Proceedings of the XVII International Ornithological Congress,* Berlin, Germany, 1978.

King, C. M. 1991. Body size-prey size relationships in European stoats *Mustela erminea*: a test case. *Holarctic Ecology* 14:173–185.

Kinloch, B. B., Jr. 1992. Distribution and frequency of a gene for resistance to white pine blister rust in natural populations of sugar pine. *Canadian Journal of Botany* 70:1319–1323.

Kinloch, B. B., Jr., and G. E. Dupper. 2002. Genetic specificity in the white pine-blister rust pathosystem. *Phytopathology* 92:278–280.

Kinloch, B. B., Jr., R. D. Westfall, E. E. White, M. A. Gitzendanner, G. E. Dupper, B. M. Ford, and P. D. Hodgekiss. 1998. Genetics of *Cronartium ribicola* IV. Population structure in western North America. *Canadian Journal of Botany* 76:91–98.

Kinloch, B. B., Jr., R. A. Sniexko, and G. E. Dupper. 2003. Origin and distribution of Cr2, a gene for resistance to white pine blister rust in natural populations of western white pine. *Phytopathology* 93:691–694.

Kinnison, M. T., M. J. Unwin, N. Bousted, and T. P. Quinn. 1998a. Population specific variation in body dimensions of adult chinook salmon (*Oncorhynchus tshawytscha*) from New Zealand and their source population, 90 years after their introduction. *Canadian Journal of Fisheries and Aquatic Sciences* 55:1946–1953.

Kinnison, M. T., M. J. Unwin, W. K. Hershberger, and T. P. Quinn. 1998b. Egg size, fecundity and development rate of two New Zealand chinook salmon (*Oncorhynchus tshawytscha*) populations. *Canadian Journal of Fisheries and Aquatic Sciences* 55:554–563.

Kinnison, M. T., M. J. Unwin, A. P. Hendry, and T. P. Quinn. 2001. Migratory costs and the evolution of egg size and number in introduced and indigenous salmon populations. *Evolution* 55:1656–1667.

Kinzie, R. A. III. 1992. Predation by the introduced carnivorous snail *Euglandina rosea* (Ferussac) on endemic aquatic lymnaeid snails in Hawaii. *Biological Conservation* 60:149–155.

Kirchner, J. W., and A. Weil. 2000. Delayed biological recovery from extinctions throughout the fossil record. *Nature* 404:177–180.

Kirkpatrick, M., and R. K. Selander. 1979. Genetics of speciation in lake whitefishes in the Allagash Basin. *Evolution* 33:478–485.

Kirkpatrick, K. J., and H. D. Wilson. 1988. Interspecific gene flow in *Cucurbita*: *C. texana* vs *C. pepo*. *American Journal of Botany* 75:519–527.

Kiyohara, T., and R. I. Bolla. 1990. Pathogenic variability among populations of the pinewood nematode, *Bursaphelenchus xylophilus*. *Forest Science* 36:1061–1076.

Klein, D. R. 1968. The introduction, increase, and crash of reindeer on St. Matthew Island. *Journal of Wildlife Management* 32:350–367.

Klepaker, T. 1993. Morphological changes in a marine population of the three-spined stickleback, *Gasterosteus aculeatus*, recently isolated in fresh water. *Canadian Journal of Zoology* 71:1251–1258.

Klinger, T. 2002. Variability and uncertainty in crop-to-wild hybridization. pp. 1–15, *in* D. K. Letourneau and B. E. Burrows (Eds.), *Genetically engineered organisms: assessing environmental and human health effects*. Boca Raton, Fla.: CRC Press.

Klinger, T., and N. C. Ellstrand. 1994. Engineered genes in wild populations: fitness of weed-crop hybrids of radish, *Raphanus sativus* L. *Ecological Applications* 4:117–120.

Klinger, T., D. R. Elam, and N. C. Ellstrand. 1991. Radish as a model system for the study of engineered gene escape rates via crop-weed mating. *Conservation Biology* 5:531–535.

Klinger, T., P. E. Arriola, and N. C. Ellstrand. 1992. Crop-weed hybridization in radish (*Raphanus sativus*): effects of distance and population size. *American Journal of Botany* 79:1431–1435.

Knops, J. M. H., D. Tilman, N. M. Haddad, S. Naeem, C. E. Mitchell, J. Haarstad, M. E. Ritchie, K. M. Howe, P. B. Reich, E. Siemann, and J. Groth. 1999. Effects of plant species richness on invasion dynamics, disease outbreaks, insect abundances and diversity. *Ecology Letters* 2:286–293.

Kogan, M. 1981. Dynamics of insect adaptations to soybeans: impact of integrated pest management. *Environmental Entomology* 10:363–371.

Kogan, M. 1991. Contemporary adaptations of herbivores to introduced legume crops. pp. 591–605, *in* P. W. Price, T. M. Lewinsohn, G. W. Fernandes, and W. W. Benson (Eds.), *Plant-animal interactions: evolutionary ecology in tropical and temperate regions.* New York: John Wiley and Sons.

Kolmer, J. A. 1996. Genetics of resistance to wheat leaf rust. *Annual Review of Phytopathology* 34: 435–455.

Kolmer, J. A. 2001. Molecular polymorphism and virulence phenotypes of the wheat rust fungus *Puccinia triticina* in Canada. *Canadian Journal of Botany* 79:917–926.

Kolmer, J. A., and Liu, J. Q. 2000. Virulence and molecular polymorphism in international collections of the wheat leaf rust fungus *Puccinia triticina*. *Phytopathology* 90: 427–436.

Komack, S., and M. R. Crossland. 2000. An assessment of the introduced mosquitofish (*Gambusia affinis holbrooki*) as a predator of eggs, hatchlings, and tadpoles on native and non-native anurans. *Wildlife Research* 27:185–189.

Koricheva, J. 2002. Meta-analysis of sources of variation in fitness costs of plant antiherbivore defenses. *Ecology* 83:176–190.

Koskinen, M. T., T. O. Haugen, and C. R. Primmer. 2002. Contemporary fisherian life-history evolution in small salmonid populations. *Nature* 419:826–830.

Kowarik, I. 1995. Time lags in biological invasions with regard to the success and failure of alien species. pp. 15–38, *in* P. Pyšek, K. Prach, M. Rejmánek, and M. Wade (Eds.), *Plant invasions—general aspects and special problems.* Amsterdam, The Netherlands: SPB Academic Publishing.

Kraaijeveld, A. R., and H. C. J. Godfray. 1999. Geographic patterns in the evolution of resistance and virulence in *Drosophila* and its parasitoids. *American Naturalist* 153:S61–S74.

Kraaijeveld, A. R., K. A. Hutcheson, E. C. Limentani, and H. C. J. Godfray. 2001. Costs of counterdefences to host resistance in a parasitoid of *Drosophila*. *Evolution* 55:1815–1821.

Krawczak, M., and J. Schmidke. 1998. *DNA fingerprinting.* Oxford, England: BIOS Scientific Publishers.

Krebs, J. W., M. L. Wilson, and J. E. Childs. 1995. Rabies—epidemiology, prevention, and future research. *Journal of Mammalogy* 76:681–694.

Kristjánsson, B. K., S. Skúlason, and L. G. Noakes. 2002. Rapid divergence in a recently isolated population of threespine stickleback (*Gasterosteus aculeatus* L.). *Evolutionary Ecology Research* 4:659–672.

Krysan, J. L., D. E. Foster, T. F. Branson, K. R. Ostlie, and W. S. Cranshaw. 1986. Two years before the hatch: rootworms adapt to crop rotation. *Bulletin of the Entomological Society of America* 32:250–253.

Kuehn, M. M., J. E. Minor, and B. N. White. 1999. An examination of hybridization between cattail species *Typha latifolia* and *Typha angustifolia* using random amplified polymorphic DNA and chloroplast DNA markers. *Molecular Ecology* 8:1981–1990.

Kullman, L. 2002. Rapid recent range-margin rise of tree and shrub species in the Swedish Scandes. *Journal of Ecology* 90:68–77.

Lacey, E. P. 1988. Latitudinal variation in reproductive timing of a short-lived monocarp, *Daucus carota* (Apiaceae). *Ecology* 69:220–232.

Lade, J. A., N. D. Murray, C. A. Marks, and N. A. Robinson. 1996. Microsatellite differentiation between Phillip Island and mainland Australian populations of the red fox *Vulpes vulpes*. *Molecular Ecology* 5:81–87.

Lane, M. D., and M. J. Lawrence. 1995. Genetics of seed dormancy in *Papaver rhoeas*. *Heredity* 75:84–91.

Larivière, S., and M. Crête. 1993. The size of eastern coyotes (*Canis latrans*): a comment. *Journal of Mammalogy* 74:1072–1074.

Lauer, T. E., and A. Spacie. 2000. The effects of sponge (*Porifera*) biofouling on zebra mussel (*Dreissena polymorpha*) fitness: reduction of glycogen, tissue loss, and mortality. *Journal of Freshwater Ecology* 15:83–92.

Leary, R. F., F. W. Allendorf, and G. K. Sage. 1995. Hybridization and introgression between introduced and native fish. American Fisheries Society Symposium 15:91–101.

Lee, C. E. 2002. Evolutionary genetics of invasive species. *Trends in Ecology and Evolution* 17:386–391.

Lee, C. E., and M. A. Bell. 1999. Causes and consequences of recent freshwater invasions by saltwater animals. *Trends in Ecology and Evolution* 14:284–288.

Leiss, K. A., and H. Müller-Schärer. 2001. Adaptation of *Senecio vulgaris* (Asteraceae) to ruderal and agricultural habitats. *American Journal of Botany* 88:1593–1599.

LeJeune, K. D., and T. R. Seastedt. 2001. *Centaurea* species: the forb that won the West. *Conservation Biology* 15:1568–1574.

Lemoine, N., and K. Böhning-Gaese. 2003. Potential impact of global change on species richness of long-distance migrants. *Conservation Biology* 17:577–586.

Lennartsson, T., P. Nilsson, and J. Tuomi. 1998. Induction of overcompensation in the field gentian, *Gentianella compestris*. *Ecology* 79:1061–1072.

Leopold, A., and S. Jones. 1947. A phenological record for Sauk and Dane Counties, Wisconsin. *Ecological Monographs* 17:81–122.

Leppäkoski, E., and S. Olenin. 2001. The meltdown of biogeographic peculiarities of the Baltic Sea: the interaction of natural and man-made processes. *Ambio* 33:202–209.

Leppäkoski, E., S. Gollasch, P. Gruszka, H. Ojaveer, S. Olenin, and V. Panov. 2002.

The Baltic—a sea of invaders. *Canadian Journal of Fisheries and Aquatic Sciences* 59:1175–1188.

Letourneau, D. K., J. A. Hagen, and G. S. Robinson. 2002. Bt-crops: Evaluating benefits under cultivation and risks from escaped transgenes in the wild. pp. 33–98, *in* D. K. Letourneau and B. E. Burrows (Eds.), *Genetically engineered organisms: Assessing environmental and human health effects.* Boca Raton, Fla.: CRC Press.

Levin, D. A. 1976. The chemical defenses of plants to pathogens and herbivores. *Annual Review of Ecology and Systematics* 7:121–159.

Levin, S. A., and J. D. Udovic. 1977. A mathematical model of coevolving populations. *American Naturalist* 111:657–675.

Levin, D. A., J. Francisco-Ortega, and R. K. Jansen. 1996. Hybridization and the extinction of rare plant species. *Conservation Biology* 10:10–16.

Levine, J. M. 2000. Species diversity and biological invasions: relating local process to community pattern. *Science* 288:852–854.

Levine, J. M., and C. M. D'Antonio. 1999. Elton revisited: a review of evidence linking diversity and invasibility. *Oikos* 87:15–26.

Levine, J. M., and C. M. D'Antonio. 2003. Forecasting biological invasions with increasing international trade. *Conservation Biology* 17:322–326.

Levine E., H. Oloumi-Sadeghi, and J. R. Fisher. 1992. Discovery of multiyear diapause in Illinois and South Dakota northern corn rootworm (Coleoptera: Chrysomelidae) eggs and the incidence of the prolonged diapause trait in Illinois. *Journal of Economic Entomology* 85:262–267.

Levine, E., J. L. Spencer, S. A. Isaid, D. W. Onstad, and M. E. Gray. 2002. Adaptation of the western rootworm to crop rotation: evolution of a new strain in response to a management practice. *American Entomologist* 48:94–107.

Lewis, M. A., and P. Kareiva. 1993. Allee dynamics and the spread of invading organisms. *Theoretical Population Biology* 43:141–158.

Lexer, C., M. E. Welch, O. Raymond, and L. H. Rieseberg. 2003a. The origin of ecological divergence in *Helianthus paradoxus* (Asteraceae): selection on transgressive characters in a novel hybrid habitat. *Evolution* 57:2012–2025.

Lexer, C., M. E. Welch, J. L. Durphy, and L. H. Rieseberg. 2003b. Natural selection for salt tolerance quantitative trait loci (QTLs) in wild sunflower hybrids: Implications for the origin of *Helianthus paradoxus*, a diploid hybrid species. *Molecular Ecology* 12:1225–1235.

Li, Y.-C., A. B. Korol, T. Fahima, A. Beiles, and E. Nevo. 2002. Microsatellites: genomic distribution, putative functions and mutational mechanisms: a review. *Molecular Ecology* 11:2453–2465.

Lia, V. V., V. A. Confalonieri, C. I. Comas, and J. H. Hunziker. 2001. Molecular phylogeny of *Larrea* and it allies (Zygophyllaceae): reticulate evolution and the probable time of creosote bush arrival in North America. *Molecular Phylogenetics and Evolution* 21:309–320.

Liebhold, A. M., W. L. MacDonald, D. Bergdahl, and V. C. Mastro. 1996. Invasion by exotic forest pests: A threat to forest ecosystems. *Forest Science Monographs* 30:1–49.

Linder, C. R., and J. Schmitt. 1995. Potential persistence of escaped transgenes: performance of transgenic, oil-modified *Brassica* seeds and seedlings. *Ecological Applications* 5:1056–1068.

Linder, C. R., I. Taha, G. J. Seiler, A. A. Snow, and L. H. Rieseberg. 1998. Long-term introgression of crop genes into wild sunflower populations. *Theoretical and Applied Genetics* 96:339–347.

Lindroth, R.L., S.-Y. Hwang, and T. L. Osier. 1999. Phytochemical variation in quaking aspen: effects on gypsy moth susceptibility to nuclear polyhedrosis virus. *Journal of Chemical Ecology* 25:1331–1341.

Lindsey, C. C. 1981. Stocks are chameleons: plasticity in gill rakers of coregonid fishes. *Canadian Journal of Fisheries and Aquatic Sciences* 38:1497–1506.

Line, R. H. 2002. Stripe rust of wheat and barley in North America: a retrospective historical review. *Annual Review of Phytopathology* 40:75–118.

Lockwood, J. L., M. P. Moulton, and S. K. Anderson. 1993. Morphological assortment and the assembly of communities of introduced passeriforms on oceanic islands: Tahiti versus Oahu. *American Naturalist* 141:398–408.

Lockwood, J. L., M. P. Moulton, and R. K. Brooke. 1996. Morphological dispersion of the introduced land-birds of Saint Helena. *Ostrich* 67:111–117.

Lockwood, J. L., T. M. Brooks, and M. L. McKinney. 2000. Taxonomic homogenization of the global avifauna. *Animal Conservation* 3:27–35.

Lodge, D. M. 1993a. Biological invasions: lessons for ecology. *Trends in Ecology and Evolution* 8:133–137.

Lodge, D. M. 1993b. Species invasions and deletions: community effects and responses to climate and habitat change. pp. 367–387, *in* P. Kareiva, J. G. Kingsolver, and R. B. Huey (Eds.), *Biotic interactions and global change.* Sunderland, Mass.: Sinauer.

Lodge, D. M. 2001. Lakes. pp. 277–312, *in* F. S. Chapin III, O. E. Sala, and E. Huber-Sannwald, *Future scenarios of global biodiversity.* New York: Springer-Verlag.

Lodge, D. M., C. A. Taylor, D. M. Holdich, and J. Skurdal. 2000. Nonindigenous crayfishes threaten North American freshwater biodiversity: lessons from Europe. *Fisheries* 25(8):7–20.

Lomolino, M. V., and R. Channell. 1995. Splendid isolation: patterns of geographic range collapse in endangered mammals. *Journal of Mammalogy* 76:335–347.

Lonsdale, W. M. 1999. Global patterns of plant invasions and the concept of invasibility. *Ecology* 80:1522–1536.

Losey, J. E., J. J. Obrycki, and R. A. Hufbauer. 2002. Impacts of genetically engineered crops on non-target herbivores: Bt-corn and monarch butterflies as a case study. pp. 144–165, *in* D. K. Letourneau and B. E. Burrows (Eds.), *Genetically engineered organisms: assessing environmental and human health effects.* Boca Raton, Fla.: CRC Press.

Losos, J. B, K. I. Warheit, and T. B. Schoener. 1997. Adaptive differentiation following experimental island colonization in *Anolis* lizards. *Nature* 387:70–73.

Losos, J. B, T. B. Schoener, K. I. Warheit, and D. Creer. 2001. Experimental studies of adaptive differentiation in Bahamian *Anolis* lizards. *Genetica* 112–113:399–415.

Lott, M. S., J. C. Volin, R. W. Pemberton, and D. F. Austin. 2003. The reproductive biology of the invasive ferns *Lygodium microphyllum* and *L. japonicum* (Schiza-eaceae): implications for invasive potential. *American Journal of Botany* 90:1144–1152.

Louda, S. M. 1998. Population growth of *Rhinocyllus conicus* (Coleoptera: Cur-culionidae) on two species of native thistles in prairie. *Environmental Entomology* 27:834–841.

Louda, S. M., and A. E. Arnett. 2000. Predicting non-target ecological effects of bio-logical control agents: evidence from *Rhinocyllus conicus*. pp. 551–567, *in* N. R. Spencer (Ed.) *Proceedings of the X International Symposium on Biological Control of Weeds,* Bozeman, Mont.: Montana State University.

Louda, S. M., and C. W. O'Brien. 2002. Unexpected ecological effects of distribut-ing the exotic weevil, *Larinus planus* (F.), for the biological control of Canada thistle. *Conservation Biology* 16:717–727.

Louda, S. M., D. Kendall, J. Connor, and D. Simberloff. 1997. Ecological effects of an insect introduced for the biological control of weeds. *Science* 277:1088–1090.

Louda, S. M., A. E. Arnett, T. A. Rand, and F. L. Russell. 2003a. Invasiveness of some biological control insects and adequacy of their ecological risk assessment and regulation. *Conservation Biology* 17:73–82.

Louda, S. M., R. W. Pemberton, M. T. Johnson, and P. A. Follett. 2003b. Nontarget effects—the Achilles' heel of biological control? Retrospective analyses to reduce risk associated with biocontrol introductions. *Annual Review of Entomol-ogy* 48:365–396.

Lounibos, L. P., R. L. Escher, and R. Lourenço-de-Oliviera. 2003. Asymmetric evo-lution of photoperiodic diapause in temperate and tropical invasive populations of *Aedes albopictus* (Diptera: Culicidae). *Annals of the Entomological Society of Amer-ica* 96:512–518.

Lovette, I. J., G. Seutin, R. E. Ricklefs, and E. Bermingham. 1999. The assembly of an island fauna by natural invasion: sources and temporal patterns in the avian colonization of Barbados. *Biological Invasions* 1:33–41.

Lucht, W., I. C. Prentice, R. B. Myneni, S. Sitch, P. Friedlingstein, W. Cramer, P. Bousquet, W. Buermann, and B. Smith. 2002. Climatic control of the high-lati-tude vegetation greening trend and Pinatubo effect. *Science* 296:1687–1689.

Lym, R. G., and R. B. Carlson. 2002. Effect of leafy spurge (*Euphorbia esula*) geno-type on feeding damage and reproduction of *Aphthona* spp.: implications for bio-logical weed control. *Biological Control* 23:127–133.

Lynch, L. D., A. R. Ives, J. K. Waage, M. E. Hochberg, and M. B. Thomas. 2002. The risks of biocontrol: transient impacts and minimum nontarget densities. *Ecologi-cal Applications* 12:1872–1882.

Mack, R. N. 1981. Invasion of *Bromus tectorum* L. into western North America: an ecological chronicle. *Agro-Ecosystems* 7:145–165.

Mack, R. N. 2003. Plant naturalizations and invasions in the eastern United States: 1634–1860. *Annals of the Missouri Botanical Garden* 90:77–90.

Mack, R. N., and M. Erneberg. 2002. The United States naturalized flora: largely the product of deliberate introductions. *Annals of the Missouri Botanical Garden* 89:176–189.

Mack, R. N., and W. M. Lonsdale. 2001. Humans as global plant dispersers: getting more than we bargained for. *BioScience* 51:95–102.

Mack, R. N., and J. N. Thompson. 1982. Evolution in steppe with few large, hooved mammals. *American Naturalist* 119:757–773.

Mack, R. N., D. Simberloff, W. M. Lonsdale, H. Evans, M. Clout, and F. A. Bazzaz. 2000. Biotic invasions: causes, epidemiology, global consequences, and control. *Ecological Applications* 10:689–710.

Macnair, M. 1987. Heavy metal tolerance in plants: a model evolutionary system. *Trends in Ecology and Evolution* 2:354–359.

Madeira, P. T., T. K. Van, K. K. Steward, and R. J. Schnell. 1997. Random amplified polymorphic DNA analysis of the phenetic relationships among world-wide accessions of *Hydrilla verticillata*. *Aquatic Botany* 59:217–236.

Madeira, P. T., C. C. Jacono, and T. K. Van. 2000. Monitoring hydrilla using two RAPD procedures and the nonindigenous aquatic species database. *Journal of Aquatic Plant Management* 38:33–40.

Magoulick, D. D., and L. C. Lewis. 2002. Predation on exotic zebra mussels by native fishes: effects on predator and prey. *Freshwater Biology* 47:1908–1918.

Magurran, A. E., B. H. Seghers, G. R. Carvalho, and P. W. Shaw. 1992. Behavioural consequences of an artificial introduction of guppies (*Peocelia reticulata*) in North Trinidad: evidence for the evolution of antipredator behaviour in the wild. *Proceedings of the Royal Society of London B* 248:117–122.

Malcolm, J. R., A. Markham, R. P. Neilson, and M. Garaci. 2002. Estimated migration rates under scenarios of global climate change. *Journal of Biogeography* 29:835–849.

Man in't Veldt, W. A., W. J. Veenbaas-Rijks, E. Ilieva, A. W. A. M. de Cock, P. J. M. Bonants, and R. Pieters. 1998. Natural hybrids of *Phytophthora nicotianae* and *P. cactorum* demonstrated by isozyme analysis and random amplified polymorphic DNA. *Phytopathology* 88:922–929.

Markiw, M.E. 1992. *Salmonid whirling disease.* Fish and Wildlife Leaflet 17. Washington, D.C.: U. S. Fish and Wildlife Service.

Maron, J., and C. Luke. 2000. Invasion and subsequent biological control of St. John's wort (*Hypericum perforatum*): rapid evolution of herbivore tolerance? Presented at the *Ecological Society of America Annual Meeting,* August 6–10. Snowbird, Utah. Washington, D.C.: Ecological Society of America.

Maron, J. L., M. Vilá, R. Bommarco, S. Elmendorf, and P. Beardsley. Forthcoming. Rapid evolution of an invasive plant. *Ecological Monographs.*

Martel, A. L., D. A. Pathy, J. B. Madill, C. B. Renaud, S. L. Dean, and S. J. Kerr. 2001. Decline and regional extirpation of freshwater mussels (Unionidae) in a small river system invaded by *Dreissena polymorpha*: the Rideau River, 1993–2000. *Canadian Journal of Zoology* 79:2181–2191.

Martel, C., A. Réjasse, M.-T. Bethenod, and D. Bourguet. 2003. Host-plant-associated genetic differentiation in northern French populations of the European corn borer. *Heredity* 90:141–149.

Marvier, M. 2002. Improving risk assessment for nontarget safety of transgenic crops. *Ecological Applications* 12:1119–1124.

Mauricio, R., and M. D. Rausher. 1997. Experimental manipulation of putative selection agents provides evidence for the role of natural enemies in the evolution of plant defense. *Evolution* 51:1435–1444.

Mauricio, R., M. D. Rausher, and D. S. Burdick. 1997. Variation in the defense strategies of plants: are resistance and tolerance mutually exclusive? *Ecology* 78:1301–1311.

Mayo, G. M., and R.T. Roush. 1997. Genetic variability of St John's wort *Hypericum perforatum* L (Clusiaceae) and the detection of resistance to a biological control agent, the eriophyid mite *Aculus hyperici* Liro (Eriophyidae). *Plant Protection Quarterly* 12:70–72.

McDonald, R. 2002. Resource partitioning among British and Irish mustelids. *Journal of Animal Ecology* 71:185–200.

McElroy, J. S., R. K. Walker, and E. van Santen. 2002. Patterns of variation in *Poa annua* populations as revealed by canonical discriminant analysis of life history traits. *Crop Science* 42:513–517.

McEvoy, P. B. 1996. Host specificity and biological control. *BioScience* 46:401–405.

McEvoy, P. B., and E. M. Coombs. 2000. Why things bite back: unintended consequences of biological weed control. pp. 167–194, *in* P. A. Follett and J. J. Duan (Eds.), *Nontarget effects of biological control*. Boston, Mass.: Kluwer Academic Publishers.

McFadyen, R. E. C. 1998. Biological control of weeds. *Annual Review of Entomology* 43:369–393.

McGinnity, P., C. Stone, J. B. Taggart, D. Cooke, D. Cotter, R. Hynes, C. McCamley, T. Cross, and A. Ferguson. 1997. Genetic impact of escaped farmed Atlantic salmon (*Salmo salar* L.) on native populations: use of DNA profiling to assess freshwater performance of wild, farmed, and hybrid progeny in a natural river environment. *ICES Journal of Marine Science* 54:1–11.

McGlynn, T. P. 1999. Non-native ants are smaller than related native ants. *American Naturalist* 154:690–699.

McIntosh, R. P. 1998. The myth of community as organism. *Perspectives in Biology and Medicine* 41:426–438.

McIntosh, A. R., and C. R. Townsend. 1994. Interpopulation variation in mayfly antipredator tactics: differential effects of contrasting predatory fish. *Ecology* 75:2078–2090.

McKenzie, J. A. 1996. *Ecological and evolutionary aspects of insecticide resistance*. Environmental Intelligence Unit. Austin, Tex.: R. G. Landes/Academic Press.

McKinney, K. K., and N. L. Fowler. 1991. Genetic adaptations to grazing and mowing in the unpalatable grass *Cenchrus incertus*. *Oecologia* 88:238–242.

McKinney, M. L., and J. L. Lockwood. 2001. Biotic homogenization: a sequential and selective process. pp. 1–17, *in* J. L. Lockwood and M. L. McKinney (Eds.), *Biotic homogenization*. New York: Kluwer Academic/Plenum Publishers.

McKinnon, J. S., and H. D. Rundle. 2002. Speciation in nature: the threespine stickleback model systems. *Trends in Ecology and Evolution* 17:480–488.

McLain, D. K., M. P. Moulton, and J. P. Sanderson. 1999. Sexual selection and extinction: the fate of plumage-dimorphic and plumage-monomorphic birds introduced onto islands. *Evolutionary Ecology Research* 1:549–565.

McMahon, R. F. 2002. Evolutionary and physiological adaptations of aquatic invasive animals: r selection versus resistance. *Canadian Journal of Fisheries and Aquatic Sciences* 59:1235–1244.

McNaughton, S. J. 1983. Compensatory plant growth as a response to herbivory. *Oikos* 40:329–336.

McPhail, J. D. 1994. Speciation and the evolution of reproductive isolation in the sticklebacks (*Gasterosteus*) of south-western British Columbia. pp. 399–437, *in* M. A. Bell and S. A. Foster (Eds.), *The evolutionary biology of the threespine stickleback*. Oxford, England: Oxford University Press.

McPheron, B. A., D. C. Smith, and S. H. Berlocher. 1988. Genetic differences between host races of *Rhagoletis pomonella. Nature* 336:64–66.

Medal, J. C., M. D. Vitorino, D. H. Habeck, J. L. Gilmore, J. H. Pedrosa, and L. P. DeSousa. 1999. Host specificity of *Heteroperreyia hubrichi* Malaise (Hymenoptera: Pergidae), a potential biological control agent of Brazilian peppertree (*Schinus terebinthefolius* Raddi). *Biological Control* 14:60–65.

Meekins, J. F., H. E. Ballard, Jr., and B. C. McCarthy. 2001. Genetic variation and molecular biogeography of a North American invasive plant (*Allaria petiolaria*, Brassicaceae). *International Journal of Plant Science* 162:161–169.

Meffe, G. K., S. C. Weeks, P. Mulvey, and K. L. Kandl. 1996. Genetic differences in thermal tolerance of mosquitofish from ambient and thermally elevated ponds. *Canadian Journal of Fisheries and Aquatic Sciences* 52:2704–2711.

Meinesz, A. 1999. *Killer algae.* Chicago, Ill.: University of Chicago Press.

Memmott, J., S.V. Fowler, Q. Paynter, A. W. Sheppard, and P. Syrett. 2000. The invertebrate fauna on broom, *Cytisus scoparius*, in two native and two exotic habitats. *Acta Oecologica* 21:213–222.

Merilä, J., M. Björklund, and A. J. Baker. 1996. The successful founder: Genetics of introduced Greenfinch (*Carduelis chloris*) populations in New Zealand. *Heredity* 77:410–422.

Messenger, P., and R. van den Bosch. 1971. The adaptability of introduced biological control agents. pp. 68–92, *in* C. B. Huffaker (Ed.), *Biological control*. New York: Plenum.

Meusnier, I., M. Valero, C. Destombe, C. Godé, E. Desmarais, F. Bonhomme, W. T. Stam, and J. L. Olsen. 2002. Polymerase chain reaction-single strand conformation polymorphism analyses of nuclear and chloroplast DNA provide evidence for recombination, multiple introductions and nascent speciation in the *Caulerpa taxifolia* complex. *Molecular Ecology* 11:2317–2325.

Meyer, K. F. 1942. The known and the unknown in plague. *The American Journal of Tropical Medicine* 22:9–36.

Meyer, S. E., and P. S. Allen. 1999. Ecological genetics of seed germination regulation in *Bromus tectorum* L. I. Phenotypic variance among and within populations. *Oecologia* 120:27–34.

Meyer, J.-Y., and J. Florence. 1996. Tahiti's native flora endangered by the invasion of *Miconia calvescens* DC. (Melastomaceae). *Journal of Biogeography* 23:775–781.

Michaud, J. P. 2002. Classical biological control: A critical review of recent programs against citrus pests in Florida. *Annals of the Entomological Society of America* 94:531–540.

Miller, R. R., J. D. Williams, and J. E. Williams. 1989. Extinctions of North American fishes during the past century. *Fisheries* 14:22–38.

Miller, G. H., J. W. Magee, B. J. Johnson, M. L. Fogel, N. A. Spooner, M. T. McCulloch, and L. K. Ayliffe. 1999. Pleistocene extinction of *Genornis newtoni*: human impact on Australian megafauna. *Science* 283:205–208.

Milne, R. I., and R. J. Abbott. 2000. Origin and evolution of invasive naturalized material of *Rhododendron ponticum* L. in the British Isles. *Molecular Ecology* 9:541–556.

Mitchell, C. E., and A. G. Power. 2003. Release of invasive plants from fungal and viral pathogens. *Nature* 421:625–727.

Moller, H. 1985. Tree wetas (*Hemideina crassicruris*) (Orthoptera: Stenopalmatidae) of Stephens Island, Cook Strait. *New Zealand Journal of Zoology* 12:55–69.

Molloy, D. P., A. Y. Karatayev, L. E. Burlakova, D. P. Kurandina, and F. Laruelle. 1997. Natural enemies of zebra mussels: predators, parasites, and ecological competitors. *Reviews in Fisheries Science* 5:27–97.

Monath, T. P. 1995. Dengue: the risk to developed and developing countries. pp. 43–58, *in* B. Roizman (Ed.) *Infectious diseases in an age of change: the impact of human ecology and behavior on disease transmission.* Washington, D. C.: National Academy of Sciences, National Academy Press.

Moodie, G. E. E. 1972. Predation, natural selection and adaptation in an unusual threespine stickleback. *Heredity* 28:155–167.

Mooney, H. A., and R. J. Hobbs (Eds.). 2000. *Invasive species in a changing world.* Washington, D.C.: Island Press.

Moore, R. J. 1975. The biology of Canadian weeds. 13. *Cirsium arvense* (L.) Scop. *Canadian Journal of Plant Science* 55:1033–1048.

Mopper, S. 1996. Adaptive genetic structure in phytophagous insect populations. *Trends in Ecology and Evolution* 11:235–238.

Moran, V. C. 1980. Interactions between phytophagous insects and their *Opuntia* hosts. *Ecological Entomology* 5:153–164.

Moritz, D. M. L., and J. W. Kadereit. 2001. The genetics of evolutionary change in *Senecio vulgaris* L.: a QTL mapping approach. *Plant Biology* 3:544–552.

Morris, L. J., J. L. Walck, and S. N. Hidayati. 2002. Growth and reproduction of the invasive *Ligustrum sinense* and native *Forestiera ligustrina* (Oleaceae): implications for the invasion and persistence of a nonnative shrub. *International Journal of Plant Science* 163:1001–1010.

Morrison, L. W. 2002. Long-term impacts of an arthropod-community invasion by the imported fire ant, *Solenopsis invicta. Ecology* 83:2337–2345.

Morrison, T. W., W. E. Lynch Jr., and K. Dabrowski. 1997. Predation on zebra mussels by freshwater drum and yellow perch in western Lake Erie. *Journal of Great Lakes Research* 23:177–189.

Moulton, M. P. 1985. Morphological similarity and coexistence of congeners: an experimental test with introduced Hawaiian birds. *Oikos* 44:301–305.

Moulton, M. P., and S. L. Pimm. 1983. The introduced Hawaiian avifauna: Biogeographic evidence for competition. *American Naturalist* 121:669–690.

Moulton, M. P., and S. L. Pimm. 1987. Morphological assortment in introduced Hawaiian passerines. *Evolutionary Ecology* 1:113–124.

Moyle, P. B., and T. Light. 1996. Biological invasions of fresh water: empirical rules and assembly theory. *Biological Conservation* 78:149–161.

Mueller-Dombois, D., and L. L. Loope. 1990. Some unique ecological aspects of oceanic island ecosystems. *Monographs in Systematic Botany of the Missouri Botanical Garden* 32:21–27.

Muir, W. M., and R. D. Howard. 2002. Methods to assess ecological risks of transgenic fish releases. pp. 355–383, *in* D. K. Letourneau and B. E. Burrows (Eds.), *Genetically engineered organisms: Assessing environmental and human health effects.* Boca Raton, Fla., CRC Press.

Müller, J. C., S. Schramm, and A. Seitz. 2002. Genetic and morphological differentiation of *Dikerogammarus* invaders and their invasion history in Central Europe. *Freshwater Biology* 47:2039–2048.

Murray, N. D. 1982. Ecology and evolution of the *Opuntia-Cactoblastis* ecosystem in Australia. pp. 17–30, *in* J. S. F. Barker and W. T. Starmer (Eds.), *Ecological genetics and evolution. The cactus-yeast-Drosophila model system.* Sydney, Australia: Academic Press.

Naeem, S., J. M. H. Knops, D. Tilman, K. M. Howe, T. Kennedy, and S. Gale. 2000. Plant diversity increases resistance to invasion in the absence of covarying extrinsic factors. *Oikos* 91:97–108.

Nalepa, T. F., D. J. Hartson, D. L. Fanslow, and G. A. Lang. 2001. Recent population changes in freshwater mussels (Bivalvia: Unionidae) and zebra mussels (*Dreissena polymorpha*) in Lake St. Clair, U. S. A. *American Malacological Bulletin* 16:141–145.

National Academy of Science. 1986. *Pesticide resistance: strategies and tactics for management.* Washington, D. C.: National Academies Press.

National Research Council. 2002. *Predicting invasions of nonindigenous plants and plant pests.* Washington, D. C.: National Academy Press.

Navajas y Navarro, M., J. Cassaing, and H. Croset. 1989. Demographie et dispersion d'une population sauvage de *Mus musculus domesticus*: comparison avec une population continentale. *Zeitschrift für Saugetierkund* 54:286–295.

Nemani, R. R., C. D. Keeling, H. Hashimoto, W. M. Jolly, S. C. Piper, C. J. Tucker, R. B. Myeni, and S. W. Running. 2003. Climate-driven increases in global terrestrial net primary production from 1982 to 1999. *Science* 300:1560–1563.

Neuffer, B., and M. Meyer-Wolff. 1996. Ecotypic variation in relation to man made habitats in *Capsella*: field and trampling area. *Flora* 191:49–57.

Neuhauser, C., D. A. Andow, G. E. Heimpelk, G. May, R. G. Shaw, and S. Wagenius. 2003. Community genetics: expanding the synthesis of ecology and genetics. *Ecology* 84:545–558.

Newcombe, G., B. Stirling, S. McDonald, and J. R. Bradshaw. 2000. *Melampsora* × *columbiana*, a natural hybrid of *M. medusae* and *M. occidentalis. Mycological Research* 104:261–274.

Newcombe, G., B. Stirling, and H. D. Bradshaw Jr. 2001. Abundant pathogenic variation in the new hybrid rust *Melampsora* × *columbiana* on hybrid poplar. *Phytopathology* 91:981–985.

Newman, R. M., and D. D. Biesboer. 2000. A decline of Eurasian watermilfoil in Minnesota associated with the milfoil weevil, *Euhrychiopsis lecontei*. *Journal of Aquatic Plant Management* 38:105–111.

Newman, R. M., M. E. Borman, and S. W. Castro. 1997. Developmental performance of the weevil *Euhrychiopsis lecontei* on native and exotic watermilfoil host plants. *Journal of the North American Benthological Society* 16:627–634.

Niemalä, P., and W. J. Mattson. 1996. Invasion of North American forests by European phytophagous insects. *BioScience* 46:741–753.

Niemelä, J., and J. R. Spence. 1991. Distribution and abundance of an exotic ground-beetle (Carabidae): a test of community impact. *Oikos* 62:351–359.

Novak, S. J., and R. N. Mack. 1993. Genetic variation in *Bromus tectorum* (Poaceae): comparison between native and introduced populations. *Heredity* 71:167–176.

Novak, S. J., and R. N. Mack. 1995. Allozyme diversity in the apomictic vine *Bryonia alba* (Cucurbitaceae): potential consequences of multiple introductions. *American Journal of Botany* 82:1153–1162.

Novak, S. J., and R. N. Mack. 2001. Tracing plant introduction and spread: genetic evidence from *Bromus tectorum* (cheatgrass). *BioScience* 51:114–122.

Novak, S. J., and A. Y. Welfley. 1997. Genetic diversity in the introduced clonal grass *Poa bulbosa* (bulbous bluegrass). *Northwest Science* 71:271–280.

Novak, S. J., R. N. Mack, and D. E. Soltis. 1991a. Genetic variation in *Bromus tectorum* (Poaceae): population differentiation in its North American range. *American Journal of Botany* 78:1150–1161.

Novak, S. J., D. E. Soltis, and P. S. Soltis. 1991b. Owenby's tragopogons: 40 years later. *American Journal of Botany* 78:1586–1600.

Novak, S. J., R. N. Mack, and P. S. Soltis. 1993. Genetic variation in *Bromus tectorum* (Poaceae): introduction dynamics in North America. *Canadian Journal of Botany* 71:1441–1448.

Obrycki, J. J., J. E. Losey, O. R. Taylor, and L. C. H. Jesse. 2001. Transgenic insecticidal corn: beyond insecticidal toxicity to ecological complexity. *BioScience* 51:353–361.

O'Hanlon, P. C., D. T. Briese, and R. Peakall. 2000. Know your enemy: The use of molecular ecology in the *Onopordum* biological control project. pp. 281–288, *in* N. R. Spencer (Ed.) *Proceedings of the X International Symposium on Biological Control of Weeds*, Bozeman, Mont.: Montana State University.

Ohmart, C. P., and P. B. Edwards. 1991. Insect herbivory on eucalypts. *Annual Review of Entomology* 36:637–657.

Olson, S. L., and H. F. James. 1984. The role of Polynesians in the extinction of the avifauna of the Hawaiian Islands. pp. 768–780, *in* P. S. Martin and R. G. Klein (Eds.), *Quaternary extinctions*. Tucson, Ariz.: University of Arizona Press USA.

Orr, M. R., and S. H. Seike. 1998. Parasitoids deter foraging by Argentine ants (*Linepithema humile*) in their native habitat in Brazil. *Oecologia* 117:420–425.

Osier, T. L., S.-Y. Hwang and R. L. Lindroth. 2000. Effects of phytochemical variation in quaking aspen *Populus tremuloides* clones on gypsy moth *Lymantria dispar* performance in the field and laboratory. *Ecological Entomology* 25:197–207.

O'Steen, S., A. J. Cullum and A. F. Bennett. 2002. Rapid evolution of escape ability in Trinidadian guppies (*Poecilia reticulata*). *Evolution* 56:776–784.

Otto, S. P., and J. Whitton. 2000. Polyploid incidence and evolution. *Annual Review of Genetics* 34:1–37.

Ovenden, J. R., and R. W. G. White. 1990. Mitochondrial and allozyme genetics of incipient speciation in a landlocked population of *Galaxias truttaceus* (Pices: Galaxiidae). *Genetics* 124:701–716.

Owen, R. B., R. Crossley, T. C. Johnson, D. Tweddle, I. Kornfield, S. Davidson, D. H. Eccles, and D. E. Engstrom. 1990. Major low levels of Lake Malawi and their implications for speciation rates in cichlid fishes. *Proceedings of the Royal Society of London B* 240:519–553.

Owenby, M. 1950. Natural hybridization and amphiploidy in the genus *Tragopogon*. *American Journal of Botany* 37:487–499.

Paige, K. N. 1992. Overcompensation in response to mammalian herbivory: from mutualistic to antagonistic interactions. *Ecology* 73:2076–2085.

Paine, T. D., and J. G. Millar. 2002. Insect pests of eucalypts in California: implications of managing invasive species. *Bulletin of Entomological Research* 92:147–151.

Paine, T. D., D. L. Dahlsten, J. G. Miller, M. S. Hoddle, and L. M. Hanks. 2000. UC scientists apply IPM techniques to new eucalyptus pests. *California Agriculture* 54(6):8–13.

Painter, E. L., J. K. Detling, and D. A. Steingraeber. 1989. Effects of grazing history, defoliation, and frequency-dependent competition on two North American grasses. *American Journal of Botany* 76:1368–1380.

Palm, M. E. 2001. Systematics and the impact of invasive fungi on agriculture in the United States. *BioScience* 51:141–147.

Palumbi, S. 2001. Humans as the world's greatest evolutionary force. *Science* 293:1786–1790.

Pappert, R. A., J. L. Hamrick, and L. A. Donovan. 2000. Genetic variation in *Pueraria lobata* (Fabaceae), an introduced, clonal, invasive plant of the southeastern United States. *American Journal of Botany* 87:1240–1245.

Parchman, T. L., and C. W. Benkman. 2002. Diversifying coevolution between crossbills and black spruce on Newfoundland. *Evolution* 56:1663–1672.

Parker, P. G., A. A. Snow, M. A. Schug, G. C. Booton, and P. A. Fuerst. 1998. What molecules can tell us about populations: choosing and using a molecular marker. *Ecology* 79:361–382.

Parkin, D. T., and S. R. Cole. 1985. Genetic differentiation and rates of evolution in some introduced populations of the house sparrow, *Passer domesticus*, in Australia and New Zealand. *Heredity* 54:15–23.

Parmesan, C. 1996. Climate and species range. *Nature* 382:765–766.

Parmesan, C., N. Ryrholm, C. Stefanescu, J. K. Hill, C. D. Thomas, H. Descimon, B. Huntley, et al. 1999. Poleward shifts in geographical ranges of butterfly species associated with regional warming. *Nature* 399:579–583.

Paterson, A. H., K. F. Schertz, Y. R. Lin, S. C. Liu, and Y. L. Chang. 1995. The weediness of wild plants: molecular analysis of genes responsible for dispersal and persistence of johnsongrass (*Sorghum halepense* L. Pers.). *Proceedings of the National Academy of Sciences USA* 92:6127–6131.

Patten, M. A., and K. F. Campbell. 1998. Has brood parasitism selected for earlier nesting in the California Gnatcatcher? *Western Birds* 29:290–298.

Patton, J. L., and P. V. Brylski. 1987. Pocket gophers in alfalfa fields: causes and consequences of habitat-related body size variation. *American Naturalist* 130:493–506.

Patton, J. L., and M. F. Smith. 1990. *The evolutionary dynamics of the pocket gopher* Thomomys bottae, *with emphasis on California populations.* University of California Publications in Zoology 123, 161 pp., Berkley, Calif.

Patton, J. L., S. Y. Yang, and P. Myers. 1975. Genetic and morphological divergence among introduced rat populations (*Rattus rattus*) of the Galapagos archipelago, Ecuador. *Systematic Zoology* 24:296–310.

Pemberton, R. W. 2000. Predictable risk to native plants in weed biological control. *Oecologia* 125:489–494.

Peñuelas, J., and I. Filella. 2001. Responses to a warming world. *Science* 294:793–795.

Peñuelas, J., I. Filella, and P. Comas. 2002. Changed plant and animal life cycles from 1952 to 2000 in the Mediterranean region. *Global Change Biology* 8:531–544.

Pergams, O. R. W., and M. V. Ashley. 2001. Microevolution in island rodents. *Genetica* 112–113:245–256.

Perry, W. L., J. E. Feder, G. Dwyer, and D. M. Lodge. 2001a. Hybrid zone dynamics and species replacement between *Orconectes* crayfishes in a northern lake. *Evolution* 55:1153–1166.

Perry, W. L., J. E. Feder, and D. M. Lodge. 2001b. Implications of hybridization between introduced and resident *Orconectes* crayfish. *Conservation Biology* 15:1656–1666.

Perry, W. L., D. M. Lodge, and J. L. Feder. 2002. Importance of hybridization between indigenous and nonindigenous freshwater species: an overlooked threat to North American biodiversity. *Systematic Biology* 51:255–275.

Peterson, R. A. 1962. Factors affecting resistance to heavy grazing in needle-and-thread grass. *Journal of Range Management* 15:183–189.

Petren, K., B. R. Grant, and P. R. Grant. 1999. A phylogeny of Darwin's finches based on microsatellite DNA length variation. *Proceedings of the Royal Society of London B, Biological Sciences* 266:321–330.

Petrie, S. A., and R. W. Knapton. 1999. Rapid increase and subsequent decline of zebra and quagga mussels in Long Point Bay, Lake Erie: possible influence of waterfowl predation. *Journal of Great Lakes Research* 25:772–782.

Phillips, P. A., and M. M. Barnes. 1975. Host race formation among sympatric apple, walnut, and plum populations of the codling moth, *Laspeyresia pomonella*. *Annals of the Entomological Society of America* 68:1053–1060.

Pimentel, D., ed. 2002. *Biological invasions: economic and environmental costs of alien plant, animal, and microbe species.* Boca Raton, Fla.: CRC Press.

Pimentel, D., L. Lach, R. Zuniga, and D. Morrison. 2000. Environmental and economic costs associated with non-indigenous species in the United States. *BioScience* 50:53–65.

Pimentel, D., S. McNair, J. Janecka, J. Wrightman, C. Simmonds, C. O'Connell, E. Wong, et al. 2001. Economic and environmental threats of alien plant, animal, and microbe invasions. *Agriculture, Ecosystems and Environment* 84:1–20.

Polley, H. W., and J. K. Detling. 1990. Grazing-mediated differentiation in *Agropyron smithii*: evidence from populations with different grazing histories. *Oikos* 57:326–332.

Pornkulwat, S., S. R. Skoda, G. T. Thomas, and J. E. Foster. 1998. Random amplified polymorphic DNA used to identify variation in ecotypes of the European corn borer (Lepidoptera: Pyralidae). *Annals of the Entomological Society of America* 91:719–725.

Porter, S. D., and D. A. Savignano. 1990. Invasion of polygyne fire ants decimates native ants and disrupts arthropod community. *Ecology* 71:2095–2106.

Potter, D. A., and D. W. Held. 2002. Biology and management of the Japanese beetle. *Annual Review of Entomology* 47:175–205.

Prokopy, R. J., S. R. Diehl, and S. S. Cooley. 1988. Behavioral evidence for host races in *Rhagoletis pomonella* flies. Oecologia 76:138–147.

Pyšek, P. 1997. Clonality and plant invasions: can a trait make a difference? pp. 405–427, *in* H. de Kroon and J. van Groenendael (Eds.), *The ecology and evolution of clonal plants*. Leiden, The Netherlands: Backhuys Publishers.

Quinn, J. A., and R. V. Miller. 1967. A biotic selection study utilizing *Muhlenbergia montana*. *Bulletin of the Torrey Botanical Club* 94:423–432.

Quinn, T. P., M. T. Kinnison, and M. J. Unwin. 2001. Evolution of chinook salmon (*Oncorhynchus tshawytscha*) populations in New Zealand: pattern, rate, process. *Genetica* 112–113:493–513.

Rafanut, C. G. 1995. *A comparative study of the Wellington tree weta,* Hemideina crassidens *(Blanchard, 1851) in the presence and absence of rodents*. M. Sc. Thesis. Victoria University, Wellington, New Zealand.

Ramakrishnan, A. P., C. C. Coleman, S. E. Meyer, and D. J. Fairbanks. 2001. *Microsatellite markers and polymorphism in cheatgrass* (Bromus tectorum *L.*). USDA Forest Service Proceedings RMRS-P-21:95–97.

Rappole, J. H., and Z. Hubálek. 2003. Migratory birds and West Nile Virus. *Journal of Applied Microbiology* 94:47S–58S.

Rappole, J. H., S. R. Derrickson, and Z. Hubálek. 2000. *Migratory birds and spread of West Nile Virus in the western hemisphere*. CDC Online 6(4):1–16. 〈http://www.cdc.gov/ncidod/eid/vol6no4/rappole.htm〉.

Ratcliffe, R. H., S. E. Cambron, K. L. Flanders, N. A. Bosque-Perez, S. L. Clement, and H. W. Ohm. 2000. Biotype composition of Hessian fly (Diptera: Cecidomyiidae) populations from the southeastern, midwestern, and northeastern United States and virulence to resistance genes in wheat. *Journal of Economic Entomology* 93:1319–1328.

Rausher, M. D. 2001. Co-evolution and plant resistance to natural enemies. *Nature* 411:857–864.

Reichard, S. H., and C. W. Hamilton. 1997. Predicting invasions of woody plants introduced into North America. *Conservation Biology* 11:193–203.

Reichard, S. H., and P. White. 2001. Horticulture as a pathway of invasive plant introductions in the United States. *BioScience* 51:103–113.

Reid, W.V., and K. R. Miller. 1989. *Keeping options alive: The scientific basis for conserving biodiversity.* Washington, D.C.: World Resources Institute.

Reimchen, T. E. 1980. Spine deficiency and polymorphism in a population of *Gasterosteus aculeatus*: an adaptation to predators? *Canadian Journal of Zoology* 58:49–61.

Reimchen, T. E. 1994. Predators and morphological evolution in threespine stickleback. pp. 240–276, in M. A. Bell and S. A. Foster (Eds.), *The evolutionary biology of the threespine stickleback.* Oxford, England: Oxford University Press.

Reimchen, T. E., and P. Nosil. 2002. Temporal variation in divergent selection on spine number in threespine stickleback. *Evolution* 56:2472–2483.

Reisenbichler, R. R., and S. P. Rubin. 1999. Genetic changes from artificial propagation of Pacific salmon affect the productivity and viability of supplemented populations. *ICES Journal of Marine Science* 56:459–466.

Rejmánek, M. 1996. A theory of seed plant invasiveness: the first sketch. *Biological Conservation* 78:171–181.

Reznick, D. N., and C. K. Ghalambor. 2001. The population ecology of contemporary adaptations: what empirical studies reveal about the conditions that promote adaptive evolution. *Genetica* 112–113:183–189.

Reznick, D. A., H. Bryga, and J. A. Endler. 1999. Experimentally induced life-history evolution in a natural population. *Nature* 346:357–359.

Rhymer, J. M., and D. Simberloff. 1996. Extinction by hybridization and introgression. *Annual Review of Ecology and Systematics* 27:83–109.

Ribera Siguan, M. A. 1996. The spread of the tropical alga *Caulerpa taxifolia* in the Mediterranean Sea. *Aliens* 3:12.

Ricciardi, A. 2001. Facilitative interactions among aquatic invaders: is an "invasional meltdown" occurring in the Great Lakes? *Canadian Journal of Fisheries and Aquatic Sciences* 58:2513–2525.

Ricciardi, A., and H. J. MacIsaac. 2000. Recent mass invasion of the North American Great Lakes by Ponto-Caspian species. *Trends in Ecology and Evolution* 15:62–65.

Ricciardi, A., and J. B. Rasmussen. 1998. Predicting the identity and impact of future biological invaders: a priority for aquatic resource management. *Canadian Journal of Aquatic and Fisheries Science* 55:1759–1765.

Ricciardi, A., F. L. Snyder, D. O. Kelch, and H. M. Reiswig. 1995. Lethal and sublethal effects of sponge overgrowth on introduced Dreissenid mussels in the Great Lakes-St. Lawrence River system. *Canadian Journal of Fisheries and Aquatic Sciences* 52:2695–2703.

Rice, K. J., and R. N. Mack. 1991. Ecological genetics of *Bromus tectorum*. I. A hierarchical analysis of phenotypic variation. *Oecologia* 77:77–83.

Richardson, B. J. 2001. Calcivirus, myxoma virus and the wild rabbit in Australia: a tale of three invasions. pp. 67–87, in G. L. Smith, W. L. Irving, J. W. McCauley, and D. J. Rowlands (Eds.), *SGM Symposium 60: New challenges to health: the threat of virus infection.* Cambridge, England: Cambridge University Press.

Richardson, D. M., N. Allsopp, C. M. D'Antonio, S. J. Milton, and M. Rejmánek. 2000. Plant invasions—the role of mutalisms. *Biological Reviews* 75:65–93.

Ricklefs, R. E., and E. Bermingham. 1999. Taxon cycles in the Lesser Antillean avifauna. *Ostrich* 70(1):49–59.

Ricklefs, R. E., and E. Bermingham. 2001. Nonequilibrium diversity dynamics of the Lesser Antillean avifauna. *Science* 294: 1522–1524.

Ricklefs, R. E., and E. Bermingham. 2002. The concept of the taxon cycle in biogeography. *Global Ecology & Biogeography* 11:353–361.

Ricklefs, R. E., and G. W. Cox. 1972. Taxon cycles in the West Indian avifauna. *American Naturalist* 106:195–219.

Ridenour, W. M., and R. A. Callaway. 2001. The relative importance of allelopathy in interference: the effects of an invasive weed on a native bunchgrass. *Oecologia* 126:444–450.

Rieseberg, L. H. 1991. Homoploid reticulate evolution in *Helianthus* (Asteraceae): evidence from ribosomal genes. *American Journal of Botany* 78:1218–1237.

Rieseberg, L. H. 1997. Hybrid origins of plant species. *Annual Review of Ecology and Systematics* 28:359–389.

Rieseberg, L. H., C. Van Fossen, and A. Desrochers. 1995. Hybrid speciation accompanied by genomic reorganization in wild sunflowers. *Nature* 375:313–316.

Rieseberg, L. H., O. Raymond, D. M. Rosenthal, Z. Lai, K. Livingstone, T. Nakazato, J. L. Durphy, A. E. Schwarzbach, L. A. Donovan, and C. Lexer. 2003. Major ecological transitions in wild sunflowers facilitated by hybridization. *Science* 301:1211–1216.

Rieske, L. K., C. C. Rhoades, and S. P. Miller. 2003. Foliar chemistry and gypsy moth, *Lymantria dispar* (L.), herbivory on pure American chestnut, *Castanea dentata* (Fam. Fagaceae) and a disease-resistant hybrid. *Environmental Entomology* 32:359–365.

Rizzo, D. M., M. Garbelotto, J. M. Davidson, G. W. Slaughter, and S. T. Koike. 2002. *Phytophthora ramorum* and sudden oak death in California: I. Host relationships. *USDA Forest Service General Technical Report PSW-GTR-184,* pp. 733–740.

Roberts, R. G., T. F. Flannery, L. K. Ayliffe, H. Yoshida, J. M. Olley, G. J. Prideaux, G. M. Laslett, et al. 2001. New ages for the last Australian megafauna: continent-wide extinction about 46,000 years ago. *Science* 292:1888–1892.

Robinson, B. W., and D. Schluter. 2000. Natural selection and the evolution of adaptive genetic variation in northern freshwater fishes. pp. 59–94, *in* T. Mosseau, B. Sinervo, and J. A. Endler (Eds.), *Adaptive genetic variation in the wild.* New York: Oxford University Press.

Robinson, B. W., and D. S. Wilson. 1994. Character release and displacement in fishes: a neglected literature. *American Naturalist* 144:596–627.

Robinson, B. W., and D. S. Wilson. 1996. Genetic variation and phenotypic plasticity in a polymorphic population of pumpkinseed sunfish (*Lepomis gibbosus*). *Evolutionary Ecology* 10:631–652.

Robinson, G. R., J. F. Quinn, and M. L. Stanton. 1995. Invasibility of experimental habitat islands in a California winter annual grassland. *Ecology* 76:786–794.

Robinson, B. W., D. S. Wilson, and A. S. Margosian. 2000. A pluralistic analysis of character release in pumpkinseed sunfish (*Lepomis gibbosus*). *Ecology* 81:2799–2812.

Roché, B. F., Jr., and C. T. Roché. 1991. Identification, introduction, distribution, ecology, and economics of *Centaurea* species. pp. 274–291, *in* L. F. James, J. O. Evans, M. H. Ralphs, and R. D. Child (Eds.), *Noxious range weeds.* Boulder, Colo.: Westview Press.

Rodda, G. H., T. H. Fritts, M. J. McCoid, and E. W. Campbell III. 1999. An overview of the biology of the brown treesnake (*Boiga irregularis*), a costly introduced pest on Pacific islands. pp. 44–79, *in* G. H. Roda, Y. Sawai, D. Chiszar, and H. Tanaka (Eds.), *Problem snake management: the habu and the brown treesnake.* Ithaca, N.Y.: Comstock Publishing Associates.

Roehrdanz, R. L. 2001. Genetic differentiation of southeastern boll weevil and Thurberia weevil populations of *Anthonomus grandis* (Coleoptera: Curculionidae) using mitochondrial DNA. *Annals of the Entomological Society of America* 94:928–935.

Roff, D. A. 1990. The evolution of flightlessness in insects. *Ecological Monographs* 60:389–421.

Rogers, W. E., and E. Siemann. 2002. Effects of simulated herbivory and resource availability on native and invasive exotic tree seedlings. *Basic and Applied Ecology* 3:297–307.

Rolff, J., and A. R. Kraaijeveld. 2001. Host preference and survival in selected lines of a *Drosophila* parasitoid, *Asobara tabida. Journal of Evolutionary Biology* 14:742–745.

Root, T. L., and S. H. Schneider. 2002. Climate change: overview and implications for wildlife. pp. 1–56, *in* S. H. Schneider and T. L. Root (Eds.), *Wildlife response to climate change.* Washington, D. C.: Island Press.

Root, T. L., J. T. Price, K. R. Hall, S. H. Schneider, C. Rosenzweig, and J. A. Pounds. 2003. Fingerprints of global warming on wild animals and plants. *Nature* 421:57–60.

Rosenzweig, M. L. 2001. The four questions: what does the introduction of exotic species do to diversity? *Evolutionary Ecology Research* 3:361–367.

Ross, H. A. 1983. Genetic differentiation of starling (*Sturnus vulgaris*: Aves) in New Zealand and Great Britain. *Journal of Zoology, London* 201:351–362.

Ross, K. G., E. L. Vargo, L. Keller, and J. C. Trager. 1993. Effect of a founder event on variation in the genetic sex-determining system of the fire ant *Solenopsis invicta. Genetics* 135:843–854.

Ross, K. G., E. L. Vargo, and L. Keller. 1996. Social evolution in a new environment: the case of introduced fire ants. *Proceedings of the National Academy of Science USA* 93:3021–3025.

Rossiter, M., J. C. Schultz, and I. T. Baldwin. 1988. Relationships among defoliation, red oak phenolics, and gypsy moth growth and reproduction. *Ecology* 69:267–277.

Rowe, M. L., D. J. Lee, S. J. Nissen, and R. A. Masters. 1997. Genetic variation in

North American leafy spurge (*Euphorbia esula*) determined by DNA markers. *Weed Science* 45:446–454.

Roy, S., J.-P. Simon, and F.-J. Lapointe. 2000. Determination of the origin of the cold-adapted populations of barnyard grass (*Echinochloa crus-galli*) in eastern North America: a total-evidence approach using RAPD DNA and DNA sequences. *Canadian Journal of Botany* 78:1505–1513.

Saint-Laurent, R., M. Legault, and L. Bernachez. 2003. Divergent selection maintains adaptive differentiation despite high gene flow between sympatric rainbow smelt ecotypes (*Osmerus mordax* Mitchell). *Molecular Ecology* 12:315–330.

Sakai, A. K., F. W. Allendorf, J. S. Holt, D. M. Lodge, J. Molofsky, K. A. With, and S. Baughman. 2001. The population biology of invasive species. *Annual Review of Ecology and Systematics* 32:305–332.

Sammons, A. E., C. R. Edwards, L. W. Bledsoe, P. J. Boeve, and J. J. Stewart. 1997. Behavioral and feeding assays reveal a western corn rootworm (Coleoptera: Chrysomelidae) variant that is attracted to soybean. *Environmental Entomology* 26:1336–1342.

Samways, M. J. 1997. Classical biological control and biodiversity conservation: what risks are we prepared to accept? *Biodiversity and Conservation* 6:1309–1316.

Sanders, R. W. 1987. Identity of *Lantana depressa* and *L. ovalifolia* (Verbenaceae) of Florida and the Bahamas. *Systematic Botany* 12:44–59.

Sato, A., C. O'hUigin, F. Figueroa, P. R. Grant, B. R. Grant, H. Tichy, and J. Klein. 1999. Phylogeny of Darwin's finches as revealed by mtDNA sequences. *Proceedings of the National Academy of Sciences USA* 96:5101–5106.

Sax, D., S. D. Gaines, and J. H. Brown. 2002. Species invasions exceed extinctions on islands worldwide: a comparative study of plants and birds. *American Naturalist* 160:766–783.

Sayyed, A. H., H. Cerda, and D. J. Wright. 2003. Could *Bt* transgenic crops have nutritionally favourable effects on resistant insects? *Ecology Letters* 6:167–169.

Schaffelke, B., N. Murphy, and S. Uthicke. 2002. Using genetic techniques to investigate the sources of the invasive alga *Caulerpa taxifolia* in three new locations in Australia. *Marine Pollution Bulletin* 44:204–210.

Schindler, D. W. 1998. A dim future for boreal waters and landscapes. *BioScience* 48:157–164.

Schluter, D. 1996. Ecological speciation in postglacial fishes. *Philosophical Transactions of the Royal Society of London B, Biological Sciences* 351:807–814.

Schluter, D. 1997. Ecological speciation in postglacial fishes. pp. 114–129, *in* P. R. Grant (Ed.), *Evolution on islands*. Oxford, England: Oxford University Press.

Schluter, D. 2000. *The ecology of adaptive radiation*. Oxford, England: Oxford University Press.

Schluter, D., and J. D. McPhail. 1992. Ecological character displacement and speciation in sticklebacks. *American Naturalist* 140:85–108.

Schluter, D., and J. D. McPhail. 1993. Character displacement and replicate adaptive radiation. *Trends in Ecology and Evolution* 8:197–200.

Schofield, E. K. 1989. Effects of introduced plants and animals on island vegetation: examples from the Galápagos Archipelago. *Conservation Biology* 3:227–237.

Schultz, J. C., D. Otte, and F. Enders. 1977. *Larrea* as a habitat component for desert arthropods. pp. 176–208 *in* T. J. Mabry, J. H. Hunziker, and J. D. R. Difeo (Eds.), *Creosote bush: biology and chemistry of Larrea in New World deserts.* Dowden, Hutchison and Ross, Stroudsberg, Pa.

Schulz, B., A.-K. Römmert, U. Dammann, H.-J. Aust, and D. Strack. 1999. The endophyte-host interaction: a balanced antagonism? *Mycological Research* 103:1275–1283.

Schwarz, D., B. A. McPheron, G. B. Hartl, E. F. Boller, and T. S. Hoffmeister. 2003. A second case of genetic host races in *Rhagoletis*? A population genetic comparison of sympatric host populations in the European cherry fruit fly, *Rhagoletis cerasi* (L.) (Diptera: Tephritidae). *Entomologia Experimentalis et Applicata* 108:11–17.

Scott, M. C., and G. S. Helfman. 2001. Native invasions, homogenization, and the mismeasure of integrity of fish assemblages. *Fisheries* 26:6–15.

Scott, J. M., and J. L. Sincock. 1985. Hawaiian birds. pp. 549–562, *in* R. L. Di Silvestro (Ed.), *Audubon wildlife report 1985.* New York: National Audubon Society.

Scott, J. M., S. Mountainspring, F. L. Ramsey, and C. B. Kepler. 1986. Forest bird communities of the Hawaiian Islands: their dynamics, ecology, and conservation. *Studies in Avian Biology* No. 9.

Seefeldt, S. S., F. L. Young, R. Zemetra, and S. S. Jones. 1999. The production of herbicide-resistant jointed goatgrass (*Aegilops cylindrica*) × wheat (*Triticum aestivum*) hybrids in the field by natural hybridization and management strategies to reduce their occurrence. *British Crop Protection Council Symposium Proceedings* No. 72:159–163.

Seehausen, O., and J. M. van Alphen. 1999. Can sympatric speciation by disruptive sexual selection explain rapid evolution of cichlid diversity in Lake Victoria? *Ecology Letters* 2:262–271.

Seehausen, O., J. M. van Alphen, and F. Witte. 1997a. Cichlid fish diversity threatened by eutrophication that curbs sexual selection. *Science* 277:1808–1811.

Seehausen, O., F. Witte, E. F. Katunzi, J. Smits, and N. Bouton. 1997b. Patterns of the remnant cichlid fauna in southern Lake Victoria. *Conservation Biology* 11:890–904.

Seehausen, O., E. Koetsier, M. V. Schneider, L. J. Chapman, C. A. Chapman, M. E. Knight, G. F. Turner, J. J. M. van Alphen, and R. Bills. 2003. Origin of the Lake Victoria cichlid species flock reconsidered: reconciling conflicting evidence with nuclear markers. *Proceedings of the Royal Society London* 270:129–137.

Seeley, R. H. 1986. Intense natural selection caused a rapid morphological transition in a living marine snail. *Proceedings of the National Academy of Sciences USA* 83:6897–6901.

Sexton, J. P., J. K. McKay, and A. Sala. 2002. Plasticity and genetic diversity may allow saltcedar to invade cold climates in North America. *Ecological Applications* 12:1652–1660.

Shea, K., and P. Chesson. 2002. Community ecology theory as a framework for biological invasions. *Trends in Ecology and Evolution* 17:170–176.

Shehata, C., L. Freed, and R. C. Cann. 2001. Changes in native and introduced bird populations on O'ahu: infectious diseases and species replacement. *Studies in Avian Biology* No. 22:264–273.

Shervis, L. J., G. M. Boush, and C. F. Koval. 1970. Infestation of sour cherries by the apple maggot: confirmation of a previously uncertain host status. *Journal of Economic Entomology* 63:294–295.

Shigesada, N., and K. Kawasaki. 1997. *Biological invasions: theory and practice.* Oxford, England: Oxford University Press.

Shonle, I., and J. Bergelson. 2000. Evolutionary ecology of the tropane alkaloids of *Datura stramonium* L. (Solanaceae). *Evolution* 54:778–788.

Sieger, L. A. 1997. The status of *Fallopia japonica* (*Reynoutria japonica*; *Polygonum cuspidatum*) in North America. pp. 95–102, *in* J. H. Brock, M. Wade, P. Pyšek, and D. Green (Eds.), *Plant invasions: studies from North America and Europe.* Leiden, The Netherlands: Backhuys Publishers.

Siemann, E., and W. E. Rogers. 2001. Genetic differences in growth of an invasive tree species. *Ecology Letters* 4:514–518.

Siemens, D. H., S. H. Garner, T. Mitchell-Olds, and R. M. Callaway. 2002. Cost of defense in the context of plant competition: *Brassica rapa* may grow *and* defend. *Ecology* 83:505–517.

Silver, H., and W. T. Silver. 1969. Growth and behavior of the coyote-like canid of northern New England with observations on canid hybrids. *Wildlife Monographs* 17:1–41.

Simberloff, D., and P. Stiling. 1996. How risky is biological control? *Ecology* 77:1965–1974.

Simberloff, D., and B. Von Holle. 1999. Positive interactions of nonindigenous species: invasional meltdown? *Biological Invasions* 1:21–32.

Simberloff, D. S., and E. O. Wilson. 1969. Experimental zoogeography of islands: A two-year record of colonization. *Ecology* 50:934–937.

Simberloff, D. S., and E. O. Wilson. 1970. Experimental zoogeography of islands: The colonization of empty islands. *Ecology* 51:278–296.

Simberloff, D., D. C. Schmitz, and T. C. Brown. 1997. *Strangers in paradise.* Washington, D. C.: Island Press.

Simberloff, D., T. Dayan, C. Jones, and G. Ogura. 2000. Character displacement and release in the small Indian mongoose, *Herpestes javanicus*. *Ecology* 81:2086–2099.

Simms, E. L. 1996. The evolutionary genetics of plant-pathogen systems. *BioScience* 46:136–145.

Simons, A. M., and M. O. Johnson. 1999. The cost of compensation. *American Naturalist* 153:683–687.

Singer, M. C., D. Ng, and C. D. Thomas. 1988. Heretability of oviposition preference and its relationship to offspring performance within a single insect population. *Evolution* 42:977–985.

Singer, M. C., C. D. Thomas, and C. Parmesan. 1993. Rapid human-induced evolution of insect-host associations. *Nature* 366:681–683.

Singer, M. C., C. D. Thomas, H. L. Billington, and C. Parmesan. 1994. Correlates of speed of evolution of host preference in a set of twelve populations of the butterfly *Euphydryas editha*. *Ecoscience* 1:107–114.

Siripattrawan, S., J.-K. Park, and D. Ó. Foighil. 2000. Two lineages of the introduced Asian freshwater clam *Corbicula* in North America. *Journal of Molluscan Studies* 66:423–429.

Skelly, D. K. 2004. Microgeographic countergradient variation in the wood frog, *Rana sylvatica*. *Evolution*.

Skelly, D. K., and L. K. Freidenburg. 2000. Effects of beaver on the thermal biology of an amphibian. *Ecology Letters* 3:483–486.

Slippers, B., M. J. Wingfield, B. D. Wingfield, and T. A. Coutinho. 2001. Population structure and possible origin of *Amylostereum areolatum* in South Africa. *Plant Pathology* 50:206–210.

Slippers, B., B. D. Wingfield, T. A. Coutinho, and M. J. Wingfield. 2002. DNA sequence and RFLP data reflect geographical spread and relationships of *Amylostereum areolatum* and its insect vectors. *Molecular Ecology* 11:1845–1854.

Smalla, K., and P. A. Sobecky. 2002. The prevalence and diversity of mobile genetic elements in bacterial communities of different environmental habitats: insights gained from different methodological approaches. *FEMS Microbiology Ecology* 42:165–175.

Smalley, E. B., R. P. Guries, and D. T. Lester. 1993. American Liberty elms and beyond: Going from the impossible to the difficult. pp. 26–45 in M. B. Sticklin and J. Sherald (Eds.), *Dutch elm disease: cellular and molecular approaches.* New York: Springer-Verlag.

Smith, D. C. 1988. Heritable divergence of *Rhagoletis pomonella* host races by seasonal asynchrony. *Nature* 336:66–67.

Smith, S. E. 1998. Variation in response to defoliation between populations of *Bouteloua curtipendula* var *cespitosa* (Poaceae) with different livestock grazing histories. *American Journal of Botany* 85:1266–1272.

Smith, T. B., and S. Skúlason. 1996. Evolutionary significance of resource polymorphisms in fishes, amphibians, and birds. *Annual Review of Ecology and Systematics* 27:111–133.

Smith, T. B., L. A. Freed, J. K. Lepson, and J. H. Carothers. 1995. Evolutionary consequences of extinctions in populations of a Hawaiian honeycreeper. *Conservation Biology* 9:107–113.

Smith, M. T., J. Bancroft, and J. Tropp. 2002. Age-specific fecundity of *Anoplophora grabripennis* (Coleoptera: Cerambicidae) on three tree species infested in the United States. *Environmental Entomology* 31:76–83.

Snow, A. A., B. Andersen, and R. B. Jorgensen. 1999. Costs of transgenic herbicide resistance introgressed from *Brassica napus* into weedy *B. rapa. Molecular Ecology* 8:605–615.

Snow, A. A., K. L. Uthus, and T. M. Culley. 2001. Fitness of hybrids between weedy and cultivated radish: implications for weed evolution. *Ecological Applications* 11:934–943.

Snow, A. A., D. Pilson, L. H. Rieseberg, M. J. Paulsen, N. Pleskac, M. R. Reagon, D. E. Wolf, and S. M. Selbo. 2003. A Bt transgene reduces herbivory and enhances fecundity in wild sunflowers. *Ecological Applications* 13:279–286.

Sobey, D. G. 1987. Differences in seed production between *Stellaria media* populations from different habitat types. *Annals of Botany* 59:543–549.

Solarz, S. L., and R. M. Newman. 2001. Variation in hostplant preference and performance by the milfoil weevil, *Euhrychiopsis lecontei* Dietz, exposed to native and exotic watermilfoils. *Oecologia* 126:66–75.

Soltis, D. E., and L. H. Rieseberg. 1986. Autopolyploidy in *Tolmiea menziesii* (Saxifragaceae): Genetic insights from enzyme electrophoresis. *American Journal of Botany* 73:310–318.

Soltis, D. E., and P. S. Soltis. 1989. Genetic consequences of autopolyploidy in *Tolmiea* (Saxifragaceae). *Evolution* 43:586–594.

Sork, V. L., K. A. Stowe, and C. Hochwender. 1993. Evidence for local adaptation in closely adjacent subpopulations of northern red oak (*Quercus rubra* L.) expressed as resistance to leaf herbivores. *American Naturalist* 142:928–936.

Southwood, T. R. E. 1961. The number of species of insect associated with various trees. *Journal of Animal Ecology* 30:1–8.

Spencer, L. J., and A. A. Snow. 2001. Fecundity of transgenic wild-crop hybrids of *Cucurbita pepo* (Cucurbitaceae): implications for crop-to-wild gene flow. *Heredity* 86: 694–702.

Spiers, A. G., and D. H. Hopcroft. 1994. Comparative studies of poplar rusts *Melampsora medusae*, *M. larici-populina* and their interspecific hybrid *M. medusae-populina*. *Mycological Research* 98:889–903.

Stace, C. A. 1991. *New flora of the British Isles.* Cambridge, England: Cambridge University Press.

Stachowicz, J. J., R. B. Whitlach, and R. W. Osman. 1999. Species diversity and invasion resistance in a marine ecosystem. *Science* 286:1577–1579.

Steadman, D. W. 1995. Prehistoric extinctions of Pacific island birds: biodiversity meets zooarcheology. *Science* 267:1123–1131.

Stearns, S. C. 1983a. A natural experiment in life history evolution: field data on the introduction of mosquitofish (*Gambusia affinis*) to Hawaii. *Evolution* 37:601–617.

Stearns, S. C. 1983b. The genetic basis of differences in life history traits among six populations of mosquitofish (*Gambusia affinis*) that shared ancestors in 1905. *Evolution* 37:618–627.

Stepien, C. A., C. D. Taylor, and K. A. Dabrowska. 2002. Genetic variability and phylogeographical patterns of a nonindigenous species invasion: a comparison of exotic vs. native zebra and quagga mussel populations. *Journal of Evolutionary Biology* 15:314–328.

Stevens, W. K. 1999. Arctic thawing may jolt sea's climate belt. *New York Times*, 7 December. Section F, p. 3.

Steward, K. K., T. K. Van, V. Carter, and A. H. Pieterse. 1984. *Hydrilla* invades Washington, D.C. and the Potomac. *American Journal of Botany* 71:162–163.

Stockwell, C. A., and S. C. Weeks. 1999. Translocations and rapid evolutionary responses in recently established populations of western mosquitofish (*Gambusia affinis*). *Animal Conservation* 2:103–110.

Stockwell, C. A., A. P. Hendry, and M. T. Kinnison. 2003. Contemporary evolution meets conservation biology. *Trends in Ecology and Evolution* 18:94–101.

Stohlgren, T. J., D. Binkley, G. W. Chong, M. A. Kalkhan, L. D. Schell, K. A. Bull, Y. Otrsuki, G. Newman, M. Bashkin, and Y. Son. 1999. Exotic plant species invade hot spots of native plant diversity. *Ecological Monographs* 69:25–46.

Stohlgren, T. J., D. T. Barnett, and J. T. Kartesz. 2003. The rich get richer: patterns of plant invasions in the United States. *Frontiers in Ecology and the Environment* 1:11–14.

Stone, C. P. 1985. Alien animals in Hawai'i's native ecosystems: toward controlling the adverse effects of introduced vertebrates. pp. 251–297, *in* C. P. Stone and J. M. Scott (Eds.), *Hawaii's terrestrial ecosystems: preservation and management.* Honolulu, Hawaii: Cooperative National Park Resources Studies Unit, University of Hawaii.

Stoner, D. S., R. Ben-Shlomo, B. Rinkevich, and I. L. Weissman. 2002. Genetic variability of *Botryllus schlosseri* invasions to the east and west coasts of the USA. *Marine Ecology Progress Series* 243:93–100.

Stowe, K. A., R. J. Marquis, C. G. Hochwender, and E. L. Simms. 2000. The evolutionary ecology of tolerance to consumer damage. *Annual Review of Ecology and Systematics* 31:565–595.

Strauss, S. Y., and A. A. Agrawal. 1999. The ecology and evolution of plant tolerance to herbivory. *Trends in Ecology and Evolution* 14:179–185.

Strayer, D. L. 1999. Effects of alien species on freshwater mollusks in North America. *Journal of the North American Benthological Society* 18:74–98.

Strong, D. R. 1974a. Rapid asymptotic species accumulation in phytophagous insect communities: the pests of cacao. *Science* 185:1064–1066.

Strong, D. R. 1974b. The insects of British trees: community equilibrium in ecological time. *Annals of the Missouri Botanical Garden* 61:692–701.

Strong, D. R. 1974c. Nonasymptotic species richness models and the insects of British trees. *Proceedings of the National Academy of Sciences USA* 71:2766–2769.

Strong, D. R. 1979. Biogeographic dynamics of insect-host plant communities. *Annual Review of Entomology* 24:89–119.

Strong, D. R., and D. A. Levin. 1975. Species richness of parasitic fungi of British tress. *Proceedings of the National Academy of Sciences USA* 72:2116–2119.

Strong, D. R., E. D. McCoy, and J. R. Ray. 1977. Time and the number of herbivore species: The pests of sugar cane. *Ecology* 58:167–175.

Strong, D. R., J. H. Lawton, and T. R. E. Southwood. 1984. *Insects on plants.* Cambridge, Mass.: Harvard University Press.

Sturm, M., C. Racine, and K. Tape. 2001. Increasing shrub abundance in the arctic. *Nature* 411:546–547.

Suarez, A. V., N. D. Tsutsui, D. A. Holway, and T. J. Case. 1999. Behavioral and genetic differentiation between native and introduced populations of the Argentine ant. *Biological Invasions* 1:43–53.

Sun, M. 1997. Population genetic structure of yellow starthistle (*Centaurea solsticialis*), a colonizing weed in the western United States. *Canadian Journal of Botany* 75:1470–1478.

Sun, M., and H. Corke. 1992. Population genetics of colonizing success of weedy rye in northern California. *Theoretical and Applied Genetics* 83:321–329.

Sun, M., and K. Ritland. 1998. Mating system of yellow starthistle (*Centaurea solsticialis*), a successful colonizer in North America. *Heredity* 80:225–232.

Sweetapple, P. J., and G. Nugent. 1999. Provenance variation in fuchsia (*Fuchsia excorticata*) in relation to palatability to possums. *New Zealand Journal of Ecology* 23:1–10.

Symstad, A. J. 2000. A test of the effects of functional group richness and composition on grassland invasibility. *Ecology* 81:99–109.

Tabashnik, B. E. 1983a. Host range evolution: the shift from native legume hosts to alfalfa by the butterfly, *Colias philodice eriphyle. Evolution* 37:150–162.

Tabashnik, B. E. 1983b. Evolution of host plant utilization in *Colias* butterflies. pp. 173–184, *in* M. D. Huettel (Ed.), *Evolutionary genetics of invertebrate behavior.* New York: Plenum.

Talbott-Roché, C., and B. F. Roché. 1991. Meadow knapweed invasion in the Pacific northwest, USA and British Columbia, Canada. *Northwest Science* 65:53–61.

Talekar, N. S., and A. M. Shelton. 1993. Biology, ecology, and management of diamondback moth. *Annual Review of Entomology* 38:275–301.

Taylor, E. B., and P. Bentzen. 1993. Evidence for multiple origins and sympatric divergence of trophic ecotypes of smelt (*Osmerus*) in northeastern North America. *Evolution* 47:813–832.

Taylor, D. J., and P. D. N. Hebert. 1993. Cryptic intercontinental hybridization in *Daphnia* (Crustaceana): the ghost of introductions past. *Proceedings of the Royal Society of London B* 254:163–168.

Tepfer, M. 2002. Risk assessment of virus-resistant transgenic plants. *Annual Review of Phytopathology* 40:467–491.

Terje, O., K. Gunnarsson, P. M. Jónasson, B. Jonsson, T. Lindem, K. P. Magnússon, H. J. Malmquist, H. Sigurjónsdóttir, S. Skúlason, and S. S. Snorrason. 1992. The arctic charr *Salvelinus alpinus* in Thingvallavatn. *Oikos* 64:305–351.

Thébaud, C., and D. Simberloff. 2001. Are plants really larger in their introduced ranges? *American Naturalist* 157:231–236.

Therriault, T. W., I. A. Grigorovich, M. A. Cristescu, H. A. M. Ketelaars, M. Viljanen, D. D. Heath, and H. J. MacIsaac. 2002. Taxonomic resolution of the genus *Bythotrephes* Leydig using molecular markers and re-evaluation of its global distribution. *Diversity and Distributions* 8:67–84.

Thibault, S. T., H. T. Luu, N. Vann, and T. A. Miller. 1999. Precise excision and transposition of piggyBac in pink bollworm embryos. *Insect Molecular Biology* 8:119–123.

Thomas, C. D., and M. C. Singer. 1998. Scale-dependent evolution of specialization in a checkerspot butterfly: from individuals to metapopulations and ecotypes. pp. 343–374, *in* S. Mopper and S. Y. Strauss (Eds.), *Genetic structure and local adaptation in natural insect populations.* New York: Chapman and Hall.

Thomas, C. D., D. Ng, M. C. Singer, J. L. B. Mallet, C. Parmesan, and H. D. Billington. 1987. Incorporation of a European weed into the diet of a North American herbivore. *Evolution* 41:892–901.

Thomas, R. E., A. M. Barnes, T. J. Quan, M. L. Beard, L. G. Carter, and C. E. Hopla. 1988. Susceptibility to *Yersina pestis* in the northern grasshopper mouse (*Onychomys leucogaster*). *Journal of Wildlife Diseases* 24:327–333.

Thomas, C. D., E. J. Bodsworth, R. J. Wilson, A. D. Simmons, Z. G. Davies, M.

Musche, and L. Conradt. 2001. Ecological and evolutionary processes at expanding range margins. *Nature* 411:577–581.

Thomas, Y., M.-T. Bethenod, L. Pelozuelo, B. Frérot, and D. Bourguet. 2003. Genetic isolation between two sympatric host-plant races of the European corn borer, *Ostrinia nubilalis* Hübner. I. Sex pheromone, moth emergence time, and parasitism. *Evolution* 57:261–273.

Thompson, J. N. 1993. Oviposition preference and the origins of geographic variation in specialization in swallowtail butterflies. *Evolution* 47:1585–1594.

Thompson, J. N. 1994. *The coevolutionary process.* Chicago, Ill.: University of Chicago Press.

Thompson, J. N. 1998. Rapid evolution as an ecological process. *Trends in Ecology and Evolution* 13:329–332.

Thompson, J. N. 1999a. What we know and do not know about coevolution: insect herbivores and plants as a test case. pp. 7–30, *in* H. Olff, V. K. Brown, and R. H. Drent (Eds.), *Herbivores: between plants and predators.* Oxford, England: Blackwell Science.

Thompson, J. N. 1999b. Specific hypotheses on the geographic mosaic of coevolution. *American Naturalist* 153:S1–S14.

Thompson, J. N. 1999c. The evolution of species interactions. *Science* 284:2116–2118.

Thompson, D. W. J., and S. Solomon. 2002. Interpretation of recent southern hemisphere climate change. *Science* 296:895–899.

Thrall, P. H., and J. J. Burdon. 2003. Evolution of virulence in a plant host-pathogen metapopulation. *Science* 299:1735–1737.

Thurber, J. M., and R. O. Peterson. 1991. Changes in body size associated with range expansion in the coyote (*Canis latrans*). *Journal of Mammalogy* 72:750–755.

Tiedje, J. M, R. K. Colwell, Y. L. Grossman, R. E. Hodson, R. E. Lenski, R. N. Mack, and P. J. Regal. 1989. The planned introduction of genetically engineered organisms: ecological considerations and recommendations. *Ecology* 70:298–315.

Ting, J. H., and J. B. Geller. 2000. Clonal diversity in introduced populations of an Asian sea anemone in North America. *Biological Invasions* 2:23–32.

Tompkins, D. M., A. R. White, and M. Boots. 2003. Ecological replacement of native red squirrels by invasive greys driven by disease. *Ecology Letters* 6:189–196.

Tooley, P. W., E. D. Goley, M. D. Carras, and N. R. O'Neill. 2002. AFLP comparisons among *Claviceps africana* isolates from the United States, Mexico, Africa, Australia, India, and Japan. *Plant Disease* 86:1247–1252.

Torchin, M. E., K. D. Lafferty, and A. M. Kuris. 2001. Release from parasites as natural enemies: increased performance of a globally introduced marine crab. *Biological Invasions* 3:333–345.

Torchin, M. E., K. D. Lafferty, A. B. Dobson, V. J. McKenzie, and A. M. Kuris. 2003. Introduced species and their missing parasites. *Nature* 421:628–630.

Townsend, C. R. 1996. Invasion biology and ecological impacts of brown trout *Salmo trutta* in New Zealand. *Biological Conservation* 78:13–22.

Townsend, C. R. 2003. Individual, population, community, and ecosystem consequences of a fish invader in New Zealand streams. *Conservation Biology* 17:38–47.

Tranel, P. J., and J. J. Wassom. 2001. Genetic relationships of common cocklebur accessions from the United States. *Weed Science* 49:318–325.

Travis, J., and R. E. Ricklefs. 1983. A morphological comparison of island and mainland assemblages of neotropical birds. *Oikos* 41:434–441.

Travis, J. M. J., and C. Dytham. 2002. Dispersal evolution during invasions. *Evolutionary Ecology Research* 4:1119–1129.

Trigiano, R. N., G. Caetano-Anollés, B. J. Bassam, and M. T. Windham. 1995. DNA amplification fingerprinting provides evidence that *Discula destructiva*, the cause of dogwood anthracnose in North America, is an introduced pathogen. *Mycologia* 87:490–500.

Trlica, M. J., and A. B. Orodho. 1989. Effects of protection from grazing on morphological and chemical characteristics of Indian ricegrass, *Oryzopsis hymenoides*. *Oikos* 56:299–308.

Trussel, G. C., and R. J. Etter. 2001. Integrating genetic and environmental forces that shape the evolution of geographic variation in a marine snail. *Genetica* 112–113:321–337.

Trussell, G. C., and M. O. Nicklin. 2002. Cue sensitivity, inducible defense, and trade-offs in a marine snail. *Ecology* 83:1635–1647.

Tsutsui, N. D., A. V. Suarez, D. A. Holway, and T. J. Case. 2000. Reduced genetic variation and the success of an invasive species. *Proceedings of the National Academy of Sciences USA* 97:5948–5953.

Tsutsui, N. D., A. V. Suarez, D. A. Holway, and T. J. Case. 2001. Relationships among native and introduced populations of the Argentine ant (*Linepithema humile*) and the source of introduced populations. *Molecular Ecology* 10:2151–2161.

Tsutsui, N. D., A. V. Suarez, and R. K. Grosberg. 2003. Genetic diversity, asymmetrical aggression, and recognition in a widespread invasive species. *Proceedings of the National Academy of Sciences USA* 100:1078–1083.

Twiddy, S. S., E. C. Holmes, and A. Rambaut. 2003. Inferring the rate and time-scale of dengue virus evolution. *Molecular Biology and Evolution* 20:122–129.

Twigg, L. E., G. R. Martin, and T. J. Lowe. 2002. Evidence of pesticide resistance in medium-sized mammalian pests: a case study with 1080 poison and Australian rabbits. *Journal of Applied Ecology* 39:549–560.

Usher, M. B., T. J. Crawford, and J. L. Banwell. 1992. An American invasion of Great Britain: the case of the native and alien squirrel (*Sciurus*) species. *Conservation Biology* 6:108–115.

Van, T. K., and P. T. Madeira. 1998. Randon amplified polymorphic DNA analysis of water spinach (*Ipomoea aquatica*) in Florida. *Journal of Aquatic Plant Management* 36:107–111.

Van der Toorn, J., and P. H. Van Tienderen. 1992. Ecotypic differentiation in *Plantago lanceolata*. pp. 269–288, *in* P. J. C. Kuiper and M. Bos (Eds.), *Plantago—A multidisciplinary study. Ecological Studies,* vol. 89. Berlin, Germany: Springer Verlag.

Van Devender, T. R. 1990. Late Quaternary vegetation and climate of the Sonoran Desert, United States and Mexico. pp. 134–165, *in* J. L. Betancourt, T. R. Van Devender, and P. S. Martin (Eds.), *Packrat middens: the last 40,000 years of biotic change.* Tucson, Ariz.: University of Arizona Press.

Van Klinken, R. D., and O. R. Edwards. 2002. Is host-specificity of weed biological control agents likely to evolve rapidly following establishment? *Ecology Letters* 5:590–596.

Van Nouhuys, S., and S. Via. 1999. Natural selection and genetic differentiation of behaviour between parasitoids from wild and cultivated habitats. *Heredity* 83:127–137.

van Riper III, C., S.G. van Riper, M.L. Goff, and M. Laird. 1986. The epizootiology and ecological significance of malaria in Hawaiian land birds. *Ecological Monographs* 56:327–344.

Van Valen, L. 1973. A new evolutionary law. *Evolutionary Theory* 1:1–30.

Vaylay, R., and E. van Santen. 2002. Application of a canonical discriminant analysis for the assessment of genetic variation in tall fescue. *Crop Science* 42:534–539.

Veit, R. R., and M. A. Lewis. 1996. Dispersal, population growth, and the Allee effect: dynamics of the house finch invasion of eastern North America. *American Naturalist* 148:255–274.

Veit, R.R., J. A. McGowan, D.G. Ainley, T.R. Wahl, and P. Pyle. 1997. Apex marine predator declines 90% in association with changing oceanic climate. *Global Change Biology* 3: 23–28.

Velkov, V.V. 2001. Stress-induced evolution and the biosafety of genetically modified microorganisms released into the environment. *Journal of Biosciences* 26:667–683.

Verlaque, M., C. F. Boudouresque, A. Meinesz, and V. Gravez. 2000. The *Caulerpa racemosa* complex (Caulerpales, Ulvophyceae) in the Mediterranean Sea. *Botanica Marina* 43:49–68.

Vermeij, G. 1982. Phenotypic evolution in a poorly dispersing snail after arrival of a predator. *Nature* 299:349–350.

Via, S. 1990. Ecological genetics and host adaptation in herbivorous insects: the experimental study of evolution in natural and agricultural systems. *Annual Review of Entomology* 35:421–446.

Via, S. 1999. Reproductive isolation between sympatric races of pea aphids. I. Gene flow restriction and habitat choice. *Evolution* 53:1446–1457.

Via, S. 2001. Sympatric speciation in animals: the ugly duckling grows up. *Trends in Ecology and Evolution* 16:381–390.

Vibrams, H. 1999. Epianthropochory in Mexican weed communities. *American Journal of Botany* 86:476–481.

Vilà, M., and C. M. D'Antonio. 1998. Fitness on invasive *Carpobrotus* (Aizoaceae) hybrids in coastal California. *Ecoscience* 5:191–199.

Vilà, M., E. Weber, and C. M. D'Antonio. 2000. Conservation implications of invasion by plant hybridization. *Biological Invasions* 2:207–217.

Vitousek, P. M., C. M. D'Antonio, L. L. Loope, M. Rejmánek, and R. Westbrooks. 1997. Introduced species: a significant component of human-caused global change. *New Zealand Journal of Ecology* 21:1–16.

Wagner, E., R. Arndt, and M. Brough. 2002. Comparison of susceptibility of five cutthroat trout strains to *Myxobolus cerebralis* infection. *Journal of Aquatic Animal Health* 14:84–91.

Waloff, N. 1966. Scotch broom (*Sarcothamnus scoparius* (L.) Wimmer) and its insect fauna introduced into the Pacific Northwest of America. *Journal of Animal Ecology* 35:293–311.

Walther, G.-R. 2000. Climatic forcing on the dispersal of exotic species. *Phytocoenologia* 30:409–430.

Walther, G.-R. 2002. Weakening of climatic constraints with global warming and its consequences for evergreen broad-leaved species. *Folia Geobotanica* 37:129–139.

Walther, G.-R., E. Post, P. Convey, A. Menzel, C. Parmesan, T. J. C. Beebee, J. M. Fromentin, O. HoeghGuldberg, and F. Bairlein. 2002. Ecological responses to recent climate change. *Nature* 416:389–395.

Wang, X.-R., R. A. Ennos, A. E. Szmidt, and P. Hansson. 1997. Genetic variability in the canker fungus, *Gremmeniella abietina*. 2. Fine-scale investigation of the population genetic structure. *Canadian Journal of Botany* 75:1460–1469.

Wangsomboondee, T., C. T. Groves, P. B. Shoemaker, M. A. Cubeta, and J. B. Ristaino. 2002. *Phytophthora infestans* populations from tomato and potato in North Carolina differ in genetic diversity and structure. *Phytopathology* 92:1189–1195.

Wares, J. P., D. S. Goldwater, B. Y. Kong, and C. W. Cunningham. 2002. Refuting a controversial case of a human-mediated marine species introduction. *Ecology Letters* 5:577–584.

Warner, R. E. 1968. The role of introduced diseases in the extinction of the endemic Hawaiian avifauna. *Condor* 70:101–120.

Warren, M. S., J. K. Hill, J. A. Thomas, J. Asher, R. Fox, B. Huntley, D. B. Roy, et al.. 2001. Rapid responses of British butterflies to opposing forces of climate and habitat change. *Nature* 414:65–68.

Warwick, S .I., J. F.Bain, R. Wheatcroft, and B. K. Thompson. 1989. Hybridization and introgression in *Carduus nutans* and *C. acanthoides* reexamined. *Systematic Botany* 14: 476–494.

Wasserman, S. S. 1986. Genetic variation in adaptation to food plants among populations of the southern cowpea weevil, *Callosobruchus maculatus*: evolution of oviposition preference. *Entomologia Experimentalis et Applicata* 42:201–212.

Weber, G. 1985. Genetic variability in host plant adaptation of the green peach aphid, *Myzus persicae*. *Entomologia Experimentalis et Applicata* 38:49–56.

Weber, G. 1986. Ecological genetics of host plant exploitation in the green peach aphid, *Myzus persicae*. *Entomologia Experimentalis et Applicata* 40:161–168.

Weiss, P. W., and S. J. Milton. 1984. *Chrysanthemonoides monilifera* and *Acacia longifolia* in Australia and South Africa. pp. 159–160, *in* B. Dell (Ed.), *Proceedings of the 4th International Conference on Mediterranean Ecosystems*. Nedlands, Australia: University of Western Australia.

Welch, M. E., and L. H. Rieseberg. 2002. Habitat divergence between a homoploid hybrid sunflower species, *Helianthus paradoxus* (Asteraceae), and its progenitors. *American Journal of Botany* 89:472–478.

Wellems, T. E. 2002. *Plasmodium* chloroquine resistance and the search for a replacement antimalarial drug. *Science* 298:124–126.

Wells, L. 1970. Effects of alewife predation on zooplankton populations in Lake Michigan. *Limnology and Oceanography* 13:556–565.

Wells, P.V., and J. H. Hunziker. 1976. Origin of the creosote bush (*Larrea*) deserts of southwestern North America. *Annals of the Missouri Botanical Garden* 63:843–861.

Werth, C. R., J. L. Riopel, and N.W. Gillespie. 1984. Genetic uniformity in an introduced population of witchweed (*Striga asiatica*) in the United States. *Weed Science* 32:645–648.

Wester, L. 1992. Origin and distribution of adventive alien flowering plants in Hawai'i. pp. 99–154, *in* C. P. Stone, C.W. Smith, and J.T.Tunison (Eds.), *Alien plant invasions in native ecosystems of Hawai'i: Management and research*. Honolulu, Hawaii: Cooperative National Park Resources Studies Unit, University of Hawaii.

Westoby, M. 1989. Selective forces exerted by vertebrate herbivores on plants. *Trends in Ecology and Evolution* 4:115–117.

Whittier, T. R., D. B. Halliwell, and S. G. Paulsen. 1997. Cyprinid distributions in northeast U.S.A. lakes: evidence of regional-scale minnow biodiversity losses. *Canadian Journal of Fisheries and Aquatic Sciences* 54:1593–1607.

Whitton, J., D. E. Wolf, A. A. Snow, and L. H. Rieseberg. 1997. The persistence of cultivar alleles in wild populations of sunflowers five generations after hybridization. *Theoretical and Applied Genetics* 95:33–40.

Wilcove, D. S., D. Rothstein, J. Dubow, A. Phillips, and E. Losos. 1998. Quantifying threats to imperiled species in the United States. *BioScience* 48:607–615.

Wilcox, B. A. 1978. Supersaturated island faunas: a species-age relationship for lizards on post-Pleistocene land-bridge islands. *Science* 199:996–998.

Wilde, G. R., and A. A. Echelle. 1997. Morphological variation in intergrade pupfish populations from the Pecos River, Texas, U.S.A. *Journal of Fish Biology* 50: 523–539.

Williams, C. K., and R. J. Moore. 1989. Phenotypic adaptation and natural selection in the wild rabbit, *Oryctolagus cuniculus*, in Australia. *Journal of Animal Ecology* 58:495–507.

Williams, J. G. K., A. R. Kubelik, K. J. Livak, J. A. Rafalski, and S. V. Tingey. 1990. DNA polymorphisms amplified by arbitrary primers are useful as genetic markers. *Nucleic Acids Research* 18:6531–6536.

Williamson, M. 1993. Invaders, weeds and the risk of genetically manipulated organisms. *Experientia* 49219–49224.

Williamson, M. 1996. *Biological invasions*. London, England: Chapman and Hall.

Willis, A. J., M. B. Thomas, and J. H. Lawton. 1999. Is the increased vigour of invasive weeds explained by a trade-off between growth and herbivore resistance? *Oecologia* 120:632–640.

Willis, A. J., J. Memmott, and R. I. Forrester. 2000. Is there evidence for the postinvasion evolution of increased size among invasive plant species? *Ecology Letters* 3:275–283.

Wilson, E. O. 1961. The nature of the taxon cycle in the Melanesian ant fauna. *American Naturalist* 95:169–193.

Wilson, E. O. 1969. The species equilibrium. pp. 38–47, *in* G. M. Woodwell and H. Smith (Eds.), *Diversity and stability in ecological systems*. Brookhaven Symposia in Biology, No. 22.

Wilson, H. D. 1990. Gene flow in squash species. *BioScience* 40:449–455.

Wilson, H., and J. Manhart. 1993. Crop/weed gene flow: *Chenopodium quinoa* Willd. and *C. berlandieri* Moq. *Theoretical and Applied Genetics* 86:642–648.

Wilson, H. D., and J. S. Payne. 1994. Crop/weed microgamete competition in *Cucurbita pepo* (Cucurbitaceae). *American Journal of Botany* 81:1531–1537.

Wingfield, M. J., B. Slippers, J. Roux, and B. D. Wingfield. 2001. Worldwide movement of exotic forest fungi, especially in the tropics and the southern hemisphere. *BioScience* 51:134–140.

Wiser, S. K., R. B. Allen, P. W. Clinton, and K. H. Platt. 1998. Community structure and forest invasion by an exotic herb over 23 years. *Ecology* 79:2071–2081.

Wolf, D. E., N. Takebayashi, and L. H. Rieseberg. 2001. Predicting the risk of extinction through hybridization. *Conservation Biology* 15:1039–1053.

Wolfe, L. M. 2002. Why alien invaders succeed: support for the escape-from-enemy hypothesis. *American Naturalist* 160:705–711.

Wonham, M. J., W. C. Walton, G. M. Ruiz, and L. D. Smith. 2000. Fish and ships: relating dispersal frequency to success in biological invasions. *Marine Biology* 136:1111–1121.

Work, T. M., J. G. Massey, B. A. Rideout, C. H. Gardiner, D. B. Ledig, O. C. H. Kwok, and J. P. Dubey. 2000. Fatal toxoplasmosis in free-ranging endangered 'Alala from Hawaii. *Journal of Wildlife Diseases* 36:205–212.

World Conservation Monitoring Centre. 1992. *Global biodiversity: status of the earth's living resources.* London, England: Chapman and Hall.

Wu, K. K., and S. K. Jain. 1978. Genetic and plastic responses in geographic differentiation of *Bromus rubens* populations. *Canadian Journal of Botany* 56:873–879.

Yela, J. L., and J. H. Lawton. 1997. Insect herbivore loads on native and introduced plants: a preliminary study. *Entomologia Experimentalis et Applicata* 85:275–279.

Yom-Tov, Y. 2001. Global warming and body mass decline in Israeli passerine birds. *Proceedings of the Royal Society of London B* 268:947–952.

Yom-Tov, Y., W. O. Green, and J. D. Coleman. 1986. Morphological trends in the brushtail possum, *Trichosurus vulpecula*, in New Zealand. *Journal of Zoology, London* 208:583–593.

Yom-Tov, Y., S. Yom-Tov, and H. Moller. 1999. Competition, coexistence, and adaptation amongst rodent invaders to Pacific and New Zealand islands. *Journal of Biogeography* 26:947–958.

Zngerl, A. R. 2003. Evolution of induced responses to herbivores. *Basic and Applied Ecology* 4:91–103.

Zangerl, A. R., and F. A. Bazzaz. 1984. Effects of short-term selection along environmental gradients on variation in populations of *Amaranthus retroflexus* and *Abutilon theophrasti*. *Ecology* 65:207–217.

Zangerl, A. R., and M. R. Berenbaum. 1993. Plant chemistry, insect adaptations to plant chemistry, and host utilization patterns. *Ecology* 74:47–54.

Zangerl, A. R., and M. R. Berenbaum. 2003. Phenotype matching in wild parsnip and parsnip webworms: causes and consequences. *Evolution* 57:806–815.

Zangerl, A. R., T. Huang, J. L. McGovern, and M. R. Berenbaum. 2002. Paradoxical shift by *Depressaria pastinacella* in North America: is enemy-free space involved? *Oikos* 98:431–436.

Zavaleta, E. S., and J. L. Royval. 2002. Climate change and the susceptibility of U.S. ecosystems to biological invasions: two cases of expected range expansion. pp. 277–341, *in* S. H. Schneider and T. L. Root (Eds.), *Wildlife response to climate change*. Washington, D.C.: Island Press.

Zeglen, S. 2002. Whitebark pine and white pine blister rust in British Columbia, Canada. *Canadian Journal of Forest Research* 32:1265–1274.

Zeisset, I., and T. J. C. Beebee. 2003. Population genetics of a successful invader, the marsh frog *Rana ridibunda* in Britain. *Molecular Ecology* 12:639–646.

Zimmerman, E. C. 1960. Possible evidence of rapid evolution in Hawaiian moths. *Evolution* 14:137–138.

Zink, R. M. 2002. A new perspective on the evolutionary history of Darwin's finches. *Auk* 119:864–871.

Ziuganov, V. V. 1995. Reproductive isolation among lateral plate phenotypes (low, partial, complete) of the threespine stickleback, *Gasterosteus aculeatus*, from the White Sea basin and the Kamchatka peninsula, Russia. *Behaviour* 132:1173–1181.

Ziuganov, V. V., and A. V. Zotin. 1995. Pelvic girdle polymorphism and reproductive barriers in the ninespine stickleback *Pungitius pungitius* (L.) from northwest Russia. *Behaviour* 132:1095–1105.

Zwölfer, H., and M. Preiss. 1983. Host selection and oviposition behaviour in west European ecotypes of *Rhinocyllus conicus* Froel. (Col., Curculionidae). *Zeitschrift für angewandte Entomologie* 95:113–122.

Glossary

Additive genetic variation. Variability on which selection can progressively modify a quantitative characteristic by increasing the frequency of particular alleles.

Agroecotypes. Weedy races of a crop or noncrop plant that are confined to the cropland habitat.

Allee effect. A reduction in population growth rate at densities below some optimum.

Allelopathy. Inhibition of the growth of one species by chemical agents released into soil or water by another species.

Allopatric speciation. See *speciation*.

Allopatry. Occurring in nonoverlapping geographical ranges.

Allopolyploidy. See *polyploidy*.

Allozyme. Different forms of an enzyme coded by different alleles at a particular genetic locus.

Amensalism. A symbiotic relationship that is detrimental to one member but harmless to the other.

Allozymes. Different forms of an enzyme coded by different alleles at a single genetic locus.

Anadromous. Aquatic organisms, usually fish, that lay eggs in fresh water but migrate to the ocean for much of their prereproductive life.

Apomixis. Production of seeds without pollination.

Assortative mating. Interbreeding of individuals having more traits in common than expected by chance.

Autopolyploidy. See *polyploidy.*

Backcross. A breeding cross between progeny and one of their earlier parental types.

Ballast water. Water taken into cargo tanks of ships that are not fully loaded to make the ship ride deeper and in more seaworthy condition.

Benthic zone. The deep water substrate habitat of an aquatic ecosystem.

Biotic homogenization. Increased similarity of biotas of different regions due to introduction of alien species.

Biotic relaxation. Decline in number of species in a recently isolated area due to an excess of extinctions over colonization by new species.

Biotype. A population or genetic race of an animal that is associated with a particular plant or animal host.

Castrator. A parasite or substance that destroys the reproductive system of an organism.

Catechin. A plant carbon-ring compound that exerts antioxidant, antimicrobial, or phytotoxic action, depending on its isomeric form.

Character displacement. The existence of greater differences between or among species in areas where they occur together compared to areas where they do not occur together.

Chitinase. An enzyme that breaks down chitin, a major component of the exoskeletons of many invertebrates.

Cladocerans. Small aquatic crustaceans commonly known as water fleas.

Clone. A group of individual organisms derived asexually from a parent and having identical genetic features.

Coevolution. Mutual evolutionary change by two or more different species as a result of their interaction.

Commensalism. A symbiotic relationship that is beneficial to one member and harmless to the other.

Compensation (for herbivory). The ability of a plant to respond to herbivore impacts so that its evolutionary fitness is not reduced. Overcompensation is a response that increases the fitness of the plant.

Congeners. Members of the same genus.

Constitutive defenses. Morphological or chemical deterrents to herbivore feeding produced by the plant as normal products of growth and development.

Counteradaptation. The evolutionary responses of members of a biotic community to a new invader species.

Cryptic species. Species that are genetically distinct but are not readily distinguished by morphological analysis.

Demographic failure. Excess of mortality over recruitment in a population leading to its decline toward extinction.

Deterrence (of herbivory). A plant's defense mechanism that functions by preventing an herbivore from consuming or damaging its tissues.

Detritus. Dead particulate organic matter.

Diapause. A period of suspended development during the larval stage of an organism.

Dimorphism. Exhibiting two distinct forms, as in size, shape, or color.

DNA polymerase. An enzyme that stimulates the replication of DNA strands.

DNA primers. Pairs of molecules consisting of short nucleotide sequences that attach to complementary sequences of DNA and stimulate the replication of the DNA section lying between their attachment points.

DNA probe. A short sequence of DNA, chosen to be complementary to a portion of a gene under analysis.

Endotoxin. A substance produced in the tissues of an organism that is toxic to its enemies.

Ecomorph. A particular body form of an organism that is associated with a certain habitat or way of life.

Ecotype. A population of a species that shows genetic adaptation to particular habitat conditions.

Electrophoresis. The separation of organic molecules of differing structure by differential migration through a substrate subjected to an electric field.

Endemic species. A species that evolved its identity in the specific region in which it occurs.

Endangerment. The reduction of the population of a species to a critical level by relationships or factors that, if continued, are likely to lead to extinction.

Endotoxin. A toxic compound that is produced inside a microorganism and is released only when the microorganism dies and breaks down.

Epistasis. The influence of alleles at one locus on the expression of alleles at a different locus.

Extinction. The disappearance of a species due to mortality that exceeds reproduction until the last individual dies or to the loss of genetic identity due to interbreeding with other species.

Extirpation. The local extinction of part of the overall population of a species.

Extrafloral nectaries. Nectar-producing structures occurring on plant parts other than flowers.

Fitness. The evolutionary success of an organism with a particular genetic makeup as measured by its contribution to the gene pool of subsequent generations.

Forb. A broad-leaved herbaceous plant.

Founder effect. The biased representation of genetic variability of a colonist population due to the fact that colonizing individuals carry only a fraction of the variability of the parental population.

Furanocoumarins. Complex chemicals produced by certain plants of the carrot family as defenses against herbivores.

Fynbos. The evergreen shrubby vegetation type of areas of Mediterranean climate in South Africa.

Genetic bottleneck. The loss of alleles of genes by genetic drift during periods when the effective breeding population of a species has been maintained at a low level for several to many generations.

Genetic drift. The change in frequency of different alleles of a gene due to random factors affecting the reproduction of individuals contributing alleles to offspring of subsequent generations.

Genetic swamping. The loss of genetic distinctiveness of a species or population by extensive interbreeding with other species or populations.

Genome. The total genetic constitution of an organism.

Genotype. The exact combination of alleles an organism possesses for one or more genes.

Gill rakers. Filter elements that are spaced so as to restrict the passage of particulate materials of certain size from the mouth cavity to the gill chamber in a fish.

Haplotype. The alleles of a set of genes or the specific sequence of genetic code shown on one chromosome.

Hardy–Weinberg expectation. The frequency of genotypes that is expected in a population of freely interbreeding individuals when the alleles for a gene are of equal fitness value.

Heterozygosity. The occurrence of different alleles of a gene on the two members of a chromosome pair.

Homoploid speciation. The hybridization of species with the same chromosome number, leading to a form that is distinct and has strong reproductive isolation without the occurrence of polyploidy.

Homozygote. The condition in which identical alleles of a gene occur on the two members of a chromosome pair.

Horizontal gene transfer. Exchange of genes directly between individuals rather than from parents to offspring.

Hybrid vigor. Enhanced growth or performance of the offspring produced by the interbreeding of different species or other distant relatives.

Hyperparasitism. Parasitism of species that are themselves parasites.

Inbreeding depression. Reduced fitness of individual offspring resulting from expression of detrimental recessive characteristics due to interbreeding of closely related parent individuals.

Induced defenses. Morphological or chemical deterrents to herbivore feeding produced by plants in direct response to tissue damage by herbivores.

Introgressive hybridization. Interbreeding between two or more species, leading eventually to the loss of genetic distinction of the species.

Invasional meltdown. The process by which successful invaders of a community or region facilitate the invasion of still other alien species.

Inversion (chromosomal). A change in chromosome structure in which a section of a chromosome becomes inverted, although it remains at the same location.

Lacustrine. Having to do with a lake environment.

Leaf-mining insects. Larval insects that feed on tissues of the interior of plant leaves.

Lemma. The lower of the paired bracts enclosing the flower of a grass.

Littoral zone. The shallow water zone near the shore of an aquatic ecosystem.

Meta-analysis. A statistical evaluation of the results of a series of different scientific studies of a specific question.

Microhabitat. The specific set of physical and biotic conditions that characterize the location occupied by individuals of a particular species.

Microsatellites. Noncoding sections of DNA in which a sequence of one to about six nucleotides is repeated along the DNA strand.

Minisatellites. Noncoding sections of DNA in which a sequence of about 9–100 nucleotides is repeated along the DNA strand.

Mitochondrial DNA. A circular DNA molecule found in mitochondria that codes for certain enzymes and RNA molecules, as well as possessing noncoding sectors.

Multivariate analysis. Statistical analysis in which variation in a variable of interest is examined as a function of variation in several other variables that are thought to be influential.

Mutualism. An interaction between two or more species that is beneficial to all.

Mycorrhizae. Fungi that form symbiotic associations with the roots of higher plants.

Otoliths. Calcareous structures occurring in the inner ear of fish.

Outcrossing. Reproduction involving exchange of reproductive cells between different individuals.

Overcompensation (for herbivory). See *compensation.*

Oviposition. Egg laying.

Pandemic. A disease epidemic that spreads worldwide.

Pappus. The modified calyx of individual flowers of plants of the sunflower family, consisting of scales, spines, or feathery bristles.

Parapatry. Occurring in adjacent geographical ranges.

Parasitoid. A parasitic arthropod in which the larva develops within the body of the host.

Parthenogenesis. Reproduction in which offspring are produced from unfertilized spores, seeds, or eggs.

Pelagic zone. The open water region of an aquatic ecosystem.

Phenolic glycosides. Organic compounds that consist of a phenol ring with an attached sugar residue.

Phenology. The seasonal pattern of growth and reproduction of an organism.

Phenotype. The realized expression or outward appearance of a particular genetic makeup.

Pheromone. A volatile organic substance produced by individuals that induces particular behavioral responses in other individuals of the species.

Photoperiod. The length of daylight at a particular time of year.

Phytophagous. Feeding on plant material.

Piscivore. An animal feeding on fish in an aquatic ecosystem.

Planktivore. An animal feeding on minute plants or animals in the open water of an aquatic ecosystem.

Pleiotropy. The influence of a gene on different characteristics of an organism.

Polyphagy. Feeding on a wide variety of food types.

Polygenic. Referring to a characteristic influenced by more than one gene.

Polymorphism. The existence of different alleles for a particular gene, or the frequency of genes with more than a single allele.

Polyploidy. The increase in the number of sets of chromosomes in individuals of one species, a process termed autopolyploidy, or an increase in the number of chromosome sets in individuals produced by interspecific hybridization, a process termed allopolyploidy. The number of sets of chromosomes is often indicated by a prefix, e.g., tetra- (4), sexta- (6), octo- (8).

Red Queen Hypothesis. Hypothesis that predators or parasites and their prey or hosts engage in an evolutionary contest to improve their respective abilities for exploitation or defense.

Refugia (glacial). Locations where species or communities survived during the periods of maximum Pleistocene glaciation.

Restriction enzymes. Enzymes that cut DNA or RNA molecules at points where specific nucleotide sequences occur.

Ruderal habitat. Terrestrial areas that are characterized by frequent physical disturbance, such as roadsides and cultivated land.

Selfing. Reproduction by self-fertilization.

Sequencing. Determining the exact nucleotide sequence of DNA or RNA strands.

Speciation. The differentiation of an ancestral species into daughter species. Allopatric speciation involves differentiation of populations that are geographically separate. Sympatric speciation involves differentiation of populations that coexist in the same region.

Supertramps. Species that are rapid colonists of isolated oceanic islands.

Symbiosis. An interaction between species in which the members (symbionts) live in intimate physical association.

Sympatric speciation. See *speciation*.

Sympatry. Occurring in the same or overlapping geographic ranges.

Taxon (pl. Taxa). Any group of organisms that is identified by a scientific name.

Taxon cycle. A repeated evolutionary and biogeographic sequence of invasion, differentiation, specialization, and extinction by members of a taxonomic group.

Thermocline. The zone at intermediate depth in a stratified lake in which rapid change in water temperature and density occurs.

Tillers. Multiple shoots produced from the base of a perennial grass.

Tolerance (to herbivory). Plant processes that compensate for damage caused by herbivore feeding.

Transgenes. Genes from one organism that have been introduced to a different organism by genetic engineering.

Translocation (chromosomal). A change in chromosome structure in which a section of a chromosome is moved to a new location.

Trichomes. Sharp plant hairs that function to discourage feeding by herbivores.

Vector. An organism that serves as an agent of dispersal or transmission of another species.

Xenodiversity. The richness of a community or biota in alien species.

Index

Abies alba (silver fir), 177–178
Abies spp. (fir), 207
Abutilon theophrasti (velvet-leaf), 106
Acacia longifolia, 100
Acacia spp. (Australian acacias), 274
Acanthiza spp. (thornbills), 252
Accumulation of species by aliens: in alien plants, 203–204; defenses and, 204; extinction and, 214–215; generalists/specialists and, 204, 206; herbivorous arthropods/crops, 204–207; herbivorous arthropods/noncrops, 207–212; host range and, 207–208; leaf miners/tree example, 202–203; parasites of alien animals, 212, 214; parasitoids of alien animals, 212–214; predators of alien animals, 212, 214; rapid evolution and, 203; species diversity and, 204; species richness and, 208
Acer campestre (maple), 207, 211
Acer platanoides (Norway maple), 280
Acer pseudoplatanus (maple), 207, 211
Achatina fulica (African snail), 222
Achatinella (tree snails), 222
Acid deposition, 277
Acridotheres tristis (common mynah), 45–46, 115
Aculus hyperici (mite), 242
Acyrthosiphon pisum (pea aphid), 129, 137, 242, 265–266
Adaptation to new habitats: by animals, 110–116; *Anolis* lizard experiment, 116; with new biotic conditions, 116–118; overview, 8–9, 118; by plants, 107–110; rapid evolution with, 106; reduced

defenses with, 116–118; smooth cordgrass example, 105–106
Additive genetic variation, 39
Adler, G.H., 110
Aedes aegypti, 159
Aedes albopictus (Asian tiger mosquito), 54, 111
Aegilops cylindrical (jointed goatgrass), 83, 154
African honey bee (*Apis mellifera scutellata*), 73
African pasture grasses, 11
African snail (*Achatina fulica*), 222
Agrawal, A.A., 129, 188
Agriculture: human-assisted dispersal and, 19, 20, 21–22; hybridization and, 71–72; pest species of, 128–132, 133; species introduction for, 22; transgenes/hybridization and, 76–88
Agroecotypes, 21–22
Ailanthus, 27
Ailanthus altissima (tree of heaven), 40
Aimophila arenaria (European beachgrass), 274
Aircraft and species dispersal, 21, 25
Alewife (*Alosa pseudoharengus*), 191–192, 196
Alfalfa (*Medicago sativa*), 180, 185–186, 242–243, 266
Algae, green (*Caulerpa*), 264–265
Allee effect, 12, 28
Allelopathy. *See* Chemical defenses
Allen, P.S., 31
Alliaria petiolata (garlic mustard), 52
Allopolyploidy, 260, 265

355

Allozyme analysis, 34, 38
Allozymes, 34
Alosa pseudoharengus (alewife), 191–192, 196
Alosa sapidissima (shad), 112
Amaranthus retroflexus (green amaranth), 106
Ambrosia trifida (giant ragweed), 124
American chestnut (*Castanea dentate*), 150–151, 172–173, 226–227
American elm (*Ulmus Americana*), 170
American mangrove (*Rhizophora mangle*), 212
American robin (*Turdus migratorius*), 282
Amplified fragment length polymorphism (AFLP), 35
Amylostereum areolatum (white rot fungus), 234
Anas platyrhynchos (mallard), 229
Anas rubripes (black duck), 229
Anastrepha ludens (Mexican fruit fly), 127
Andow, D.A., 206, 207
Aneides ferreus (clouded salamander), 47–48
Aneides vagrans (wandering salamander), 48
Animal adaptation to aliens: brown trout/mayfly, 188–189; to ecosystem engineers, 200; introduced diseases, 197–200; invertebrates and, 189–193; native vertebrates and, 193–197; potential of, 201; predation, 189–197; Red Queen Hypothesis, 189
Animal species (aliens): genetic variability of, 32–33, 42–46; introductions of (overview), 23–24; traits of, 26, 27
Annual bluegrass (*Poa annua*), 108
Anolis sagrei, 116
Anophleles mosquito, 158
Anoplophora glabripennis (Asian long-horned beetle), 127
Anthonomus grandis (boll weevil), 129–130
Antibiotic resistance, 84
Antigenic shift, 158
Antillean crested hummingbird (*Orthorhynchus cristatus*), 254
Ant species genetic variability, 43
Apache trout (*Oncorhynchus apache*), 219–220
Aphidius ervi (parasitoid wasp), 137, 242–243
Aphthona spp. (weevil), 241
Apios americanaI (groundnut), 261

Apis mellifera scutellata (African honey bee), 73
Apium graveolens (celery), 82
Aplodinotus grunniens (freshwater drum), 247
Apples: *Malus pumila,* 121–122; *Malus sylvestris,* 180–181
Aquatic invertebrates genetic variability, 42–43
Arabidopsis thaliana, 78, 85, 164–165
Arbutus menziesii (madrone), 148
Arctic char (*Salvelinus alpinus*), 139
Argentine ant (*Linepithema humile*): aggression and, 32–33, 137; biological control of, 59–60; as extinction threat, 222–223; genetic variability of, 32–33, 43; source area of, 53–54, 59–60
Aricia agestis (brown argus butterfly), 283
Arnett, A.E., 240
Arriola, P.E., 76–77
Artemisia vulgaris (mugwort), 266
Asclepias spp. (milkweeds), 86, 123
Asian clams (*Corbicula fluminea*), 27, 226
Asian long-horned beetle (*Anoplophora glabripennis*), 127
Asian sea anemones (*Diadumene lineate*), 43
Asian swamp eel (*Monopterus albus*), 50
Asian tiger mosquito (*Aedes albopictus*), 54, 111
Asparagus (*Asparagus officinalis*), 82
Aspergillus niger, 84
Atalopedes campestris (Sachem skipper), 279
Atlantic salmon (*Salmo salar*), 73, 228–229
Auerbach, M., 202
Aurelia (jellyfish), 49
Australian acacias (*Acacia* spp.), 274
Australian eucalypts (*Eucalyptus* spp.): herbivory release in, 99; introduction of, 23, 274
Australian flax (*Linum marginale*), 149, 153
Australian paperbark (*Melaleuca quinquenervia*), 23, 211–212, 273–274
Austrian pine (*Pinus nigra*), 126
Autopolyploidy, 260, 261
Avena barbata. See Slender wild oat
Avian malaria, 198–199, 227
Avian malaria pathogen (*Plasmodium relictum*), 151, 198–199
Avian pox, 227
Aythya affinis (lesser scaup), 246
Aythya marila (greater scaup), 246

Bacillus thuringiensis. See Bt gene
Bactrocera dorsalis (Oriental fruit fly), 127
Badyaev, A.V., 114
Balloon vine (*Cardiospermum corindum*), 182, 183–184
Baltimore checkerspot butterfly (*Euphydryas phaeton*), 177
Banana (*Musa paradisiaca*), 266
Bananaquit (*Coereba flaveola*), 254
Barbados bird fauna, 254–256
Barley (*Hordeum vulgare*), 84
Barley leaf blotch fungus (*Rhynchosporium secale*), 156
Barnyard grass (*Echinochloa crus-galli*), 22, 107
Barred owl (*Strix varia*), 226
Bathyplectes curculionis (parasitic wasp), 240
Beans (*Phaseolus* spp.), 84
Beaver (*Castor canadensis*), 200
Beeches (*Nothofagus* spp.), 211
Beering, D.J., 284
Beets (*Beta vulgaris*), 82
Belsky, A.J., 163, 164
Benkman, C.W., 250
Berberis spp., 154
Berberis vulgaris (common barberry), 154
Berenbaum, M.R., 125
Bergelson, J., 165
Berger, J., 118
Bergman's Rule, 113
Berlinger, J.E., 76
Bermuda grass (*Cynodon dactylon*), 82
Bernays, E.A., 121, 124–125
Berthold, P., 284
Beta macrocarpa, 82
Beta vulgaris (beets), 82
Biodiversity: factors affecting, 92–93; herbicide use and, 86; invasibility and, 92–96
Biological control: alien genetic variability and, 60; coevolution and, 244; ecological adaptation by control species, 239–241; extinction risks and, 223, 231; host counteradaptations and, 241–243; host shifts with, 127, 137, 232–233, 234–238; hyperparasitism and, 214; introduction source areas and, 59–60; precautions for, 243–244; regulation and, 244; risks with, ix, x, 233–234
Biological Invasions, x

Biota of North American Program, 93
"Biotic homogenization," 217, 275
Biotic relaxation, 270–271
Biotic resistance hypothesis, 96
Biotypes/races: of apple fly maggot, 180–181; of creosote bush, 253; herbivore adaptation (aliens), 123–124, 129–132, 178, 186–187
Birches (*Betula* spp.), 169
Birks, H.J.B., 208
Bittersweet (*Solanum dulcamara*), 132
Blackcap (*Sylvia atricapilla*), 283
Black cottonwood (*Populus trichocarpa*), 74–75
Black duck (*Anas rubripes*), 229
Black-eyed pea (*Vigna unguiculata*), 129
Black-faced grassquit (*Tiaris bicolor*), 254
Black nightshade (*Solanum nigrum*), 181
Black rat (*Rattus rattus*), 115, 145, 192–193
Black spruce (*Picea mariana*), 250
Black-whiskered vireo (*Vireo altiloquus*), 254
Blaustein, A.R., 193, 194
Bloater (*Coregonus hoyi*), 196
Blossey, B., 102, 116–117, 118
Blue catfish (*Ictalurus furcatus*), 247
Bluegill sunfish (*Lepomis macrochirus*), 68, 141, 280–281
Blumstein, D.T., 117–118
Body size: adaptations and, 134–135, 145–146; cold/warm climates and, 113
Boiga irregularis (brown tree snake), 222
Boll weevil (*Anthonomus grandis*), 129–130
Bosmina polyploidy, 265
Botryllus schlosseri (sea squirt), 52–53, 95
Bouteloua curtipendula (side-oats grama), 167–168
Bouteloua spp., 166
Bowers, M.D., 177
Bradley, N., 278
Brassica campestris, 83
Brassica napus (oilseed rape), 80, 83, 84
Brassica oleracea (broccoli), 129
Brassica oleracea (cabbage), 239
Brassica rapa (field mustard), 83, 117
Brazilian pepper (*Schinus terebinthifolius*), 27, 211, 273–274
Bremia lactucae (downy mildew), 156
Briske, D.D., 166
Broccoli (*Brassica oleracea*), 129
Brome grasses (*Bromus* spp.), 274

Bromus hordaceus (soft brome), 67

Bromus mollis (soft brome), 30, 108

Bromus rubens (red brome), 109

Bromus tectorum. See Cheatgrass

Brook trout (*Salvelinus fontinalis*), 219

Brown argus butterfly (*Aricia agestis*), 283

Brown citrus aphid (*Toxoptera citricida*), 243

Brown-headed cowbird (*Molothrus ater*),
    196–197

Brown mussel (*Perna perna*), 43

Brown tree snake (*Boiga irregularis*), 222

Brown trout (*Salmo trutta*), 73, 188–189,
    198

Bruchid seed beetle (*Stator limbatus*), 176

Brushtail opossum (*Trichosurus vulpecula*),
    116, 146, 170

Brylski, P.V., 185

Bryonia alba (white bryony), 40

Bt gene: nontarget species effects of, 85, 86;
    pest resistance to, 86–87, 128; regulation
    and, 87; use in crop species, 79; wild
    plant effects of, 81

Bubuculus ibis (cattle egret), 20–21

Bucephala albeola (bufflehead), 246

Bufflehead (*Bucephala albeola*), 246

Bufo marinus (cane toad), 223, 236, 238

Bulbous bluegrass (*Poa bulbosa*):
    adaptation/reproduction shift, 108;
    genetic variability of, 42

Bullfrog (*Rana catesbeiana*), 103, 193–194,
    223

Bunch grass, 89–90

Burr medic (*Medicago polymorpha*), 107

Bursaphelenchus xylophilus (pine wood
    nematode), 151

Bush crickets, 28–29

Butterfly species: climatic zones shift, 279;
    seasonal activity changes, 278. *See also*
    individual species

Butternut canker (*Sirococcus clavigignenti-
    juglandacearum*), 46, 52, 60

Byington, T.S., 161

Bythotrephes longimanus (long-spined water
    flea), 56, 68–69

Cabbage (*Brassica oleracea*), 239

Cabbage butterfly (*Pieris rapae*), 127, 239

Cabbage looper (*Trichoplusia ni*), 165

Cacao (*Theobroma cacao*), 205–206

Cactoblastis cactorum, 237–238, 239–240, 244

Calidris alpina (dunlin), 64

California bay laurel (*Umbellularia
    californica*), 148, 171

California cordgrass (*Spartina foliosa*), 70–71

California gnatcatcher (*Polioptila californica*),
    197

California ground squirrel (*Spermophilus
    beecheyi*), 200

Callosobruchus maculatus (southern cowpea
    weevil), 129

Camarhynchus spp. (tree finches), 261

Camelina sativa (false flax), 22

Canada thistle (*Cirsium arvense*): adaptation
    of, 31, 109; biological control and, 237;
    insect fauna of, 209–210

Cane toad (*Bufo marinus*), 223, 236, 238

Canis familiaris (dog), 74

Canis latrans. See Coyote

Canis lupus (gray wolf), 74, 146

Canis lycaon (eastern wolf), 146

Canis rufus (red wolf), 146

Canis simiensis (Ethiopian wolf), 74

Capsella bursa-pastoris (shepherd's purse),
    168–169

Carcinus (European crabs), 49

Carcinus aestuarii, 49

Carcinus aestuarii (European green crab),
    101

Carcinus maenas (European green crab), 49,
    101, 189–191

Cardiospermum corindum (balloon vine), 182,
    183–184

Cardiospermum halicacabum (heartseed vine),
    182, 183

Carduelis chloris (greenfinch), 45

Carduus, 67

Carduus nutans (musk thistle), 127–128,
    236, 240

Carduus pycnocephalus (Italian thistle), 209

Caribbean elaenia (*Elaenia martinica*), 254

Carib grackle (*Quiscalus lugubris*), 254–255

Carino, D.A., 103

Carman, J.G., 166

Carpobrotus chilensis (sea fig), 71

Carpobrotus edulis (sea fig), 71

Carpodacus mexicanus (house finch), 12–115,
    113

Carroll, Lewis, 189

Carroll, S.P., 3, 39–40

Carrot (*Daucus carota*), 82

Carthamus tinctorius (safflower), 243–244
Cassey, P., 27
Castanea crenata (Japanese chestnut), 202, 203
Castanea dentata (American chestnut), 150–151, 172–173, 226–227
Castanea mollisima (Chinese chestnut), 172
Castor canadensis (beaver), 200
Casuarinas (*Casuarina* spp.), 27, 212, 273–274
Cats: *Felis catus,* 192–193, 224, 227; *Felis sylvestris,* 74
Cattail, narrowleaf (*Typha angustifolia*), 263
Cattail, North American broadleaf (*Typha latifolia*), 263
Cattail, white (*Typha glauca*), 263
Cattle egret (*Bubuculus ibis*), 20–21
Caulerpa (green algae), 264–265
Caulerpa taxifolia (marine algae), 55, 110
Celery (*Apium graveolens*), 82
Cenchrus spp., 166
Centaurea diffusa (diffuse knapweed), 26, 89–90, 100
Centaurea maculosa (spotted knapweed), 100
Centaurea repens (Russian knapweed), 100
Centaurea solsticialis. See Yellow starthistle
Centaurea spp. (star thistles), 65, 67, 274
Centrarchidae hybrids, 68
Cephus cinctus (wheat stem sawfly), 123
Ceratitis capitata. See Mediterranean fruit fly
Cercopagis pengoi (spiny cladoceran), 57–58, 59
Cervus elaphus (red deer), 229
Cervus nippon (sika deer), 229
Cespitose grasses, 168
Channell, R., 221
Channer, A.G. de R., 240
Character displacement, 134, 136–137, 266–267
Character release, 136
Charlock mustard (*Sinapis arvensis*), 109
Cheatgrass (*Bromus tectorum*): adaptation of, 31, 109; genetic variability of, 41; multiple introductions of, 55–56
Chelone glabra (turtlehead/balmony), 177
Chemical defenses: adaptation/reduction in, 117; coevolution and, 122; of diffuse knapweed, 89–90, 100; to gypsy moth, 162; invasiveness and, 26
Chenopodium quinoa (quinoa), 84

Cherry laurel (*Prunus laurocerasus*), 272–273
Cherry species (*Prunus*), 181
Chesson, P., 95
Chestnut blight (*Cryphonectria parasitica*), 150–151, 170, 172, 226–227
Chinese chestnut (*Castanea mollisima*), 172
Chinese mitten crab (*Eriocheir sinensis*), 53
Chinese tallow tree (*Sapium sebiferum*), 30–31, 117, 274
Chinook salmon (*Oncorhynchus tshawytscha*), 73–74, 111–112
Chitinases/chitinase inhibitors, 152–153
Chloroleucon ebano (Texas ebony), 176
Chloroplast DNA analysis, 38
Chondrilla juncea (rush skeletonweed), 242
Choristoneura murinana, 177–178
Chromosome doubling effects, 63, 64, 65
Chrysanthemoides monilifera, 100
Chrysolina quadrigemina, 232–233, 241–242
Chrysoperla carnea (green lacewing), 86
Cinnabar moth (*Tyria jacobaeae*), 237
Cinnamomum glanduliferum (Nepal camphor tree), 273
Cirsium arvense. See Canada thistle
Cirsium canescens (Platte thistle), 237, 238
Cirsium pitcheri (pitcher's thistle), 237
Cirsium spp., 127–128, 236–237
Cirsium undulatum (wavyleaf thistle), 237
Claviceps africana (sorghum ergot), 52
Claviceps purpurea (ergot fungus), 64
Clement, S.L., 210
Climacteris spp. (tree-creepers), 252
Climbing ferns (*Lygodium* spp.), 25
Clonal growth and invasiveness, 26
Clouded salamander (*Aneides ferreus*), 47–48
Coast horned lizard (*Phrynosoma coronatum*), 32
Coast live oak (*Quercus agrifolia*), 171
Coconut palm (*Cocos nucifera*), 266
Cocos nucifera (coconut palm), 266
Codling moth (*Laspeyresia pomonella*), 121–122, 130
Cody, Martin, 17–19
Coereba flaveola (bananaquit), 254
Coevolution: alien release from, 92, 97–102; biodiversity and, 257; biological control and, 244; "cold/hot spots" of, 122, 125, 250; counteradaptation/integration and, 246–247; of creosote bush/insects, 253; factors affecting, 90–91;

Coevolution (*continued*): gene-for-gene pattern (host/pathogen), 152–153, 156, 171; host-parasite taxon cycle, 257; integration and, 246–247; invasibility and, 90–91, 92, 95, 97–102; of plants/herbivores, 122–123; stability/predictability and, 91–92, 93; views on, 90

Colias philodice (sulfur butterfly), 180

Colletotrichum sublinolum (sorghum anthracnose), 156

Collinsia parviflora, 174–176

Colonization: by humans, 22, 24. *See also* Establishment

Colorado pinyon (*Pinus edulis*), 172

Colorado potato beetle (*Leptinotarsa decimlineata*), 132, 133

Columbina passerina (common ground dove), 254

Commensal relationships, 149–150

Common barberry (*Berberis vulgaris*), 154

Common blue butterfly (*Zizina labradus*), 228

Common carp (*Cyprinus carpio*), 247

Common chickweed (*Stellaria media*), 30

Common ground dove (*Columbina passerina*), 254

Common mynah (*Acridotheres tristis*), 45–46, 115

Common St. John's wort (*Hypericum perforatum*): adaptation of, 107; biological control and, 232–233, 241–242

Common vole (*Microtus arvalis*), 54

Community alteration: biotic homogenization and, 275; conservation and, 284–286; in ecosystem functions, 274–276; global climate change and, 272–273, 276–281, 283–284; invasional meltdown, 275–276; overview, 272–274; southern Alps, 272–273

Compensation/overcompensation to herbivory, 163–164

Competition (aliens) evaluation, 248–249

Compsilura concinnata, 235

Conocephalus discolor (long-winged cone-head), 29

Conservation, 15, 284–286

Constitutive defenses, 162–163, 165, 169

Copper redhorse (*Moxostoma hubbsi*), 247

Corbicula clams, 50

Corbicula fluminea (Asian clams), 27, 226

Coregonus clupeiformis (lake whitefish), 140

Coregonus hoyi (bloater), 196

Coregonus spp., 140–141

Corn earworm (*Helicoverpa zea*), 127

Cornell, H.V., 202, 213

Corn poppy (*Papaver rhoeas*), 109

Cornus florida (flowering dogwood), 50–51

Cornus kousa (Japanese dogwood), 51

Cornus nuttallii (Pacific dogwood), 50–51

Cornus spp., 50–51, 170, 180

Corvus brachyrhynchos (crow), 157

Corvus hawaiiensis (Hawaiian crow), 227

Cotesia glomerata (wasp), 239

Cotoneasters (*Cotoneaster* spp.), 273

Cotton: (*Gossypium hirsutum*), 79, 80; (*Gossypium* spp.), 84, 130; (*Gossypium thurberi*), 130

Cottontail rabbits (*Sylvilagus* spp.), 233, 240–241

Coturnix coturnix (European quail), 229–230

Coturnix japonica (Japanese quail), 229–230

Counteradaptation/integration: coevolution and, 246–247; ecological adjustments, 247–250; Hawaiian birds, 248–250; of hosts/biological control, 241–243; Lesser Antilles bird fauna, 254–257; long-term evolutionary responses, 252–257; overview, 10, 14, 245–247; red crossbills/conifers, 250–251; short-term evolutionary responses, 250–252; Tasmania bird fauna, 251–252; West Indies bird fauna, 254–257; zebra/quagga mussels and, 245–246

Cousyn, C., 192

Cow parsnip (*Heracleum lanatum*), 125

Coyote (*Canis latrans*): adaptations of, 146; hybridization of, 74, 146; increased range of, 146, 282; as rabies reservoir, 157

Crataegus spp. (hawthorns), 180–181

Crawley, M.J., 102

Crayfish: hybridization of, 72; plague of, 227; in United States, 225. *See also Orconectes*

Creeping St. John's wort/Aaron's beard (*Hypericum calycinum*), 232–233

Crenicichla alta (pike cichlid), 195–196

Creosote bush (*Larrea tridentata*), 252–253

Crepis tectorum (narrowleaf hawksbeard), 94–95

Crête, M., 146

Cristescu, M.E.A., 58

Cronartium occidentale (pinyon pine blister rust), 172

Cronartium ribicola (white pine blister rust), 154–155, 171–172, 227

Crop mimicry, 21–22

Crop seed contamination, 21–22, 24

Crow (*Corvus brachyrhynchos*), 157

Cryphonectria parasitica (chestnut blight), 150–151, 170, 172, 226–227

Cryptic species, 46, 48–51

Cucurbita spp. (squash), 82, 84

Curly dock (*Rumex crispus*), 107

Cutthroat trout (*Oncorhynchus clarki*): Apache trout and, 219–220; hybridization of, 228; predation by, 144; whirling disease and, 198

Cwynar, L.C., 28

Cynodon dactylon (Bermuda grass), 82

Cynomys spp. (prairie dog), 199

Cyperus spp. (flatsedges), 235

Cyprinodon bovinus (Leon Springs pupfish), 228

Cyprinodon pecosensis (Pecos pupfish), 228

Cyprinodon variegatus (sheepshead minnow), 228

Cyprinus carpio (common carp), 247

Cytisus scoparius (Scotch broom), 99, 210

Daehler, C.C., 103, 105

Daktulosphaira vitafoliae (grape phylloxera), 54

Danaus plexippus. See Monarch butterfly

D'Antonio, C.M., 5

Daphnia: galeata, 72; *lumholtzi,* 53; *magna,* 192; polyploidy of, 265; *retrocurva,* 191–192

Darwin's finches, 260–261

Datura stramonium (jimson weed), 165–166

Daucus carota (carrot), 82

Daucus carota (wild carrot), 107

Davis, M.A., 94

Dayan, T., 136–137

Deladenus siricidicola, 234

Dengue virus, 137, 138, 159–160

Dennill, G.G., 235

Depressaria pastinacella (parsnip webworm), 125

Deterrence by plants, 162–163

Diabrotica barberi (northern corn rootworm), 130–131

Diabrotica virgifera (western corn rootworm), 130

Diadumene lineata (Asian sea anemones), 43

Diamond, J., 145

Diamondback moth (*Plutella xylostella*), 87, 128

Diapause extensions, 130

Diffuse knapweed (*Centaurea diffusa*), 26, 89–90, 100

Dipodomys ingens (giant kangaroo rat), 248

Discula destructiva (dogwood anthracnose), 50–51, 170

Disease agents (alien): animal adaptation to, 197–200; of animals (overview), 151, 156–157; dispersal of, 20; evolution of, ix, 149–151; host/vector responses, 160; of humans, 157–160; plant adaptations to, 170–173; of plants (overview), 148–149, 150–151, 151–156; predator adaptations to, 137–138; release from, 98–99; rust fungi, 153–155. *See also* specific disease agents

Disease agents: evolution of, 149–150; extinction/extirpation and, 226–227; host resistance/agent virulence, 149, 152–153, 154; plant adaptations to, 170–173

Dispersal: across geographical barriers, 20; of aliens (overview), 7–8; ballast of ships and, 24, 42–43, 49, 53, 59; crop seed contamination and, 21–22, 24; by deliberate introduction, 22–24; evolutionary adaptations for, 19–21, 28–29; expansion/invasion phase of, 27; genetic variability and, 31; human-assisted dispersal, 24–25; as inadvertent human-assisted, 21; by locomotion, 20; natural vs. human-assistance, 19–21; overview, 19–21; plant use of animals and, 20; by ships, 21, 24–25, 42–43, 52; water transport for, 19, 20; by wind, 17–18, 19, 25; wind dispersal/seed morphology, 17–18

Disturbance: invasibility and, 95; species diversity and, 92–93

DNA fingerprints, 46
DNA fragment length polymorphism
    analyses, 34–36
DNA/RNA sequencing, 38
Dog (Canis familiaris), 74
Dogwood. See Cornus
Dogwood anthracnose (Discula destructiva),
    50–51, 170
Douglas-fir (Pseudotsuga menziesii), 149
Downy mildew (Bremia lactucae), 156
Dreissena bugensis. See Quagga mussel
Dreissena polymorpha. See Zebra mussel
Drosophila subobscura. See Fruit fly
Drug resistance and malaria, 158
Duckweeds (Lemna spp.), 19
Dunlin (Calidris alpina), 64
Dutch elm disease (Ophiostoma ulmi):
    extirpation by, 227; hybridization
    and, 69–70; plant genetic variation and,
    170

Eastern cottonwood (Populus deltoides),
    74–75
Eastern white pine (Pinus strobus), 155
Eastern wolf (Canis lycaon), 146
Ebola virus, 160
Echinochloa crus-galli (barnyard grass), 22,
    107
Ecological impact overview (alien species), 4
Ecology of Invasions by Animals and Plants, x
Economic costs (alien species): blight
    fungus of maize, 151; overview, 5; of
    potato late blight, 4
Ecosystem engineers, 200
Ecosystem function alteration, 274–276
Ecotypic adaptations, 107–108
Edith's checkerspot butterfly (Euphydryas
    editha), 174–176, 279
Ehrlich, P.R., 27
Eichhornia crassipes (water hyacinth), 224,
    238
Elaenia martinica (Caribbean elaenia), 254
Eleagnus angustifolia (Russian olive), 23, 248,
    274
Eleagnus pungens (silverberry), 273
Eleusine spp. (millet), 84
Ellstrand, N.C., 66, 76–77
Elms (Ulmus spp.), 169
Elton, Charles, ix–x, 92
Elymus smithii (western wheatgrass), 127

Endangerment: description of, 220. See also
    Extinction/extirpation
Endophytes, 150
Enemy release hypothesis, 92, 95, 97–102
English walnuts (Juglans regia), 121–122
Epistasis, 9, 39–40
Ergot fungus (Claviceps purpurea), 64
Erinaceus europaeus (hedgehogs), 192–193
Eriocheir sinensis (Chinese mitten crab), 53
Erysiphe graminis (powdery mildew of
    wheat/barley), 156
Escherichia coli, 149
Esox lucius hybrids (northern pike), 68
Esox masquinogy hybrids (muskellunge), 68
Establishment: evolutionary adaptations for,
    19–21, 29–31; seed traits and, 17–18, 30,
    31
Ethiopian wolf (Canis simiensis), 74
Eucalyptus, 212. See also Australian eucalypts
Eugandina rosea (rosy wolfsnail), 222
Euhrychiopsis lecontei (weevil), 185
Euphorbia esula (leafy spurge), 42, 241
Euphydryas editha (Edith's checkerspot
    butterfly), 174–176, 279
Euphydryas phaeton (Baltimore checkerspot
    butterfly), 177
Eurasian collared dove (Streptopelia decaocto),
    21
Eurasian water milfoil (Myriophyllum
    spicatum), 185
European beachgrass (Aimophila arenaria),
    274
European brown trout (Salmo trutta),
    151
European corn borer (Ostrinia nubilalis),
    131, 266
European crabs (Carcinus), 49
European green crab: Carcinus aestuarii,
    101; Carcinus maenas, 49, 101, 189–191
European hare (Lepus europaeus), 146
European laurel (Laurus nobilis), 272–273
European periwinkle (Littorina littorea), 59
European pines (Pinus spp.), 274
European pine shoot beetle (Tomicus
    piniperda), 126
European quail (Coturnix coturnix), 229–230
European rabbit (Oryctolagus cuniculus), 115,
    128, 146, 233, 240–241
European starling (Sturnus vulgaris):
    dispersal/establishment of, 20–21;

genetic variability of, 38–39, 45; parasites of, 101–102, 214

Eutrophication, 224

Evolutionary change: interactions of aliens/natives, 119; by natives (overview), 9–10, 13–14; overview, ix–x, xi, 1–2, 5–7, 10–11, 61–62

Extinction: description of, 220; Pleistocene glaciation/Lesser Antilles, 255; recovery from, 270; speciation and, 269–271; species accumulation by aliens, 214–215

Extinction/extirpation: Apache trout, 219–220; competition/hybridization interaction, 230; disease agents and, 226–227; due to predation/herbivory, 221–224; human activities and, 13, 220–221, 269–270; hybridization and, 227–230; interspecific competition and, 224–226; overview, xi–xii, 12–13, 219, 220–221; threat summary table, 221

Extirpation: description of, 220. *See also* Extinction/extirpation

Fabaceae family, 129

Facultative forms (microorganisms), 149

Fallopia species/varieties, 66–67

False flax (*Camelina sativa*), 22

Felis catus (cat), 192–193, 224, 227

Felis sylvestris (cat), 74

Fennel (*Foeniculum vulgare*), 184

Fescue (*Festuca arundinacea*), 106

Festuca arundinacea (fescue), 106

Ficedula hypoleuca (pied flycatcher), 284

Field gentian (*Gentianella campestris*), 164

Field mustard (*Brassica rapa*), 83, 117

Filchak, K.E., 181

Finches, ground (*Geospiza* spp.), 261

Finches, tree (*Camarhynchus* spp.), 261

Fir (*Abies* spp.), 207

Fir canker, 52

Fire ant (*Solenopsis invicta*), 247–248, 283

Flamegold tree (*Koelreuteria elegans*), 182, 183–184

Flatsedges (*yperus* spp.), 235

Flaviviruses, 159

Flax (*Linum usitatissimum*), 22

Flecker, A.S., 191

Foeniculum vulgare (fennel), 184

Forestiera ligustrina, 103

Forestry and species introduction, 22–23

Founder effect: Argentine ant example, 32–33; description of, 8; genetic variability and, 38–40; self-fertilization and, 30

Fountain grass (*Pennisetum setaceum*), 103

Foxes (*Vulpes* spp.), 157

Freidenberg, L.K., 200

Freshwater drum (*Aplodinotus grunniens*), 247

Frost grape (*Vitis riparia*), 54

Fruit fly (*Drosophila subobscura*): geographical cline of, 111; parasitoid interactions, 136

Fry, J.D., 129

Fry, W.E., 148

Fuchsia excorticata (tree fuchsia), 170

Fungal diseases: genetic variability and, 46; hybridization and, 69–70, 74–75, 151–152; introduction sources and, 50–51, 52; overcoming resistance by, 156; release from, 100. *See also* specific diseases

Funk, D.J., 124–125

Furanocoumarins, 125

Fusarium circinatum (pitch canker), 170–171

Galaxias, 188–189

Galaxias truttaceus, 267

Gall tissue induction, 176

Gambusia affinis. See Mosquitofish

Gambusia spp.: biological control and, 236; hybridization of, 228

Garlic mustard (*Alliaria petiolata*), 52

Gasparich, G.E., 56

Gasterosteus aculeatus (threespine stickleback), 141–142, 143–144, 267

Gene-for-gene pattern (host/pathogen), 152–153, 156, 171

Genetic analysis: cryptic species and, 48–51; disproving human introductions, 59; introduction source areas and, 46, 47–48, 51–55; invasion routes and, 57–59

Genetic bottlenecking: example of, 108; from founder populations, 30, 38

Genetic drift: Asian tiger mosquito, 111; smooth cordgrass example, 106

Genetic engineering. *See* Transgenes/hybridization

Genetic variability: additive genetic variation, 39; among alien animals, 32–33, 42–46; among alien microorganisms, 46; among alien plants, 40–42; Argentine ant example, 32–33; biological control and, 60; founder effect and, 38–40; herbivory/alien plants, 174, 176, 178; hybridization and, 64, 65; invasiveness and, 46; plants response to disease, 170–173

Genetic variability assessment: allozyme analysis, 34; chloroplast DNA analysis, 38; DNA fragment length polymorphism analyses, 34–36; DNA/RNA sequencing, 38; microsatellite analysis, 36–37; mitochondrial DNA analysis, 37; overview, x–xi, 33–34

Gentianella campestris (field gentian), 164

Geographic location and species diversity, 92

Geospiza spp. (ground finches), 261

Geranium molle (wild geranium), 283

Giant kangaroo rat (*Dipodomys ingens*), 248

Giant ragweed (*Ambrosia trifida*), 124

Gil-ad, N.L., 63

Glaciation retreat/colonization, 250, 251, 267–268

Global climate change: climate zone shifts and, 278–281; community alteration with, 272–273, 276–281, 283–284; components of, 276–277; invasive/noninvasive species, 280–281; marine ecosystems and, 277; overview, 10–11, 15; phenology changes with, 278, 282–283, 285; shifting ranges and, 281–283, 284, 285; terrestrial ecosystems and, 277, 278–280

Global consequences overview, 217–218

Glossy privet (*Ligustrum lucidum*), 273

Glucosinolates, 165

Glycine max. See Soybean

Glycosides, 169

Goat's beard (genus *Tragopogon*), 66, 258–259, 261

Goeden, R.D., 209

Goldenrain tree (*Koelreuteria paniculata*), 182, 183

Goldwire (*Hypericum concinnum*), 233

Goodwin, B.J., 27

Goodwin, S.B., 148

Gossypium. See Cotton

Gould, F., 128, 129

Gowen, S.R., 240

Graham, M., 121

Grape phylloxera (*Daktulosphaira vitafoliae*), 54

Grasshopper mice (*Onychomys leucogaster*), 199–200

Gray, A.J., 17

Gray-breasted silvereye (*Zosterops lateralis*), 115

Grayling (*Thymallus thymallus*), 112

Gray squirrel (*Sciurus carolinensis*), 21, 226

Gray wolf (*Canis lupus*), 74, 146

Greater scaup (*Aythya marila*), 246

Green amaranth (*Amaranthus retroflexus*), 106

Greenfinch (*Carduelis chloris*), 45

Green lacewing (*Chrysoperla carnea*), 86

Green peach aphid (*Myzus persicae*), 129

Green sunfish (*Lepomis cyanellus*), 68, 280–281

Groundnut (*Apios americana*), 261

Groundsel (*Senecio cambrensis*), 263–264

Groundsel (*Senecio vulgaris hibernicus*), 263–264

Groundsel, common (*Senecio vulgaris*): adaptation of, 109; establishment of, 30, 31; speciation and, 263–264

Growth (aliens vs. natives), 102–103

Guppy (*Poecilia reticulata*), 194–196

Gypsy moth (*Lymantria dispar*): American chestnut and, 172–173; biological control and, 235; extirpation by, 224; host shifts of, 127; plant adaptations/responses to, 161–162, 169–170

Habitat fragmentation: global climate change and, 280; invasiveness and, 11, 28; species numbers and, 271

Habitat generalism, 27

Hairy cat's ear (*Hypochoeris radicata*), 18

Hakeas, 274

Hamilton, C.W., 27

Hampea, 129–130

Harrison, G.D., 179

Havill, N.P., 170

Hawaii: biological control and, 236, 238;

bird beaks/competition, 249–250; competition of introduced species, 248–250; extinctions and, 221–223, 225, 227, 249; introduced species and, 23, 248–250, 274; species invasiveness in, 27

Hawai'i 'amakihi (*Hemignathus virens*), 199

Hawaiian crow (*Corvus hawaiiensis*), 227

Hawkins, B.A., 202, 213

Hawkins, B.C., 235

Hawthorns (*Crataegus* spp.), 180–181

Heartseed vine (*Cardiospermum halicacabum*), 182, 183

Hedgehogs (*Erinaceus europaeus*), 192–193

Hedrick, R.P., 198

Hedylepta spp. (moth), 266

Helianthus. *See* Sunflowers

Helicoverpa zea (corn earworm), 127

Hemignathus flavus (O'ahu 'amakihi), 199

Hemignathus virens (Hawai'i 'amakihi), 199

Hemileuca maia (silk moth), 235

Hendry, A.P., 268

Heracleum lanatum (cow parsnip), 125

Herbicide resistance: selection for, 85; transgenes/hybridization and, 77, 79, 83, 85

Herbivore adaptation (aliens): biotypes/races of, 123–124, 129–132, 178, 186–187; codling moth example, 121–122; coevolution of plants/herbivores, 122–123; crop rotation and, 130; from Europe to North America, 126–127; host shifts by, 121–122, 124–128; by insect arthropods, 128–132; ongoing evolution, 132–133; specialization by, 123–125

Herbivore adaptation (natives) to alien plants: crop plants, 177, 179–181; Edith's checkerspot butterfly example, 174–176; hosts shifts, 176–178; insects/noncrop plants, 181–185; opportunities vs. challenges, 187; pocket gophers, 176, 185–186; speciation and, 186–187

Herbivory adaptations by plants: evolutionary responses, 161, 162–164; gypsy moth example, 161–162; herbaceous plants/grazing animals, 166–169; herbaceous plants/herbivorous invertebrates, 164–166; overview, 173; in woody plants, 169–170

Herbivory release, 98–100

Herpestes javanicus. *See* Indian mongoose

Hessian fly (*Mayetiola destructor*), 127, 131–132

Heteropogon contortus (pili grass), 103

Hevea brasiliensis (rubber tree), 206

Hill, G.E., 114

Hill, J.K., 28

Hochberg, M.E., 234

Holly-leaved barberry (*Mahonia aquifolium*), 272–273

Holt, R.D., 234

Homoploid hybrid speciation, 262, 263

Honeyeater: *Myzomela pammelaena,* 145; *Myzomela schlateri,* 145

Honeysuckle (*Lonicera* spp.), 184, 273

Honnay, O., 280

Hordeum vulgare (barley), 84

Horse nettle (*Solanum carolinense*), 132, 133

Horticulture: hybridization with, 71–72; species introduction and, 22, 23, 24

Horton, D.R., 179–180

House finch (*Carpodacus mexicanus*), 12–115, 113

House mouse (*Mus musculus*): adaptations to new habitat, 110, 115, 145; speciation and, 269

House sparrow (*Passer domesticus*): adaptation to new habitats, 112–113; aliens' reduced parasitism, 101–102; dispersal/establishment of, 20–21; parasite accumulation of, 214; West Nile virus and, 157

Hoyle, S.T., 25

Huxel, G. R., 230

Hybridization: for agriculture, 71–72; between alien animals, 67–68; between alien/native animals, 72–74; between alien/native microbial species, 74–75; between alien/native plants, 70–72; between alien plants, 66–67; competition/hybridization interaction, 230; complexity of consequences, 64, 65; extinction/extirpation and, 227–230; for horticulture, 71–72; introgressive hybridization, 228, 230; between microbial species, 68–70; overview, xi, 63–66; significance of, ix, 75; speciation with, 259–264. *See also* Transgenes/hybridization

Hybrid sport fish, 68

Hybrid vigor, 64–65

Hydrilla (*Hydrilla verticillata*), 51

Hylobius transversovittatus (root-feeding beetle), 117

Hypera brunneipennis (weevil), 240

Hypericum calycinum (creeping St. John's wort/Aaron's beard), 232–233

Hypericum concinnum (goldwire), 233

Hypericum perforatum. See Common St. John's wort

Hyperparasitism, 214, 238

Hypochoeris radicata (hairy cat's ear), 18

Ictalurus furcatus (blue catfish), 247

I'iwi (*Vestiaria coccinea*), 197

Imura, O., 206, 207

Inbreeding depression, 30, 108

Indian mongoose (*Herpestes javanicus*): for biological control, 236, 238; evolutionary adaptation of, 134–135, 146; extirpations by, 222

Indian rice grass (*Oryzopsis hymenoides*), 166

Indirect defense, 164

Induced defense, 162–163

Influenza virus, 158–159

Inouye, D.W., 282

Insecticides, 85

Insect pollination and transgenes, 78

Insular communities: extinction and, 220–221, 223; invasibility and, 96–97; species and, 266–267; species diversity and, 92; taxon cycles and, 257. *See also* Island communities

Integration. *See* Counteradaptation/integration

Intracontinental vs. intercontinental aliens, 285

Introduction source areas: biological control and, 59–60; genetic analysis and, 46, 47–48, 51–55; with multiple introductions, 55–57; overview, 47–48, 60

Introgressive hybridization, 65, 228, 230

Invasibility: coevolved relationships and, 90–91; diffuse knapweed example, 89–90; escape from coevolved relationships, 92, 95, 97–102; insular communities and, 96–97; mutualistic relationships and, 103–104; natural selection and, 104; plant traits and, 25–27; resources and, 94, 95, 96; species diversity and, 92–96; stability/predictability and, 91–92, 93

Invasional meltdown, 275–276

Invasion/differentiation patterns: of Lesser Antilles, 254–257; taxon cycle of, 257; understanding of, 253–254; of West Indian islands, 254–257

Invasion routes, 57–59

Invertebrate herbivore specialization, 123, 125–126

Ipomopsis aggregata (scarlet gilia), 164

Island communities: extinction and, 220–223; taxon cycles and, 257. *See also* specific areas

"Island syndrome" (adaptation), 110

Italian thistle (*Carduus pycnocephalus*), 209

Jackman, Todd, 47–48

Jack pine (*Pinus banksiana*), 126

Jadera haematoloma. See Soapberry bug

Jander, G., 165

Japanese beetle (*Popilia japonica*), 165–166, 169

Japanese blue oak (*uercus glauca*), 211

Japanese chestnut (*Castanea crenata*), 202, 203

Japanese dogwood (*Cornus kousa*), 51

Japanese quail (*Coturnix japonica*), 229–230

Jarvinen, A., 284

Jellyfish (*Aurelia*), 49

Jimson weed (*Datura stramonium*), 165–166

Johnsongrass (*Sorghum halepense*): as hybrid, 67; transgenes/hybridization, 76–77, 78, 82

Jointed goatgrass (*Aegilops cylindrica*), 83, 154

Jones, S., 278

Juglans cinerea (North American butternut), 46, 52

Juglans regia (English walnuts), 121–122

Kay, S.H., 25

Kelly, C.K., 284

Kennedy, T.A., 94

Kiesecker, J.M., 193, 194

King, W.B., 220

Kiore (*Rattus exulans*), 145, 192–193, 221

Klinger, T., 81

Knops, J.M.H., 94

Knotweeds (*Fallopia* species/varieties), 66–67
Koelreuteria elegans (flamegold tree), 182, 183–184
Koelreuteria paniculata (goldenrain tree), 182, 183
Kogan, M., 210
Koricheva, J., 117
Kraaijeveld, A.R., 136
Kristjánsson, B.K., 143–144
Kudzu (*Pueraria lobata*), 39

Lace bug (*Teleonemia scrupulosa*), 238
Lactuca muralis (wall-lettuce), 18
Lake whitefish: *Coregonus clupeiformis,* 140; *Coregonus* spp., 140–141
Lampetra minima (Miller Lake lamprey), 223
Lantana camara, 227–228, 238
Lantana camara × *L. depressa,* 71, 228
Lantana depressa, 227–228
Larch (*Larix*), 207
Largemouth bass (*Micropterus salmoides*), 223, 280–281
Larinus planus (weevil), 237
Larivière, S., 146
Larix (larch), 207
Larrea divaricata, 252–253
Larrea tridentata (creosote bush), 252–253
Laspeyresia pomonella (codling moth), 121–122, 130
Lates nilotica (Nile perch), 223–224
Laurus nobilis (European laurel), 272–273
Lawton, J.H., 211
Leaf-mining insects, 202–203, 210–211
Leafy spurge (*Euphorbia esula*): biological control and, 241; genetic variability of, 42
Lemna spp. (duckweeds), 19
Lens esculenta (lentil), 22
Lentil (*Lens esculenta*), 22
Leon Springs pupfish (*Cyprinodon bovinus*), 228
Leopold, A., 278
Lepidoptera and Bt gene, 85, 86
Lepomis cyanellus (green sunfish), 68, 280–281
Lepomis gibbosus (pumpkinseed), 141, 247
Lepomis macrochirus (bluegill sunfish), 68, 141, 280–281
Lepomis microlophus (redear sunfish), 247

Leptinotarsa decimlineata (Colorado potato beetle), 132, 133
Lepus europaeus (European hare), 146
Lesser Antillean bullfinch (*Loxigilla noctis*), 254
Lesser Antilles bird fauna, 254–257
Lesser scaup (*Aythya affinis*), 246
Levine, J.M., 5
Levins, R., 110
"Liberty elm," 170
Light, T., 91–92
Ligustrum lucidum (glossy privet), 273
Ligustrum sinense, 103
Limber pine (*Pinus flexilis*), 171
Linepithema humile. See Argentine ant
Linum marginale (Australian flax), 149, 153
Linum usitatissimum (flax), 22
Lithocarpus densiflorus (tanoak), 48, 148, 149
Little blue stem (*Schizachryium scoparium*), 166–167
Littorina littorea (European periwinkle), 59
Littorina obtusata, 190
Littorina snails, 190–191
Lively, C.M., 188
Lobelia, 197
Lockwood, J.L., 219
Lodge, D.M., 27
Lodgepole pine: *Pinus contorta,* 28, 280; *Pinus murrayana,* 251
Lomolino, M.V., 221
Long-spined water flea (*Bythotrephes longimanus*), 56, 68–69
Long-winged cone-head (*Conocephalus discolor*), 29
Lonicera, 67
Lonsdale, W.M., 93
Louda, S.M., 240
Lovette, I.J., 254
Loxia curvirostra/percna (red crossbills), 250–251
Loxigilla noctis (Lesser Antillean bullfinch), 254
Luke, C., 242
Lupines (*Lupinus* spp.), 155
Lycopersicon esculentum (tomato), 3–4, 129
Lygodium spp. (climbing fern), 25
Lymantria dispar. See Gypsy moth
Lyssavirus, 157
Lythrum salicaria. See Purple loosestrife

MacArthur, Robert, 93

MacDonald, G.M., 28

Mack, R.N., 89

Macropus eugenii (Tammar wallabies), 117–118

Madeira, P.T., 36, 51

Madrone (*Arbutus menziesii*), 148

Maggot, apple fly (*Rhagoletis* spp.), 180–181, 265

Magnaporthe grisea (rice blast fungus), 156

Mahonia aquifolium (holly-leaved barberry), 272–273

Mahonia spp., 154

Maize (*Zea mays*): pests of, 130, 131, 151, 266; transgenes and, 79, 80, 86, 87; weed hybridization, 84

Malacosoma disstria (tent caterpillars), 169

Malaria, 158. *See also* Avian malaria

Malcolm, J.R., 281

Mallard (*Anas platyrhynchos*), 229

Malus pumila (apple), 121–122

Malus sylvestris (apple), 180–181

Maple: *Acer campestre,* 207, 211; *Acer pseudoplatanus,* 207, 211

Marenzelleria (marine polychaete worms), 48–49

Marine algae (*Caulerpa taxifolia*), 55, 110

Marine polychaete worms (*Marenzelleria*), 48–49

Marino, P.C., 235

Marmota flaviventris (yellow-bellied marmot), 282

Maron, J., 242

Marsh frog (*Rana ridibunda*), 45

Marsupial wolf (*Thylacinus cyanocephalus*), 117–118

Martin, T.E., 114

Mauricio, R., 165

Mayetiola destructor (Hessian fly), 127, 131–132

Mayfly (*Nesameletus ornatus*), 188–189

Mayfly drift-feeding, 191

McFadyen, R.E.C., 235

McMahon, R.F., 27

McPhail, J.D., 267

Meadow rue (*Thalictrum* spp.), 153

Medicago polymorpha (burr medic), 107

Medicago sativa (alfalfa), 180, 185–186, 242–243, 266

Mediterranean fruit fly (*Ceratitis capitata*):

actions against, 57; genetic variability of, 44, 57; host shifts of, 127; multiple introductions of, 56–57

Melaleuca quinquenervia (Australian paperbark), 23, 211–212, 273–274

Melampsora lini (rust), 149, 153

Melampsora medusae, 74

Melampsora occidentalis, 74

Melampsora × columbiana, 74–75

Meloidogyne, 240, 243

Memmott, J., 210

Mephitis spp. (skunks), 157

Messenger, P., 240

Metrioptera roeselii (Roesel's bush cricket), 29

Metrosideros polymorpha (Ohia tree), 197

Mexican fruit fly (*Anastrepha ludens*), 127

Meyer, S.E., 31

Miconia calvescens, 225

Micropterus salmoides (largemouth bass), 223, 280–281

Microsatellite analysis, 32, 36–37

Microsatellites, 36

Microtus arvalis (common vole), 54

Milk thistle (*Silybum marianum*), 209

Milkweeds (*Asclepias* spp.), 86, 123

Miller, K.R., 220

Miller Lake lamprey (*Lampetra minima*), 223

Millet: *Eleusine* spp., 84; *Setaria* spp., 84

Mimicry in agroecotypes, 21–22

Mitchell, C.E., 100

Mite (*Aculus hyperici*), 242

Mitochondrial DNA analysis, 37

Molothrus ater (brown-headed cowbird), 196–197

Monarch butterfly (*Danaus plexippus*): Bt endotoxin and, 86; milkweed and, 86, 123

Monopterus (swamp eels), 49–50

Monopterus albus (Asian swamp eel), 50

Monterey pine (*Pinus radiata*), 170–171, 274

Morrison, L.W., 247–248

Mosquito: *Aedes aegypti formosus/aegypti,* 137–138; *Culex quinquefasciatus,* 198

Mosquitofish (*Gambusia affinis*): adaptation of, 112, 113; as biological control, 238; effects on native species, 223; hybridization of, 228; rapid evolution in, 142–143

Moth (*Hedylepta* spp.), 266
Mountain muhly (*Muhlenbergia montana*), 166
Moxostoma hubbsi (copper redhorse), 247
Moyle, P.B., 91–92
Mugwort (Artemisia *vulgaris*), 266
Muhlenbergia montana (mountain muhly), 166
Musa paradisiaca (banana), 266
Muskellunge (*Esox masquinogy*) hybrids, 68
Musk thistle (*Carduus nutans*), 127–128, 236, 240
Mus musculus. See House mouse
Mustela erminea (stoat/short-tailed weasel), 146, 192–193
Mutualistic relationships:
  description/examples of, 149, 150;
  herbivory and, 163–164; invasibility and,
  103–104
Mycorrhizal fungi, 103
Myoporum sandwicense (naio), 238
Myriophyllum sibericum (water milfoil), 185
Myriophyllum spicatum (Eurasian water milfoil), 185
Myxobolus cerebralis, 151
Myxobolus cerebralis (whirling disease), 151, 197–198
Myxomatosis, 233, 240–241, 243
Myzomela pammelaena (honeyeater), 145
Myzomela schlateri (honeyeater), 145
Myzus persicae (green peach aphid), 129

Naeem, S., 94–95
Naio (*Myoporum sandwicense*), 238
Narrowleaf hawksbeard (*Crepis tectorum*), 94–95
Neochetina eichhorniae (weevil), 238
Neositta spp. (sittellas), 252
Nepal camphor tree (*Cinnamomum glanduliferum*), 273
Nesameletus ornatus (mayfly), 188–189
Nesogobius melanostomus (round goby), 55
Newman, R.M., 185
Nicklin, M.O., 190
Nilaparvata lugens (rice planthopper), 124
Nile perch (*Lates nilotica*), 223–224
Ninespine stickleback (*Pungitius pungitius*), 144–145
Nitrogen-fixing organisms, 103, 150
North American barberries, 154

North American butternut (*Juglans cinerea*), 46, 52
Northern corn rootworm (*Diabrotica barberi*), 130–131
Northern pike (*Esox lucius*) hybrids, 68
Norway maple (Acer *platanoides*), 280
Norway rat (*Rattus norvegicus*), 145
Nothofagus spp. (beeches), 211
Nötzold, R., 102, 116–117, 118
Nugent, G., 170

O'ahu 'amakihi (*Hemignathus flavus*), 199
Oaks. *See Quercus* species
Oat crown rust (*Puccinia coronata*), 153
Oceanographic Museum of Monaco, 110
Odocoileus virginianus (white-tailed deer), 146
Odontesthes spp. (silverside fish), 267
Ohia tree (*Metrosideros polymorpha*), 197
Oilseed rape (*Brassica napus*), 80, 83, 84
Oncorhynchus apache (Apache trout), 219–220
Oncorhynchus clarki. See Cutthroat trout
Oncorhynchus nerka (sockeye salmon), 268–269
Oncorhynchus spp. (Pacific salmon), 73
Oncorhynchus tshawytscha (chinook salmon), 73–74, 111–112
Oncorynchus mykiss. See Rainbow trout
Onopordum, 67
Onychomys leucogaster (grasshopper mice), 199–200
Ophiostoma forms/subspecific forms, 69–70
Ophiostoma ulmi. See Dutch elm disease
Opuntia spp. (prickly pear cacti), 176, 212, 237–238, 239–240
Orconectes propinquus, 72, 230
Orconectes rusticus, 72, 225, 230
Orconectes spp. and hybridization, 228
Orconectes virilis, 72
Oreochromis (tilapia) hybrids, 67–68
Oriental fruit fly (*Bactrocera dorsalis*), 127
Orthorhynchus cristatus (Antillean crested hummingbird), 254
Oryctolagus cuniculus (European rabbit), 115, 128, 146, 233, 240–241
Oryza spp. (rice), 22, 84
Oryzopsis hymenoides (Indian rice grass), 166
Osmerus mordax (rainbow smelt), 139–140, 196, 268

O'Steen, S., 195, 196
Ostrinia nubilalis (European corn borer), 131, 266
Outcrossing and establishment, 30
Overton, Jacob, 17–19
Owenby, Marion, 258
Oxford ragwort (Senecio squalidus), 263
Oxyura jamaicensis (ruddy duck), 229
Oxyura leucocephala (white-headed duck), 229

Pacific salmon (Oncorhynchus spp.), 73
Pantinaca sativa (wild parsnip), 125
Papaver rhoeas (corn poppy), 109
Papilio zelicaon (western anise swallowtail butterfly), 184
Pararge aegeria (speckled wood butterfly), 28
Parasites: adaptations of, 136, 137; of alien animals, 212, 214; aliens reduced load of, 100–102; dispersal of, 20
Parasitic castrator, 101
Parasitic wasp (Bathyplectes curculionis), 240
Parasitoids: adaptations (aliens) of, 136, 137; of alien animals, 212–214; alien hosts of natives, 193
Parasitoid wasp (Aphidius ervi), 137, 242–243
Parchman, T.L., 250
Parsnip webworm (Depressaria pastinacella), 125
Parthenogenetic reproduction, 126, 129
Partula spp., 222
Passer domesticus. See House sparrow
Pasturella penetrans, 240, 243
Pathogenic microorganisms, 149
Patton, J.L., 185
Pea aphid (Acyrthosiphon pisum), 129, 137, 242, 265–266
Pears (Pyrus communis), 121
Pecos pupfish (Cyprinodon pecosensis), 228
Pectinophora gossypiella (pink bollworm), 88
Pelsor, M., 94
Pemberton, R.W., 127, 235
Pennisetum setaceum (fountain grass), 103
Perna perna (brown mussel), 43
Pesticide resistance: diamondback moth and, 128; of disease vectors, 158; genetic engineering and, 86–87, 88
Pest management, 178
Petroica rodinogaster (pink robin), 251–252

Petromyzon marinus (sea lamprey), 196, 223
Phaseolus, 84
Phoridae flies, 60, 101
Phrynosoma coronatum (coast horned lizard), 32
Phyllonorycter, 212, 213
Phytophthora: hybrids, 70; nicotianae × cactorum, 74; rapid evolution of, 155–156; sojae, 155–156
Phytophthora infestans. See Potato late blight
Phytophthora ramorum. See Sudden oak death fungus
Picea abies (spruce), 207
Picea glauca (white spruce), 277–278
Picea mariana (black spruce), 250
Pied flycatcher (Ficedula hypoleuca), 284
Pieris rapae (cabbage butterfly), 127, 239
Pike cichlid (Crenicichla alta), 195–196
Pili grass (Heteropogon contortus), 103
Pine species: seed characteristics/invasiveness, 26. See also individual species
Pine wood nematode (Bursaphelenchus xylophilus), 151
Pink bollworm (Pectinophora gossypiella), 88
Pink robin (Petroica rodinogaster), 251–252
Pin oak (Quercus palustris), 149
Pinus albicaulis (whitebark pine), 155
Pinus banksiana (jack pine), 126
Pinus cembra (Swiss stone pine), 280
Pinus contorta (lodgepole pine), 28, 280
Pinus edulis (Colorado pinyon), 172
Pinus flexilis (limber pine), 171
Pinus lambertiana (sugar pine), 155, 171, 172
Pinus monophylla (singleleaf pinyon), 172
Pinus monticola (western white pine), 155, 171–172
Pinus murrayana (lodgepole pine), 251
Pinus nigra (Australian pine), 126
Pinus ponderosa (ponderosa pine), 126
Pinus radiate (Monterey pine), 170–171, 274
Pinus resinosa (red pine), 126
Pinus spp. (European pines), 274
Pinus strobiformis (southwestern white pine), 171
Pinus strobes (eastern white pine), 155
Pinus sylvestris (Scotch pine), 126, 282
Pinyon pine blister rust (Cronartium occidentale), 172
Pitch canker (Fusarium circinatum), 170–171

Pitcher's thistle (*Cirsium pitcheri*), 237

Plague (*Yersinia pestis*), 199–200

Plane tree (*Platanus* spp.), 212, 213

Plant adaptations: to alien diseases, 170–173. *See also* Herbivory adaptations by plants

Plantago lanceolata (ribwort plantain), 168, 174–176, 177

Planthopper *Prokelisia marginata,* 105–106

Plasmodium relictum, 151, 198–199

Plasmodium spp., 158

Platanus spp. (plane tree), 212, 213

Platte thistle (*Cirsium canescens*), 237, 238

Pleistocene glaciation retreat/colonization, 250, 251, 267–268

Plum (*Prunus domestica*), 121–122

Plutella xylostella (diamondback moth), 87, 128

Poa annua (annual bluegrass), 108

Poa bulbosa. See Bulbous bluegrass

Poecilia reticulata, 223

Poecilia reticulate (guppy), 194–196

Polioptila californica (California gnatcatcher), 197

Polymerase chain reaction (PCR), 35, 36

Polyphagous species, 123

Polyploidy and speciation, 259–260, 265

Ponderosa pine (*Pinus ponderosa*), 126

Popilia japonica (Japanese beetle), 165–166, 169

Poplars (*Populus* spp.), 169, 170

Populus deltoids (eastern cottonwood), 74–75

Populus tremuloides (trembling aspen), 169

Populus trichocarpa (black cottonwood), 74–75

Pornkulwat, S., 131

Porter, S.D., 247

Potato (*Solanum tuberosum*): pests of, 3–4, 132, 133; transgenes and, 79

Potato late blight (*Phytophthora infestans*): evolution and, 3–4; host resistance/pathogen virulence, 156; interbreeding potential, 151–152, 156; migration of, 148

Powdery mildew of wheat/barley (*Erysiphe graminis*), 156

Power, A.G., 100

Prairie dog (*Cynomys* spp.), 199

Predation: animal adaptation to aliens, 189–197; extinction/extirpation and, 221–224

Predator adaptations (aliens): animal disease vectors, 137–138; aquatic vertebrate predators, 138–145; divergent forms in fish, 139–145; invertebrate predators, 137; mongoose example, 134–135; overview, 147; prey interactions, 135–137; terrestrial vertebrate predators, 145–146

Prickly pear cacti (*Opuntia* spp.), 176, 212, 237–238, 239–240

Primula, 74

Procyon lotor (raccoon), 157

Prokelisia marginata (planthopper), 105–106

Prunus (cherry species), 181

Prunus domestica (plum), 121–122

Prunus laurocerasus (cherry laurel), 272–273

Pseudacteon spp., 101

Pseudotsuga menziesii (Douglas-fir), 149

Puccinia chondrillina (rust), 242

Puccinia coronata (oat crown rust), 153

Puccinia graminis (wheat stem rust), 153, 154

Puccinia striiformis (wheat/barley stripe rust), 153, 154

Puccinia triticina (wheat leaf rust), 153–154

Pueraria lobata (kudzu), 39

Pumpkinseed (*Lepomis gibbosus*), 141, 247

Pungitius pungitius (ninespine stickleback), 144–145

Purple loosestrife (*Lythrum salicaria*): herbivory of, 209; host shifts and, 176; native/alien growth of, 102; reduced defenses and, 117

Pyracantha, 212

Pyrus communis (pears), 121

Quagga mussel (*Dreissena bugensis*): counteradaptation/integration and, 245–246; extirpation by, 225–226; genetic variability of, 43

Quercus acutissima (sawtooth oak), 202–203, 210–211

Quercus agrifolia (coast live oak), 171

Quercus cerris, 211

Quercus glauca (Japanese blue oak), 211

Quercus ilex, 207

Quercus nigra (water oak), 202

Quercus palustris (pin oak), 149

Quercus petraea, 207

Quercus robur, 207, 211
Quercus rubra (red oak), 149, 161–162, 169
Quercus spp., 148, 169, 211
Quinoa (*Chenopodium quinoa*), 84
Quiscalus lugubris (Carib grackle), 254–255

Rabbit hemorrhagic disease (RHD), 241
Rabies virus, 157
Raccoon (*Procyon lotor*), 157
Radish (*Raphanus sativus*), 81
Raffa, K.F., 170
Ragweed aphid (*Uroleucon ambrosiae*), 124–125
Ragwort (*Senecio inaequidens*), 12
Rainbow smelt (*Osmerus mordax*), 139–140, 196, 268
Rainbow trout (*Oncorynchus mykiss*): Apache trout and, 219–220; prey adaptations to, 191; whirling disease and, 198
Rana aurora (red-legged frog), 193–194
Rana catesbeiana (bullfrog), 103, 193–194, 223
Rana ridibunda (marsh frog), 45
Rana sylvatica (wood frog), 200
Random amplified polymorphic DNA analysis (RAPD), 35–36
Rangifer tarandus (reindeer), 248
Raphanus raphanistrum (wild radish), 83–84
Raphanus sativus (radish), 81
Rats (*Rattus* spp.), 146
Rattus exulans (kiore), 145, 192–193, 221
Rattus norvegicus (Norway rat), 145
Rattus rattus (black rat), 115, 145, 192–193
Rausher, M.D., 165
Red brome (*Bromus rubens*), 109
Red clover (*Trifolium pretense*), 242–243
Red crossbills (*Loxia curvirostra/percna*), 250–251
Red deer (*Cervus elaphus*), 229
Redear sunfish (*Lepomis microlophus*), 247
Red fire ant (*Solenopsis wagneri*), 43–44
Red fox (*Vulpes vulpes*), 45, 224, 230
Red-legged frog (*Rana aurora*), 193–194
Red oak (*Quercus rubra*), 149, 161–162, 169
Red pine (*Pinus resinosa*), 126
Red Queen Hypothesis, 189
Red squirrel (*Sciurus vulgaris*), 226, 250–251
Red wolf (*Canis rufus*), 146
Redwood (*Sequoia sempervirens*), 149, 227

Reichard, S.H., 27
Reid, W.V., 220
Reimchen, T.E., 145
Reindeer (*Rangifer tarandus*), 248
Relaxation (biotic), 270–271
Reproduction system shift, 107–108
Reproductive performance, 103
Resource use in invasion phase, 26
Restriction enzymes, 34–35
Restriction fragment length polymorphism (RFLP), 35
Reznicek, A.A., 63
Rhagoletis spp., 180–181, 184, 265
Rhinocyllus conicus (weevil), 127–128, 236–237, 238, 240
Rhizophora mangle (American mangrove), 212
Rhododendron, 67, 148
Rhododendron ponticum, 211
Rhynchosporium secale (barley leaf blotch fungus), 156
Ribes spp., 155
Ribwort plantain (*Plantago lanceolata*), 168, 174–176, 177
Ricciardi, A., 276
Rice: *Oryza* sativa, 22; *Oryza* spp., 84
Rice blast fungus (*Magnaporthe grisea*), 156
Rice planthopper (*Nilaparvata lugens*), 124
Ricklefs, R.E., 256
Rieseberg, L.H., 262
Robinson, B.W., 134, 136
Roesel's bush cricket (*Metrioptera roeselii*), 29
Roff, D.A., 28
Root-feeding beetle (*Hylobius transversovittatus*), 117
Rorippa austriaca × *R. sylvestris,* 71
Rose clover (*Trifolium hirtum*), 108–109
Rosy wolfsnail (*Eugandina rosea*), 222
Round goby (*Nesogobius melanostomus*), 55
Rubber tree (*Hevea brasiliensis*), 206
Rubus: alceifolius × *roridus,* 71; fungal attacks on, 70
Ruddy duck (*Oxyura jamaicensis*), 229
Rumex crispus (curly dock), 107
Rush skeletonweed (*Chondrilla juncea*), 242
Russian knapweed (*Centaurea repens*), 100
Russian olive (*Eleagnus angustifolia*), 23, 248, 274
Russian thistle (*Salsola tragus*), 209

Rust: *Melampsora lini,* 149, 153; *Puccinia chondrillina,* 242
Rust fungi and rapid evolution, 153–155
Rye (*Secale cereale*), 67

Saccharum officinarum (sugar cane), 84, 204–205
Sachem skipper (*Atalopedes campestris*), 279
Safflower (*Carthamus tinctorius*), 243–244
Salinity tolerance: selective pressures for, 29; species introductions and, 24
Salix (willows), 66
Salmo hybrids, 68
Salmo salar (Atlantic salmon), 73, 228–229
Salmo trutta (brown trout), 73, 188–189, 198
Salmo trutta (European brown trout), 151
Salsify (*Tragopogon* species), 66, 258–259, 261
Salsola tragus (Russian thistle), 209
Salt cedar. *See* Tamarisk (*Tamarix* spp.)
Salt marsh cordgrass (*Spartina maritime*), 63
Salvelinus alpinus (arctic char), 139
Salvelinus fontinalis (brook trout), 219
Salvelinus hybrids, 68
Sapium sebiferum (Chinese tallow tree), 30–31, 117, 274
SARS corona virus, 160
Savignano, D.A., 247
Sawtooth oak (*Quercus acutissima*), 202–203, 210–211
Scarlet gilia (*Ipomopsis aggregate*), 164
Schierenbeck, K.A., 66
Schinus terebinthifolius (Brazilian pepper), 27, 211, 273–274
Schizachryium scoparium (little blue stem), 166–167
Schizachryium spp., 166
Schluter, D., 137, 139, 267
Sciurus carolinensis (gray squirrel), 21, 226
Sciurus vulgaris (red squirrel), 226, 250–251
Scotch broom (*Cytisus scoparius*), 99, 210
Scotch pine (*Pinus sylvestris*), 126, 282
Sea fig: *Carpobrotus chilensis,* 71; *Carpobrotus edulis,* 71
Sea lamprey (*Petromyzon marinus*), 196, 223
Sea squirt (*Botryllus schlosseri*), 52–53, 95
Secale cereale (rye), 67
Secale montanum, 67
Seed dormancy, 26, 31

Seed morphology: dispersal and, 17–18; invasive phase and, 25–26
Seehausen, O., 260
Selective pressure: dispersal and, 17–18, 28–29; establishment and, 17–18, 28–29
Self-fertilization: genetic variability and, 40; selective pressure for, 29–30
Senecio: denticulatus ssp. *vulgaris,* 31; new species of, 261; *triangularis,* 237
Senecio cambrensis (groundsel), 263–264
Senecio inaequidens (ragwort), 12
Senecio jacobeae (tansy ragwort), 237
Senecio squalidus (Oxford ragwort), 263
Senecio sylvaticus (woodland ragwort), 17
Senecio vulgaris. See Groundsel, common
Senecio vulgaris hibernicus (groundsel), 263–264
Sequoia sempervirens (redwood), 149, 227
Serin (*Serinus serinus*), 283–284
Serinus serinus (serin), 283–284
Sesame (*Sesamum indicum*), 238
Sesamum indicum (sesame), 238
Setaria spp. (millet), 84
Sexual dimorphism, 27
Shad (*Alosa sapidissima*), 112
Shea, K., 95
Sheepshead minnow (*Cyprinodon variegatus*), 228
Shehata, C., 199
Shepherd's purse (*Capsella bursa-pastoris*), 168–169
Shonle, I., 165
Siberian elm (*Ulmus pumila*), 23
Side-oats grama (*Bouteloua curtipendula*), 167–168
Siemens, D.H., 117
Sika deer (*Cervus nippon*), 229
Silene latifolia (white campion), 98–99, 210
Silk moth (*Hemileuca maia*), 235
Silverberry (*Eleagnus pungens*), 273
Silver fir (*Abies alba*), 177–178
Silver-leaf nightshade (*Solanum eleagnifolium*), 179
Silverside fish (*Odontesthes*) spp., 267
Silybum marianum (milk thistle), 209
Simberloff, D., 102–103, 136–137, 202, 214, 232, 275–276
Sinapis arvensis (charlock mustard), 109
Singleleaf pinyon (*Pinus monophylla*), 172
Sirex noctilio (wood wasp), 234

Sirococcus clavigignenti-juglandacearum (butternut canker), 46, 52, 60

Sittellas (*Neositta* spp.), 252

Skelly, D.K., 200

Skunks (*Mephitis* spp.), 157

Slender wild oat (*Avena barbata*): adaptation of, 109; genetic variability of, 42; shift toward outcrossing, 108

Smith, S.E., 167

Smooth cordgrass (*Spartina alterniflora*): adaptation to new habitat, 29–30, 105–106; hybridization of, 70–71; speciation and, 264

Snow, A.A., 83

Soapberry bug (*Jadera haematoloma*): epistasis and, 39–40; shift to noncrop plants, 182–184

Soapberry tree (*Sapindus saponaria*), 182

Sockeye salmon (*Oncorhynchus nerka*), 268–269

Soft brome: *Bromus hordaceus*, 67; *Bromus mollis*, 30, 108

Solanum carolinense (horse nettle), 132, 133

Solanum dulcamara (bittersweet), 132

Solanum eleagnifolium (silver-leaf nightshade), 179

Solanum nigrum (black nightshade), 181

Solanum sp., 152

Solanum tomatillo (tomatillo), 181

Solanum tuberosum. See Potato

Solenopsis invicta (fire ant), 247–248, 283

Solenopsis wagneri (red fire ant), 43–44

Sorghum, 52, 131

Sorghum anthracnose (*Colletotrichum sublinolum*), 156

Sorghum bicolor, 76–77, 78, 82

Sorghum ergot (*Claviceps africana*), 52

Sorghum halepense. See Johnsongrass

Southern blue butterfly (*Zizina oxyleyi*), 228

Southern cowpea weevil (*Callosobruchus maculatus*), 129

Southwestern white pine (*Pinus strobiformis*), 171

Southwood, T.R.E., 207, 208

Soybean (*Glycine max*): genetic engineering and, 84; herbivory and, 206, 210; pests and, 130, 155–156

Spartina alterniflora. See Smooth cordgrass

Spartina alterniflora, 63

Spartina anglica, 63–64, 261

Spartina foliosa (California cordgrass), 70–71

Spartina maritima (salt marsh cordgrass), 63

Spartina townsendii, 63

Spathiphyllum, 74

Speciation: with alien invasions (overview), 14–15; in animals (overview), 265–269; cichlid fishes of Africa, 260; coevolution and, 257; Darwin's finches, 260–261; extinction and, 269–271; of green algae (*Caulerpa*), 264–265; native herbivores/alien plants and, 186–187; new ecosystems from, 271; overview, 258–261; in plants (overview), 261–265; polyploidy and, 259–260, 265; of sunflowers, 262–263; *Tragopogon* spp., 258–259

Speckled wood butterfly (*Pararge aegeria*), 28

Spermophilus beecheyi (California ground squirrel), 200

Sphenodon spp. (tuataras), 221

Spiny cladoceran (*Cercopagis pengoi*), 57–58, 59

Spotted knapweed (*Centaurea maculosa*), 100

Spotted owl (*Strix occidentalis*), 226

Spruce (*Picea abies*), 207

Squash: *Cucurbita pepo*, 82; *Cucurbita* spp., 84

Stachowicz, J.J., 95

Star thistles (*Centaurea* spp.), 274

Stator limbatus (bruchid seed beetle), 176

Stearns, S.C., 112, 142–143

Stellaria media (common chickweed), 30

Stepien, C.A., 32

Stiling, P., 232

Stipa spp., 166

Stoat/short-tailed weasel (*Mustela erminea*), 146, 192–193

Stohlgren, T.J., 93

Streptopelia decaocto (Eurasian collared dove), 21

Striga asiatica (witchweed), 40

Strix occidentalis (spotted owl), 226

Strix varia (barred owl), 226

Strong, D.R., 105, 204, 207–208

Sturnus vulgaris. See European starling

Subterranean clover (*Trifolium subterranean*), 30, 108–109

Sudden oak death fungus (*Phytophthora ramorum*): extirpation and, 227; spread of, 148–149, 151, 171

Sugar cane (*Saccharum officinarum*), 84, 204–205
Sugar pine (*Pinus lambertiana*), 155, 171, 172
Sulfur butterfly (*Colias philodice*), 180
Sunflowers: common (*Helianthus annuus*), 78, 81, 262, 263; *Helianthus anomalus*, 262; *Helianthus deserticola*, 262; prairie (*Helianthus petiolaris*), 262, 263; puzzle (*Helianthus paradoxus*), 262–263
"Supertramps," 145
Swamp eels (*Monopterus*), 49–50
Sweetapple, P.J., 170
Swiss stone pine (*Pinus cembra*), 280
Sylvia atricapilla (blackcap), 283
Sylvilagus spp. (cottontail rabbits), 233, 240–241

Tamarisk (*Tamarix* spp.): hybridization of, 67; introduction of, 23; invasiveness of, 27, 274, 283; use by native species, 248
Tamarix ramosissima, 107
Tammar wallabies (*Macropus eugenii*), 117–118
Tannins, 169
Tanoak (*Lithocarpus densiflorus*), 48, 148, 149
Tansy ragwort (*Senecio jacobeae*), 237
Tasmania bird fauna, 251–252
Taxon cycle, 257
Teleonemia scrupulosa (lace bug), 238
Tent caterpillars (*Malacosoma disstria*), 169
Tetranychus urticae (two-spotted spider mite), 128–129, 265
Tetraploids, 261–262
Texas ebony (*Chloroleucon ebano*), 176
Thalictrum spp. (meadow rue), 153
Thébaud, C., 102–103
Thelohania solenopsae, 248
Theobroma cacao (cacao), 205–206
Thomomys bottae (valley pocket gopher), 176, 185–186
Thompson, J.N., 125, 184, 245, 272
Thornbills (*Acanthiza* spp.), 252
Threespine stickleback (*Gasterosteus aculeatus*), 141–142, 143–144, 267
Through the Looking Glass (Carroll), 189
Thylacinus cynocephalus (marsupial wolf), 117–118
Thymallus thymallus (grayling), 112
Tiaris bicolor (black-faced grassquit), 254

Tiedje, J.M., 76
Tiger muskellunge, 68
Tilapia (*Oreochromis*) hybrids, 67–68
Tillering pattern and grazing, 167–168
Time lags (alien impacts), 12
Tolerance to herbivory, 163–164, 166, 168
Tolmiea menziesii, 261–262
Tomatillo (*Solanum tomatillo*), 181
Tomato (*Lycopersicon esculentum*), 3–4, 129
Tomato blight, 148
Tomicus piniperda (European pine shoot beetle), 126
Torchin, M.E., 100–101
Toxoplasma gondii, 227
Toxoplasmosis, 227
Toxoptera citricida (brown citrus aphid), 243
Trachycarpus fortunei (windmill palm), 273
Tragopogon, genus (goat's beard/salsify), 66, 258–259, 261
Transgenes/hybridization: agriculture and, 76–88; antibiotic resistance, 84; counterevolution and, 86–87; crops/crop weedy races, 81–82; crops/other plants, 82–84; ecological implications of, 84–86; fitness cost and, 81, 85; future trends in, 87–88; herbicide resistance and, 77, 79, 83, 85; higher trophic level effects, 86; insecticides and, 85; microorganisms and, 84; natural enemies of crop pests and, 85; overview, 76–80; pesticide resistance and, 86–87, 88; problems with, ix, 77–80; regulatory issues, 87; transgene functions, 77, 78–79
Travis, J., 256
Tree-creepers (*Climacteris* spp.), 252
Tree fuchsia (*Fuchsia excorticata*), 170
Tree introductions, 22–23
Tree of heaven (*Ailanthus altissima*), 40
Tree snails (*Achatinella*), 222
Trelease, William, 278
Trembling aspen (*Populus tremuloides*), 169
Trichoplusia ni (cabbage looper), 165
Trichosurus vulpecula (brushtail opossum), 116, 146, 170
Trifolium hirtum (rose clover), 108–109
Trifolium pratense (red clover), 242–243
Trifolium repens (white clover), 110
Trifolium subterranean (subterranean clover), 30, 108–109
Trigiano, R.N., 50

Triticum spp. (wheat), 83, 84

Trussell, G.C., 190

Tsutsui, N.D., 47

Tuataras (*Sphenodon* spp.), 221

Tubificid worms (Tubifex spp.), 151, 197–198

Turdus migratorius (American robin), 282

Turtlehead/balmony (*Chelone glabra*), 177

Two-spotted spider mite (*Tetranychus urticae*), 128–129, 265

Typha angustifolia (narrowleaf cattail), 263

Typha glauca (white cattail), 263

Typha latifolia (North American broadleaf cattail), 263

Ulmus americana (American elm), 170

Ulmus pumila (Siberian elm), 23

Ulmus spp. (elms), 169

Ultraviolet radiation, 277

Umbellularia californica (California bay laurel), 148, 171

Uroleucon ambrosiae (ragweed aphid), 124–125

Valley pocket gopher (*Thomomys bottae*), 176, 185–186

Van, T.K., 36

Van den Bosch, R., 240

Van Nouhuys, S., 239

Velvet-leaf (*Abutilon theophrasti*), 106

Vermeij, G., 190

Vertebrate herbivore specialization, 123, 125

Vestiaria coccinea (I'iwi), 197

Vetch (Vicia sativa), 22

Via, S., 174, 239, 258

Viburnum, 148

Vicia sativa (vetch), 22

Vigna unguiculata (black-eyed pea), 129

Vikings, 269

Vireo altiloquus (black-whiskered vireo), 254

Virus spread, 156–157

Vitis riparia (frost grape), 54

Vitis vulpina (winter grape), 54

Von Holle, B., 275–276

Vulpes spp. (foxes), 157

Vulpes vulpes (red fox), 45, 224, 230

Wall-lettuce (*Lactuca muralis*), 18

Wandering salamander (*Aneides vagrans*), 48

Wasp (*Cotesia glomerata*), 239

Water hyacinth (*Eichhornia crassipes*), 224, 238

Water milfoil (*Myriophyllum sibericum*), 185

Water oak (*Quercus nigra*), 202

Wavyleaf thistle (*Cirsium undulatum*), 237

Weber, G., 129

Weevils: *Aphthona* spp., 241; *Euhrychiopsis lecontei,* 185; *Hypera brunneipennis,* 240; *Larinus planus,* 237; *Neochetina eichhorniae,* 238; *Rhinocyllus conicus,* 127–128, 236–237, 238, 240

Wells, L., 191

Western anise swallowtail butterfly (*Papilio zelicaon*), 184

Western corn rootworm (*Diabrotica virgifera*), 130

Western wheatgrass (*Elymus smithii*), 127

Western white pine (*Pinus monticola*), 155, 171–172

West Indies bird fauna, 254–257

West Nile virus, 157, 159

Wetas, 192–193

Wheat: Hessian fly and, 131–132; *Triticum aestivum,* 83; *Triticum* spp., 84

Wheat/barley stripe rust (*Puccinia striiformis*), 153, 154

Wheat leaf rust (*Puccinia triticina*), 153–154

Wheat stem rust (*Puccinia graminis*), 153, 154

Wheat stem sawfly (*Cephus cinctus*), 123

Whirling disease (*Myxobolus cerebralis*), 151, 197–198

Whitebark pine (*Pinus albicaulis*), 155

White bryony (*Bryonia alba*), 40

White campion (*Silene latifolia*), 98–99, 210

White clover (*Trifolium repens*), 110

White-headed duck (*Oxyura leucocephala*), 229

White pine blister rust (*Cronartium ribicola*), 154–155, 171–172, 227

White rot fungus (*Amylostereum areolatum*), 234

White spruce (*Picea glauca*), 277–278

White-tailed deer (*Odocoileus virginianus*), 146

Wilcove, D.S., 220, 221

Wilcox, B.A., 270

Wild carrot (*Daucus carota*), 107

Wild geranium (*Geranium molle*), 283

Wild parsnip (*Pantinaca sativa*), 125
Wild radish (*Raphanus raphanistrum*), 83–84
Williamson, M., 87
Willis, A.J., 102
Willows (*Salix*), 66
Wilson, D.S., 134, 136
Wilson, E.O., 214
Wilson, Paul, 146
Windmill palm (*Trachycarpus fortunei*), 273
Winter grape (*Vitis vulpina*), 54
Witchweed (*Striga asiatica*), 40
Wolfe, L.M., 98, 210
Wood frog (*Rana sylvatica*), 200
Woodland ragwort (*Senecio sylvaticus*), 17
Wood wasp (*Sirex noctilio*), 234
World Conservation Monitoring Centre, 220

Xenodiversity, 273–274

Yela, J.L., 211
Yellow–bellied marmot (*Marmota flaviventris*), 282

Yellow fever virus, 137, 138, 159
Yellow starthistle (*Centaurea solsticialis*): adaptation/reproduction shift, 108; biological control and, 243–244; genetic variability of, 42; herbivory of, 210; invasibility factors, 95
Yersinia pestis (plague), 199–200
Yom-Tov, Y., 145, 284

Zangerl, A.R., 125
Zea mays. See Maize
Zebra mussel (*Dreissena polymorpha*): adaptation to new habitat, 27, 110–111; counteradaptation/integration and, 245–246, 247; extirpation by, 225–226; genetic variability of, 43
Zimmerman, E.C., 266
Ziuganov, V.V., 144
Zizina labradus (common blue butterfly), 228
Zizina oxyleyi (southern blue butterfly), 228
Zosterops lateralis (gray-breasted silvereye), 115